NEW CENTURY BIBLE COMMENTARY

General Editors

RONALD E. CLEMENTS
(Old Testament)

MATTHEW BLACK
(New Testament)

The Gospel
of
LUKE

THE NEW CENTURY BIBLE COMMENTARIES

Other titles in preparation

NEW CENTURY BIBLE COMMENTARY

Based on the Revised Standard Version

The Gospel of LUKE

E. EARLE ELLIS

Wm. B. Eerdmans Publ. Co., Grand Rapids

Marshall, Morgan & Scott Publ. Ltd., London

Original edition © Thomas Nelson & Sons Ltd. 1966
This revised edition © Marshall, Morgan & Scott 1974
Softback edition published 1981

Wm. B. Eerdmans Publishing Company
255 Jefferson Ave. S.E., Grand Rapids, Mich. 49503
and
Marshall, Morgan & Scott
A Pentos company
1 Bath Street, London ECIV 9LB
ISBN 0 551 00849 0

Library of Congress Cataloging in Publication Data
Ellis, Edward Earle.
The Gospel of Luke.

(New century Bible commentaries)
Reprint of the ed. published by Oliphants, London,
which was issued in series: New century Bible.
Bibliography: p. xiii
Includes index.
1.   Bible.   N.T.   Luke — Commentaries.   I.   Bible.
N.T. Luke.   English.   Revised Standard.   1980.
II.   Title.   III.   Series: New century Bible commentary.
IV.   Series: New century Bible.
[BS2595.3.E4   1980]   226′.407   80-18294
ISBN 0-8028-1863-3

To the Memory of
Frank J. Neuberg
who, in his inimitable way,
taught students to live with the prophets
and ask questions

οὐκ ἔνι ᾿Ιουδαῖος οὐδὲ ῞Ελλην
ἐν Χριστῷ

CONTENTS

PREFACE

In words Austin Farrer (p. 30) used of another Gospel, Luke 'is neither a treatise nor a poem, but it is more like a poem than a treatise'. Luke is an historian, but he can be appreciated best when he is recognized also as a theologian and *littérateur*. In this conviction some attention has been given in the following pages to the theological emphases of the Gospel and to its literary structure.

The old adage that the biblical commentator elaborates the obvious and bypasses the difficult is not without basis: but, we hope, it is not entirely true. The present commentary, intended for clergy and laymen as well as for students, has not attempted an exhaustive treatment of Luke's text. It does seek, however, to illuminate the major lines of thought in each passage, and it gives some detailed attention to issues that are stimulating the current study of Luke–Acts. The references to other works and sources are designed to benefit students without excessively encumbering the general reader. With present-day research in view considerable space has been devoted to 'introduction'. The commentary can be best understood when read in the light of the introductory material.

It is a pleasure to write these words where, in the academic year 1961–2, the substance of this book was written. The charm of Marburg is equalled only by the vigour of its theological climate. In such an atmosphere a commentator fully appreciates how dependent he is on the work of his colleagues, especially those with whom he disagrees. May I express my appreciation also to those in Marburg who, by many kindnesses, aided in the completion of this volume. I am especially grateful to Professor W. G. Kümmel and to Fräulein Herbst, Librarian of the *Theologisches Seminar*, for their gracious and helpful assistance. For beneficial criticisms and corrections of the manuscript I am indebted to Professors B. Rigaux, V. M. Rogers, and A. F. Walls.

Collegium Philippinum   E. Earle Ellis
Marburg, Summer 1964

PREFACE TO THE SECOND EDITION

The present revision adds two special notes and makes a number of amendments in the commentary, incorporating the results of more recent Lukan studies. The date of the Gospel and the relationship of the twelve to the apostles receive further attention. While taking seriously the criticism of several reviewers, I remain persuaded that the Gospel was written not far from AD 70. I have endeavoured to state more clearly the reasons for my opinion. On the second matter I am no longer convinced that Luke equates the twelve and the apostles, with Ac. 14: 4, 14 forming an exceptional variation. A special note sets forth my change of mind.

As before, the commentary intends primarily to present the mind of Luke, as far as I am able to discern it. It does not attempt a thorough sifting of the teachings (or events) of the earthly ministry of Jesus from the elaboration of traditioners or of the exalted Lord. This approach reflects in part the character of the commentary, in part a doubt that today's critical tools (or the writer's mastery of them) are always adequate to make an historical analysis of this kind. I hope to address the question in a forthcoming essay in the *Festschrift* for Professor Conzelmann.

Reading the commentary a decade after its first writing, I am again conscious of its deficiencies. In the light of this I am the more grateful to the readers whose kind reception of the volume has now called forth a second edition. A word of appreciation is due also to the editors of the *Encyclopaedia Britannica* (Chicago, 1974) and of the *Dictionary of Christian Ethics* (Grand Rapids, 1973), in whose works the substance of some of the added material first appeared, and to the publisher and editors for the extensive labour of resetting the book and for patiently awaiting and indulging my sometimes pedantic alterations.

New Brunswick, Christmas 1973   E. Earle Ellis

LIST OF ABBREVIATIONS

BOOKS OF THE BIBLE

OLD TESTAMENT (*OT*)

Gen.	Jg.	1 Chr.	Ps.	Lam.	Ob.	Hag.
Exod.	Ru.	2 Chr.	Prov.	Ezek.	Jon.	Zech.
Lev.	1 Sam.	Ezr.	Ec.	Dan.	Mic.	Mal.
Num.	2 Sam.	Neh.	Ca.	Hos.	Nah.	
Dt.	1 Kg.	Est.	Isa.	Jl	Hab.	
Jos.	2 Kg.	Job	Jer.	Am.	Zeph.	

APOCRYPHA (*Apoc.*)

1 Esd.	Tob.	Ad. Est.	Sir.	S 3 Ch.	Bel	1 Mac.
2 Esd.	Jdt.	Wis.	Bar.	Sus.	Man.	2 Mac.
(=4 Ezra)			Ep. Jer.			

NEW TESTAMENT (*NT*)

Mt.	Ac.	Gal.	1 Th.	Tit.	1 Pet.	3 Jn
Mk	Rom.	Eph.	2 Th.	Phm.	2 Pet.	Jude
Lk.	1 C.	Phil.	1 Tim.	Heb.	1 Jn	Rev.
Jn	2 C.	Col.	2 Tim.	Jas	2 Jn	

DEAD SEA SCROLLS

1QIs^a	First Isaiah Scroll
1QIs^b	Second Isaiah Scroll
1QLevi	Second Testament of Levi
1QpHab	Habakkuk Commentary
1QS	Rule of the Community (Manual of Discipline)
1QSa (=1Q28a)	Rule of the Community (Appendix)
1QSb (=1Q28b)	Collection of Benedictions
1QM	War of the Sons of Light against the Sons of Darkness
1QH	Hymns of Thanksgiving
4QFlor	Florilegium, Cave 4
4Qtest	Messianic Testimonia, Cave 4
4Q patr	Patriarchal Blessing, Cave 4

CD　　　　　　　　Fragments of a Zadokite work (Damascus
　　　　　　　　　　Document)

BABYLONIAN TALMUD TRACTATES

Aboth	Aboth	Meg.	Megillah	Shab.	Shabbath
B.B.	Baba Bathra	Naz.	Nazir	Shek.	Shekalim
B.K.	Baba Kamma	Ned.	Nedarim	Suk.	Sukkah
Ber.	Berakoth	Nid.	Niddah	Ta.	Ta'anith
Edu.	Eduyoth	Peah	Peah	Tamid	Tamid
Hag.	Hagigah	Pes.	Pesahim	Yeb.	Yebamoth
Kid.	Kiddushin	Sanh.	Sanhedrin	Yoma	Yoma

OTHER ABBREVIATIONS

T Sota	Tosephta, Sota	Mek.	Mekilta
R.	Midrash Rabbah	Test.	Testaments of the Twelve
j	Jerusalem Talmud		Patriarchs
Jubil.	Jubilees		

BIBLIOGRAPHY

AHG	*Apostolic History and the Gospel. Essays [for] F. F. Bruce*, edited by W. W. Gasque, Exeter, 1970.
AJT	*American Journal of Theology*
ANT	*New Testament Apocrypha*, 2 vols., edited by E. Hennecke–W. Schneemelcher, Philadelphia, 1963, 1965
ASTI	*Annual of the Swedish Theological Institute.*
AV	*Authorized Version.*
Aland	K. Aland, *Synopsis Quattuor Evangeliorum*, Stuttgart, 1967.
Albright	W. F. Albright, *History, Archaeology and Christian Humanism*, New York, 1964.
Arndt	W. F. Arndt and F. W. Gingrich, *A Greek–English Lexicon of the New Testament . . .*, Chicago, 1957.
BA	*The Biblical Archaeologist Reader*, edited by G. E. Wright, Garden City, 1961.
BC	*The Beginnings of Christianity*, 5 vols., edited by F. J. Foakes Jackson and K. Lake, London, 1920–33.
BJRL	*Bulletin of the John Rylands Library.*
BR	*Biblical Research.*
BZ	*Biblische Zeitschrift.*
Bailey	J. A. Bailey, *The Traditions Common to the Gospels of Luke and John*, Leiden, 1963.
Barrett	C. K. Barrett, *The Holy Spirit and the Gospel Tradition*, London, 1947.
Barrett, *Historian*	C. K. Barrett, *Luke the Historian in Recent Study*, London, 1961.
Barrett, *Essays*	C. K. Barrett, *New Testament Essays*, London, 1972.
Barth	K. Barth, *Church Dogmatics, I*, 2, Edinburgh, 1956.
Barthélemy	D. Barthélemy and J. T. Milik, *Qumran Cave I*, Oxford, 1955.
Baur	F. C. Baur, *Paul*, 2 vols., London, 1876.
Beasley-Murray	G. R. Beasley-Murray, *Jesus and the Future*, London, 1954.
Bib.	*Biblica.*

Black   M. Black, *An Aramaic Approach to the Gospels and Acts*, Oxford, 3rd edn, 1967.

Black, *Scrolls*   M. Black, *The Scrolls and Christian Origins*, London, 1961.

Blackman   E. C. Blackman, *Marcion and his Influence*, London, 1948.

Blinzler   J. Blinzler, *The Trial of Jesus*, Westminster (Md.), 1959.

Bornkamm   G. Bornkamm, *Jesus of Nazareth*, New York, 1960.

Brown   S. Brown, *Apostacy and Perseverance in the Theology of Luke*, Rome, 1969.

Brownlee   W. H. Brownlee, *The Dead Sea Manual of Discipline*, New Haven, 1951.

Bruce   F. F. Bruce, *The Acts of the Apostles: Greek Text*, London, 1951.

Bruce, *Exegesis*   F. F. Bruce, *Biblical Exegesis in the Qumran Texts*, Grand Rapids, 1959.

Bruce, *Saviour*   F. F. Bruce, 'Our God and Saviour' . . . *The Saviour God*, edited by S. G. F. Brandon, Manchester, 1963, pp. 51–65.

Bultmann   R. Bultmann, *The History of the Gospel Tradition*, New York, 1963 (1931).

Bultmann, *Existence*   R. Bultmann, *Existence and Faith*, New York, 1960.

Bultmann, *John*   R. Bultmann, *The Gospel of John*, Philadelphia, 1971.

Bultmann, *Theology*   R. Bultmann, *Theology of the New Testament*, 2 vols., London, 1952, 1955.

Burney   C. F. Burney, *The Aramaic Origin of the Fourth Gospel*, Oxford, 1922.

Butler   B. C. Butler, *The Originality of St. Matthew*, Cambridge, 1951.

CAP   R. H. Charles, *The Apocrypha and Pseudepigrapha of the Old Testament*, 2 vols., Oxford, 1913.

CBG   *Collationes Brugenses et Gandavenses.*

CBQ   *Catholic Biblical Quarterly.*

CI   *Current Issues in New Testament Interpretation*, in honour of O. Piper, New York, 1962.

CIB   *Current Issues in Biblical and Patristic Interpretation*, in honour of M. C. Tenney, Grand Rapids, edited by G. F. Hawthorne, 1974.

CN   *Coniectanea Neotestamentica XI* in honorem A. Fridrichsen, Lund, 1947.

Cadbury   H. J. Cadbury, *The Making of Luke–Acts*, New
                            York, 1927.
Cadbury, *Style*   H. J. Cadbury, *The Style and Literary Method of
                            Luke*, Cambridge, 1920.
Caird   G. B. Caird, *Saint Luke*, London, 1963.
Carrington   P. Carrington, *The Primitive Christian Calendar*,
                            Cambridge, 1952.
Cartledge   D. R. Cartledge and D. L. Dungan, *Sourcebook
                            [for] Comparative Study of the Gospels*, Missoula,
                            Mont., 1972.
Childs   B. S. Childs, *Myth and Reality in the Old Testa-
                            ment*, London, 1960.
Colpe   C. Colpe, *Die religionsgeschichtliche Schule*, Göt-
                            tingen, 1961.
Conzelmann   H. Conzelmann, *The Theology of St Luke*,
                            London, 1960.
Cranfield   C. E. B. Cranfield, *The Gospel according to St
                            Mark*, Cambridge, 1959.
Creed   J. M. Creed, *The Gospel according to St. Luke*,
                            London, 1930.
Cross   F. M. Cross, *The Ancient Library of Qumran*,
                            Garden City (N.Y.), 1961.
Cullmann   O. Cullmann, *The Early Church*, London, 1956.
Cullman, *Christology*   O. Cullmann, *The Christology of the New Testa-
                            ment*, London, 1959.
Cullmann, *Salvation*   O. Cullmann, *Salvation in History*, London, 1967.
Cullmann, *Immortality*   O. Cullmann, *Immortality of the Soul or Resurrec-
                            tion of the Dead*, London, 1958.
Cullmann, *Peter*   O. Cullmann, *Peter*, New York, 1958.
Cullmann, *State*   O. Cullmann, *The State in the New Testament*,
                            London, 1957.
Cullmann, *Time*   O. Cullmann, *Christ and Time*, Philadelphia,
                            1950.
Cullmann, *Worship*   O. Cullmann, *Early Christian Worship*, London,
                            1953.
DSS   Dead Sea Scrolls.
Dalman   G. Dalman, *Jesus–Jeschua*, London, 1929.
Dalman, *Words*   G. Dalman, *The Words of Jesus*, Edinburgh,
                            1902.
Daube   D. Daube, *The New Testament and Rabbinic
                            Judaism*, London, 1956.
Davies   W. D. Davies, *Paul and Rabbinic Judaism*,
                            London, 1948.

Davies, *Sermon*   W. D. Davies, *The Setting of the Sermon on the Mount*, Cambridge, 1964.

Derrett   J. D. M. Derrett, *Law in the New Testament*, London, 1970.

Dial.   *Dialogue with Trypho.*

Dibelius, *Acts*   M. Dibelius, *Studies in the Acts of the Apostles*, London, 1956.

Dibelius, *Botschaft*   M. Dibelius, *Botschaft und Geschichte I*, Tübingen, 1953.

Dibelius, *Tradition*   M. Dibelius, *From Tradition to Gospel*, London, 1934.

Dion. Hal.   Dionysius of Halicarnassus, *Roman Antiquities.*

Dodd   C. H. Dodd, *The Parables of the Kingdom*, London, 1935.

Dupont   J. Dupont, *The Sources of Acts*, London, 1964.

EL   *L'evangile de Luc. Memorial L. Cerfaux*, ed. F. Neirynck, Gembloux, 1973.

ELT   A. Edersheim, *The Life and Times of Jesus the Messiah*, 2 vols., London, 1887.

ERE   *Encyclopaedia of Religion and Ethics*, edited by J. Hastings, 13 vols., Edinburgh, 1908–26.

ET   *Expository Times.*

ETL   *Ephemerides Theologicae Lovanienses.*

ETS   *Erfurter Theologische Studien.*

EvT   *Evangelische Theologie.*

Easton   B. S. Easton, *Early Christianity*, Greenwich (Conn.), 1954.

Edersheim   A. Edersheim, *The Temple*, London, 1960 (1900)

Edsman   C. M. Edsman, *Le baptême de feu*, Uppsala, 1940.

Ellis   E. E. Ellis, *Paul's Use of the Old Testament*, Edinburgh, 1957.

Ellis, *Eschatology*   E. E. Ellis, *Eschatology in Luke*, Philadelphia 1972.

Ellis, *Interpreters*   E. E. Ellis, *Paul and his Recent Interpreters*, Grand Rapids, 1961.

Ellis, *John*   E. E. Ellis, *The World of St John*, London, 1965.

Eus.   Eusebius, *The Ecclesiastical History.*

FBK   P. Finne, J. Behm, W. G. Kümmel, *Introduction to the New Testament*, Nashville, 1966.

Farmer   W. R. Farmer, *The Synoptic Problem*, New York, 1964.

Farrar   F. W. Farrer, *St Luke*, Cambridge, 1912.

Farrer   A. Farrer, *A Study in Mark*, London, 1951.
Farrer, *Matthew*   A. Farrer, *St Matthew and St Mark*, London, 1954.
Fascher   E. Fascher, *ΠΡΟΦΗΤΗΣ*, Giessen, 1927.
Flender   H. Flender, *St. Luke, Theologian of Redemptive History*, Philadelphia, 1967.
Frend   W. H. C. Frend, *Martydom and Persecution in the Early Church*, Oxford, 1965.
Fuller   R. H. Fuller, *The Mission and Achievement of Jesus*, London, 1954.
Funk   F. Blass, A. Debrunner, R. W. Funk, *A Greek Grammar of the New Testament*, Chicago, 1961.
Gärtner   B. Gärtner, *The Areopagus Speech and Natural Revelation*, Uppsala, 1955.
Gärtner, *Temple*   B. Gärtner, *The Temple and the Community in Qumran and the New Testament*, Cambridge, 1965.
Geldenhuys   N. Geldenhuys, *Commentary on the Gospel of Luke*, Grand Rapids, 1951.
Gerhardsson   B. Gerhardsson, *Memory and Manuscript*, Uppsala, 1961.
Gerhardsson, *Samaritan*   B. Gerhardsson, *The Good Samaritan*, Lund. 1958.
Gerhardsson, *Testing*   B. Gerhardsson, *The Testing of God's Son*, Lund, 1966.
Goguel   M. Goguel, *Jesus and the Origins of Christianity*, 2 vols, New York, 1960 (1933).
Goppelt   L. Goppelt, *Jesus, Paul and Judaism*, New York, 1964.
Goudoever   J. van Goudoever, *Biblical Calendars*, Leiden, 1959.
Grant   R. M. Grant, *After the New Testament*, Philadelphia, 1967.
Gressmann   H. Gressman, *Von Reichen Mann und Armen Lazarus*, Berlin, 1918.
Grobel   K. Grobel, *Formgeschichte und synoptische Quellenanalyse*, Berlin, 1937.
Grundmann   W. Grundmann, *Das Evangelium nach Lukas*, Berlin, 1959.
Guignebert   C. Guignebert, *The Jewish World in the Time of Jesus*, London, 1939.
Guilding   A. Guilding, *The Fourth Gospel and Jewish Worship*, Oxford, 1960.

HA	*Apophoreta, Festschrift für E. Haenchen*, Berlin, 1964.
HC	*Historicity and Chronology in the New Testament*, D. E. Nineham *et al.*, London, 1965.
HDAC	*A Dictionary of the Apostolic Church*, 2 vols., edited by J. Hastings, Edinburgh, 1915.
HDCG	*A Dictionary of Christ and the Gospels*, 2 vols., edited by J. Hastings, Edinburgh, 1906.
HTR	*Harvard Theological Review.*
Hadas	M. Hadas, *Ancilla to Classical Reading*, New York, 1954.
Haenchen	E. Haenchen, *The Acts of the Apostles*, Philadelphia, 1971.
Hagner	D. A. Hagner, *The Use of the Old and New Testaments in Clement of Rome*, Leiden, 1973.
Hanson	R. P. C. Hanson, *The Acts*, Oxford, 1967.
Harnack, *Acts*	A. Harnack, *The Date of the Acts and of the Synoptic Gospels*, London, 1911.
Harnack, *Luke*	A. Harnack, *Luke the Physician*, London, 1907.
Harris	J. R. Harris, *The Origin of the Prologue to St. John's Gospel*, Cambridge, 1917.
Hartman	L. Hartman, *Prophecy Interpreted*, Lund, 1966.
Hastings	A. Hastings, *Prophet and Witness in Jerusalem*, London, 1958.
Hawkins	J. C. Hawkins, *Horae Synopticae*, Oxford, 1909.
Hengel	M. Hengel, *Was Jesus a Revolutionist?*, Philadelphia, 1971.
Higgins	A. J. B. Higgins, *The Lord's Supper in the New Testament*, London, 1952
Higgins, *Christology*	A. J. B. Higgins, 'Aspects of New Testament Christology', *Promise and Fulfilment, Essays presented to S. H. Hooke*, edited by F. F. Bruce, Edinburgh, 1963.
Hill	D. Hill, *The Gospel of Matthew*, London, 1972.
Hobart	W. K. Hobart, *The Medical Language of St. Luke*, Grand Rapids, 1954 (1882).
Hodgson	P. C. Hodgson, *The Formation of Historical Theology*, New York, 1966.
Holm-Nielsen	S. Holm-Nielsen, *Hodayot: Psalms from Qumran*, Aarhus, 1960.
Hort	B. F. Westcott and F. J. A. Hort, 'Notes on Select Readings', *The New Testament . . . Introduction and Appendix*, London, 1882.

IB	*The Interpreter's Bible*, edited by G. A. Buttrick, Nashville, 1952–7.
IEJ	*Israel Exploration Journal.*
Int.	*Interpretation.*
Iren.	Irenaeus, *Against Heresies.*
JBL	*Journal of Biblical Literature.*
JQR	*Jewish Quarterly Review.*
JRS	*Journal of Roman Studies.*
JTC	*Journal for Theology and the Church.*
JTS	*Journal of Theological Studies.*
Jaubert	A. Jaubert, *The Date of the Last Supper*, New York, 1965.
Jeremias, *Eucharistic Words*	J. Jeremias, *The Eucharistic Words of Jesus*, rev. edn., New York, 1966.
Jeremias, *Jerusalem*	J. Jeremias, *Jerusalem in the Time of Jesus*, London, 1969.
Jeremias, *Prayer*	J. Jeremias, *The Lord's Prayer*, Philadelphia, 1964.
Jeremias, *Servant*	J. Jeremias, and W. Zimmerli, *The Servant of God*, London, 1959.
Jeremias, *Theology*	J. Jeremias, *New Testament Theology*, London, 1971.
Jeremias, *Nations*	J. Jeremias, *Jesus' Promise to the Nations*, London, 1958.
Jeremias, *Parables*	J. Jeremias, *The Parables of Jesus*, rev. edn, New York, 1963.
Jeremias, *Sermon*	J. Jeremias, *The Sermon on the Mount*, London, 1961.
Jervell	J. Jervell, *Luke and the People of God*, Minneapolis, 1972.
Johnson	A. R. Johnson, *Sacral Kingship in Ancient Israel*, Cardiff, 1955.
Johnson, *Genealogies*	M. D. Johnson, *The Purpose of the Biblical Genealogies*, Cambridge, 1969.
Jos. *Ant.*	Josephus, *The Antiquities of the Jews.*
Jos. *c. Apion.*	Josephus, *Against Apion.*
Jos. *Life*	Josephus, *The Life of Flavius Josephus.*
Jos. *War*	Josephus, *The Jewish War.*
Klausner	J. Klausner, *The Messianic Idea in Israel*, New York, 1955.
Knox, *Acts*	W. L. Knox, *The Acts of the Apostles*, Cambridge, 1948.
Knox, *Gospels*	W. L. Knox, *The Sources of the Synoptic Gospels*, 2 vols., Cambridge, 1953, 1957.

Knox, *Marcion* J. Knox, *Marcion and the New Testament*, Chicago, 1942.

Köster, H. Köster, *Synoptische Überlieferung bei den apostolichen Vätern*, Berlin, 1957.

Kosmala H. Kosmala, *Hebräer-Essener-Christen*, Leiden, 1959.

Kraus H. J. Kraus, *Psalmen*, 2 vols., Neukirchen, 1960.

Kümmel W. G. Kümmel, *Promise and Fulfilment*, London, 1957.

Kümmel, *Man* W. G. Kümmel, *Man in the New Testament*, London, 1963.

Kurtz D. C. Kurtz, *Greek Burial Customs*, London, 1971.

LAE A. Deissmann, *Light from the Ancient East*, New York, 1927.

LQ *Library Quarterly.*

LXX *The Septuagint.*

Laurentin R. Laurentin, *Structure et théologie de Luc I–II*, Paris, 1957.

Leaney A. R. C. Leaney, *The Gospel According to St. Luke*, London, 1958.

Lietzmann-Kümmel H. Lietzmann, W. G. Kümmel, *An die Korinther I, II*, Tübingen, 1949.

J. B. Lightfoot J. B. Lightfoot, *The Apostolic Fathers: S. Clement of Rome*, 2 vols., London, 1890.

R. H. Lightfoot R. H. Lightfoot, *Locality and Doctrine in the Gospels*, London, 1937.

Lindars B. Lindars, *New Testament Apologetic*, London, 1961.

Linnemann E. Linnemann, *Parables of Jesus*, London, 1966.

Lohmeyer E. Lohmeyer, *The Lord of the Temple*, Edinburgh, 1961.

Lohse B. Lohse, *Das Passafest der Quartadezimaner*, Gütersloh, 1953.

Lövestam E. Lövestam, *Son and Saviour*, Lund, 1961.

Lövestam, *Wakefulness* E. Lövestam, *Spiritual Wakefulness in the New Testament*, Lund, 1963.

MB *Mélanges Bibliques* en l'honneur de A. Robert, Paris, 1957.

MBR *Mélanges Bibliques B. Rigaux*, Gembloux, 1970.

MC *Mysterium Christi*, ed. G. K. A. Bell, London, 1930.

MM   J. H. Moulton and G. Milligan, *The Vocabulary of the Greek Testament*, Grand Rapids, 1950.

Machen   J. G. Machen, *The Virgin Birth*, New York, 1930.

Manson, *Sayings*   T. W. Manson, *The Sayings of Jesus*, London, 1949.

Manson, *Studies*   T. W. Manson, *Studies in the Gospels and Epistles*, Manchester, 1962.

Manson, *Teaching*   T. W. Manson, *The Teaching of Jesus*, Cambridge, 1951.

Manson   W. Manson, *The Gospel of Luke*, London, 1930.

Manson, *Jesus*   W. Manson, *Jesus the Messiah*, London, 1943.

Mansoor   M. Mansoor, *The Thanksgiving Hymns*, Leiden, 1961.

Marshall   I. H. Marshall, *Luke: Historian and Theologian*, Exeter and Grand Rapids, 1970.

Martin   W. J. Martin, 'Dischronologized Narrative in the Old Testament', *Congress Volume* (*V.T. Suppl.* 17), Leiden, 1969.

McCasland   S. V. McCasland, *By the Finger of God*, New York, 1951.

McNamara   M. McNamara, *The New Testament and the Palestinian Targum to the Pentateuch*, Rome, 1967.

McNeile   A. H. McNeile, *New Testament Teaching in the Light of St Paul's*, Cambridge, 1923.

McNeile, *Matthew*   A. H. McNeile, *The Gospel according to St Matthew*, London, 1915.

Metzger   B. M. Metzger, *The Text of the New Testament*, 2nd edn., Oxford 1968.

E. Meyer   E. Meyer, *Ursprung und Anfänge des Christentums*, 3 vols., Berlin, 1921–3.

R. Meyer   R. Meyer, *Hellenistisches in der rabbinischen Anthropologie*, Stuttgart, 1937.

Miller   D. G. Miller, *The Gospel of Luke*, Richmond, 1959.

Moffatt   J. Moffatt, *The New Testament. A New Translation*, New York, 1935.

Moore, A. L.   A. L. Moore, *The Parousia in the New Testament*, Leiden, 1966.

Moore   F. G. Moore, *The Roman's World*, New York, 1936.

Morgenthaler   R. Morgenthaler, *Die lukanische Geschichtsschreibung als Zeugnis*, 2 vols., Zürich, 1949.

Moule	C. F. D. Moule, *An Idiom Book of New Testament Greek*, Cambridge, 1953.
Munck	J. Munck, *Paul and the Salvation of Mankind*, Richmond, 1960.
Munck, *Acts*	J. Munck, *Acts*, Garden City (N.Y.), 1967.
NBD	*New Bible Dictionary*, edited by J. D. Douglas, London, 1962.
NEB	*The New English Bible.*
NES	*Neotestamentica et Semitica . . . in honour of M. Black*, ed. E. E. Ellis and M. Wilcox, Edinburgh, 1969.
NoT	*Novum Testamentum.*
NP	*Neotestamentica et Patristica* für O. Cullmannn, Leiden, 1962.
NS	*Neutestamentliche Studien* für R. Bultmann, Berlin, 1954.
NTA	*New Testament Abstracts.*
NTAF	*The New Testament in the Apostolic Fathers*, ed. J. V. Bartlet, *et al.*, Oxford, 1905.
NTE	*New Testament Essays* in memory of T. W. Manson, Manchester, 1959.
NTS	*New Testament Studies.*
Noack	B. Noack, *Das Gottesreich bei Lukas*, Uppsala, 1948.
Norden	E. Norden, *Agnostos Theos*, Stuttgart, 1956 (1913).
OS	*Studies in the Synoptic Problem*, ed. W. Sanday, Oxford, 1911.
Oesterley	W. O. E. Oesterley, *The Gospel Parables in the Light of their Jewish Background*, New York, 1936.
O'Neill	J. C. O'Neill, *The Theology of Acts in its Historical Setting*, rev. edn., London, 1970.
PC	*Peake's Commentary on the Bible*, edited by M. Black, London, 1962.
Pauly	*Paulys Real-encyclopädie.*
Pedersen	J. Pedersen, *Israel* 2 vols., London, 1959.
Perrin	N. Perrin, *The Kingdom of God in the Teaching of Jesus*, Philadelphia, 1963.
Pesch	R. Pesch, *Naherwartungen. Tradition und Redaktion in Mk 13*, Düsseldorf, 1968.
Phillips	J. B. Phillips, *The New Testament in Modern English*, London, 1958.
Piper	O. Piper, *The Biblical View of Sex and Marriage*, New York, 1960.

Plummer	A. Plummer, *Gospel According to St. Luke*, Edinburgh, 1922 (1896).
RB	*Revue biblique.*
RHPR	*Revue d'Histoire et de Philosophie religieuses.*
RGG	*Religion in Geschichte und Gegenwart*, 3rd edn, 6 vols., edited by K. Galling, Tübingen, 1957–1962.
RSV	Revised Standard Version.
RV	Revised Version.
Ramsay	W. M. Ramsay, *The Bearing of Recent Discovery on the Trustworthiness of the New Testament*, London, 1915.
Rehkopf	F. Rehkopf, *Die lukanische Sonderquelle*, Tübingen, 1959.
Reicke	B. Reicke, *The Gospel of Luke*, Richmond, 1964.
Reicke, *Era*	B. Reicke, *The New Testament Era*, Philadelphia, 1968.
Rengstorf	K. H. Rengstorf, *Das Evangelium nach Lukas*, Göttingen, 1949.
Riesenfeld	H. Riesenfeld, *The Gospel Tradition*, Philadelphia, 1970.
Riesenfeld, *Jesus*	H. Riesenfeld, *Jésus Transfiguré*, København, 1947.
Ringgren, *Qumran*	H. Ringgren, *The Faith of Qumran*, Philadelphia, 1963.
Ringgren	H. Ringgren, *Word and Wisdom*, Lund, 1947.
Ristow	H. Ristow, ed., *Der historische Jesus und der kerygmatische Christus*, Berlin, 1960.
H. W. Robinson	H. W. Robinson, *Inspiration and Revelation in the Old Testament*, Oxford, 1946.
J. M. Robinson	J. M. Robinson, *A New Quest of the Historical Jesus*, London, 1959.
W. C. Robinson	W. C. Robinson, Jr., *Der Weg des Herrn*, Hamburg, 1964.
Ropes	J. H. Ropes, *The Synoptic Gospels*, Cambridge, 1960 (1934).
Rostovtzeff	M. Rostovtzeff, *The Social and Economic History of the Roman Empire*, 2 vols., Oxford, 2nd edn, 1957.
SBK	H. L. Strack und P. Billerbeck, *Kommentar zum Neuen Testament aus Talmud und Midrasch*, 6 vols., München, 1954–56 (1926–28).
SBT	*Babylonian Talmud*, Socino edn., London, 1961.
SE	*Studia Evangelica*, edited by K. Aland, Berlin, 1959.

SEA   *Svensk Exegetisk Årsbok.*
SG   *Studies in the Gospels*, edited by D. E. Nineham,
                 Oxford, 1957.
SJT   *Scottish Journal of Theology.*
SL   *Studies in Luke–Acts*, edited by L. E. Keck,
                 Nashville, 1966.
SS   *Synoptische Studien* für A. Wikenhauser, Mün-
                 chen, 1953.
SSNT   *The Scrolls and the New Testament*, edited by
                 K. Stendahl, New York, 1957.
ST   *Studia Theologica.*
Sahlin   H. Sahlin, *Der Messias und das Gottesvolk*,
                 Uppsala, 1945.
Schlatter   A. Schlatter, *Das Evangelium des Lukas*, Stutt-
                 gart, 1960 (1931).
Schlatter, *Matthäus*   A. Schlatter, *Der Evangelist Matthäus*, Stuttgart,
                 1959 (1929).
Schleiermacher   F. Schleiermacher, *Ueber die Schriften des Lukas*,
                 Berlin, 1817.
Schlier   H. Schlier, *Principalities and Powers in the New
                 Testament*, Edinburgh, 1961.
Schmidt   K. L. Schmidt, *Der Rahmen der Geschichte Jesu*,
                 Berlin, 1919.
Schmithals   W. Schmithals, *Gnosticism in Corinth*, Nashville,
                 1971.
Schmithals, *Paul*   W. Schmithals, *Paul and James*, London, 1965.
Schniewind   J. Schniewind, *Die Parallelperikopen bei Lukas
                 und Johannes*, Darmstadt, 1958 (1914).
Schramm   T. Schramm, *Der Markus-Stoff bei Lukas*, Cam-
                 bridge, 1971.
Schürer   E. Schürer, *A History of the Jewish People*, 6 vols.,
                 Edinburgh, 1919 (1885).
Schürmann   H. Schürmann, *Das Lukasevangelium. Erster
                 Teil*, Freiburg, 1969.
Schürmann I   H. Schürmann, *Der Passahmalbericht, Lk. 22 :15–
                 18*, Münster, 1953.
Schürmann II   H. Schürmann, *Der Einsetzungsbericht, Lk. 22 :
                 19–20*, Münster, 1955.
Schürmann III   H. Schürmann, *Jesu Abschiedsrede, Lk. 22 : 21–
                 38*, Münster, 1957.
Schweizer   E. Schweizer, *Church Order in the New Testament*,
                 London, 1961.
Selwyn   E. C. Selwyn, *St Luke the Prophet*, London, 1901.

Shedd   R. P. Shedd, *Man in Community*, London, 1958.
Sherwin-White   A. N. Sherwin-White, *Roman Society and Roman
                         Law in the New Testament*, Oxford, 1963.
Stauffer   E. Stauffer, *Jesus and his Story*, London, 1960.
Stendahl   K. Stendahl, *The School of St Matthew*, Uppsala,
                         1954 (2nd edn., 1969).
Stenning   J. F. Stenning, *The Targum of Isaiah*, Oxford,
                         1953.
Stewart   R. A. Stewart, *Rabbinic Theology*, Edinburgh,
                         1961.
Stonehouse   N. B. Stonehouse, *The Witness of Luke to Christ*,
                         Grand Rapids, 1953.
Stonehouse, *Origins*   N. B. Stonehouse, *Origins of the Synoptic Gospels*,
                         Grand Rapids, 1963.
Stonehouse, *Paul*   N. B. Stonehouse, *Paul before the Areopagus*,
                         Grand Rapids, 1963.
Strecker   G. Strecker, *Der Weg der Gerechtigkeit*, Göttin-
                         gen, 1962.
Streeter   B. H. Streeter, *The Four Gospels*, London, 1924.
TC   *La tradition chrétienne*, Mélanges M. Goguel,
                         Paris, 1950.
TCER   *Twentieth Century Encyclopedia of Religious Know-
                         ledge*, edited by L. A. Loetscher, 2 vols., Grand
                         Rapids, 1955.
TLZ   *Theologische Literaturzeitung*.
TR   *Theologische Rundschau*.
TS   *Theological Studies*.
TU   *Texte und Untersuchungen*.
TDNT   *Theological Dictionary of the New Testament*,
                         edited by G. Kittel, Grand Rapids, 1963–   ).
TZ   *Theologische Zeitschrift*.
Talbert   C. H. Talbert, *Luke and the Gnostics*, Nashville,
                         1966.
Taylor   V. Taylor, *Behind the Third Gospel*, Oxford, 1926.
Taylor, *Mark*   V. Taylor, *The Gospel according to St. Mark*,
                         London, 1959.
Taylor, *Luke*   V. Taylor, *The Passion Narrative of St Luke*,
                         Cambridge, 1972.
Thielicke   H. Thielicke, *Theological Ethics*, 2 vols., Phila-
                         delphia, 1966, 1969.
Thompson   G. H. P. Thompson, *Luke*, Oxford, 1972.
Torrey   C. C. Torrey, *Documents of the Primitive Church*,
                         New York, 1941.

Toynbee   J. M. C. Toynbee, *Death and Burial in the Roman World*, London, 1971.

van der Loos   H. van der Loos, *The Miracles of Jesus*, Leiden, 1968.

van Unnik   W. C. van Unnik, *Tarsus or Jerusalem*, London, 1962.

Walton   B. Walton, *Biblia Sacra Polyglotta*, 6 vols., London, 1656.

Wellhausen   J. Wellhausen, *Einleitung in die drei ersten Evangelien*, 2nd edn, Berlin, 1911.

Weymouth   R. F. Weymouth, *The New Testament in Modern Speech*, London, 1908.

Wilckens   U. Wilckens, *Die Missionsreden der Apostelgeschichte*, Neukirchen, 1961.

Wilcox   M. Wilcox, *The Semitisms of Acts*, Oxford, 1965.

Wilder   A. Wilder, *Early Christian Rhetoric*, London, 1964.

Williams   C. S. C. Williams, *Alterations to the Text of the Synoptic Gospels and Acts*, Oxford, 1951.

Williams, *Acts*   C. S. C. Williams, *The Acts of the Apostles*, New York, 1957.

Wilson, R. M.   R. M. Wilson, *The Gnostic Problem*, London, 1958.

Wilson, S. G.   S. G. Wilson, *The Gentiles and the Gentile Mission in Luke–Acts*, Cambridge, 1973.

Winter   P. Winter, *On the Trial of Jesus*, Berlin, 1961.

Wuellner   W. Wuellner, *The Meaning of 'Fishers of Men'*, Philadelphia, 1967.

ZKT   *Zeitschrift für katholische Theologie.*

ZNTW   *Zeitschrift für die neutestamentliche Wissenschaft.*

ZTK   *Zeitschrift für Theologie und Kirche.*

Zahn   T. Zahn, *Introduction to the New Testament*, 3 vols., Grand Rapids 1953 (1909).

Zeller   E. Zeller, *The Acts of the Apostles*, 2 vols., London, 1875.

INTRODUCTION

to

The Gospel of Luke

1. THE LITERARY CHARACTER OF THE GOSPEL

THE UNITY OF LUKE–ACTS

The Gospel of Luke appears in the New Testament as the first volume of a two-volume work, Luke–Acts, dedicated to one Theophilus (1 : 3; Ac. 1 : 1). Although separated in our Bibles today, in all probability these two books originally formed one literary unit. Their common authorship is attested by Church traditions from the latter part of the second century (cf. Muratorian Canon; Iren. 3, 1, 1). J. C. Hawkins (pp. 174–93) tested this tradition by a minute comparison of the language and style of Luke and Acts. This and more recent research (e.g., H. J. Cadbury) revealed a great similarity between the two books. There is today a virtual consensus of critical opinion that 'the same hand is responsible for the final compilation both of the Acts and the Gospel' (Knox, *Acts*, p. 14).

Luke–Acts was a two-volume 'narration' (*diēgēsis*; 1 : 1), formally dedicated 'to Theophilus'. It was intended not just for Christian communities but also, in the words of Dibelius (*Acts*, p. 135), 'for the book market'. Furthermore, Luke is shown to be an historian and theologian as well as a *littérateur*. He relates Christianity to the general course of world events (2 :1; 3 : 1; Ac. 5 : 36ff.; 11 :28) and traces its progress from Jerusalem to Rome. The same theological motifs are woven through both volumes. Most important, the unity of Luke–Acts requires that questions of style, purpose, authorship, and date be considered from the perspective of the whole work.

THE LANGUAGE AND STYLE OF LUKE

In an examination of *The Style and Literary Method of Luke* (pp. 36–39) Cadbury found that the proportion of classical Greek expressions used by Luke was comparable to other authors of antiquity. Indeed, in many passages Luke's style is about the best in the New Testament and confirms that his 'literary abilities were of a superior order' (B. M. Metzger, *IB* VII, 47). This fact can be observed by a comparison of Luke with the Gospel of Mark. When he uses Mark as a source (see below), the author of the third Gospel not infrequently improves the style of his predecessor. By the use of participial constructions and by changes in word order Luke expresses himself more in keeping with the literary good taste of his day. Also, his omission and alteration of some words may have this end in view. For example, 'hosanna' and 'abba' (Mk 11 : 9; 14 : 36) are eliminated, and some Markan hebraisms are given Greek equivalents: zealot (6 : 15), skull (23 : 33), 'teacher' for 'rabbi' (but see on 3 : 12).

However, there is another side to the coin. Some of Luke's linguistic characteristics do not conform to the picture of a polished Hellenist writing literary Greek. Hebraisms, e.g., 'it came to pass that', are more abundant in Luke than in the other Gospels. Two sections, Lk. 1–2 and Ac. 1–12, have a pervasive Semitic colouring. Usually, Luke's Semitic idiom is attributed to his source materials, whose style he retained (e.g., Wilcox, pp. 180–4; Bruce, pp. 18–21; but see below, pp. 51ff.). This is the most likely explanation even though some recent writers think otherwise. Grundmann (p. 23) suggests that Luke purposely uses the idiom of the Septuagint, the popular Greek version of the Old Testament, because 'he wants to relate holy history in the style of Holy Scripture'. Others believe that Luke deliberately archaized his style to retain an historical Palestinian flavour (cf. Wilckens, p. 26; H. J. Cadbury, BC v, 420). But this conclusion involves a number of improbabilities. It is contrary to Luke's known practice when he alters Mark (above); and it is difficult to see why the story of the Palestinian Church (Ac. 1–12) should be more 'flavoured' than Jesus' Galilean mission or Paul's Jerusalem speech (Ac. 22). The sporadic appearance of Semitic idiom in Lk. 3–24 must be explained in terms of written sources (see below, pp. 27f.). In all likelihood the same is true for Lk. 1–2 and Ac. 1–12.

Luke's alterations probably were towards a better Greek style, sometimes, perhaps, by using other traditions. The Evangelist appears to follow his sources carefully, exhibiting his own style most profusely in 'introductory' verses (Grobel, pp. 73ff.; cf. Manson, *Studies*, p. 57; P. Winter, *ST* 8, 1955, 170f.). But he must not, because of this, be thought of merely as an editor, faithfully transmitting collected materials. Earlier studies of Luke's style have emphasized its value as evidence for the historical and linguistic background of Luke–Acts. Today, increasing attention is being given to the theological implications of Luke's manner of presentation. From this approach arises the above suggestion that the Evangelist is writing a continuation of the acts of God related in the Old Testament. But, rather than his style, Luke's use or non-use of certain terms and his selection and alteration of sources are clearer indicators of his theological purpose. These matters are a part of two larger questions, the historical and the theological nature of the Lukan writings. Together, these questions have motivated most of the current research into the literary character of Luke.

LUKE AS HISTORIAN

Luke (1 : 1–4) proposes to give 'an orderly account' of the beginnings of Christianity. Such a claim assumes that his work is historical writing, and it raises two questions. First, is Luke's conception of history and historiography valid? Second, does Luke prove to be a good historian? These two questions cannot be separated. For example, if the writing of history is understood to be a chronological listing of facts, then Luke's reputation as an historian will depend on these criteria. But these criteria have little importance for an evaluation of Luke if the writing of history may properly include an interpretative function and a thematic (rather than a chronological) presentation.

The Nature of the Problem

Recent biblical research discloses the complexity of this issue. A century ago the Tübingen scholar F. C. Baur interpreted the book of Acts as a second-century compromise between the Gentile followers of Paul and the Judaizing followers of Peter and the Jerusalem church. Since the earlier, artificial 'apostolic' setting was dominated by an overriding theological *Tendenz*, Acts' value as history was virtually nil. An English admirer of Baur, W. M. Ramsay, was largely responsible for bringing the Tübingen school's historical estimate of Acts into disrepute. He found that the 'legendary' historical and geographical notices in Lukes–Acts proved, in case after case, to accord with the geography and archaeological data that he found in Asia Minor. Reversing his earlier opinion, Ramsay became a polemical defender of 'Luke

the historian'. It was an ironic tribute to him that Lk. 2 : 1ff.
(q.v.), earlier dismissed because of its historical inaccuracies, now
was rejected by some scholars because it was too accurate. (Luke
supposedly invented Mary's journey to Jerusalem to conform to
the census custom; Ramsay, p. 273.) With a few possible exceptions, e.g., the order of the revolts in Ac. 5 : 36f., Luke–Acts
exhibits in its secular-historical and geographical notices an intimate knowledge and a remarkable accuracy. To this extent
Ramsay's judgment is well established (cf. Hanson, pp. 2–11).

Reinforced by Harnack (*Luke*, p. 25) the 'newer criticism' led to
a higher historical estimate of Luke–Acts on the Continent. Appropriately enough, the highest compliment for 'Luke the historian'
came from the historian E. Meyer (1, 2f.), who compared him to
the great Greek historiographers. However, because of the continuing influence of the Tübingen school and the propensity for
philosophical reconstructions, the implications of Ramsay's research were not always appreciated by continental scholarship.
Thus today, Luke's geographical knowledge (this time of Palestine) again is denied by some. Their interpretation of the texts is
questionable (see below, p. 148; see on 17 : 11), but it is possible
that Luke's demonstrated knowledge of Asia Minor did not extend
to Palestine. Against this possibility is Luke's evident concern for
accuracy elsewhere (cf. Cadbury, pp. 240–5).

Attention has shifted in recent years from Luke's accuracy to a
more comprehensive question, the kind of historical writing that
Luke–Acts represents. Luke attaches considerable importance to
witnesses. For him authenticity is a theological motif as well as an
historical method (1 : 1–4). The bearing of interpretation upon
such authenticity assumes an important place in current discussion. In the speeches in Acts some scholars argue that in the last
analysis Luke is not an historian but a preacher who creates the
speeches for theological purposes (Dibelius, *Acts*, pp. 183f.; cf.
Wilckens, pp. 187f.). But, as I. H. Marshall (pp. 21–52) has
shown, this strong dichotomy rests on questionable assumptions.
To be a concerned theologian does not necessarily make Luke a
less concerned historian (cf. Barrett, *Historian*, p. 39; A. Ehrhardt,
ST 12, 1958, 67). It is likely that in Acts, as he does in the Gospel,
Luke draws upon earlier documents and in the speeches also gives
'at least the gist of what was really said on the various occasions'
(Bruce, p. 21; cf. Gärtner, p. 33; H. J. Cadbury, *BC* v, 405ff.). At

the same time Luke's own contribution to their form and content is quite apparent. This issue has been carried into the study of the Gospel by H. Conzelmann's stimulating work, *The Theology of St. Luke*. As Conzelmann's title implies, such studies seek primarily to discern Luke's theological convictions and interests. To do this they must discover, first of all, the methods by which Luke incorporates his interpretation into his materials.

History and Interpretation in Luke

In the present generation perhaps no question has exercised New Testament students more than the relation of history and interpretation in the Gospels. This issue has been central in the search for the intention of the Evangelists, in the analysis of their literary forms and sources, and in the quest for the precise character and content of the pre-resurrection mission of Jesus. (For recent and varied approaches to the subject cf. Gerhardsson; C. F. D. Moule in *NTE*, pp. 165–79; Riesenfeld, pp. 1–29; Ristow; J. M. Robinson; Wilder, pp. 17–25; in *CI*, pp. 38–52). Only two observations on the matter can be offered here. They are the role of chronology in the structure of Luke and the significance of an interpretative procedure termed *midrash pesher*.

(*a*) *Chronology and the Structure of Luke*. As early as the second century some Church fathers thought that a part of Matthew's excellence as a Gospel writer lay in the fact that he, unlike Mark, wrote in chronological order (cf. Eus. 3, 39, 15f.). Later it became almost axiomatic that the Gospel narrations should be chronological. In the nineteenth century this was the common assumption upon which the 'accuracy' of the Gospel was attacked or defended. However, the ancient Hellenistic world recognized that chronological narration was only one of many literary methods, one which was not always the most desirable (Daube, p. 416). The rabbis went even further. They were convinced that the Old Testament often was not in chronological order. For example, the Egyptians' threats against Israel (Exod. 15 : 9) occurred after they already were destroyed (Exod. 15 : 1–8). The orders of creation in Genesis 1 and 2 were chronologically different. Also, Ezekiel's vision (Ezek. 1) could not have preceded his call (Ezek. 2); the prophet rearranged the texts. Consequently, the rabbis fashioned

a rule for biblical studies: there is no before and after in Scripture
(cf. *Mek.* on Exod. 15 : 9; Martin, pp. 179–86).

This principle of biblical interpretation probably was current in
the New Testament period. In rearranging their materials without regard for chronological sequence the Gospel writers follow a
common literary practice, a practice considered appropriate even
in the Old Testament Scripture itself (Daube, pp. 410, 417). Thus
Luke can alter the chronological (and geographical) setting of, for
example, the temptations (4 : 1–13), the healing at Jericho
(18 : 35), and the prophecy of Peter's denial (22 : 34, 39; cf. Mk
14 : 26–31). The procedure is not arbitrary, nor is it erroneous.
Luke simply subordinates chronological (and geographical) interests to theological and literary motifs. Sometimes this involves
a symbolic alteration (see below, pp. 30ff).

F. W. Farrar (pp. xxxixff.) wrote that attempts to arrange the
Gospel of Luke according to a theological theme had failed. In
spite of individual displacements Luke's words 'to write in order'
(1 : 3) referred mainly to chronological order. This expressed a
widespread conviction in Farrar's generation. In spite of evidence
to the contrary this judgment continues to be followed in some
recent commentaries (e.g. Geldenhuys).

The problem, however, entails more than individual chronological displacements, as the structure of Luke's central division
clearly shows (9 : 51–19 : 44; see below, pp. 34 ff., 146–9). It is very
doubtful that Luke intends to give a chronological sequence at all
except in the broadest outline. Miss Guilding (pp. 138f., 230f.)
believes that Luke's episodes sometimes follow the order of the
Old Testament lections read in Jewish (and Christian) worship
services. Other writers see the influence of various theological
interests upon the organization of the Gospel (e.g., Conzelmann;
Farrer, pp. 53–6; Morgenthaler, 1, 191–5; P. Schubert, *NS*). The
present commentary suggests that a comprehensive thematic structure is present in Luke's Gospel. Whatever the relative merit of
these proposals, they show at least that the judgment of Farrar's
time was premature and must be carefully reconsidered.

(*b*) *Midrash Pesher.* Recent studies have shown that some Old
Testament quotations in the New Testament are characterized by
an interpretative (*pesher*) text-form in which the New Testament
writer's commentary (*midrash*) is incorporated into the quotation

itself (cf. Stendahl, pp. 183–202; Ellis, pp. 139–47; Lindars, pp. 15–28). The modification of the text and the shift in its application adapt the citation to the writer's own day and to his specific interest and audience. This procedure and the resulting text form have been termed a *midrash pesher*. Strictly speaking, it goes beyond a simple interpretative alteration of the text. In *midrash pesher* the author contemporizes the text, fitting it to its 'fulfilment' in the writer's own time. B. Gärtner (*ST* 8, 1954, 6f., 13ff.) would restrict the definition and use of the term even more precisely.

There is reason to believe that this hermeneutical method was employed not only in citations from the Old Testament but also in the handling of the Gospel traditions. Sometimes it is difficult to know whether a textual alteration contains a 'fulfilment' motive or whether it is a simple interpretative elaboration. For example, the addition of 'king' in the citation in 19 : 38 and the change of a 'Q' saying from 'follow me' to 'preach the kingdom of God' (9 : 60) are simple adaptations to Luke's theme. However, the addition of 'daily' to the command to take up the cross appears to shift the saying to the post-resurrection situation of the Church. Also, the alterations in 3 : 16 ('holy spirit and fire') and 12 : 11 ('authorities') probably were made in a post-Pentecost and diaspora Christianity. Such changes assume that these pre-resurrection sayings find their fulfilment in 'the time of the Church'.

This activity was not confined to the Evangelists but appears to have been practised by (other) Christian prophets whose oracles and *midrash pesher* the Evangelists use (see on 13 : 34f.; 21 : 20–24; the special note at 11 : 49–51). There is no evidence, however, that this was a liberty taken casually. (There also was a concern for 'the facts as they were'. One sees this, for example, when Luke (9 : 28) alters Mark's six days to 'about' eight days.) Also, it was not apparently an activity engaged in by the Christian community as a whole. Otto Piper's words are in order: 'The time has come to de-mythologize the myth of a creative collectivity called "die Gemeinde" [the community]' (*JBL* 78, 1959, 123). However, the creactive activity which does appear in the Gospels must be explained, and it should be done in a manner appropriate to the prophetic and charismatic character of the early Christian movement. Prophetic oracles and the '*pesher*-ing' of pre-resurrection sayings form a part of that creativity.

*   *   *

These observations tell us something about the nature of the Gospels and of the traditions lying behind them. The Gospel tradition did not merely preserve Jesus' words and deeds. It proclaimed them. For some years after the resurrection, the traditions of the Lord were interpreted and applied to the life of the Church by men 'gifted' and authorized for this task. The Evangelists continued this process and brought it into a firm and final shape. Some would seek in the Gospels a map of all the journeys of Jesus and a chronological sketch of his mission. But the Evangelists were not court-reporters, nor were they newspaper correspondents sending wire dispatches from the scene. They conceive their task to be something quite different. They are concerned to interpret and transmit the traditions in the light of their understanding of Messiah's message and of the needs of their readers.

In the DSS and in the New Testament, Old Testament sayings are not the occasion for creating events, but rather they are interpreted in the light of known events (see F. F. Bruce, *BJRL* 43, 1960–1, 350ff.; Davies, *Sermon*, p. 208f.; Lindars, p. 25; B. Gärtner *ST* 8, 1955, 12). Although there are differences, one might expect a similar attitude (in Palestine) toward the Gospel sayings. This supposition is strengthened by the presence of the same hermeneutical procedures in the Gospel traditions. That is, the creative element in the formation of the Gospel traditions probably should not be understood, as it is in some of the older form criticism, as the creation of events. Rather it is, in considerable measure at least, an employment of interpretative alterations and of a kind of *midrash pesher*. In this frame of reference the events already are at hand. The creative element lies more in the sayings and in the literary structure, elaboration, and application given to the events and sayings in the Gospels. See on 7 : 36–50.

THE THEOLOGY OF LUKE

The investigations mentioned above have shown that the Evangelist is a careful historian, and it is not his method, nor that of his predecessors, to invent events to serve their interests. Nevertheless, within the context of historical narration Luke has a distinctive message to give. Because of the nature of his task he does not present his message, his theology, in the direct form of a creed or doctrinal treatise. Yet his beliefs and teachings may be recognized

in various ways. Obviously Luke–Acts is not the account of a dis-
interested observer and recorder. The topical emphases, the selection and alteration of the sources, and the structure and progress
of the story appear to be carefully planned by the author. They
all have an interpretative function, revealing and highlighting the
teachings that Luke wishes to convey.

The main theme of the Gospel is the nature of Jesus' messiahship and mission. As the outline below indicates, this theme is
developed by a series of episodes (see below, pp. 32–6). These
episodes give a 'witness' to the meaning of Jesus' person, and of
the coming kingdom of God that he preaches. Central to this
witness is the part played by the Holy Spirit.

The Role of the Holy Spirit

The emphasis given to the Holy Spirit in the Lukan writings has
frequently been observed. Fundamentally, 'witness' in the Gospel
is the witness of the Spirit, most often through the acts and teachings of Jesus (4 : 31–22 : 53) but also through Old Testament and
contemporary prophets (1 : 5–2 : 40; 3 : 16; see below, p. 28).
The Spirit is the same 'Spirit of the Lord' who spoke through the
prophets (4 : 18; Ac. 1 : 16), but he now appears in a new role.
This role determines the meaning of Jesus' messiahship and of his
message of the kingdom of God. What the Spirit foretold through
the prophets he now has accomplished through Messiah. Jesus of
Nazareth, the decisive figure in this new act of the Spirit, is
Spirit conceived (1 : 35) and Spirit confirmed (3 : 22). He proclaims his message through the Spirit (4 : 18; 10 : 21; 11 : 20; Ac.
1 : 2) and, after his resurrection, mediates the Spirit to his followers
(24 : 49; Ac. 2 : 33).

The Messiahship of Jesus

Luke is concerned not to prove Jesus' messiahship but to show the
nature of it. A number of traditional terms for Messiah are applied
to Jesus: he is the Son of God (3 : 21f.), the Son of David (20 : 41–
44), the Son of man (5 : 24), and the suffering Servant (4 : 17–19;
Ac. 3 : 13). Luke leaves the definition of these titles to the content
that Jesus' acts and sayings gave them. The person of Messiah is
defined in terms of his mission.

Luke points to the uniqueness of Jesus in a number of ways. His whole life, death, and resurrection are one continuing fulfilment of prophecy (see below, pp. 30f., 67, 265). He has a divine origin and a unique relation to God; he does works that only God can do (1 : 35; 2 : 49; 10 : 22; see below, p. 99). Jesus, in a word, is 'the Lord' whose name is decisive for man's salvation (24 : 47; Ac. 4 : 12).

The acts and teachings of Jesus testify that he is the instrument through whom God will accomplish both redemption and judgment. The role of Jesus and the sphere of his authority are pictured in two diverse images, Israel and Adam, the nation and the whole of humanity. He will execute judgment on both (3 : 17; Ac. 17 : 31). More importantly, he also is the redeemer of both. As the fulfilment of the hope of the nation, he is the king who inherits the throne of David (1 : 32). He is the prophet like Moses who reconstitutes the twelve tribes of Israel and through his death and resurrection brings about a new 'exodus' of salvation (6 : 12–16; 9 : 31; Ac. 3 : 22). He is identified with the nation at his baptism (3 : 22) and dies as the suffering servant of Israel (see on 22 : 7–38). In his resurrection he is the new temple in whom the true Israel of God inheres (see the special note at 19 : 45–20 : 18), and at the end of this age he will 'restore the kingdom to Israel' (Ac. 1 : 6).

On the other hand, a number of traits in Luke–Acts indicate that the Evangelist also views Jesus, even as Paul did, as the counterpart to Adam (cf. Grundmann, p. 3; Gärtner, p. 251ff.). Like Adam, Jesus is the Son of God, created by God's Spirit (3 : 38). His resurrection marks an 'eighth day' (see on 24 : 13), the beginning of a new creation into which Jesus' followers are incorporated (see on 5 : 24; 23 : 43). Luke's use of this imagery discloses his understanding of the relation between Jesus and his disciples. It also bears upon the larger question of the relation of Christianity to Judaism and to the world (see below).

The Gospel of Luke teaches, and the Book of Acts amply illustrates, that the fate of Jesus is the fate of his followers. If he is attested by God and rejected by men, so are they (see below, p. 18). If he has no resting place in this world (9 : 58), they too are destined to wander, preaching the kingdom of God. The disciples are commanded to carry their cross after Jesus (9 : 23), and his persecution marks the beginning of their own (22 : 35ff.). Even Christian martyrdom is described in terms reminiscent of

the death of Jesus (23 : 34; Ac. 7 : 60). These parallels are not to
be understood merely as an existential imitation of Jesus but as
the working out of a corporate relation to Jesus. Jesus' disciples
have his Spirit, proclaim his message, bear his cross and share his
glory because they are, in Paul's idiom, 'the body of Christ' whose
destiny is bound up 'with' Christ (22 : 28ff.; see on 23 : 43). Although Luke does not use the Pauline idiom, his thought pattern
is very close, if not identical, to the Apostle's.

The goal toward which Jesus moves is to be 'received up' to
God through death and resurrection (9 : 31, 51; Ac. 1 : 2). Luke,
like the author of the Fourth Gospel, apparently views Messiah's
death and resurrection as essentially one event that accomplishes
his glorification (see on 13 : 32f.). Because Jesus is the prototype
of the Christian, the Christian life also is always a life in the
process of being glorified. Therefore, unlike Paul, Luke develops
no distinct and separate *theologia crucis* in his portrayal of the lives
of Jesus' followers: Christian suffering is suffering with Jesus (cf.
Ac. 9 : 4f.) and is the appointed path to glorification (see on
12 : 1–12; Ac. 14 : 22). In the final analysis this also is Paul's
conclusion: 'We suffer with him in order that we may also be
glorified with him' (Rom. 8 : 17).

The Kingdom of God

The person of Jesus originates and defines the company who will
share God's glorious and mighty redemption. The message of Jesus
announces this redemption, 'the good news of the kingdom of God'
(4 : 43; cf. Mk 1 : 15). This theme becomes prominent in the Gospel of Luke in connection with the mission of the kingdom of God
(8 : 1ff.). In the subsequent division of the Gospel (9 : 51–19 : 44) it
is the dominant motif.

The theme of the kingdom of God has its roots in the teaching of
Jesus and in pre-Christian Judaism. The imminent appearance of
the reign of God was a lively hope in first-century Palestine. It was
expected to establish righteousness and peace, to bring divine
judgment upon the world, and to deliver and exalt the nation of
Israel. Studies of the sayings of Jesus have shown that he shared
this hope and claimed to be the Son of man who would establish
the kingdom (cf. Perrin, pp. 104ff.; see on 5 : 24). But Jesus qualified the popular expectation in a number of ways. He rejected a

political interpretation of God's kingdom. It was not in rivalry with Caesar, nor could it be identified with Jewish nationalism. Jesus depicted the kingdom rather as a new order of creation that would deliver men from sin and death and bring the present age to a catastrophic end. The new creation, like the present one, would be brought into being by the mighty power of the Spirit of God. The unique and revolutionary aspect of Jesus' message was his assertion that in his ministry this new creation already was breaking in upon the present age: 'If it is by the finger of God that I cast out demons, then the kingdom of God has come upon you' (11 : 20; cf. Mt. 12 : 28; Kümmel, pp. 105ff.; cf. Hengel, pp. 20–35).

Luke underlines and develops Jesus' teaching about the kingdom especially at two points. Like the Fourth Evangelist, he affirms the two-stage manifestation of the kingdom, and accents its manifestation in the present (see below, pp. 162f., 200f.; on 23 : 42f.; Ellis, *John*, pp. 37–42, 74f.) Also Luke interprets the role of the Spirit in the Church as being similar to his role in Jesus' pre-resurrection mission: the Spirit constitutes a continuing presence of the kingdom of God in the post-resurrection Church. (In Acts the term 'kingdom of God' is used only of a future event. But Luke's understanding of the matter is evident in the 'acts' of the Spirit and especially in the temple typology; cf. Ac. 5 : 16 with Ac. 10 : 38; the special note at 19 : 45–20 : 18; cf. Barrett, p. 101). Like Paul and Jesus, Luke regards the Holy Spirit as the mediator of the reign of God, 'the anticipation of the end in the present' (Cullmann, *Time*, p. 72; Ellis, *Interpreters*, pp. 37–40). The Spirit's presence, therefore, obviates any anxiety about the time of the kingdom's glorious and public manifestation in the future (Ac. 1 : 8 (*alla*); cf. Conzelmann, p. 136).

Within this frame of reference 'to preach the kingdom' (9 : 60; 16 : 16) means for Luke not only that the message of the kingdom is present (Conzelmann, p. 122). It means also that in the events produced by the Spirit in Jesus' pre- and post-resurrection missions the kingdom itself is being manifested (see on 10 : 9, 17ff.; 11 : 31f.; 16 : 16; 17 : 20f.; 23 : 32–49). Like the creative word of God in Genesis (1 : 3), the word of the kingdom contains within it the reality of the new creation itself. Nevertheless, the kingdom also remains in the future, and its coming is associated with the *parousia*, the glorious appearance of Jesus at the close of the age

(19 : 11; 22 : 18; cf. 11 : 2; Ac. 1 : 7, 11). Luke is quite interested in distinguishing these two stages in the manifestation of the reign of God.

As the bearer of the kingdom, Jesus' present mission is one of redemption and not of destruction (see on 9 : 51–56). This becomes apparent in his conflict with the demonic realm. Satan, of course, is always 'God's Devil', serving God's purpose and having no independent authority (cf. Conzelmann, pp. 156f.). But the power of Satan and his demonic kingdom (11 : 18; 13 : 11, 16) extends over mankind and is subject only to the power of the kingdom of God (4 : 5ff.; Ac. 19 : 15f.; 26 : 18). The power of the Spirit begins to break the dominion of the demons and to banish them to their proper abode (see on 8 : 31; 10 : 18f.). Perhaps this is understood as a prelude to their destruction (4 : 34), but Luke does not pursue the question. His total emphasis is the redemption of men from demonic powers.

In the present time the word of the kingdom brings to men deliverance from the power of Satan, the bestowal of messianic peace (10 : 5), forgiveness of sins (5 : 20; Ac. 2 : 38), and the proclamation of 'the acceptable year of the Lord'. (Significantly, Lk. 4 : 19 omits the following line of the quotation, 'and the day of vengeance of our God'; Isa. 61 : 2.) Nevertheless, the present manifestation of the kingdom does not bring final redemption. The faithful disciple now receives 'manifold more', but eternal life awaits the 'age to come' (18 :30). Also, the present is a time of testing and the prelude to a future redemption (see below, p. 163; cf. 21 : 28; Ac. 14 : 22). Because the powers of the coming age are now being manifested, the present, in contrast to the past, has become a time of decision and division (9 : 57–62; 12 : 49ff.; Ac. 17 : 30). By their response to the kingdom message men reveal whether they are destined for the life of the age to come (8 : 1–18; Ac. 13 : 46, 48).

The future revelation of the kingdom consummates the redemption of Jesus' followers. More important, it is 'the wrath to come', a time of judgment and destruction (3 : 7, 17). Thus, in the Gospel Jesus' message of redemption is also in large measure a warning both to the rejector and to faithless disciples (see below, pp. 179, 187). The Judge will be God himself (cf. 12 : 5; 20 : 16). But Jesus, who now is God's instrument of redemption, at his future appearance will be God's instrument of judgment (cf.

12 : 46; Ac. 10 : 42; 17 : 31). Although the judgment awaits the last
day, tokens of it appear in the present. For example, the destruction of Jerusalem is so interpreted and, therefore, is closely related
to the future revelation of the kingdom (cf. 13 : 6–9; 21 : 5–38).
Also, the fate of Judas and of Ananias and Sapphira may exemplify the judgment of all unfaithful disciples (Ac. 1, 5).

Christianity and the World

(a) *Luke's Understanding of History.* Of the Evangelists Luke alone
has a second volume of the 'acts' of Jesus' post-resurrection mission
through the Church. Also, more than the others, he places the pre-
resurrection mission in the wider context of world history (2 : 1f.;
3 : 1). Most significantly, he presents the mission and message of
Jesus as the decisive historical event by which all God's acts of
redemption and judgment are to be understood (Ac. 2 : 33, 36;
17 : 30f.). Luke is properly called a 'theologian of redemptive
history' (E. Lohse, *EvT* 14, 1954–5, 256ff.). That is, he regards
history to be the realm of God's redemptive activity and interprets
the movement and goal of history by this fact. This raises two
further questions. How does Luke understand the structure and
progress of redemptive history? How does he relate redemptive
history to the world in which he lives and writes?

The important work of H. Conzelmann (pp. 149f., 170) has
drawn attention to the Lukan scheme and has interpreted it as a
three-stage history of salvation: the period of the prophets, the
period of Jesus, and the period of the Church. The period of
Jesus is unique. It is separate from that of the Church in that it is a
special time of salvation (4 : 18f.), protected from the activity of
Satan (Conzelmann, pp. 36, 170, 195). While there are distinctions
between the pre- and post-resurrection missions (see on 24 :33–
53), the kind of division that Conzelmann makes is questionable
(cf. P. S. Minear, *SL*, pp. 121–5). Satan is, as a matter of fact,
active in the pre-resurrection mission and in a manner similar to his
activity in the Church (see on 22 : 3). Also, there seems to be no
reason to limit the time of fulfilment, the 'today' of Jesus' mission,
to the pre-resurrection or pre-passion period (4 : 21; see on 23 : 43;
cf. 2 C. 6 : 2). The post-resurrection mission is still the mission of
Jesus (Ac. 1 : 1, 'began'; 9 : 4). In it the same message is proclaimed and the Spirit and the 'name' of Jesus have still the same
function. Cf. 4 : 18; 10 : 21; Ac. 1 : 8; 3 : 16; H. Schürmann, *ETS*

12, 1962, 69n; Barrett, p. 101; W. C. Robinson, p. 29; Haenchen, pp. 130ff.

The pre-resurrection mission of Jesus is a time of unique events, but for Luke it inaugurates and belongs to the same 'time of salvation' in which Luke's readers live. Only this explains, for example, the fact that the Evangelist can contemporize the pre-resurrection sayings of Jesus and mix among them oracles from the exalted Jesus (see on 11 : 49–51). Luke's structure of redemptive history consists in the time of promise ('the law and the prophets') followed by the time of fulfilment ('the kingdom of God'). The latter begins with the mission of Jesus and the Church (see on 16 : 16; 24 : 33–53), but it is consummated only at the *parousia*. Therefore Luke's scheme may be represented as follows: the time of promise, the manifestation of the kingdom in the present age, the future manifestation of the kingdom in 'the age to come' (18 : 30). Cf. Ac. 17 : 30f.

It is important for Luke to show the relation of Christianity to the world because God's kingdom, as it is manifest in the Church, overlaps and occurs within the continuing course of this age. Luke's interest in history and in the world is determined by his theological understanding of history and the world. This is true even when apologetic and political considerations also are present as, for example, in the relation of Christianity to Judaism and to the Roman Empire (cf. Conzelmann, pp. 148f.).

(*b*) *The Church and Judaism.* The rejection of Jesus by religious Judaism was already a problem in the pre-resurrection mission. Jesus answered it by referring his disciples to the Scriptures. The nation has always rejected its prophets and, moreover, it is God's purpose for Messiah to suffer and be rejected (e.g. 8 : 10; 9 : 22; Mk 6 : 4). The third Gospel gives considerable attention to both these matters. In the post-resurrection mission the Jewish rejection of the gospel became final, and Luke makes this fact a continuing motif (see below, pp. 61f).

The subject is important to the Evangelist for several reasons. First, the Jewish rejection is the occasion for giving the gospel to the Gentiles and, therefore, a turning point in the progress of redemptive history (Ac. 13 : 46; cf. Rom. 1 : 16; 11 : 11). Also, it forms a part of a large question, 'who will receive the kingdom of God?' (see below, pp. 109f., 187, 200f.; cf. 1 C. 1 : 26ff.). Finally,

the Jewish rejection of Messiah is the vantage point from which
God's rejection of Judaism and the Church's relation to Judaism
are to be understood. Broadly speaking, all these interests are a
part of Paul's theology. Possibly they reflect the Apostle's influence upon Luke. But Luke develops the ideas independently and
with a different purpose in view.

Perhaps with an eye toward the Church's relations with the
Roman state, Luke effectively distinguishes Christianity from
Judaism, and he lays bare the evil and groundless nature of the
Jewish antagonism to the followers of Messiah (cf. Conzelmann,
pp. 138–44). Theologically, Luke views the relationship of Judaism
and Christianity from two perspectives. On the one hand, the
Church and Judaism share the same Scriptures and have a common heritage in redemptive history. The gospel is nothing more
than 'the hope of Israel' that is ever again offered 'to the Jew
first' (Rom. 1 : 16; cf. Ac. 13 : 46; 28 : 17–20). Judaism's conversion remains a special object of the Church's mission, and even
its unfaithfulness foreshadows the Church's own sin.

On the other hand, while Judaism and Christianity are insepar-
ably coupled, their divorce is equally real and decisive. The
Church, and no longer Judaism, embodies the true Israel, the
people of God. That is, the 'people for his name' now include
Gentiles as well as Jews (Ac. 15 : 14). Ideally, the people of God,
the *laos*, should be identical with the Jewish nation; and Luke
most frequently uses the term in this way (cf. N. A. Dahl, *NTS* 4,
1957–8, 324ff.; Schweizer, pp. 63f.). But this only serves to emphasize the consequences of Jewish rejection. Acceptance of Messiah
is the true mark of 'a son of Abraham' (see on 19 : 1–10; 3 : 8f.).
Those who reject him 'shall be destroyed from the people' (Ac.
3 : 23). Israel, the people of God, continues in the messianic community (cf. Ac. 1 : 6), but the rejecting Jewish nation has excluded
itself from 'the people' and has come under divine judgment.

God's rejection of Judaism is shown especially in two events of
redemptive history. God's presence now dwells in a new temple
and Jerusalem, because of its rejection of Messiah, will be destroyed. See on 23 : 26–31; the special note at 19 : 45–20 : 18. For
Luke the judgment of Judaism exemplifies God's future judgment
on all apostasy and evil. Thus, the destruction of Jerusalem is
closely related to the judgment of the last day (see above, pp. 14f.).
And Jesus' warnings to an unrepentant Judaism can be applied

to unfaithful churchmen of Luke's own time (e.g., 12 : 10; 13 : 1–9; cf. 1 C. 10 : 1–11.).

(c) *The Church in the World.* The Church's relation to the world, like its relation to Judaism, has both political and theological ramifications. Politically, Luke refutes the Jewish charge that Christianity is a subversive element in the Empire. Pilate recognizes that Jesus' kingship is non-political. Similarly, the Roman authorities in Greece and Asia testify that Paul has committed no criminal offence (23 : 4; cf. 22 : 49ff.; Ac. 18 : 14f.; 26 : 31f.). As a law-abiding Roman citizen, Paul illustrates Jesus' maxim that the legitimate claims of Caesar are not in conflict with the claims of God (20 : 25; cf. Conzelmann, pp. 137–40).

The theological relationship of the Church and the world, that is, the present political, social, and natural order, is more complex, and at first impression it is ambiguous. Positively, the world and 'everything in it' are created by God and subject to his rightful lordship. At his future appearance Jesus will effect a 'universal restoration' of that lordship (Ac. 3 : 21 *NEB*; 14 : 15; 17 : 24ff.; cf. Rom. 8 : 18–22; Mt. 19 : 28). Nevertheless, the kingdoms of the world presently have been delivered to the dominion of Satan (4 : 6). While they exercise a legitimate authority, to which Christians are subject, the nations belong essentially to 'this age'. Therefore, both Jesus and his disciples are destined to be persecuted by them (12 : 11; 21 : 12; see on 22 : 3, 47–53).

The situation of the Church in the world is governed by Luke's understanding of redemptive history. The kingdom of God, although presently manifest in the world, is never identified with it. The sons of the kingdom are always distinguished from the 'sons of this age' (cf. 12 : 29f.; 16 : 8; 20 : 34f.). Consequently, the 'universalism' of Luke, for which his Gospel is justly noted, is not be be mistaken for a redemption of all men or of the present world order. Rather it means that all men, no less than the Jews, now are offered the good news of the kingdom of God and stand under God's demand for decision (Ac. 17 : 30f.). All who respond to the kingdom's message will receive the resurrection life of the coming age. Those who adhere to the world will share in the judgment and death under which it exists and to which it is destined (12 : 13–34; 17 : 26–33; 21 : 26–8).

THE TEXT OF THE GOSPEL

Important Textual Questions

New Testament students are very fortunate in having a comparatively large number of manuscripts of great antiquity and excellent quality. For the vast majority of passages, the Greek Testament that we have is essentially identical with the text of the author himself. Nevertheless, individual textual problems remain to be solved. For Luke–Acts the differences between two textual families, the Western and the Alexandrian, pose the major difficulty. The Alexandrian text-type now can be traced as far back as the late second-century (B. M. Metzger, *ET* 73, 1961–2, 203), and in all likelihood the Western text, best represented by Codex Bezae (D), is equally primitive (cf. A. F. J. Klijn, *NoT* 3, 1959, 22ff.). Each of these families has been championed as the truest representative of Luke's original manuscript. In the last century the British scholars Westcott and Hort classed the Western text as secondary. However, on the Continent F. Blass argued that both text-types were original. The Alexandrian text of the Gospel represented Luke's first draft, written perhaps in Caesarea; the Western text was a revision issued by the Evangelist in Rome. This theory—and a similar one for Acts—has not found general acceptance, but the past fifty years have witnessed a sharp qualification of the estimate placed on the Western text by Westcott and Hort.

In recent discussion, A. J. Wensinck, who favours Blass's theory of two autographs, contends that the Western text is a more faithful representation of Aramaic, the language of Jesus and of the earliest Christian documents (cf. Black, pp. 29–34). It is possible, of course, that any Aramaic text behind Codex D was a later retranslation from a Greek text (Torrey, pp. 128f.). However, this explanation is cumbersome. C. S. C. Williams (p. 54) raises a more important objection: the Western text, at least in Acts, does not conform to the style of Luke–Acts elsewhere (*contra*: Zahn III, 13f.). The problem of the original text of Luke remains unresolved. But M. Black (pp. 33f.) rightly concludes that the readings of the Western text have to be examined 'without any presuppositions being entertained about the best single manuscript source for the earliest text'. The merit of the individual reading, rather than the pedigree of its family, should be the decisive factor for determining the correct text.

Textual studies in the Aramaic background of Gospel traditions not only help to determine the original text of Luke and his sources, but also clarify the character and intention of 'Gospel' writing. M. Black (p. 275) has shown that in a number of passages 'the Gospels are not just the interpretation of translators; they are also the "Targum" of Evangelists'. We may believe that this 'targumizing', or interpretative paraphrasing, sometimes served a theological purpose. Black's conclusions thus give added force to the observations made above (pp. 7ff.) on *midrash pesher*.

Important Textual Variants in Luke

A number of the more important textual variants in Luke are indicated below. Their significance and the questions that they raise are discussed in the Commentary.

(a) *Variants in the Western text that are absent from (or different in) the Alexandrian text.*
    (1) The heavenly voice at Jesus' baptism (3 : 22).
    (2) Jesus' word to a Sabbath-breaker (6 : 5).
    (3) Jesus' reply to the comparison of his mission with Elijah's (9 : 55).
    (4) The longer text of the Lord's prayer (11 : 2–4).
    (5) Jesus' agony and vision of the angel (22 : 43f.).

(b) *Variants in the Alexandrian text that are absent from the Western text.*
    (1) The comparison of healing on the Sabbath to the rescue of a son (14 : 5).
    (2) The title 'sons of God' for those who attain the resurrection (20 : 36).
    (3) The longer text of the institution of the Lord's Supper (22 : 19b–20).
    (4) Jesus' ascension into heaven (24 : 51).
    (5) The disciples' worship of the resurrected Jesus (24 : 52).

(c) *Other variants.*
    (1) Passages bearing on the virgin-conception of Jesus (1 : 34; 2 : 5, 41).

(2) A petition in the Lord's Prayer for the coming of the
Holy Spirit (11 : 2).

(3) The story of the woman taken in adultery (21 : 38).'

(4) Jesus' prayer for those who crucified him (23 : 34).

2. THE ORGANIZATION AND STRUCTURE OF THE GOSPEL

THE FORMATION OF THE GOSPELS

Fifty years ago most New Testament scholars believed that in the
'two-document hypothesis' the relationship of the first three
Gospels had found a broadly definitive solution. According to this
hypothesis, Matthew and Luke were dependent upon two primary
documents, the Gospel of Mark and 'Q'; Q was inferred from
passages common to Matthew and Luke which did not occur in
Mark. To this foundation Matthew and Luke added their own
special traditions, 'M' and 'L' respectively, to complete their Gospels. If M and L are regarded as documents (Streeter, pp. 227–70),
a 'four-document hypothesis' results:

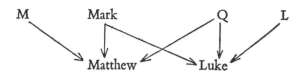

The two-document (or four-document) hypothesis has remained
dominant in New Testament studies, but two developments in the
past generation have brought it under increasing question.
Directly, a persistent minority of scholars has raised important
objections to the chronological priority of Mark (cf. Farmer, pp.
118–77, 196f.), and a larger number has questioned the existence
of a Q document. Indirectly, the emergence of form criticism, that
is, the analysis of the individual literary units of the Gospels, has
undermined some of the assumptions underlying the two-document hypothesis.

Extensive and detailed parallels in the non-Markan sections of
Matthew and Luke make it highly probable that common written

traditions lie behind them. These traditions (Q) usually have been conceived to be one document. As it is reconstructed, Q consists of a collection of Jesus' sayings, prefaced by an account of his baptism, but without the Passion story. F. F. Bruce (*NBD*, p. 486; cf. Streeter, p. 291) compares it to an Old Testament prophetic book that gives the prophet's call and his oracles but omits mention of his death. T. W. Manson (*Sayings*, pp. 17ff.) and others have identified it with 'Matthew's oracles' mentioned by Papias early in the second century (cf. Eus. 3, 39, 16). These suggestions are plausible enough if it is assumed that such a document existed. But very little has been done to demonstrate that Q was one document. It is not sufficient to point to Semitic phraseology and conflicts with the Pharisees (W. C. Allen, *OS*, pp. 236, 241f.). Nor does the common sequence, in Matthew and Luke, of *some* Q episodes necessarily point to the unity of the *whole* material (so, V. Taylor, *JTS* N.s. 3, 1952, 129f.; *FBK*, p. 51). Because of the lack of distinctive criteria by which the Q material may be identified, no agreement exists on its precise nature or content. There is, therefore, some justification in the gibe of S. Petrie (*NoT* 3, 1959, 28ff.) that 'Q is only what you make it'. Certainly there is little or no clear evidence for the widely held view that the passages common to Matthew and Luke are derived from one document.

The tenuous character of Q made it suspect in the eyes of some scholars even at the height of its popularity (cf. Ropes, p. 93). In recent years the doubts have increased. A. Farrer (*SG*, pp. 55ff.) has contended that the Q material in Luke may be accounted for by Luke's use of Matthew and, therefore, without recourse to a hypothetical document (similarly, Butler, pp. 60f.). This argument is supported, although not proved, by passages in which Luke agrees with Matthew against a parallel text in Mark (cf. N. Turner, *SE*, p. 234). But other evidence weighs heavily against Farrer's explanation of Luke's agreements with Matthew. Some Q material that is united in Matthew is scattered in Luke, and some that is scattered in Matthew is united in Luke. Although it is possible that Luke fitted Matthean material to his own outline, the rearrangement is quite unlike Luke's use of Mark. This at least raises questions about a theory of simple dependence of Luke on Matthew. Four other considerations virtually rule out this possibility and require in some Q passages the hypothesis that Luke

used a source or sources on which the First Evangelist also was
dependent.

(1) A few non-Matthean settings of Q passages (e.g., 11 : 1) do
not appear to be editorial.
(2) Some non-Matthean variations in the immediate context are
most probably derived from Luke's source. For example, the
formula, 'the wisdom of God said' (11 : 49), never occurs elsewhere and is scarcely, as B. C. Butler (p. 35) thinks, a re-
phrasing of Matthew. The same is true of 7 : 1 (cf. Mt. 7 : 28).
(3) H. J. Cadbury (*Style*, pp. 83ff.) and H. Schürmann (*ZKT* 75,
1953, 344n; 76, 1954, 83–93) have shown that Luke tends to
avoid repetitions. Instances of repetitious phraseology in
7 : 19f. and 11 : 47f. are very probably not editorial, and they
are not from Matthew. They can be explained otherwise only
by reference to a Q source. Similarly, the repetition of 'you
build' in 11 : 47f. is neither Lukan nor from Matthew: apparently the words, 'you build' (11 : 48) and 'you are sons
of' (Mt. 23 : 31), are variant renderings of the same Aramaic
phrase (Black, *Gospels*, pp. 11f.). The Lukan form of 7 : 3ff.
presents a similar situation. R. Morgenthaler (1, 50) points to
some 'Lukan' repetitions (e.g., 19 : 31, 34; 22 : 40, 46). These
instances, however, do not affect the general validity of the
conclusions above. Most of Morgenthaler's examples may be
repetitions already present in Luke's sources.
(4) Some Matthean sayings presuppose a non-Markan source that
appears in Luke. Compare the variant 'watch' (*phulakē*), in
Mt. 24 : 43 with Lk. 12 : 38 (cf. H. Schürman, *NTS* 6, 1959–
60, 208).

Although Farrer's explanation of the Q material is not satisfactory, the question that he poses cannot be evaded. Is the Q-
document hypothesis really necessary? Considerable research into
the formation of the Gospel tradition suggests that it is not. Form
criticism has shown it to be probable that the Gospel traditions were
first written as short tracts. Very soon, if not at the beginning, the
individual units were joined to give sayings and/or stories on a
similar theme or to tell what Jesus did at a given place or time
(e.g., 8 : 40–56; cf. Manson, *Sayings*, p. 13). Traces of earlier collections remain visible in the Gospels (see below, pp. 27ff.) and,

on the other hand, the earlier groupings often are rearranged by the Evangelists to fit their own themes and purposes. Under the two-document hypothesis Q is represented as an intermediate stage document in the formation of the Gospel traditions. The evidence of form criticism and the intermixed placement of the Q (and L) material in the Gospels themselves point to a more probable alternative. The non-Markan material common to Matthew and Luke (Q) was not a single document but, at most, a stratum of tradition (cf. Dibelius, *Tradition*, pp. 234f.; G. Bornkamm, *RGG* II, 756). Probably it is best understood as several short independent tracts, cycles of tradition upon which Matthew and Luke drew (cf. C. K. Barrett, *ET* 54, 1942–3, 320ff.; Knox, *Gospels*, II, 3ff., 47). Sometimes both Evangelists had the same tract in hand. Sometimes, as the differences between them indicate, they used variant forms of that tradition. With these considerations in mind the sources of the third Gospel may now be examined.

THE SOURCES OF LUKE

A General Classification of the Sources

The very close and ordered parallels with large sections of Mark make it virtually certain that the Evangelist had a copy of the second Gospel before him. The other sources may be defined broadly as traditions used in common with Matthew (Q) and with John and traditions peculiar to Luke (L). The episodes in Luke may be classified according to source as below. One must allow, of course, for Lukan alterations *ad hoc* and by the fusing of different sources. Also, there may be an overlapping of sources in which Luke has, for example, both Markan and L or Markan and Q accounts of the same narrative (cf. Schramm, p. 186). Also some L material, such as 12 : 35–38, is probably only a portion of a Q source unused by Matthew. The classification therefore, has a fixed element of uncertainty and is offered only as a general guide.

THE EPISODES OF THE GOSPEL OF LUKE

Arranged according to their sources

Q	Mark	L
		1 : 5–2 : 52
3 : 1–20		3 : 1–20 in part?

Q	Mark	L
3 : 21–22		
		3 : 23–38
4 : 1–13		
		4 : 14–30
	4 : 31–44	
		5 : 1–11
	5 : 12–6 : 16	6 : 12–16 in part?
6 : 17–7 : 10		
		7 : 11–17
7 : 18–35		
		7 : 36–50
	8 :1–18 in part	8 : 1–18 in part
9 : 18–45 each episode in part?	8 : 19–9 : 50	
		9 : 51–56
9 : 57–62		
10 : 1–20 in part		10 : 1–20 in part
10 : 21–24		
		10 : 29–42
11 : 1–54 each episode in part		11 : 1–54 each episode in part
12 : 1–12		
12 : 13–34 in part		12 : 13–34 in part
12 : 35–48		
12 : 49–59 each episode in part		12 : 49–59 each episode in part
		13 : 1–9
13 : 10–35 each episode in part		13 : 10–35 each episode in part
14 : 16–24 in part?		14 : 1–24
14 : 25–17 : 10 each episode in part		14 : 25–17 : 10 each episode in part
		17 : 11–19
17 : 20–37 in part		17 : 20–37 in part
		18 : 1–14
	18 : 15–43	
		19 : 1–10
19 : 11–27 in part?		19 : 11–27
	19 : 28–44 in part	19 : 28–44 in part

Q	Mark	L
	19 : 45–21 : 4	
	21 : 5–38 in part	21 : 5–38 in part
	22 : 1–6	
	22 : 7–38 in part	22 : 7–38 in part
	22 : 39–46	22 : 39–46 in part?
	22 : 47–23 : 56 each episode in part	22 : 47–23 : 56 each episode in part
		24 : 1–53

The Nature and Relationship of the Sources

Since B. H. Streeter (pp. 201–22), it has been rather popular in British and American scholarship to regard Q+L (less Lk. 1–2) as the original Gospel, a proto-Luke, to which the Markan material was added (recently, Caird, pp. 23–7). The task facing the advocates of proto-Luke is like that posed by the Q-document hypothesis: the unity of the source must be established by reliable criteria. V. Taylor (pp. 68f., 172f.; *Luke*, pp. 8–30, 125f) seeks to do this, but the unity that he deduces appears to be nothing more than the unity of the Gospel of Luke itself. F. Rehkopf (pp. 87, 91–9), attacking the central problem, makes a valiant attempt to isolate a pre-Lukan vocabulary that is common to Q and L. It is doubtful, however, that his methodology is adequate to establish the limits, or the existence, of a proto-Luke (cf. H. Schürmann, *BZ* 5, 1961, 270, 285f.; W. C. Robinson, p. 52f.). Besides other objections to this hypothesis (cf. S. M. Gilmour, *JBL* 67, 1948, 143–52), the non-Markan sections of Luke presuppose the context and order of the present Gospel (cf. Conzelmann, pp. 28n, 33, 60ff.). Therefore, proto-Luke could have been hardly more than a selection of notes and tracts that Luke fitted to his present format.

It is more usual, and more probable, to regard Mark as the foundation document to which the Evangelist added the Q and L materials. Favouring this is the fact that the central division of Luke most likely is built upon the Markan journey scaffolding. But Luke's own contribution must not be underrated. If Mark forms the skeleton for the progression of parts of the Gospel, it does not determine the structure of the whole (see below). Luke's

alteration and omission of parts of Mark show that it, no less
than the Q and L traditions, is subservient to Luke's purposes.
Doubtless there are a number of reasons for the Markan omissions
(cf. Grundmann, pp. 8f.). But the primary reason is that no one
document is really the foundation for the third Gospel. All the
sources are quarries from which the Evangelist selects and adapts
material to serve his own end. The 'Gospel according Luke' is a
considerable achievement, an achievement that in plan, as well as
in publication, belongs to Luke.

Distinctive Elements in the Q and L Traditions

Several efforts have been made in recent years to identify individual sources within the Q and L materials. The results of these
studies suggest the following general classification: traditions in
common with the Gospel of John; traditions exhibiting a similar
linguistic, structural, or thematic character; personal sources of
the Evangelist.

Only the Gospels of Luke and John give prominence to Samaria,
place the prediction of Peter's denial at the Last Supper, speak
of two angels at the tomb, and identify the severed *right* ear of the
high priest's servant. They alone mention Mary and Martha,
Judas the son of James, Annas the high priest, and the satanic
possession of Judas Iscariot. These and other affinities are not of
such a nature as to indicate an immediate relationship between
the Gospels (*contra:* Bailey, p. 4n). J. Schniewind (pp. 95ff.) has
shown that they point rather to common traditions on which Luke
and John drew. Schniewind thinks that these were only oral
traditions (so P. Parker, *NTS* 9, 1962–3, 336). But the possibility
of some written materials also should be taken into account.

A number of investigations have revealed a remarkable amount
of Hebraic idiom in some sections of Luke (cf. F. Neirynck, *EL*,
pp. 179–93). Very probably the traditions used in the infancy
narratives (1 : 5–2 : 40), at least, rest directly upon written
Hebrew sources (cf. Schlatter, p. 201; Laurentin, p. 13; P. Winter,
NTS 1, 1954–5, 121). In the opinion of E. Schweizer (*TZ* 6, 1950,
183) and R. Laurentin (pp. 17f.) they have affinities with the
sources or milieu of the Fourth Gospel. Schweizer maintains that
this 'hebraizing' source may be recognized in several other L
passages: 5 : 1–11; 7 : 11–17, 36–50; 8 : 1–3; 9 : 51–56; 11 : 27f.;

13 : 10–17; 14 : 1–6; 17 : 11–19; 19 : 1–10; 23 : 50–24 : 53. These
verses reveal a striking linguistic affinity. Whether they are from
one written source remains an open question, especially in the
light of their thematic diversity, and the question applies equally
to the more homogeneous Passion narrative (cf. Grobel, p. 104).
The identification of a source on the basis of the structure of the
Lukan episodes (cf. W. R. Farmer, *NTS* 8, 1961–2, 301–16) is
even more difficult since the hand of the Evangelist may be
responsible.

It is quite possible that Luke's sources included a collection (or
collections) of contemporary prophetic oracles. In the Jewish mind
the Holy Spirit was primarily the spirit of prophecy. The absence
of prophecy, therefore, signified nothing less than the departure
of the Holy Spirit (*Sanh.* 11a; cf. *T. Sota* 13 : 2; *SBK* I, 127).
Luke's emphasis on the Holy Spirit is connected in some measure
with an interest in contemporary prophecy. For example, the
quotation of Joel in Ac. 2 : 18 is '*pesher*-ed', apparently by the
Evangelist, to stress the importance of prophecy among the current
Pentecostal 'fulfilments' (see above, pp. 7ff.). Similarly, the first
two chapters of the Gospel are built around the renewal of prophecy at the dawn of the messianic era. In common with the
Fourth Evangelist, Luke underlines the role of Jesus as prophet
(cf. Hastings, pp. 50–75; Fascher, p. 178). This is evident in the
attitude of Jesus' hearers, in the Lord's estimate of himself (13 : 28,
33; cf. Dahl, *SL*, p. 141), and in the Evangelist's editorial settings
(4 : 1; 10 : 21). Given these facts, it is not surprising to find in
Luke evidence of Christian prophetic oracles, some of which
appear to originate in the primitive Jerusalem church (see on
11 : 49–51). Oracles expressing a similar theme (e.g., 11 : 49–51;
13 : 34f.; 21 : 20–24) may have been derived from a common
source. But here, too, the unity of the material is not certain.

In conclusion, there are affinities between some passages of the
Q and L material which accord with the supposition that the
passages came from one pre-Lukan translator or source, but in no
case is there sufficient evidence to establish this. In each case the
degree of probability is difficult to assess.

If the author of Luke–Acts is Luke the physician and companion of Paul (see below), he very likely obtained information
from persons directly involved in the events he records. Indeed,
Luke claims to have received traditions from eyewitnesses (1 : 2).

A. Harnack (*Luke*, pp. 156f.) has called attention to Philip and his daughters. During his visit with them (Ac. 21 : 8f.: 'we') Luke received a first-hand account and perhaps some written traditions about the Samaritan mission (9 : 52–56; Ac. 8 : 5).

The Evangelist also had personal contacts in Jerusalem (Ac. 21 : 17). Jerusalem is the source of a number of the Q and L traditions, judging by the setting of the episodes and the point of view of the narration (e.g., 2 : 38; see on 13 : 1–9; 17 : 11). The two facts may not be unrelated. Also it may be, for example, that Joanna (8 : 3) is Luke's informant about Herod's household (23 : 8–10) and that Cleopas (24 : 18) told him of the walk to Emmaus. The linguistic character of the latter passage, at least, indicates that it already was in written Greek form when Luke obtained it; for the Evangelist, who can write good Greek, very likely would employ Semitic idiom only out of deference to a written source. The eyewitnesses that Luke knew probably were not immediate oral sources for the Gospel narrative, but they may have transmitted to Luke, or served to confirm, traditions already in written form (cf. D. E. Nineham, *JTS* 9, 1958, 13–25; Wilcox, pp. 83, 111, 180ff.).

THE STRUCTURE OF LUKE

Recent Approaches to the Structure of Luke

The discovery of the structure of the Gospel requires, first of all, some criterion by which it may be subdivided. As long as the Gospel is viewed as a running *chronological* account, the major subdivisions are easily secured: the infancy narratives (1–2); the Galilean mission (3 : 1–9 : 50); the journey to Jerusalem (9 : 51–19 : 44); the Jerusalem ministry, the passion, death, and resurrection (19 : 45–24 : 53). It has been shown above (pp. 6f.) that this view of the Gospel fails to explain Luke's ordering of his materials. Nonetheless, the general divisions achieved by this method are not necessarily incorrect.

V. Taylor (pp. 91f.) and, more emphatically, R. H. Lightfoot (pp. 78ff., 132–43) and H. Conzelmann (pp. 19–94) have pointed to *geographical* elements as an important factor in the composition of the Gospel. This results in a similar threefold division: Galilee, the journey, Jerusalem. While making a contribution, this view also has its limitations. The journey motif of the central division of the Gospel is given an undue importance (see below, pp. 147f.), and both Conzelmann (pp. 40f.) and A. Schlatter (p. 51) doubt that the Galilean mission is intended as a geographical limitation (cf. 4 : 44 'Judea'). Also, the infancy narratives do not fit the scheme very well. They are, however, integral to the plan of the Gospel (cf. Laurentin, p. 14; Minear, *SL*, pp. 114–18). E.g., the relation of John and Jesus in Lk. 1–2 seems to be the foundation for the later references to the meaning of the Baptist's ministry (3 : 1–20; 7 : 18–35; 16 : 16), and the prophecy motif in Luke 1–2 has its sequel in the last section of the Gospel (see below, pp. 31, 67f.).

A change of *source* is commonly used to discover Luke's structure. Here, too, recur some of the divisions already noted. For example, as the chart above (pp. 25f.) indicates, one block of Markan material ends at 9 : 50, another begins at 19 : 45. However, two sources sometimes appear within one episode. This shows that Luke, in the words of Farrer (*SG*, p. 63), is not collecting sources but building an edifice. Similarly, the common stylistic features of Luke–Acts, noted above (pp. 2f.), illustrate the author's adaptation of all the material to a unified whole. This includes even the sections retaining a strong Hebraic flavour (E. Schweizer, *TZ* 6, 1950, 165). Certainly, a knowledge of the sources is a valuable aid in ascertaining the structure of Luke. It is, however, important to remember that the sources are servants of the Evangelist and do not necessarily determine the ordering of the material.

Structure and Theme in Luke

In addition to the above factors, thematic patterns also may offer a clue to the total structure. The building-blocks of such patterns are the individual episodes of the Gospel. Most of them can be identified with a high degree of probability. The thematic groupings of episodes are less apparent, but a close investigation along these lines is rewarding. The first and rather obvious section is the infancy narrative (1 : 5–2 : 40). As the analysis below (pp. 32f.) shows, it falls into a sixfold series of visions and prophecies. The seventh episode, the visit of the child Jesus to the temple, is distinct from them in theme and linguistic character (cf. Sahlin, pp. 308ff.). Placed with the succeeding material, it forms an integral part of five or six episodes attesting the messiahship of Jesus. This second

section begins with Jesus' witness in the temple and closes with
his witness in the synagogue at Nazareth (2 : 41–4 : 30). Apparently it is a transition piece. In it the setting of Jesus' Galilean
mission is secured, and the meaning of it is defined.

The first block of Markan material begins a series of twenty-
four acts of Messiah (4 : 31–9 : 50). These episodes make up the
Galilean mission and conclude the first division of the Gospel.
Apart from Lk. 5 : 1–11 and six episodes in Lk. 6 : 12–7 : 50, they
are based upon the Gospel of Mark. In subdividing the material
the non-Markan section (6 : 12–7 : 50) provides a well-defined
starting point. It is marked by a shift in theme as well as a change
of source (see below, pp. 109f.). The preceding episodes (4 : 31–6 :
11) are unified by the motif of the authority of Jesus. The general
theme of 8 : 1–9 : 50 is the 'kingdom of God' mission, but the subdivisions of the section are less clear. Perhaps it is one block of
episodes. On the other hand, the introductory note, 'the Twelve
were with him' (8 : 1), may be a deliberate counterpart to the
sending out of the Twelve at 9 : 1 (cf. Plummer, p. 116). In Mark
(6 : 6b) also the mission of the Twelve appears to represent a
point of transition. Probably Lk. 9 : 1 begins a successive and
climatic stage in the Galilean mission.

The central division of the Gospel (9 : 51–19 : 44) exhibits a
similar episodic arrangement (see below, pp. 149f). However, the
subdivisions of the material may depend more on the framework
of 'the journey to Jerusalem' than on a shift in theme or in the
source used. The question is difficult, since Luke's major sources,
Q and L materials, are not available for comparison.

The final division (19 : 45–24 : 53) is marked by a return to the
Jerusalem setting in which Luke's story began. Two other facts
also are reminiscent of the infancy narrative. The first and most
clearly marked section (19 : 45–21 : 38) is set in the temple; the
last (23 : 26–24 : 53) gives prominence to prophecy. Both Markan
and other sources are visible throughout this division of the Gospel.
But the change of scene and theme are more significant pointers to
the Evangelist's intentions. Using these criteria, the material may
be divided into three sections (see below, p. 227). Part of the
'Passion narrative' approaches a running account. At these places
the identification of the episodes—if not the episodic character of
the material itself—becomes rather difficult and uncertain.

In recent years such scholars as Conzelmann, Farrer (*Matthew*, pp. 53–6), Morgenthaler, and P. Schubert (*NS*, pp. 178–86) have argued that Luke's theological interests have influenced the structure of his Gospel. The above observations accord with this approach, and they show that Luke often has selected and structured his materials with a thematic purpose in view. To this end he shifts some passages from their setting in his sources (e.g., 4 : 16–30; 8 : 1–3). A part of the Gospel manifests a sixfold combination of episodes and of sections, a literary device that others have observed in Mark (Carrington, p. 22; Pesch, p. 54), Acts (F. V. Filson, *BR* 9, 1964, 26), Matthew and the rabbinic literature (cf. Davies, *Sermon*, pp. 300–2). The rest yields to this arrangement without great difficulty although the intention of the Evangelist is less clear. Thus while the repetitive 'sixes' in the analysis below do reflect some editorial shaping, the basic pattern is not (consciously) the commentator's. The episodical character and, in large measure at least, the structural arrangement appear to represent the intention of Luke himself.

The structure of the third Gospel probably is not without a symbolic and perhaps a liturgical significance. At least, symbolic elements are woven into the structure. In this regard the 'eighth day' motif, the eight meal scenes, and the six prophecies of Jerusalem's destruction are suggestive. See on 23 : 26–31; 24 : 13–32. The meaning of Luke's episodes, moreover, must be sought not only in an analysis of the individual passages but also with a view to his literary intention. Properly this should include an analysis of the book of Acts, a task that has not been attempted here. Judging from the Gospel alone, the inclusion, exclusion, and ordering of the episodes is determined by Luke's total intent much more than usually has been supposed.

An Analysis of the Gospel of Luke

3. THE ORIGIN AND AUTHORITY OF THE GOSPEL

THE CANONICITY OF LUKE

The Historical Basis

The Gospel of Luke is read today because the Christian community recognized it as part of its canon, its 'rule' of faith. The concept of 'Scripture' and 'canon' was present in the Church from the beginning as a part of its Jewish heritage. However, the basis for the inclusion of Luke within this category of sacred writings is not readily apparent. 'Many' (1 : 1) whose 'Gospels' were not so recognized wrote earlier than the third Evangelist. Furthermore, Luke was not an apostle, and he makes no greater claim than to write an accurate and orderly account (1 : 1–4). Probably the 'word of God' status accorded Luke's writings had a twofold basis, his association with the Apostle Paul and his own ministry in the primitive Church.

As O. Cullmann (pp. 66–75) and B. Gerhardsson (pp. 288–306) have shown, the teaching of Paul is given and received as nothing less than the Word of God (1 Th. 2 : 13). As an apostle, Paul's tradition is 'from the Lord', the revealed word of the risen Jesus. This is so whether the teaching is an immediate revelation or an interpreted transmission of Jesus' teachings. Such is the background of the unique status accorded the apostolic tradition by the second-century Church. Writing against the Gnostic heresy, Irenaeus (3, 1, 1; 3, 14, 1; c. AD 180) insists that to find 'perfect knowledge' of the gospel one must go to the writings of the apostles. Then he identifies Luke as 'the follower of Paul who put down in a book the gospel preached by that one'. This is the probable import of Justin Martyr's (Dial. 103 : 19; c. AD 160) comment that the 'Memoirs' of Jesus' ministry were composed 'by apostles and by those who followed them', that is, Mark and Luke, the followers of Peter and Paul, respectively (cf. Creed, p. xiii). The witness of Tertullian (c. Marcion 4 : 2) at the beginning of the third century is similar. These passages show that by the latter half of the second century Luke's Gospel was widely associated with Paul's apostolic authority. This tendency reached full flower two centuries later when Paul's phrase, 'my gospel', was widely believed to refer to Luke (Eus. 3, 4, 7; Rom. 16 : 25; 2 Tim. 2 : 8; cf. 2 C. 8 : 18). The 'apostolic' character of Luke also may be

inferred from the Evangelist's preface. However, perhaps significantly, there is no mention of Paul. Luke introduces this Gospel
as the narration of the 'Word of God' delivered to him by the
eyewitnesses (see on 1 : 2, 4).

The anti-Marcionite prologue of Luke, composed about the time
of Irenaeus, also describes Luke as a 'disciple of the apostles' and
companion of Paul, but in connection with the writing of the
Gospel it states that Luke was 'moved by the Holy Spirit'.
Ephraem of Syria and other fourth-century witnesses identify
Luke with the prophet 'Lucius of Cyrene' mentioned in Ac. 13 : 1
(cf. Bruce; see below, pp. 53f.). This interpretation of the verse is
questionable (cf. H. J. Cadbury, *BC* v, 489–95). However, other
elements in Luke–Acts, suggest that a genuine tradition of 'Luke
the prophet' may lie behind the identification of Luke with Lucius
of Cyrene. For example, Luke gives considerable attention to the
phenomenon of Christian prophecy, and he incorporates oracles of
Christian prophets into his writings (see on 11 : 49–51). Did Luke
also have the gift of prophecy? It is tempting to think that he did.
If he was so regarded by those who received his writings, the value
placed upon them did not arise originally from his association
with the Apostle Paul (see below, p. 54).

The Earliest Witnesses

Parallels to Lukan verses occur in a number of extra-canonical
writings of the late first and early second century. In some cases
they are brief and fragmentary, and it is difficult to say whether
they allude to the third Gospel or just reflect a Lukan source or a
similar tradition. The few instances in 1 *Clement* (e.g., 13 : 2; 48 : 4;
Lk. 6 : 38; 1 : 75, 79), Ignatius (*ad Polyc.* 2 : 1f; Lk. 6 : 32), the
Didache (16 : 1; Lk. 12 : 35), and an Unknown Gospel (*ANT* 1, 97),
may be of this nature. However, Plummer (p. lxxvi) and Jeremias
(*ANT* 1, 95), respectively, see a probable allusion to Luke in the last
two instances; Grant (p. 42), in Ignatius. In spite of the arguments of
J. C. O'Neill (pp. 29–44) it remains very likely that Justin Martyr,
writing at the middle of the second century, used the third Gospel
or a harmony derived from it. Cf. *I Apology* 19 : 6; 33 : 5; 34 : 2;
Dial. 78 : 4f.; 81 : 4; 100 : 5; 103 : 6; 105 : 4; 51 : 3; 76 : 6; Lk.
18 : 27; 1 : 31f.; 2 : 2; 2 : 1–5; 20 : 35f.; 1 : 35, 38; 3 : 22D; 23 : 46;
16 : 16; 10 : 19; Zeller, 1, 114–38.

Among apocryphal writings from the first half of the second century, allusions to Luke are virtually certain in the *Gospel of Peter* and *Epistula Apostolorum* (*ANT* 1, 184, 198ff.; cf. 213ff.; cf. Creed, p. xxvi). There is a probable reference to Lk. 12 : 33 in the recently discovered *Gospel of Truth* 33 : 15–18 (AD 150?) and a certain one to Lk. 10 : 34 in the *Gospel of Philip* 126 : 7 (before AD 180?). The *Gospel of Thomas* 65–6, is probably dependent on the Lukan text form of Lk. 20 : 9–18 (cf. E. E. Ellis *ZNTW* 62, 1971, 102).

If 1 Tim. 5 : 18 refers to a Lukan source, the earliest reference to Luke itself as Scripture is probably from AD 120–140 in 2 *Clement* 13 : 4 (cf. Lk 6 : 32, 35). This passage is possibly from a pre-Lukan tradition, but against this is the evident acquaintance of 2 *Clement* with Luke elsewhere (cf. Köster, pp. 75f., 84; 2 *Clement* 4 : 5, 6 : 1). Sometimes the quotation is taken to refer to a 'word of Christ' and not to be a citation of a Gospel as Scripture (cf. Köster, p. 65). Apart from the fact that this dichotomy has a rather modern ring to it, other evidence on balance favours a reference here to a written authority. First, 2 *Clement* (2 : 4) cites a synoptic tradition elsewhere as Scripture. More significantly, the introductory formula, 'says God', can introduce either a prophet's oracle or a citation of Scripture (Ac. 2 : 17; Rev. 1 : 8; Bar. 5 : 12; cf. Mt. 19 : 4f.; 1 *Clement* 33 : 6; Ellis, pp. 107–12). But it never is used to refer simply to a transmitted saying of Jesus (J. B. Lightfoot, II, 242f.). Finally, the term, 'the oracles', mentioned in the preceding verse, is commonly used of Scripture or of divine utterances in Scripture (Ellis, p. 20n). In any case the term cannot be restricted to oral tradition (cf. Justin, *Dial.* 18 : 1; Eus. 3, 39, 16).

In conclusion, the third Gospel was widely used as an authority in the Church by the middle of the second century. The date is somewhat earlier if one accepts the above interpretation of 2 *Clement* 13 : 4. The inclusion of Luke in Marcion's canon at *c.* AD 140 also suggests that it had an authoritative status at that time (see below, p. 55). One cannot exclude the possibility that Luke was recognized as 'holy word' earlier, even from the beginning. But this question is part of a larger topic, the problem of the canon.

THE AUTHORSHIP OF LUKE

The Tradition

The present title, 'According to Luke', is not original. However, Luke's name was in all likelihood placed upon the Gospel at the very beginning. See on 1 : 1–4. A Syrian commentary which, according to Rendel Harris, reflects the original 'Western Text' (c. AD 120), reads at Ac. 20 : 13, 'I, Luke and those with me'. F. F. Bruce (p. 5) and F. C. Conybeare (BC III, 443n) also leave open the possibility that this was the original Western reading. The first clear and certain external reference to the authorship of Luke–Acts appears about AD 180 in Irenaeus (3, 1, 1; 3, 14, 1). That writer identifies the author as Luke the physician and companion of Paul. A similar identification occurs about the same time in the Muratorian Canon and in the 'anti-Marcionite' prologue to the Gospel. Despite some judicious criticisms by Haenchen (pp. 8ff.), it remains probable that the prologue originated independently of, and at least as early as, Irenaeus (cf. W. F. Howard, ET 47, 1935–6, 534–8). However, its present form may be a later expansion (cf. R. G. Heard, JTS N.S. 6, 1955, 9ff.). It read as follows:

> Luke is a man from Antioch, Syria, a physician by profession. He was a disciple of the apostles, and later he accompanied Paul until his martyrdom. Having neither wife nor child, he served the Lord without distraction. He fell asleep in Boeotia at the age of eighty four, full of the Holy Spirit.
>
> Moved by the Holy Spirit, Luke composed all of this Gospel in the districts around Achaia although there were already Gospels in existence—one according to Matthew written in Judea and one according to Mark written in Italy. He reveals this fact in the prologue: that other Gospels were written before his and that it was imperative that an accurate account of the divine plan be set forth for the Gentile believers. This was necessary in order that they might neither be distracted by Jewish myths nor, deceived by heretical and vain phantasies, depart from the truth.
>
> Therefore, right at the beginning Luke took up the birth of John because this was a most necessary matter. John is the beginning of the Gospel. He was the forerunner of the Lord and his partner in the preparation of the gospel, in the administration of the baptism, and in the fellowship of the Spirit. The prophet with this ministry is mentioned in the Twelve (Minor Prophets).

Afterwards the same Luke also wrote 'the Acts of the Apostles'. Still later the Apostle John, one of the Twelve, wrote the Revelation on the isle of Patmos and after these things the Gospel.

(For the Greek text cf. Aland, p. 553)

The tradition of Lukan authorship is generally attested from the beginning of the third century. It was never disputed. The second-century tradition carries considerable weight, especially because it identifies the author with a relatively insignificant person.

The New Testament evidence agrees with the tradition. Paul occasionally mentions Luke the physician as his colleague (Col. 4 : 14; 2 Tim. 4 : 11; Phm. 24). The Gospel prologue affirms that the author was not an eyewitness to the events he relates (1 : 2). The attention given to Antioch (Ac. 11 : 19–30; 13 : 1ff.; 15 : 30ff.) and the unnecessary mention of Lysanias and Philip (3 : 1) may (or may not) reflect the interest of a native of that area.

In part the tradition is drawn from the New Testament. H. J. Cadbury (*BC* II, 261; cf. Haenchen, p. 10n) conjectures that the second-century Church deduced the Lukan authorship itself by observing the 'we' passages (e.g., Ac. 16 : 10ff.), and then selecting a companion of Paul who best fitted them. This is a teasing possibility but not an entirely convincing one. Irenaeus (3, 1, 1; 3, 14, 1) is concerned to show only Luke's intimate relation to Paul. The Lukan authorship of Luke–Acts apparently is an assumption common to him and his Marcionite opponents, although later Marcionites attributed Marcion's Gospel to Christ. Indeed, the Gospel title, 'According to Luke', is certainly earlier than AD 180 (see on 1 : 1–4). If the authorship had been disputed or had been a novel idea, Irenaeus could not have argued as he does.

Moreover, Marcion himself probably received the same tradition. He recognized only Paul as a true apostle, yet he accepted an abbreviated Gospel of Luke in his canon of Scripture. This implies that the Gospel was associated with Paul at that time (*c.* AD 140). It is not impossible that within seventy or eighty years the author of Luke–Acts was forgotten and a new name found without leaving a trace of a contrary opinion. It also is not impossible that before the mid-second century, when Christian writers were notoriously unconcerned to cite New Testament authors, some, by shrewd detective work, discovered the 'unknown' author of Luke–Acts. However, at most this line of reasoning is an exercise in improbabilities, and its appeal will be limited largely to those who on other grounds find Lukan authorship to be unacceptable. In all likelihood, the second-century tradition is essentially correct although, as will be observed below (p. 51), it may have suffered from exaggeration.

The Current Discussion

(a) *The Background.* A century ago F. C. Baur (I, 103f., 129–37, 175) and his 'Tübingen School' drove a strong wedge between the Paul presented in Acts and the Apostle's own witness in his letters. Baur mentioned the un-Pauline character both of Acts' presentation of the death of Christ (Ac. 13 : 26–41) and of the philosophical ideas in the Areopagus Speech (Ac. 17), and he stressed the conflicting attitudes toward the Law in Acts and in Galatians. Baur (I, 12) concluded that 'we can no longer maintain the authorship of Luke for the Acts of the Apostles, at least in the form in which we possess the work'. In his opinion Acts was a second-century synthesis, mediating a quarrel between Jewish Christianity and the followers of Paul. When this reconstruction proved to be untenable, the research moved toward a reconsideration of the traditional view of Lukan authorship (cf. Munck, pp. 69–86). But there was by no means a consensus against Baur (cf. A. C. McGiffert, *BC* II, 394f.), and some of his arguments find continuing support today among a significant number of scholars (e.g. C. K. Barrett, *NTS* 17, 250–4; 20, 243).

At the beginning of this century the 'newer criticism' came down firmly in favour of Lukan authorship. While recognizing differences between the Paul of Acts and of the letters, A. Harnack (*Luke*, pp. 139–45) complained that both the differences and their significance were overdrawn. 'Without any justification [critics] have made the highest demands of a companion of St. Paul—he must thoroughly understand St. Paul, he must be of congenial disposition and free from prejudice, he must be absolutely trustworthy and his memory must never fail' (p. 122n). Both Harnack (*Luke*, p. 142, 147) and B. H. Streeter (pp. 561f.) pointed out that the picture of Luke as the 'disciple' of Paul is not drawn from the New Testament but from the later Fathers. In the New Testament Luke is only a sometime companion of the Apostle and, therefore, should not be required to reflect Pauline theology.

K. Lake raised an exegetical objection to Baur's interpretation of Acts. 15. Baur failed to see Luke's 'distinction between the Law as a source of salvation—it was not this for anyone—and the Law as a command of God—this it was for the Jew but not for the Gentile'. Lake (*HDAC* I, 29) concluded that in this respect Acts gives 'a faithful representation of St Paul's own views'. Certainly, for Acts no less than for Paul the Law is an unbearable yoke which cannot bring salvation and which is not to be placed upon Gentile Christians (Ac. 13 : 39; 15 : 10, 19). But where in Acts is the Law a command of God for Jewish Christians? Like the temple, circumcision is not only insufficient but under judgment (Ac. 7 : 8, 51). Paul's relation to the Jewish cult is totally by way of concession to the 'Hebrew' brothers (e.g., Ac. 16 : 3f.; 21 : 21–26) or an expression of his own custom as a Jewish Christian (e.g., Ac. 18 : 18). This accurately reflects the attitude in Paul's letters in which he never disparages the voluntary keeping of the Law by Jewish Christians (Rom. 14 : 20f.; 1 C. 7 : 18ff.; 9 : 20). This fact had good practical as well as theological reasons (see below, pp. 52f.). Lake overstated the case, but his conclusion was valid.

More important than the 'newer criticism's' rebuttal of the Tübingen school was its own contribution to the research. This contribution was notable in two areas, the medical terminology of Luke–Acts and the 'we' passages in Acts. W. K. Hobart, building on earlier studies, showed that of the New Testament writings Luke's work contained a relatively high proportion of medical terms. He inferred that the author must have been a physician. Harnack (*Luke*, pp. 175–98) reached a similar conclusion. In a sharp critique of these studies H. J. Cadbury (*BC* II, 349–55; *Style*, pp. 39–72) cited examples of the same terminology in non-medical writers and questioned the basis of any argument built upon an alleged professional vocabulary. On the whole Cadbury makes the better case. The vocabulary proves nothing about the profession of the author of Luke–Acts although it is congenial with the tradition that he was a physician. To this extent the studies of Hobart and Harnack gave critical support to the patristic testimony.

The first person in the prefaces (1 : 3; Ac. 1 : 1) reappears in a number of 'we' passages in Ac. 11 : 28D; 16 : 10–17; 20 : 5–21 : 18; 27 : 1–28 : 16. In no other part of Acts are the peculiarities of the vocabulary and style of the author of the whole work so accumulated and concentrated as they are in the 'we' sections

(Harnack, *Acts*, p. 12; cf. Dibelius, *Acts*, p. 136). There is, there-fore, a reasonable presumption that these sections represent points in the narrative at which the author of Luke–Acts was present. Their occurrence is too occasional and unobtrusive to be an arti-ficial claim to 'eyewitness' status, and there are few, if any, parallels in ancient writings for a writer to use another's notes in this fashion (cf. A. D. Nock, *Gnomon* 25, 1953, 502f.; the travel report in Ammianus Marcellinus 18, 6, 5). The exclusion of the author and the 'many' from the 'eye-witnesses' (1 : 1) is not a real objection; in this respect the prologue refers only to the events in the Gospel. So, Schürmann, p. 4.

This presumption—and the case for Lukan authorship—is strengthened by another observation. Persons important for the author of Luke–Acts are found in the Pauline letters mentioning Luke or in the 'we' sections of Acts. They include Philip (Ac. 8 : 4ff.; 21 : 8), Mark (Ac. 15 : 36ff.; Col. 4 : 10, 14; 2 Tim. 4 : 11; Phm. 24), Priscilla, Aquila, Trophimus, Tychicus, Aristarchus (Ac. 18 : 18; 20 : 4; Col. 4 : 7, 10ff.; 2 Tim. 4 : 12, 19f.).

Alternative interpretations of the 'we' passages continue to be offered by some scholars. The most common one ascribes the pas-sages to someone else's diary, later used by the author of Luke–Acts (e.g., H. Windisch, *BC* II, 343f.; Kümmel, FBK, p. 131). Apart from the objection above, is it probable that an author who thoroughly reworked another's notes would neglect to change the pronoun? E. Haenchen (*ZTK* 58, 1961, 365f.; ET in *JTC* I, 1965, 99) answers that the 'we' is retained deliberately to certify a decisive moment in the Pauline mission (Ac. 16) and to give the reader a sense of participation in Paul's journey (Ac. 27, 28). But these explanations are, at best, secondary alternatives. They become live options only if one presupposes on other grounds that a co-worker of Paul could not have written Luke–Acts. The most natural explanation is that the 'we', like the 'I' of the prefaces, refers to the author of the two volumes to Theophilus'. Cf. Dupont, pp. 126–32.

(*b*) *The Continuing Debate*. Outside Germany the judgment of Streeter and Harnack has generally prevailed. While problems remain in relating Acts to Paul's letters, critical analysis confirms the tradition of Lukan authorship. This view has received no little support from the assent of the historian, E. Meyer (III, 17–36) and the long considered conversion of the Harvard classicist, A. D. Nock (*Gnomon* 25, 1953, 502). Among German scholars, however, the argument against Lukan authorship has been vigorously renewed. The revival draws its greatest support from the Bultmann school, but its influence extends beyond that group. For example, the verdict of Dibelius in favour of Luke has been reversed by his pupil, W. G. Kümmel (FBK, p. 130).

The renewed 'case against the tradition' was sparked by the trenchant essay of P. Vielhauer (*EvT* 10, 1950–1, 1–15 = *SL*, pp. 33–50). Representative of a much larger body of opinion, his argument is predicated upon theological differences between Luke–Acts and Paul in four specific areas: Natural Theology, the Law, Christology, and Eschatology. In addition, Kümmel (FBK, p. 129) notes the absence in Acts of Paul's 'Apostle' title, which the Corinthian letters emphasize. Others argue that the assignment to Peter of 'the gospel to the circumcised' (Gal. 2 : 7) conflicts with a Pauline synagogue ministry as presented in Acts (but cf. 1 C. 9 : 20; 2 C. 11 : 24; see below, pp. 52f.). Generally, however, the objections to Lukan authorship follow the fourfold pattern of Vielhauer.

Following E. Norden (cf. p. 128) and M. Dibelius (*Acts*, pp. 26–77) Vielhauer interprets Paul's Areopagus speech in Acts 17 from the background of Greek philosophy. The speech develops, in the words of Haenchen (p. 529), 'a doctrine of the religious status of the Gentiles' based on their natural relation to God. For Acts the heathen, unknowing, worship and live 'in God'; for Paul, knowing God, they glorify him not (Rom. 1 : 21).

But Luke does not mean that mankind has by nature a *redemptive* life 'in God' (see on 20 : 38). The 'ignorance motif' in Luke–Acts is rooted in Semitic thought and is not a state of innocence but of guilt (see on 23 : 34). Before Acts 17 can be used to show that it is 'unthinkable that a missionary companion of Paul could have ascribed to him these radically different views of God and salvation' (Kümmel, FBK, p. 130), the philosophical interpretation of the texts must be justified. In an impressive and in large measure convincing argument B. Gärtner (p. 249) rejects this interpretation. He finds that the conceptual background of the speech is largely Jewish and at no point 'clashes with what is otherwise known of Paul's theology'. Although disputed (cf. E. Grässer, *TR* 26, 1960, 141ff.), Gärtner's arguments have not

been answered. Also, the creators of the philosophical interpretation upon which Vielhauer rests his argument did not, ironically,
draw Vielhauer's conclusions. Dibelius accepted Lukan authorship, and Norden later admitted that the speech could be Pauline
(cf. Meyer, III, 92n).

The alleged contradictory attitude toward the Mosaic Law in
Paul and in Acts is for the most part Tübingen revisited (see
above). The strongest point made is the absence in Acts of the
Pauline emphasis upon freedom from the Law. Less convincingly,
for Paul's Jerusalem visits these scholars follow the traditional
equation, Ac. 15 = Gal. 2, and then cite the problems raised by
that equation as evidence for the unhistorical character of Acts
(e.g. Kümmel, FBK, pp. 128f.). It might be more fruitful to use
another equation, say, Ac. 11 = Gal. 2 (cf. Williams, *Acts*, pp.
24–30). Sometimes the argument approaches a legalistic fervour
to keep Paul unlegalistic. For example, when Vielhauer (p. 8)
asserts that, *contra* Ac. 16 : 3, circumcision for Paul was never a
matter of indifference, does he mean that Paul opposed circumcision for Jewish Christians (cf. 1 C. 7 : 19)?

There is greater validity in the contention that the Christology
of Paul in Acts is neither Pauline nor Lukan but early Christian.
Paul's emphasis on the 'cosmic Christ' and on the theology of the
cross are missing. (These ideas do appear occasionally: e.g.,
22 : 19f.; Ac. 20 : 28; see on 23 : 43; above, p. 11; special note,
p. 230. And the Evangelist has reasons for his different emphasis;
see above, p. 12.) There is little basis, however, for finding an un-
Pauline 'adoptionist Christology' in Ac. 13 : 33 when the same
thought is present in Rom. 1 : 4. For Luke, Messiah's unique relation to God is not an 'adopted' characteristic at all: Jesus has
divine origins (see above, pp. 10f.). Cf. C. F. D. Moule, *SL*, pp.
159–85.

E. Haenchen (pp. 112–16) sees additional discrepancies: Unlike
Paul's letters, Acts presents Paul as a miracle worker and a great
orator who offends Jews by 'disseminating an age-old Jewish
doctrine' of resurrection. But Paul's letters also make reference to
his miraculous powers (cf. Rom. 15 : 18f.; 1 C. 5 : 4f.; 2 C. 4 : 7;
12 : 9, 12; 13 : 4; 1 Th. 1 : 5) even if, as letters, they do so in a different
manner. Paul's oratory leaves the Athenians unmoved, gives Fes-
tus the impression that Paul is mad, puts Eutychus to sleep, and
otherwise fails to hold his audience (Ac. 17 : 32, 26 : 24; 20 : 9; 14 : 4;

22 : 22; 23 : 1f.). These texts are hardly consonant with the presentation of an 'outstanding orator', and other texts also are suggestive
more of persistence than of eloquence. The (Pharisaic) doctrine
of resurrection becomes an issue only as a debating point (Ac.
23 : 6) and, as Haenchen admits, Acts elsewhere presents Paul's
disputes within a context found in his letters: salvation for Gentiles
apart from the ritual law (Ac. 13 : 38f., 48ff.; 15 : 2; 21 : 20f., 28).
Given a closer look, then, these objections to the Lukan portrait
of Paul do not appear to be well founded, and the same may be
said of Luke's alleged exclusion of Paul from the circle of apostles
(see the special note at 9 : 1).

Vielhauer and his colleagues make their strongest case when
arguing for the independent character of Luke's theology. However, they do not weigh heavily enough Kümmel's (FBK, p. 129)
significant admission that it is impossible to know how well Paul's
companions knew his theology or how far they chose to emphasize
it. Vielhauer's exegesis of Acts is less satisfactory. When he has
difficulty in recognizing Luke's Paul, this writer often finds a
similar difficulty in recognizing Vielhauer's Luke.

Exegetical questions remain a most important key—and obstacle—to achieving a consensus of opinion on the authorship of
Luke–Acts. But the New Testament student does not come to
exegesis straight from the womb. Preceding the explanation or
'exegesis' of the texts, and in the midst of it, a pre-understanding of
the texts is present. It influences both his exegetical analysis and
his total perspective. Today the decisive factor affecting any pre-
understanding of Luke–Acts is eschatology, that is, the end of the
age and the manifestation of the new age of the kingdom of God.
This issue has played a most important role in recent questions
about the authorship of the third Gospel.

(c) *The Eschatological Perspective.* With the demise of the Tübingen
school a number of scholars, recently J. Munck, L. Goppelt, and
W. Schmithals (*Paul*), have offered new reconstructions of Paul's
relationship to the Jerusalem church. In the nature of the case the
book of Acts is bound up with this issue. However, in keeping
with the trend in New Testament studies generally most attention
today is directed to a different question. How do the Evangelist
and the Apostle Paul view the end of the age? That is, what is the
relationship of their 'eschatologies'?

At the beginning of this century J. Weiss and A. Schweitzer pictured Jesus as an apocalyptic preacher who expected the end of the world in his generation. R. Bultmann, whose writings have had considerable influence in more recent decades, accepted this view. But he regarded the cosmic catastrophe to be only a mythical framework. According to Bultmann (*Theology*, I, 23ff.) and his followers the real meaning of Jesus' message was his calling men to decision, by which the future age, the kingdom of God, would be manifested in the individual life. Paul's teaching is essentially the same. But for Paul the death and resurrection of Jesus have made the 'new age' a present possibility. The future or 'eschatological' age becomes present in one's 'existential' commitment in faith (Bultmann, *Existence*, 124, 196ff., 255ff.; cf. J. M. Robinson's elaboration, pp. 114f., 122–5, and especially in his German edition, pp. 178–82). For Paul, eschatology is not a process of time but a paradoxical contemporaneity of the present and the future (P. Vielhauer, *EvT* 10, 1950–1, 12f.).

Luke–Acts, these theologians continue, stands in sharp contrast to the eschatology of Paul. Seeking to solve the problem of the 'delay' of the *parousia*, the return of Jesus, the third Evangelist sets forth a history of salvation in which Jesus' mission becomes the midpoint (Bultmann, *Existence*, p. 238; Conzelmann, pp. 131–6). In this context Luke represents an eschatology that, temporally and theologically, stands at some distance from Paul. He scarcely could have been the companion of the Apostle.

Like Baur in the last century, these theologians have used a modern philosophical key to make a far-reaching reconstruction of the New Testament writings. Like Baur, they interpret Acts as a belated mediation of a Church problem. A century ago the problem was the conflict between Jewish and Gentile Christianity. Today it is eschatology. But also like Baur they use presuppositions that, exegetically, have become increasingly suspect to many New Testament students. The reconstruction is particularly vulnerable in two areas, its apocalyptic picture of Jesus and its existentialist interpretation of Paul.

Today it is widely recognized that Schweitzer's apocalyptic picture of Jesus was incorrect. For Jesus, no less than for Paul and Luke, the kingdom of God was a present as well as a future reality (see on 10 : 1–20; 11 : 14–28; cf. Perrin, pp. 87ff., 159; Ellis, *Interpreters*, pp. 32ff.). Consequently, the sequel of Schweitzer's view, the crucial 'delay' of the *parousia*, likewise was an exaggeration. Paul's near-term expectation of the return of Jesus is not substantially different from Luke's longer-term perspective. Paul can, indifferently, identify himself with the dead or with the living at the *parousia* (1 Th. 4 : 15; 5 : 10; Rom. 14 : 8f.; 1 C. 6 : 14; Phil. 1 : 20ff.). For him (1 Th. 5 : 1ff.), as for Luke (18 : 8; Ac. 1 : 6f.), it is not the time but the certainty and suddenness of the *parousia* that is significant. Luke does place greater emphasis upon the continuing role of the Church in this age. Partly, this is occasioned by an 'apocalyptic heresy' that posed a greater threat in his situation (see on 17 : 20–37). Partly, Luke's ordered, schematic presentation allows him to give full play to a 'salvation history' theme. But J. Munck (pp. 36–55) and P. Borgen (*CBQ* 31, 1969, 168–82) have shown the presence of the same theme in Paul, however one may judge Munck's specific interpretation of it. In the nature of Paul's writings the theme becomes explicit only on occasion, e.g., Rom. 9–11. But it is there. These facts raise serious doubts about an existentialist interpretation of Paul.

Furthermore, this interpretation is achieved only by making expendable what for Paul was of the essence: the historical, temporal character of the resurrection both of Jesus in AD 33 and of his followers at the *parousia*. Without this essence faith would be a vanity and eschatological existence only a delusion, a prelude to despair (1 C. 15 : 17ff.). To Paul's mind eschatological existence cannot be separated from history or from time. For it is rooted in the resurrection of Jesus 'on the third day' (see special note at 24 : 1–12). In both Paul and Luke the Spirit is the mediator of the *future* in the present. He is 'sent' and in the Christian as 'first fruits' and as 'anticipation' of the coming age (Gal. 4 : 6; Rom. 8 : 23; 2 C. 5 : 5; cf. 1 C. 15 : 20).

It is, therefore, difficult to accept E. Schweizer's (p. 95) distinction between the function of the Spirit in Luke as the power to carry out a specific historical task (e.g., Ac. 1–8) and the function of the gifts of the Spirit in Paul (e.g., 1 C. 12–14; Eph. 4 : 11f.). For both writers the eschatological presence of the Spirit is within the continuing historical process. For both the role of the Spirit explains the meaning of the *interval* between the resurrection and the *parousia* of Jesus (see above, pp. 13–16; see on 23 : 43). Whatever differences there are between Paul and Luke, they do not appear to warrant Schweizer's conclusion that, unlike Luke, Paul viewed the Church in its eschatological character to be 'taken out of time and place' (p. 104; cf. TDNT vi, 409f.)

The existentialist understanding of Paul is a fascinating philosophical reconstruction. But it does not reach to the rationale underlying Paul's 'existential' language. The tension between the 'present' and the 'future' is not a modern philosophical paradox. Indeed, the key to Paul's eschatology cannot be found in existentialist philosophy at all. It lies rather in his very Semitic understanding of human existence as both a corporate and an individual reality (cf. Ellis, *NTS* 6, 1959–60, 212–16; Davies, pp. 102–10; Shedd, pp. 56ff., 193, 195ff.). Eschatological existence is, first of all, an event in AD 33 at a garden tomb into which the Christian is incorporated. Because an existentialist interpretation does not perceive the Semitic background of Paul's thought here, it fails to appreciate the historical and the corporate basis of eschatological existence. Cf. also Cullmann, *Salvation*, pp. 125f., 239–68; Ellis, *Eschatology*, pp. 11–14.

(*d*) *Conclusion.* In all probability the author of Luke–Acts was known, and known as Luke, from the first. The critical questions are directed at the second-century identification of this Luke with the companion of Paul. The chief complaint is twofold. First, Luke–Acts gives a different picture of Paul than that in his letters. Second, Luke's own theology is not 'Pauline'.

It is conceivable that a companion would present Paul independent of his letters and in some diversity from them. But would a post-apostolic admirer of the Apostle have done so? The apocryphal 'Acts' and 'Apocalypse' of Paul show that later writers clothed their 'Paul' with clear allusions to his letters. The independent cast of Luke–Acts argues against authorship by a later admirer. It lends some support to Lukan authorship, for only a colleague would write the story without recourse to Paul's letters.

To answer this question W. G. Kümmel (FBK, pp. 132f., 130) contends that the author of Luke–Acts did not use Paul's letters because he was unacquainted with them. This is questionable: but if so, it poses a further problem. Would someone who did not know Paul well or his letters at all choose Paul as the hero of the Gentile mission? This is possible if the author was a sometime companion of the Apostle. It is less credible if he had 'a total lack of relationship to Paul'. Also it is not sufficient to urge that he found a diary of a companion of Paul. Heroes are seldom made by reading other people's diaries.

In a number of areas Luke and Paul share a common theological viewpoint. But A. Plummer (p. xliv) correctly labels the parallels generally as common Christian teaching. The recent analysis of the differences between Luke and Paul only emphasizes what Harnack and Streeter said earlier: the Evangelist was not the disciple of Paul. In their battle with Gnosticism the second-century Fathers had a special interest in tying authority to the apostles and, therefore, Luke–Acts to Paul. Probably they exaggerated the relation between Luke and Paul.

It is ironical that those most sceptical of the second-century tradition of Lukan authorship incautiously accept the second-century tradition of Luke's discipleship to Paul. Perhaps this reflects a tendency to read into the Pauline circle the rabbinic (and modern) predilection for theological 'schools'. In any case it is a poor argument that requires a companion of Paul—and of other Christian leaders—to be a follower of Pauline thought. This objection to Lukan authorship, like the first one, becomes a case of the dog biting its master. Luke's theological independence actually favours the view that he was the Apostle's co-worker and his contemporary, as indeed he claims to be (1 : 2; see above, pp. 37f.).

'The case against the tradition' is always the sign of a lively theological enterprise. Often it points the way to a more accurate understanding of the New Testament. If it is not persuasive for the authorship of Luke–Acts, it is nonetheless valuable; for the questioning serves the very useful function of bringing the tradition to the bar of criticism. Without the debate the authorship of Luke–Acts would rest on much less certain grounds. With it one has better reasons for affirming Lukan authorship than at any previous time. Apart from the major Pauline letters the authorship of no section of the New Testament has better critical support than that of the two volumes to Theophilus by Luke the physician and companion of Paul.

St Luke the Evangelist

(a) *His Racial Background.* The New Testament gives very little direct information about Luke. Indirectly, the Evangelist's language and style display a good command of Greek but, nevertheless,

they have convinced a number of scholars that he was a Jew.
B. Reicke (p. 22) and W. F. Albright (p. 296, Munck; *Acts*, pp.
264–7) are more recent additions to an impressive list of names.
In the last generation A. Schlatter (p. 151) identified Luke's
speech as Palestinian, and E. C. Selwyn (*Expositor* 7, 1909, 551)
flatly stated that 'no Gentile could ever have obtained' Luke's
intimate knowledge of Old Testament phraseology. From the
purpose of Acts, B. S. Easton (p. 115) reached the same conclusion: Luke was a Jewish Christian. A. H. McNeile (pp. 132f.)
argued that Luke was a Hellenist, that is, a Jew who adopted
Greek customs. This accords with his attention and attitude to the
temple and to the 'Hellenists' of Ac. 6–8. C. F. Burney (pp. 10f.)
was inclined to the same opinion but was held back by one passage,
Col 4 : 10f., 14.

The large majority of scholars believe that Luke was a Gentile.
Although appeal is made to Luke's good Greek, Col. 4 : 10f., 14 is
the only strong argument for the prevailing view. Luke is excluded
from those 'of the circumcision'. However, the meaning of the
passage is not at all clear. One need not, with C. F. D. Moule
(p. 31) and C. C. Torrey (*AJT* 23, 1919, 66n), only call attention
to the ambiguous wording of Col 4 : 11. There is a more important
question: who are those 'of the circumcision'? In some passages
the phrase can mean simply 'the Jews' (e.g., Rom. 4 : 12). But
there is no instance with the certain meaning, 'Jewish Christians'.
F. F. Bruce (p. 228) thinks that outside Acts the phrase refers to
Judaizers, that is, Jewish Christians who wanted to impose the
Mosaic Law upon Gentile believers. This meaning fits Gal. 2 : 12
and Tit. 1 : 10 ('the circumcision party', *RSV*). But it is impossible
at Col. 4 : 11.

O. Cullmann (*SSNT*, p. 26; cf. Schmithals, *Paul*, pp. 21–8) correctly sees a religious rather than a racial or linguistic distinction
between the 'Hebrews' and the 'Hellenists' in Ac. 6 : 1 (however
one may judge his elaboration of it). This may offer a clue for the
present question. The distinctiveness of those 'of the circumcision'
probably is not racial but ritual. (See E. E. Ellis, 'Those of the
Circumcision, *TU* 102 (1968), 390–9.)

Pre-Christian Judaism displays differing attitudes toward the
observance of ritual laws (cf. Guignebert, pp. 80f., 227). Likewise
among Jewish Christians some were 'zealous for the law' and some,
like Paul, were ritually lax (Ac. 21 : 20ff.; 1 C. 9 : 19ff.). The latter

were the 'Hellenists'. The former, we may suppose, were 'the circumcision party'. But not all of them sought to impose the Law on Gentiles. Only the Judaizers, a segment of the ritually strict group, attempted to extend the ritual party lines into Gentile Christianity. Paul absolutely opposed this segment. But he was glad to work with others of the circumcision party, he evangelizing the 'Hellenists' and the Gentiles, and they, the 'Hebrews' = 'the circumcision'.

Although not provable, this explanation accounts for the New Testament use of the phrase. To identify those 'of the circumcision' merely as Jewish Christians does not. Without that identification the evidence that Luke was a Gentile disappears. There is no proof, of course, that he was not. But the balance of probabilities favours the view that Luke was a hellenistic Jew. This leaves open the possibility that Luke is the Lucius (Paul's cousin?) mentioned in Rom. 16 : 21. Like Silas and Silvanus, Luke and Lucius were alternate forms of the same name (H. J. Cadbury, *BC* v, 491f.; *LAE*, pp. 437f.; Ramsay, pp. 370–81).

(b) *His Home and Ministry.* The anti-Marcionite prologue given above (pp. 40f.) identifies Luke as a native (or resident) of Antioch, Syria. This tradition, found also in later sources (e.g., Eus. 3, 4, 6), finds some support in the attention given to that area in Luke–Acts. See above, pp. 38f., 41. Drawing a fine line, R. H. Connolly (*JTS* 37, 1936, 383) detects some northern Syrian idiom in passages for which the Evangelist (and not his source) is responsible. Also, the 'we' passage in the Western text of Ac. 11 : 28, if not original, is an early second-century testimony to Luke's relationship to Antioch. R. Bultmann (*NTE*, p. 77) suspects another 'we' passage underlying a text in Ac. 13 : 1f., although other solutions to the problem are possible. To identify Luke with the Lucius of Cyrene in this passage is possible (Reicke, pp. 12–21), but it is Luke's practice elsewhere to leave his name unmentioned. On balance, the tradition connecting Luke with Antioch is early and reasonable, although the support for it is limited (cf. Leaney, pp. 3f.; A. Strobel, *ZNTW* 49, 1958, 131–4; Wilcox, p. 183). A less likely suggestion, popular a generation ago, puts Luke's home in Philippi. There, presumably, Luke was left and later rejoined Paul (Ac. 17 : 1; 20 : 6).

Accounts of Luke's ministry generally are limited to his role as a co-worker with Paul and as a Christian writer. Some evidence suggests that his ministry arose out of an important charismatic gift. Long ago E. C. Selwyn (pp. 275–325; *Expositor* 7, 1909, 552f.) argued that Ac. 1–12 exhibited literary patterns characteristic of a prophet's writing. The Evangelist also shows a great interest in New Testament prophets and prophecy (see above, pp. 7f., 28f.), and he emphasizes Jesus' role as 'prophet' (see on 19 : 32). From these facts it is inviting to suppose that Luke was a Christian prophet with contacts among others exercising the same gift. This is supported by Origen's statement (*Homily on Lk.* 1 : 1) that Luke 'wrote from the Holy Spirit' and the similar comment of the Prologue (see above, p. 40).

The locale of Luke's ministry is known mainly from his association with Paul. He was with the Apostle in Philippi and perhaps for a time in Ephesus; he accompanied him to Jerusalem and later to Rome (Ac. 16 : 10ff.; 21 : 17; 28 : 16). Probably he was present at Paul's martyrdom in Rome (2 Tim. 4 : 6, 11). The prologue cited above (p. 40) is the earliest account of Luke's own death in Boeotia, Greece. According to Jerome, Luke's bones were moved from there to Constantinople (cf. *contra vigil.* 5; *de vir. illus.* 7).

Later legends about Luke are plentiful but are of doubtful value. In the third century he was mentioned as the brother 'whose praise is in the Gospel' (cf. 2 C. 8 : 18 *AV*). Some writers identified him with one of the Seventy and with the companion of Cleopas (10 : 1; 24 : 18; but cf. 1 : 2). The tradition that Luke was a painter is very late (cf. Plummer, pp. xxif.).

Luke is most famous, of course, as the author of Luke–Acts. Other less certain achievements also are ascribed to him. Origen (Eus. 6, 25, 14) cites an opinion of his day that Luke wrote the letter to the Hebrews (cf. C. M. P. Jones, *SG*, pp. 113–43). A few New Testament manuscripts name the Evangelist as Paul's secretary in writing 2 Corinthians. Some modern scholars assign him the same role in the Pastoral letters (cf. C. F. D. Moule, *BJRL* 47, 1965, 430–52). Whatever the worth of these opinions, Luke's greatness in the history of Christianity will always find its true measure in his two volumes to Theophilus.

THE OCCASION OF THE WRITING OF LUKE

The Date

(a) *General Considerations.* The Gospel of Luke was written after
Mark, which Luke uses, and before Acts, Luke's 'second word' to
Theophilus. A few writers still put the publication of Acts well
into the second century, a view advocated in Germany a hundred
years ago. Arguing that Luke in its present form is an enlargement of
a Gospel used by Marcion, J. Knox (*Marcion,* pp. 110ff., 120f.) dates
it after AD 140. This view has a rather low level of probability (cf.
Blackman, pp. 38–41; O'Neill, pp. 19ff.). Among other objections
the non-Marcion sections, for example, Lk. 1–2, are essential to
the basic plan of the Gospel. They cannot be explained as a later
appendage (see above, pp. 26f.; P. S. Minear, *SL,* pp. 111–30).
Recently, J. C. O.'Neill (p. 21) has dated Acts at *c.* AD 115–30.
But his view rests on rather narrow grounds and is not persuasive.

The majority of scholars today date Luke's Gospel in one of
two periods, AD 60–65 or AD 70–90. The argument that Luke used
the historian, Josephus (AD 93), was never fully convincing (H. J.
Cadbury, *BC* II, 357). Today it is seldom pressed. If one accepts
(against Williams, *Acts,* pp. 12f.) the usual view that the Gospel
was written before Acts, any date after AD 90 faces serious difficulties. A comparison of Luke–Acts with the 'early catholic' letters
of 1 *Clement* (AD 95) and Ignatius (AD 117) reveals a sharply different
perspective (Haenchen, p. 49; Barrett, *Historian,* p. 76). But, then,
different theologies could exist at the same time in different places.
Another consideration is perhaps more significant. By the turn of
the century Paul's letters had a wide and important currency.
Yet the author, whose hero in Acts is Paul, makes no allusions to
them. Also, if 1 *Clement* reflects an acquaintance with Acts, as
seems probable (cf. Hagner, pp. 256–63), and if Ignatius alludes to
Acts, as W. L. Knox thinks (*Acts,* p. 2), it indicates that Luke's
second volume, 'if not "Holy Scripture", was a Christian classic
well before AD 117'. Cf. 1 *Clem.* 5 : 6f. with Acts 26; 1 *Clem* 2 : 1
with Acts 20 : 35; 1 *Clem.* 18 : 1 with Acts 13 : 22 (1 Sam. 13 : 14
+ Ps. 88 : 21).

(b) *Current Viewpoints.* Several facts favour the earlier date advocated, among others, by Harnack, Bruce, Munck, E. R. Good-
enough (*SL,* p. 58), and Sahlin (pp. 46, 23–7; see the literature cited

there). Acts mentions no events after AD 63, not even the destruction of Jerusalem in AD 70, the death of James in AD 62, or the death of Paul. Also, the abrupt ending of Acts may indicate the time of its composition, that is, at the end of Paul's imprisonment. Lastly, could Luke give such a friendly picture of Rome after Nero's persecution of AD 64? Cf. Thompson, pp. 8ff.

The reasons given for the early date are plausible, but they are not compelling. Acts is not a complete history, and the inclusion of events is largely governed by Luke's theme and purpose. If a part of his purpose is to show the political innocence of Christianity, the exclusion of Nero's persecution or Paul's execution is quite conceivable. But the omission of the destruction of Jerusalem is not (see below). It remains a strong argument against dating Luke–Acts after that event.

Advocates of a date after AD 70 rest their case primarily on two contentions, a knowledge of the destruction of Jerusalem reflected in Lk. 21 : 20–24 and the 'late' theological climate of Luke–Acts. It is true that Luke's description of the fall of Jerusalem is more specific than Mark's. But it would be uncritical to assume that a specific prediction that comes true must have been made after the event. C. H. Dodd (*JRS* 37, 1947, 49f.) has demonstrated that the Lukan oracle is composed of Old Testament phraseology without any evidence of alterations after AD 70. See on 21 : 20–24. It is difficult to say whether Luke's theology, specifically his eschatology and his attack on gnostic-type influences, reflects a situation after AD 70.

A number of scholars, recently represented by Profs. Conzelmann (*SL*, pp. 298–309) and Haenchen (pp. 112–16), have dated Luke–Acts around the turn of the first century. Haenchen appeals primarily to Luke's differences from Paul, a matter discussed above (see pp. 45–51). Conzelmann seeks a more broadly based reconstruction but, like Haenchen, also assumes that theological differences from Paul must be interpreted in terms of chronological distance (p. 307). He regards the external evidence to be inconclusive (p. 300) and rests his case on certain internal criteria: Luke's perspective on the Christian mission; his exclusion of Paul from the apostolate (see on 9 : 1); his placing of himself in the 'third generation', separated from the eye-witnesses by the 'collectors' or by Paul (see on 1 : 2). Apart from exegetical problems,

Conzelmann's reconstruction of 'Luke's place in the development
of early Christianity' contains two questionable assumptions: that
theological differences necessarily imply a chronological development; and that Luke stands in a third generation making a 'comprehensive synthesis' of components from the original period, the
Jewish-Christian community and the Gentile church (pp. 306f.).
In the context of German theology such assumptions are reminiscent of F. C. Baur's interpretation of early Christianity in terms
of an Hegelian philosophy of history (cf. also Haenchen, pp. 115f.,
629ff.). They are not, of course, consciously employed to conform
historical data to an Hegelian mould—nor were they by Baur (cf.
Hodgson, pp. 3f.). But they do witness to the continuing power of
Hegelian thought for the mind of the German historian. The
reconstruction, consequently, will be viewed with some hesitation
by those who do not share its philosophical suppositions.

(c) *Assessment*. On the whole, the early date has more in its favour.
However, two considerations make it improbable that Luke was
published before the outbreak of the Neronian persecution and of
the Jewish rebellion (AD 66). First, if Lk. 11 : 49–51 (q.v.) refers
to an event of AD 67–68, as is argued below, that is the earliest
date possible. Also, Lk. 21 : 20–24 (q.v.), although probably not
a prophecy after the event, indicates a changed situation from
Mark. It is best understood if dated after the beginning of the
Jewish rebellion. No longer must the Church's reader have special
insight, as he must in Mk. 13 : 14, to 'understand' and interpret
Jesus' oracle. Before the war Luke's wording would have brought
complete Jewish rejection and opposition. Afterward moderate
Jews would have listened. In addition, the clarified prophecy
would show interested Roman officials that Christianity was not
party to the revolt.

The above reasons, if valid, preclude a dating of Luke prior to
the late sixties. Although a precise *terminus ad quem* is more difficult
to determine, a number of considerations suggest a publication
date not much after that time. They vary in force but, taken
together, they raise a rather substantial degree of probability.
There is, among the external evidence, some likelihood that about
the turn of the century Luke and/or Acts was known to Clement
of Rome and Ignatius of Antioch (see above, p. 55). While it cannot be pressed, it should be considered along with other criteria.

Parallel themes and concepts in other early Christian literature may offer some clue to the date of Luke–Acts. But such comparisons are often ambiguous and must be weighed with caution. For example, a similar mission praxis, e.g., of Christian 'brothers' working and travelling in groups (Ac. 11 : 12; 13 : 3ff.; 15 : 25ff.; 28 : 15), is reflected both in Paul's letters (1 C. 16 : 10ff.) and in Ignatius (*Phila.* 11 : 1f.; *Smyr.* 12 : 1). Which is more significant for Luke's situation? Other aspects of this theme and the fact that Luke purports to represent the Pauline period favour K. G. Kuhn's conclusion: 'The depiction of Paul's missionary work in Acts is always in exact agreement with the current situation. Since it is so true to life, there is no reason to doubt its historicity' (*TDNT* vi, 744).

Compared with Mark, Luke strikingly emphasizes the fate of the Christian to suffer. There is some indication that he addresses current persecutions of extreme severity that apparently have caused much apostasy and some misguided expectations of an immediate return of Jesus. See on 12 : 1–10; 13 : 34; 18 : 1–8; 21 : 19; 22 : 28. By itself this does not take us very far. For Luke applies Christ's warnings equally to Christian leaders who, content with the 'delay' in his coming, have become corrupt (see on 12 :41–48). Furthermore, persecution that is instigated by unbelieving Jews is characteristic not only of the pre-AD 70 Church (1 Th. 2 : 14ff.) but also of the time of Justin (*Dial.* 17 : 96; cf. 2 *Apol.* 12), and apparently it is common to the whole period AD 33–135 (cf. Frend, pp. 168f., 178–86). However, only two periods of persecution in the first century are remembered for their severity, the sixties by Nero and the nineties by Domitian, extended into the provinces as a promulgation of edicts show (Tert. *Apol.* 5, 1, 7 : *leges*; Suet. *Nero* 16 : *instituta, suppliciis*). The intervening reigns of the Flavian emperors were relatively uneventful (cf. Frend, p. 211; Melito, in Eus. 4, 26, 9). The time of persecution that is of interest to Luke is indicated by his association of this theme with the destruction of Jerusalem.

After AD 70 'Jerusalem ceased to be the directing centre of the Christian mission' (Frend, p. 171). Even more, for the diaspora-Church it apparently ceased to be of any significance at all. Apart from Paul, the Gospels, and Acts, the name appears only four times in the New Testament and then only with reference to the 'heavenly' city. It is also absent from the Apostolic Fathers except

for a cultic reference in 1 *Clem.* 41 : 2. In the Apologists it appears
only in Justin, who speaks of the gospel going out from Jerusalem
(e.g., 1 *Apol.* 39 : 3; 45 : 5; cf. Lk. 24 : 47; *Ascen. Isa.* 11 : 22) and
of its desolation (particularly) in AD 135 (e.g., *Dial.* 16 : 2; 40 : 2;
92 : 2). Among the apocryphal writings only *Epistula Apostolorum*
(33) makes a reference to the fall of Jerusalem. To summarize, in
the Christian literature that can be clearly dated between AD 90
and the mid-second century, Jerusalem's name and fame virtually
disappear. In the writings of Luke one encounters an entirely
different situation.

Luke–Acts contains some ninety references to Jerusalem, almost
twice as many as all the rest of the New Testament. Luke stresses
the centrality of Jerusalem in the life of Jesus and in the burgeon-
ing post-resurrection mission of the Church. More than any Gospel
he underscores the judgment of God upon the city. In this regard
he includes a six-fold repetition of Jesus' prophecies against
Jerusalem, a repetition that strongly suggests an issue of widespread current interest (see on 23 : 28ff.). This probability is
strengthened by the purpose of Luke's writings which, among
other things, appears to be to answer the question, 'Why has God
rejected the Jewish nation?' These emphases indicate that Luke–
Acts reflects a transition period in which the role and fate of
Jerusalem was a problematic, living issue. This would have been
eminently the case at the time of the Jewish war of AD 66–70. A
generation later, at least in the diaspora-Church, the issue was
long past and apparently evoked little interest.

The authorship of Luke–Acts gives a general, though less precise indication of its date. Authorship, as C. S. C. Williams rightly
observed (*ET* 73, 1961–2, 133), cannot simply be left in the air
'as though our answer were unrelated to the problem how late
the theological environment was in which Luke wrote. 'If the
author was Paul's co-worker, as has been maintained above, he
may have written in the eighties but probably not as late as the
nineties of the first century. It is easier to suppose that he wrote
closer to the events with which his account closes, i.e., the sixties
or seventies.

The dating of the Gospel must satisfy a number of conditions,
(1) There apparently was a crisis sufficient to give rise to a widespread apocalyptic fever. (2) There was apostasy in persecution
sufficient to cause despair of the very existence of the faith. (3)

The judgment on Jerusalem was a focus of Christian concern; of equal concern was the failure of the national mission to Judaism and its theological corollary, God's rejection of the nation. (4) There was a pressing need to affirm the political innocence of Christianity. At the same time Christians must be assured of the Church's abiding theological relation to Jerusalem (see above, pp. 17f., 32). (5) The Gentile mission was introduced but not developed: Ac. 28:28b 'seems to reflect the time of the author [in which] the Gentile mission is really only beginning' (Jervell, p. 63). One period fits this combination of circumstances better than any other. Perhaps it is the only period that fits very well. Most probably, the Gospel of Luke was published during or shortly after the Jewish rebellion or, in T. W. Manson's words, 'round about AD 70' (*Studies*, p. 67).

The Purpose

A time-honoured thesis holds that the Lukan writings were intended to be a defence brief for the trial of Paul. This is difficult to accept, especially since in content and plan Luke–Acts is largely irrelevant for Paul's trial. H. Sahlin (pp. 34ff.) may be right in identifying Ac. 16–28 as an apology for Paul, later incorporated into Luke–Acts. But his argument for the same motive in the whole of Luke's writing is less than convincing (pp. 44ff.). Barrett's objection is well put: 'No Roman official would ever have filtered out so much of what to him would be theological and ecclesiastical rubbish in order to reach so tiny a grain of relevant apology' (*Historian*, p. 63). The same objection applies in substantial measure against B. H. Streeter (pp. 535, 539), who argued that Luke wished to present the case for Christianity to the Roman aristocracy. Whatever secondary effects the Evangelist's work had on the 'book market', it was written primarily for the Church, on issues important for the Church.

The purpose of Luke must be sought in connection with other questions about the Gospel, its date, its theological emphases, and its recipients. Luke–Acts, of course, may have enabled Christians to counter charges that they were subversive or party to the Jewish revolt. On the other hand, it sets forth the Church as the true heir of Judaism, rooted in Jerusalem and, consequently, a legitimate religion in the empire. But these issues do not appear to be primary, at least in the Gospel. More significant are three theological concerns of the Church of Luke's day.

The de-historicizing of the Gospel events by gnosticizing Christians is one theological aberration that Luke addresses. H. Schürmann (*ETS* 12, 1962, 43ff.), probably correctly, has characterized the Gospel as an instruction book for Christians, especially against such influences (cf. C. H. Talbert, *NTS* 14, 1967–8, 259–71; see on 1 : 4; the special note at 24 : 1–12). Secondly, the eschatology of Luke is a corrective for those who viewed the kingdom of God only in terms of an immediate return of Jesus. See above, pp. 12–15; on 17 : 20–37; 21 : 5–38. The third and most pervasive motif in Luke–Acts is the relationship of Judaism and Christianity. From Simeon's prophecy (2 : 34f.) and Messiah's 'inaugural' address in Nazareth (4 : 16–30) to Paul's final word of judgment on Judaism (Ac. 28 : 25ff.) the awful fact of the Jews' rejection of their Messiah is continually brought to the attention of the reader. The principal purpose of the Lukan writings very likely is to be found in this dominant theme.

As noted above (pp. 16ff.), Luke presents the problem of the Jewish rejection of Messiah in the context of salvation history. Using the same pattern, Paul spoke to this pressing concern a decade earlier in his letter to the Romans (9–11). P. Borgen (*CBQ* 31, 1969, 168–82) may not be far from the mark in regarding Luke's writings as an elaboration of Paul's thesis. The Jews have been rejected because of their unbelief; and their rejection has occasioned, in the purpose of God, an accelerated and successful mission among the Gentiles. That mission has provoked the Jews to be 'jealous', 'disobedient', and 'contrary', saving some but 'hardening' most (Ac. 13 : 45; 14 : 2; 17 : 5; 19 : 9; Rom. 9 : 18; 10 : 21; 11 : 14; cf. Ac. 21 : 20). Like Rom. 11 : 25f., Lk. 21 : 24 may look to a future 'grafting in' again of the Jewish people into the Israel of God. The parallels are not such as to indicate that Luke used Rom. 9–11, but there is a common pattern of ideas.

Two other facts are amenable to this interpretation of Luke's purpose. God's rejection of Judaism would have been of the greatest concern to proselyte and Jewish Christians at the probable date that Luke–Acts was written; and it is probable that Luke is writing to a diaspora Christianity in which 'the Jewish Christians form a respected and influential element [and] the foundation of the church' (Jervell, p. 175). Also, in the references to government officials the emphasis is not so much upon Rome's friendliness as upon Judaism's perverse and persistent antagonism (23 : 20f.; Ac. 12 : 3; 13 : 6ff., 27f.; 18 : 12ff.; 24 : 27; 25 : 9).

The Circumstances

Presumably Luke remained in Rome until Paul's death (cf. 2 Tim. 4 : 6, 11), and some late manuscripts name that city as the provenance of the Gospel. Others mention Greece, and this is the witness of the prologue cited above (p. 40). Little can be said about the destination of Luke–Acts. In the Gospel the translated names (e.g., 6 : 15; 23 : 33) show only that the destination was outside Palestine. The attention given to Rome and to Antioch is suggestive, but little more.

In this context one can venture only a very tentative reconstruction of the circumstances. At Paul's death Luke returns to the East, encouraged by Theophilus to complete his project. He has a copy of Mark and most of his other materials in hand. To these he adds (in Antioch? cf. Ac. 11 : 27) recent oracles of Jerusalem prophets, which is this time of crisis eloquently speak the Word of God to the churches. With his sources complete, Luke settles in Greece and sets about his task.

THE GOSPEL ACCORDING TO LUKE

Structure. The prologue is primarily the preface for the Gospel (cf. Haenchen, p. 136; Schürmann, p. 4), but Acts is probably also in view (cf. Higgins, *AHG*, pp. 78–91). It follows the type of introduction generally used by Greek writers of the period (cf. H. J. Cadbury, *BC* II, 490f.). The pattern may be compared with the Jewish historian, Josephus:

> In my history . . ., most excellent Epaphroditus, I have made sufficiently clear . . . the antiquity of our Jewish race. Since, however, I observe that a considerable number of persons . . discredit the statements . . ., I consider it my duty to devote a brief treatise to all these points (*c. Apion.* 1, 1).
>
> In the first volume of this work, my most esteemed Epaphroditus, I demonstrated the antiquity of our race, . . . (*c. Apion*, 2, 1; cf. Ac 1:1).

In addition, Luke's prologue contains a distinct poetic rhythm. The simple and balanced form of the words displays considerable literary skill and beauty. It also offers an insight into the writer's meaning.

> Inasmuch as many have undertaken
> to complile a narrative . . .
>   just as [the eyewitnesses] delivered to us . . .
> it seemed good to me also . . .
> to write an orderly account . . .
>   that you may know the truth . . .

Teaching. Although his own endeavour presupposes some inadequacy in the 'Gospels' of his predecessors, Luke does not disparage their efforts. Indeed, he is one of their company, and his work is an improved parallel to their own. He presents his Gospel as a very human composition: it is a meticulous collection, arrangement, and interpretation of selected data. At the same time the 'word' (1 : 2) that he transmits is no less than the Word of God. See above, pp. 37f., 53f.

Title. The title, 'According to Luke', appears in the best manuscripts. Its present form originated when a church had two Gospels and desired to distinguish them or, at the latest, when the

Gospels were a collected unit. Similar titles appear on the recently
discovered Gnostic 'Gospels' of Thomas and Philip. The *titulus*
was often omitted by first-century writers, but on literary works
it was added immediately afterwards. 'Private libraries had become as common as baths in the houses of the rich.' Before placing
a book-roll in the library, it would be tagged for. ready reference
with a title and the author's name (cf. Hadas, p. 25). In all likelihood Luke's volumes were so tagged by Theophilus since this
was the common custom. 'The most significant contribution
which the Greeks made to cataloguing was the use of the author
of a work for its entry. . . . in the Orient the traditional entry for
a book is its title' (R. F. Strout, *LQ*, 1956, 7). Cf. Moore, p. 223;
Seneca, *de tranquil. animi* 9 : 4ff.; Suetonius, *de grammaticis* 6: the
author's name 'is given in numerous catalogues and superscrip-
tions (*indicibus et titulis*) with one "l", but he writes it with two'.

I. many: they are not identified, but Mark is certainly one of
them. They are not ultimate authorities on which Luke is dependent (whatever his use of them) but contemporaries whose
relation to the events is no better grounded than his own.

2. delivered (*paredosan*)**:** i.e. in both oral and written form.
Both may be implied by the second-century writer, Papias. He
refers to Mark as 'the interpreter of Peter' and Matthew as the
composer of 'oracles in the Hebrew dialect' (Eus. 3, 39, 15f.).
O. Cullmann (pp. 59–75) has shown that in the primitive Church
the delivered tradition (*paradosis*) had a well-defined and technical
significance. It was nothing less than revelation, imparted by
Christ himself.

to us (*hēmin*)**:** probably not just the Christian community (so,
Schürmann) but specifically including Luke who is, thus, a
'second generation' Christian in contact with, the 'eyewitnesses'
of the mission of Jesus. Cf. Heb. 2 : 3. Contrast 1 *Clem.* 42 : 1:
'The apostles received the gospel for our benefit' (*hēmin*).

Eyewitnesses and ministers, one group, are distinguished
from the 'many', although a person might belong to both groups.
Luke numbers himself among the latter. The reference to 'eyewitnesses' is a calculated answer to an explicit concern. It reflects
the conviction that the Christian faith is rooted not in speculative
creation but in historical reality. 'An ancient writer would no
more claim the authority of eyewitnesses without expecting his
statement to be believed than a modern' (Creed).

word (*logos*): i.e. Word of God or Word of the Lord. This includes not only the essential Christian proclamation but also the acts and teachings of Jesus. Cf. Ac. 10 : 36–43; Gerhardsson, pp. 223ff.

3. followed . . . closely: i.e. by investigation (Stonehouse, *Origins*, pp. 118–28) or by observation (H. J. Cadbury, *NTS* 3, 1956–7, 131f.). The former is preferable, for 'eyewitnesses' most probably is to be taken literally and Luke distinguishes himself from them (cf. Kümmel, FBK, p. 127). But Luke has acquired such familiarity with the facts and has 'so kept in touch with them that his witness is practically contemporary witness' (MM, p. 486). **an orderly account:** i.e. a connected whole, whether the sequence is chronological, logical, or otherwise (see above, pp. 29f.). **Theophilus** ('friend of God') was a proper name used by Gentiles and Jews (cf. Jos. *Ant.* 18, 5, 3). Most probably he was Luke's patron who defrayed the cost of composing and publishing Luke–Acts. The title, 'most excellent', may indicate that he was an official or socially prominent person. Or it may be only a courteous form of address. Since Luke is following a literary convention, the secular title (rather than a Christian greeting) does not reveal whether or not Theophilus was a Christian.

4. informed: i.e. 'instructed' by Christians (cf. Ac. 18 : 25; Rom. 2 : 18). The 'things' (*logōn*) probably are to be equated with the 'word' of God in verse 2. But the emphasis upon the 'truth' or 'certainty' of the teaching presupposes denials or heretical perversions of it. In some considerable measure Luke's purpose is to counter heretical misinformation (cf. H. J. Cadbury, *BC* II, 510) as well as to verify and supplement fragmentary Christian teaching (Stonehouse, p. 44).

In part gnostic-type groups may be in mind. They arose within the Church, claimed to have secret apostolic tradition, and denied a bodily resurrection. In the Gospel Luke stresses a bodily resurrection. In Acts he appeals to Paul's 'public' gospel and to the Apostle's warning against false teachers (see p. 40; the special note at 24 : 1–12). Cf. Ac. 20 : 20, 27, 30; E. Käsemann, *ZTK* 54, 1957, 20; Haenchen, pp. 596f.; H. Schürmann, p. 3; *ETS* 12, 1962, 51f.; Talbert, p. 56n.

THE MESSIAHSHIP AND MISSION OF JESUS 1 : 5–9 : 50

The Dawn of the Messianic Age 1 : 5–2 : 40

Structure and Background. The sixfold division of the section consists of three prophecies and three visions. Each vision also includes an angelic prophecy. Like other parts of the Gospel, the thrust of the episodes often lies in the appended or concluding portion. Similarly, proof from prophecy, as P. Schubert has observed, is 'a dominant feature of the literary structure of the Gospel as a whole' (*NS*, p. 178).

In contrast to the classical Greek of the prologue, the infancy narratives abound in Hebraisms. Most probably they rest on Hebrew or Aramaic documents. This substratum is as ancient as any material in the New Testament and probably belongs to Luke's frequently used Jerusalem traditions. Luke has interpreted it and moulded it into a unified whole. But his usage elsewhere, for example, of the Markan tradition, gives reason to suppose that he has handled it with care and accuracy. Cf. P. Winter, *NTS* 1, 1954–5, 111–21; *ZNTW* 47, 1956, 217ff.; R. M. Wilson, *SE*, pp. 251ff.; C. S. Mann, HC, p. 54f.; but see P. Benoit, *NTS* 3, 1956–7, 191, 194.

The frequent allusions to the Old Testament and the lyrical form of the prophetic hymns invite comparison with the psalms of Qumran, and the possibility must be left open that these hymns already were circulating among disciples during the ministries of Jesus and of the Baptist. More likely, however, they originated, or at least took firm form, in the prophetic activity of the earliest Christian community (cf. Wilder, p. 75). In the knowledge of the prophetic, messianic manifestations attendant upon the births of John and Jesus the 'writing prophets' of the (Jerusalem) Church give appropriate expression and interpretation to them. In A. Harnack's (*Acts*, p. 55n) opinion the remarkable role of Mary in this section goes back to the impression that she made on the circle in which the narratives were collected.

Teaching. The infancy narratives of Matthew present Messiah as the royal seed who fulfils the words of the ancient prophets. Luke emphasizes Messiah's advent as an event that calls forth a fresh outpouring of the gift of prophecy (see the special note on

1 : 26–38). This is the character of the episodes about which the story gathers. In the nature of the case the angels are 'spokesmen for God'. But Mary, Zechariah, and Simeon also exercise the prophetic function (cf. also 1 : 76; 2 : 36).

In accordance with a continuing Lukan motif (cf. Ac. 2 : 17f.) both the prophecies and the visions herald the dawning of the messianic era. The Semitic, Old Testament background of the stories shows that it is wide of the mark to seek their meaning in Greek myths or miracle stories. It is also doubtful that the infancy narratives are an imaginary accommodation of Jesus and the Baptist to Old Testament texts. This would leave unexplained the considerable attention to historical detail, and it would reverse a prevailing order of priority in the use of the Old Testament in first-century Judaism (see above, p. 9). Any accommodation probably would have been in the direction of shaping the biblical texts to actual current events. Indeed, for Luke the factual character of the narratives is essential to their significance for his theme. Jesus is the all-important fact. He is the interpretative key who unlocks the Old Testament and reveals its meaning. We may suppose that the original collectors of the stories were guided by similar considerations.

THE VISION IN THE TEMPLE I : 5–25

Structure. The episodes of the 'infancy Gospel' reveal very similar literary patterns. Following the historical setting (5–10) a vision (or prophecy) is presented (11–20); the passage is concluded by a short epilogue (21–25). In the presentation of the visions a set pattern also is noticeable: the angel's identity (11), fear (12), the fear dispelled by the angel's message (13–17), doubt (18), the doubt answered by a sign (20).

Background. The incense offering took place twice daily, early morning and mid-afternoon (Exod. 30 : 7f.). To be the offering priest was an honour which some priests never received and none were permitted more than once. As the sacrificed animal burned outside, the offering priest poured incense over a live coal on the altar within the Holy Place. As the smoke arose, he prayed some set prayer for the blessing, peace, and messianic redemption of Israel:

> Appoint peace, goodness, and blessing
> Grace, mercy, and compassion
> For us and for all Israel, thy people . . .
> Blessed be thou, Jehovah,
>   who blesseth thy people Israel with peace
>   (Cf. Edersheim, pp. 168f.)

Emerging from the building, the priest concluded the service with
a benediction upon the assembled people:

> The Lord bless thee, and keep thee:
> The Lord make his face to shine upon thee,
>   and be gracious unto thee:
> and give thee peace
>   (Num. 6 : 24–26 AV)

Zechariah's sacrifice occurred during the reign of Herod, a
Roman appointee over the satellite kingdom of Judea. Later
historians called him 'the Great', but his subjects only tempered
their hate with one good memory: he began rebuilding the
temple. In this temple, toward the close of Herod's reign, Luke's
story begins.

Teaching. Zechariah belongs to 'Abijah', the eighth of twenty-four
ancient priestly orders. He is distinguished in having a wife also
of priestly stock. As the crowning experience of his life he stands
alone in the Holy Place to offer incense. In the stillness an angel
appears and speaks his message (13–17). Zechariah will have a
son whose birth will answer both his personal and his priestly
prayers. No ordinary prophet, John will take a special vow and
receive a special grace (15). But his greatness will rest in the
character of his message (see on 3 : 1–20; 7 : 18–35). In requesting
a sign the priest follows good precedent (Gen. 15 : 18; Exod.
4 : 1ff.). But to his objection 'I am old' the angel counters, 'I am
Gabriel' ('man of God'). Because of his distrust the sign is given
in the form of a judgment (20). Cf. Gen. 15 : 8, 13.

Completing the week's service assigned to his order, Zechariah
returned home (cf. 1 : 39f.). Thus the country priest, held in
benevolent contempt by the more eminent ecclesiastics, fulfilled
the proverb, 'God resists the proud, but gives grace to the humble'
(Jas 4 : 6).

5. Judea is used of all Palestine. Cf. 4 : 44; 23 : 5.

6. righteous: i.e. in the traditional Old Testament sense of the word. See on 18 : 9–14.

9. temple: see on 21 : 5.

11. The name **angel of the Lord** derives from the angel's function and is not necessarily to be identified with any particular angel. He speaks and acts for God, especially in God's covenant relationship with Israel. Cf. Gen. 22 : 15; Exod. 3 : 2; 1 Kg. 19.

12. fear: see on 8 : 37.

13. prayer (*deēsis*): stresses special petition in contrast to the general worship (*proseuchē*) of the people.

14ff. Note the poetic parallelism.

15. Instead of **wine** John's stimulant from birth onward is the **Holy Spirit.** His abstinence is similar to the practice of the ancient Nazirite order (Num. 6; Jg. 13 : 5; 1 Sam. 1 : 11). But in the Old Testament the Spirit came upon men only intermittently. In the former quality, therefore, John stands within the prophetic tradition; in the latter he foreshadows the messianic era (cf. Jn 14 : 17; Ac. 2; Eph. 5 : 18; 1*QH* 9 : 30ff.).

17. In the spirit of Elijah: John is the fulfilment of Mal. 4 : 5 but with a qualification which defines the popular expectation of an Elijah *redivivus*. See on 1 : 76; 7 : 27; 9 : 7f.; cf. *SBK*, IV, 779ff. Although some interpreters view the Elijah prophecy as having another fulfilment prior to the *parousia*, the New Testament writers never apply it in this fashion (cf. Rev. 11 : 3ff.).
before him: i.e. God. The coming of God himself was a part of the Jewish messianic expectation. Cf. Mal. 3 : 1; *CAP* on *Test. Simeon* 6 : 5–8; Rev. 21 : 3. See on 2 : 10f.

19. Names were given to angels only from the time of the Exile (586–516 BC). They were symbolic and probably were related to their function. **Gabriel**, who foretold Messiah's coming (Dan. 9 : 25), now proclaims the event and, in popular Christian tradition, will 'sound the trumpet' at the *parousia*.

22. vision: see on 3 : 21f.

24f. hid herself: i.e. concealed her pregnancy. The neighbours could only guess at the joyful secret that put new light in her eyes and a lilt in her voice. And, no doubt, such a change was presupposed. The 'reproach' of childlessness was deeply felt in Judaism.

THE VISION OF MARY **1 : 26–38**

Structure. The literary structure of this vision parallels that of the preceding passage. In poetic phrasing the angel's message describes the human (32f.) and divine (35f.) character of Mary's child. As messianic heir to David's throne he will be called by a royal title, 'Son of the Most High' (Ps. 2 : 7; 89 : 26f.). As the virgin's child this title will signify something more, a unique and mysterious unity with Jehovah, God.

Background. A Jewish engagement resulted in a marital status which, though unconsummated, was as sacred as marriage itself. In this context neither Matthew (1 : 16) nor Luke (2 : 33) sees any incompatibility between Jesus' sonship to Joseph and the virgin birth. This is not the result of their forced interpolation of the virgin birth into the (original) story but probably is rooted in the realism of Semitic thinking (see on 2 : 33). On the theory of pagan derivation of the virgin birth story see Machen (pp. 317–79); for the texts cf. Cartledge.

Teaching. Mary's question (34) assumes that the prophecy is to be fulfilled immediately in the normal manner of conception. Luke uses it to make explicit the earlier allusion to the virgin birth (27, 31) and the unique status signified by it. The reality of the incarnation is not dependent upon a virgin birth. God could have done otherwise. But since God ordained a miraculous conception, Luke sees Jesus' hidden deity appropriately manifested in it. But see Barth, pp. 172–202.

In a similar, though different, manner God's power has been manifested in Elizabeth's pregnancy. Thus, the angel not only gives a sign to Mary but suggests a confidant with whom she may share her strange and wondrous experience (36–38). To the declaration, 'No word (*rhēma*) from God shall be void of power' (*RV*), Mary replies, 'So let it be with your word (*rhēma*) to me'. These words of submission, destined to shape many an artist's brush and poet's song, held both sorrow and joy for her own life and marked the fulfilment of the prophets' dreams.

A Special Note: Jesus, John, and Late Jewish Messianic Expectation

According to some Jewish tradition the prophetic gift ceased at the close of the Old Testament period, but its presence or revival was generally expected in the messianic times (cf. 1 Mac. 14:41; Jos. *c. Apion.* 1, 41; *Ta.* 8a; but see R. Meyer, *TDNT* VI, 812–28; see above, pp. 12f.). It is not unnatural, therefore, that the attention of Jewish messianism should focus in considerable measure upon 'the prophet'. Besides the reappearance of Elijah as Messiah's forerunner (*SBK* IV, 764ff.; *ELT* II, 706ff.), the coming of a prophet 'like unto Moses' was generally anticipated. Sometimes the latter figure was identified with Messiah. In addition, a resurrected prophet or prophets and the coming of the Messiah(s) of Aaron and Israel were messianic expectations in parts of pre-Christian Judaism (1QS 9:11; *Test. Levi* 18:2ff.; 4 Ezra 2:17; *SBK* II, 479, 626).

Luke shows considerable interaction with these views, as well as with the more ancient expressions of Israel's messianic hope. See on 9:28–36. Jesus is the prophet 'like unto Moses' (Ac. 3:22). And probably his Davidic messiahship is equivalent to the Messiah of Israel mentioned above. See on 1:32; 18:38f.; 20:41–44. But the identification of Jesus with a resurrected prophet is rejected, and the Elijah prophecy is applied solely to the Baptist (1:17). A Messiah of Aaron concept also is rejected, but Luke does recognize a priestly role for Jesus in his use of Psalm 110 (cf. Heb. 6:20). This priesthood is Davidic for, to use the words of F. F. Bruce, 'it is extremely probable that after David's capture of Jerusalem he and his successors regarded themselves as heirs to the ancient royal priesthood exercised by Melchizedek and other pre-Israelite rulers of that city' (*NTS* 2, 1955–6, 181; *Exegesis*, p. 75n; cf. Kraus, II, 760).

Luke 1–2 emphasizes the dawning messianic era as a time of the renewal of prophecy. These chapters also set Jesus and John in contrast. Probably this is Luke's way of clarifying the confused and intermingled messianic expectations which continued even in the Judaism of his day (cf. Ac. 18:24f.; 19:1ff.). The contrast is not a polemic to show Jesus' superiority to the Baptist; it is rather a contrast of roles. There is no Messiah of Aaron, but in the Baptist the priestly tribe does contribute to the fulfilment of the messianic hope. John is important not only for his relationship to

Messiah's mission but also for the vision and prophecy that occurred at his birth. These revelations point to the character of the
coming messianic era.

A priestly pride in the role of John would be strongly in evidence
in churches in the neighbourhood of Jerusalem (and Qumran?),
and perhaps only there. Luke notes that many priests in Jerusalem
accepted Jesus' messiahship (Ac. 6 : 7). It is not improbable that
he found the traditions of John the Baptist in this circle.

27. house of David: i.e. of Davidic descent and therefore of
the tribe of Judah.

28f. 'Blessed are you' (margin) is absent in the best manuscripts.
The salutation announces the gracious attitude of the Lord toward Mary, the 'favoured' one. As is the case elsewhere (1 : 38,
48), Mary is described as receiving grace not as endowed with
the power to give grace. The message (*aspasmos*), more than the
vision, occasions her startled perplexity. See on 1 : 41.

31. The verse is virtually a quotation of Isa. 7 : 14 with 'Imman-
uel' changed to **Jesus** (= 'The Lord is salvation', or 'The Lord
is saviour'). Cf. Mt. 1 : 21, 23. In Luke the virgin birth appears
only in this primitive Hebrew-flavoured episode and plays a very
minor role in Luke's presentation of Jesus' messiahship. The
teaching is absent in the earliest writers to the hellenistic Church
(e.g., Paul and Mark) and seems to have no place in most of the
earlier post-apostolic writings. This suggests that the virgin birth
was much less important for the earliest Christians than for the
later Church. It also suggests that it was not a tradition created
by hellenistic Christianity to popularize Jesus as a new 'god'. It
looks more like a tradition of the early Palestinian Church which
was publicly avoided to prevent Jewish offence and 'Greek' misunderstanding of Jesus and his messiahship. It became important
to publicize the tradition as a counter to tendencies that, in
time, denied Jesus' humanity ('Docetists') or his divine origin
('Adoptionists') or his legitimacy (Jewish polemic). See above,
p. 68; special note at 24 : 1–12; cf. E. Stauffer, *NES*, pp. 119–28.

32. throne: an allusion to 2 Sam. 7 : 12, 16. Cf. 2 C. 6 : 18;
Heb. 1 : 5; 4*QFlor* 1 : 7, 10f.

33f. no end: in popular conception the Davidic Messiah was
thought to have only a temporary reign. Like Luke, the Qumran
sect (4*QFlor*), using the same passage (2 Sam. 7 : 10–14), combines

the messianic 'Son of God' with everlasting kingship. Cf. Lövestam, pp. 93f.; see on 3 : 21f.

34. The verse is omitted by one fifth-century Latin manuscript.
Streeter (pp. 267f.) is impressed with the 'possibility' that this
isolated reading is original. Harnack (*Luke*, p. 111n) also omits
the verse. But such a rendering destroys the parallelism between
this announcement and the one to Zechariah (1 : 18). And it
makes pointless the comparison with Elizabeth's miraculous conception (1 : 36; cf. Williams, pp. 28ff.; Machen, pp. 120ff.). It
also is of little use to speculate whether Luke's source lacked the
verse and, therefore, a reference to the virgin conception. A
theology of the sources is always precarious and often misleading:
the Lukan addition (if 1 : 34 is such) may have been drawn from
elsewhere in the same source.

35. The Holy Spirit who was active in bringing the first
creation into being (Gen. 1 : 2) is the agency through which the
new creation is born in Jesus the Messiah. Barrett (pp. 20–24)
finds no instance in Judaism of the Spirit's activity in *begetting*
a child. But, as he recognizes, in Ezek. 37 : 14 God's Spirit creates
resurrection life. Cf. Jdt. 16 : 14; 2 *Bar.* 21 : 4. Barrett may draw
too fine a distinction between the Spirit 'creating' and 'causing
to conceive'. For, in fact, a barren womb was equated with death
(¹ Sam. ¹ : 5f.) and life from it was regarded as a creative,
miraculous act (cf. E. E. Ellis, *NBD*, p. 736). Paul in Rom. 4 : 17ff.
compares the conception of Sarah with a resurrection from the
dead (cf. Gal. 4 : 27ff.; Dibelius, *Botschaft*, pp. 28f.). It is not unlike
the case of Mary, for Luke does not present the virgin conception
as a 'mating' of the Holy Spirit with Mary. Rather God's Shekinah
presence 'overshadows' her. This idea most probably is derived
from Old Testament antecedents (cf. Daube, pp. 5–9, 32ff.).
Son of God: because of the miraculous conception and, therefore, signifying divine origin. Cf. Dibelius, *Botschaft*, p. 16. See on
22 : 70.

38. handmaid: cf. 1 Sam. 1 : 11 LXX.

THE PROPHECY OF MARY I : 39–56

Structure. Strictly speaking, the episode is 'the prophecies of Elizabeth and Mary'. But it stands in close conjunction with the preceding passage, and the dominant element is the Magnificat.

Believing 'Mary' (46) to be an interpolation, some scholars assign
the hymn to Elizabeth. But this judgment is opposed to the mass
of manuscript evidence and reflects a misunderstanding of the
literary structure of the episode. As he does elsewhere (see pp. 76f.,
82f., 179, 181, 277), Luke uses the concluding part of an episode
to elaborate and underline the first part. Therefore it is very
unlikely that Luke would have Elizabeth sing her own praise.
The passage is closely related to the annunciation (1 : 26–38), and
there is no return to a 'John the Baptist' motif.

The Magnificat (46–55) takes its name from the Latin Vulgate,
the 'Authorized Version' of the medieval Church. A lyrical poem
modelled upon Old Testament (and Qumran?) psalms, it has a
special affinity to the Song of Hannah (1 Sam. 2 : 1–10; cf. Lk.
1 : 38; P. Winter, *BJRL* 37, 1954, 328–47). It expresses Mary's
joyous gratitude for her personal blessing (46–48), God's gracious-
ness to all who reverence him (49–50), his special love for the
lowly (51–53) and for Israel (54f.). The last half of the poem
describes God's victory in terms of a national deliverance from
human oppressors. This is a recurrent note in pre-Christian
messianism. The New Testament writers do not deny it, but they
redefine it and transfer it to Messiah's *parousia*.

Teaching. The Lord is 'Saviour' in his Old Testament role as the
deliverer of Israel (cf. Hab. 3 : 18; Ps. 106 : 21). Those mighty
acts of old are doubtless in mind. But foremost in the Virgin's
thoughts is a messianic deliverance, a new mighty act of God,
whose meaning surpasses her comprehension. In this she is to
share: 'God my Saviour' (47). Even more, and this is the cause
of her song, God has deigned to choose her, a peasant maid, to
fulfil the hope of every Jewish woman. For in Judaism that which
gave deepest meaning to motherhood was the possibility that her
son might be the Deliverer.

In his messianic redemption God 'has manifested his supreme
strength' (51, Weymouth). The specific object of his mercy is
Israel 'his servant' (*pais*; cf. Ac. 3 : 13, 26; 4 : 27, 30). His action
is not the whim of a moment but the fulfilment of a promise made
to Abraham: 'I will give to you and to your descendants . . . the
land . . . for an everlasting possession' (Gen. 17 : 8).

39f. Like many of the priests, Zechariah lived outside Jerusalem. See on 10 : 30ff. Perhaps Mary and Joseph also previously

resided in this region. This would account for the close friendship between Elizabeth and Mary that is assumed here, as well as for the locality of Jesus' birth and early life. Cf. 2 : 3f.; Mt. 2 : 13, 16, 21f.

41, 44f. The **greeting** (*aspasmos*) was no mere 'hello' (*chaire*, cf. 1 : 28f.) but a ceremonial act whose significance lay in the content of the message. Cf. Mk 15 : 18; H. Windisch, *TDNT* I, 496ff. As Luke the physician perhaps knew, an emotional experience of the mother can cause a movement of the foetus. Elizabeth sees in this a confirmation of the Holy Spirit and a connection with her own pregnancy. She expresses this in the idyllic phrase, **The babe . . . leaped for joy**.

42f. All mothers are **blessed;** but **among women** Mary stands forth alone as the recipient of a unique blessing.

47. Saviour: see on 2 : 11.

50. fear him: cf. Ps. 103 : 17. Fear of God is 'the Old Testament description of piety' (Plummer).

51–53. As is often the case in the Old Testament, the future acts of God are viewed as already accomplished. The promise of God has the efficacy of the act itself (cf. Gen. 17 : 5). His word is the word of power. God will reverse the status of men in the coming age. In sovereign purpose he 'puts down' and 'exalts'. Thereby he manifests both his justice and his great mercy.

54f. Is there reflected here the Old Testament distinction between the nation and the remnant? The contrast in 1 : 51–53 may be only between the Jewish nation and the Gentile overlords. But for Luke and his readers the Christian interpretation of such concepts as 'Israel', 'servant', and 'seed' (= posterity) certainly is not absent. Probably it enters into his understanding and interpretation of Mary's prophecy. Cf. 24 : 21, 26; Ac. 1 : 6; 3 : 13, 26; Jn 8 : 39; Gal. 3 : 16, 29.

56. three months, i.e. until John's birth. The episodes, which chronologically overlap, often are marked by conclusions similar to this verse. Cf. 1 : 24f., 38, 80; 2 : 20, 40, 52.

THE PROPHECY OF ZECHARIAH **1 : 57–80**

Structure. The passage has two major divisions, the narrative (57–66) and the appended 'Benedictus' (67–79). Like the other prophecies of Luke 1–2, the Benedictus is named from the initial

word of the Latin version. In Luke's scheme it is the central motif
to which the narrative forms a prologue. The conclusion (80) ties
the incident to the wider story of the Baptist.

The prophecy has two sections. The first (68–75), in successive
parallelisms, extols God for his messianic deliverance and rejoices
in its results. The second (76–79) describes the place that John
has in this mighty act of God. The switch from the third person
to the second (76) is a literary device, frequent in Jewish writings,
by which the force of the poem is intensified. Cf. Isa. 63 : 10–19;
Mt. 5 : 10f., Daube, pp. 200f.

Background. In Hebrew prophecy the prophet often expresses
his message as an elaboration or application of former revelations.
For example, certain Psalms dwell upon the Exodus (Ps. 105).
And later prophets occasionally draw upon the words of earlier
writers (cf. Mic. 4 : 4; Zech. 3 : 10). Composed in this pattern,
the Benedictus paraphrases or alludes to a number of Old Testament passages.

In the Old Testament a name recalled a memorable occasion
or, if God gave it, indicated the person's character or destiny.
Cf. Gen. 17 : 5; 32 : 28; Exod. 2 : 10; 1 Sam. 1 : 20. By the first
century the first-born son of a Jewish family frequently was
named after the father or grandfather. The circumcision and
naming of John, therefore, was a significant occasion. Cf. Jos.
Ant. 14, 1, 3; Tobit 1 : 9.

Teaching. Even before the ceremony the kinsfolk doubtless 'were
calling' (59, *ekaloun*) the child 'little Zechariah'. They are as-
tounded when Zechariah confirms Elizabeth's word: 'his name is
John' (= 'The Lord is gracious'). The ceremony is not to choose
a name but to confirm a name that already has been given.
With the accompanying miracle it forms a climactic setting (65f.)
for the following oracle.

The Baptist will prepare Messiah's 'ways'. Messiah's work is
defined as a deliverance from 'fear' and from 'sins'. This goes
beyond a political redemption to picture the messianic salvation
in religious, priestly terms quite appropriate to the priest Zechariah. For while the mass of Jews viewed Messiah as a political
deliverer, his priestly role is not absent from Judaism. See the
special note at 1 : 26–38.

59. eighth day: Abraham's new name was given at his circumcision, but this does not appear to be the usual Old Testament custom. In the Hellenistic world the child was named seven to ten days after birth. Probably the Jewish practice was an adoption of this culture-form. Cf. Pauly 32 (1935), 1615f.

circumcise: according to an ancient Jewish custom the child was circumcised upon a chair called the 'throne of Elijah' with the hope that he might be the long-awaited prophet (Mal. 3 : 1; 4 : 5). 'If, in the New Testament age, some messianic symbolism was applied to any male child—whether or not it took just this form of "throne of Elijah"—it becomes far easier to fit the narratives of the adoration of the Magi or the shepherds into a Jewish milieu. The same is true of the miracle which Luke says happened at the circumcision of the Baptist, whom the Gospel, in its present form at least, does clearly assimilate to Elijah' (Daube, p. 22).

62f. made signs (*enneuō*)**:** was Zechariah both deaf and dumb? The word may mean only a covert beckoning (cf. Jn 13 : 24; Ac. 24 : 10: *neuō*). But it also may reveal what was implicit in the earlier episode: cf. *kōphos* in 1 : 22; 7 : 22.

writing tablet: from Old Testament times small wooden boards, covered with a film of wax, were used. Cf. Ezek. 37 : 16, 20; *SBK* II, 108.

65f. The twofold reaction is very human: they were awed and they gossiped. The 'things', i.e. events (*rhēma*), became 'common talk' (*NEB*). Probably they played their part in the acceptance which the Baptist later received as a prophet of God (7 : 26; 20 : 6).

68, 71f. has redeemed: see on 1 : 51-53, 54f. For Luke and his readers such concepts as 'Israel' (see on 24 : 13-32, 21), 'people', 'enemy', 'covenant' (see on 22 : 19*b*, 20) have a transformed, Christian significance. The language is that of the Old Testament in which God's ancient acts of salvation are seen as patterns, and therefore prophecies, of his messianic redemption. E.g., Ps. 106 : 10, 45; cf. 1 Pet. 2 : 9.

68f. As an animal's strength is in its horn so God is a **horn** in effecting his mighty act of salvation (Ps. 18 : 2; cf. Dt. 33 : 17; 1*QH* 9 : 28f.). The ancient title for God is applied to Messiah. In the Old Testament there is an undefined fusion of Yahweh and his 'messenger'. This may be present here. Cf. Jg. 6 : 11-23;

13 : 21f.; Mal. 3 : 1; E. Hill, *SE*, pp. 191, 195f.; W. H. Brownlee, *NTS* 3, 1956–7, 196f.

house of David: cf. 1 : 32; 2 : 4.

74f. The Magnificat describes a reversal of political and economic status in the coming age (1 : 52f.). The 'Benedictus' speaks of the ethical transformation to be effected by the messianic redemption.

76. ways: i.e. of Messiah or of God in the messianic redemption. Cf. Mal. 3 : 1; 4 : 5; Isa. 40 : 3; Mk 1 : 2; see on 7 : 18–35.

77f. salvation: i.e. which either consists in forgiveness of sins or brings forgiveness of sins upon repentance (cf. 3 : 3; 24 : 47). The latter is directly connected with John's preaching; the former is the ultimate effect of his work.

dayspring (margin) (*anatolē*): This may be only a figure for the coming or 'arising' of Messiah or of God (cf. P. Winter, *ST* 7, 1953, 160f.). More probably it is a name for Messiah (cf. Zech. 3 : 8; 6 : 12 LXX; Jer. 23 : 5). Found only here in the New Testament, it has a special significance for the context. Messiah is a light-giver who leads into life and peace those who are in the 'darkness' of death. See special note at 11 : 29–36; cf. Isa. 9 : 1f.; 42 : 7; 59 : 8f.; Mt. 4 : 16; 2 Pet. 1 : 19.

79f. way: see on 20 : 21.

grew: cf. 2 : 40, 52; 1 Sam. 2 : 26.

wilderness: did his sojourn include, as some believe (A. S. Geyser, *NoT* 1, 1956, 70–5), participation in a monastic or religious community such as Qumran? At present, the question cannot be answered with assurance. Cf. F. F. Bruce, *NTS* 2, 1955–6, 189.

THE VISION OF THE SHEPHERDS **2 : 1–20**

Structure and Background. The setting (1–5) and the birth of Jesus (6f.) are a prologue to the story of the shepherds (8–20). Only Luke relates a story coincident with Messiah's birth. He does not give the time of year. But the sheep at pasture indicate that the time was not midwinter, and the enrolment probably coincided with a major religious festival. The traditional Christmas date, 25 December, most likely arose later, perhaps to coincide with the birth of the year. Or perhaps a pagan festival was appropriated just as pagan new year festivals are appropriated today for 'watchnight' services. Cf. Cullmann, pp. 21–36.

In Messiah's ministry God revealed his message primarily to the poor and outcasts. See on 6: 20–26; 10: 21–24. Thus, at his birth the angels' song came to simple shepherds (8–20). As a class they were not held in high regard, exhibiting a gypsy-like tendency to confuse other people's property with their own (cf. *SBK*). Possibly, however, these were a religious group who provided sheep for the temple sacrifices. If so, their comprehension and reception of the angels' message is more understandable.

Teaching. Previously the angelic announcements were directed to those who received the visions. This message is for all 'the people' of God. They represent the faithful multitude who from ancient time until that day longed for the messianic deliverance.

At Jesus' birth the 'hour' of redemption has arrived (see on 10 : 21; 23 : 43). The angels' benediction (14) expresses a reality that has become manifest in an event:

> To God in the highest, glory!
> To his people on earth, peace!

The splendour of the vision is in sharp contrast to the commonness of the event (16). But having seen the *thing* (*rhēma*, 15) that has happened they make known the *saying* (*rhēma*, 17) told them by the angel.

1f. In keeping with his historical perspective Luke relates the birth to the context of the Roman world. Writing at *c.* AD 90, the historian Josephus (*Ant.* 17, 13) reports that Quirinius as 'legatus' or governor, conducted a census in Syria in AD 6–7. Palestine was a subdistrict of that province. Josephus and Tacitus (*Annals* III, 48) mention neither his governorship nor a census in the period of Luke's narrative (*c.* 9–4 BC). But an inscription discovered in Antioch may refer to Quirinius as the leading military official, virtually the Emperor's viceroy, in Syria during this earlier period (Ramsay, pp. 275–300; but cf. G. Ogg, PC, p. 728; H. E. W. Turner, HC, pp. 60–5). It is likely that Luke refers to him in this capacity (*hēgemoneuontos*, cf. 2 : 1). In spite of the silence of Josephus, there seems to be no good reason to dismiss Luke's account although Quirinius may be mistakenly associated with it. However, if Lk. 2 : 1f. has reference only to an initial enrolment, the census itself may have been in process throughout the period

9 BC–AD 6 (cf. Grundmann; Stauffer, pp. 27–36). Cf. Sherwin-White, pp. 162–71.

4. city of David: Joseph had a family as well as a tribal relationship to David. Mary's former home also may have been in this region (1 : 39).

5. with child: this presupposes their legal marital status. In describing Mary as 'betrothed' Luke may wish to indicate that the marriage is yet unconsummated. Cf. Mt. 1 : 25. A few manuscripts term Mary 'his wife'. Although probably not original, the reading only states what the circumstances presuppose. It has no bearing on the question of the virgin conception. See on 2 : 33.

6f. When the rooms were filled and the animals were at pasture, an **inn** would improvise quarters for the poorer people in the animal courtyard. In such circumstances Mary gave birth and cradled her son **in a manger,** i.e. a feeding trough. In ancient Christian tradition the stable is pictured as a courtyard or a cave. Cf. Justin, *Dial.* 78. It reflects the relative poverty of the couple and emphasizes that the humiliation of our Lord did not begin at Calvary. Cf. 9 : 58; J. D. M. Derrett, *TU* 112 (1974), 90–4.
firstborn: if Luke had wished to indicate that Mary had no other children, he would have used *monogenēs* (cf. 7 : 12).

10. Be not afraid: see on 1 : 5–25; 8 : 37.

11. Saviour: the background of the term is in the descriptions given to God and the national leader in the Old Testament and Judaism (P. Winter, *ST* 12, 1958, 106). In Luke the word occurs elsewhere only in the Magnificat, referring to God. It is found most often in the Pastorals and 2 Peter. It may be significant that they, like the present passage, use the term in connection with the deity of Jesus (Tit. 2 : 13; 2 Pet. 1 : 1).

This usage may reflect the Christian response to the Emperor cult which regarded him as a divine 'saviour'. However, such a response was possible because, from the beginning, the 'saviourhood' of Messiah was assumed by the primitive Christian community. This assumption drew on the royal messianic expectations of Israel. Characteristically, God was the 'saviour' of Israel. But as the Lord's 'anointed' (= 'messiah') the king was 'a potent extension of the divine personality' and intimately associated with Yahweh's salvation of the nation (Johnson, pp. 14, 122f.; cf. Bruce, *Saviour*, p. 52). See on 19 : 38.

this day: i.e. the day of messianic salvation. See on 23 : 43.
Christ the Lord: the term identifies Messiah as Yahweh, although the nature of the identification is left undefined. Cf. *Ps. Sol.* 17 : 36; *Test. Levi* 2 : 11 (*CAP* II, 650n, 305n); Heb. 1 : 10ff. See on 1 : 68f.

14. 'Men of God's good pleasure' is the better attested reading. It is parallel to *laos* (people) in verse 10 and refers to those upon whom God's redemptive mercy has been bestowed and with whom he is well pleased. Cf. 3 : 22; 1*QH* 4 : 32f.; 11 : 9; E. Vogt, *SSNT*, pp. 114–17. The 'peace' which the angels announce is not the external and transient *Pax Romana*. It is the peace which heals the estrangement between sinful men and a holy God. Cf. Isa. 9 : 6f.; Rom. 2 : 10. Contrast 19 : 38. Cf. Metzger, pp. 229f.

18f. wondered: unlike the miracle at the Baptist's birth, this story would make no sustained impression: 'only a shepherd's tale, you know'. But Mary 'treasured up' (*AV*) these things in her heart. Luke may intimate that she later revealed them in the Church.

THE PROPHECY IN THE TEMPLE **2 : 21–40**

Structure. The naming of Jesus (21) and the temple ritual (22–24) introduce the main point of the episode. It is the witness of Simeon and Anna to the Christ-child (25–38). While no prophecy of Anna is mentioned, it is implied that her thanksgiving (38) arises from a prophetic knowledge of Jesus' messiahship. In the case of Simeon three specific 'acts of the Spirit' occur (26ff.). He is assured that he will live to 'see' Messiah. He recognizes in Jesus the fulfilment of the promise. And he utters a prayer which, in the context, clearly is to be regarded as prophetic.

Background. Under the law a woman was ceremonially unclean and strictly segregated for seven days after the birth of a son. For a month longer she could neither visit nor take part in religious services. Cf. Lev. 12. At that time she was to offer a dove or pigeon to expiate her uncleanness and a lamb as a burnt offering of general worship. For the latter sacrifice the poor might substitute a dove. Since they were near Jerusalem, Mary performed these rites personally in the temple. In this setting Simeon utters his prophetic oracle.

Teaching. The words of Simeon include a prayer (29–32) and a prophecy spoken to Mary (34f.). The joy of the prayer is in stark contrast to the warning of the prophecy. Messiah, the instrument of Israel's glory, will cause division and be rejected by 'many in Israel'. Cf. 12 : 49–53; 20 : 9–18; Rom. 9 : 33. In this prophecy the concept of a suffering Messiah first appears in Luke's story. Jesus will be attacked, for the kind of redemption he represents will not be welcomed by all. This will bring anguish to Mary, but through the opposition men will be brought to decision. And thus their real selves, their hidden selves, will be uncovered.

21. circumcised: his first shedding of blood, like his last, identified him with his people. The Lord Messiah not only came to the sons of Adam, he became a son of Adam. Cf. Mt. 3 : 15; Rom. 8 : 3; Heb. 2 : 14–18.
Jesus ('Yahweh is saviour'): to be named by God before birth was of great significance. For Luke and Matthew (1 : 21) it pointed to the nature of Jesus' destiny. See on 1 : 57–80; cf. Gen. 17 : 19.

22f. Firstborn males were the property of God. Since the priestly tribe of Levi had been set apart in their stead, the firstborn in other tribes could be 'ransomed' through the payment of a nominal redemption price to the priest. Cf. Num. 8 : 15ff.; 18 : 16. The analogy to Hannah's dedication of Samuel is secondary at most. Cf. 1 Sam. 1 : 24ff. **Their purification** may go with the following **they** and, in loose idiom, refer to Joseph and Mary.

25. Holy Spirit or 'a spirit which was holy': in Jewish tradition the Holy Spirit was equated with the 'spirit of prophecy'. See the special note at 1 : 26–38. Cf. 1*QS* 4 : 21f.

26. see: see on 9 : 9. The parallel wording at 9 : 27 suggests that Luke relates the two promises. He may imply that Simeon 'saw' the kingdom of God (30).

28ff. According to an ancient Jerusalem custom parents brought their child to the temple for an aged rabbi to bless and pray for it (*SBK*). It may have been in this context that Jesus was placed in the arms of Simeon. As a slave addressing his sovereign (*despota*), Simeon requests dismissal from duty. God's 'salvation', a term applied to the messianic deliverance, has now become visible in the child of a peasant maid.

32f. Gentiles: cf. Isa. 49 : 6; Ac. 1 : 8; Rom. 15 : 8ff. Joseph and Mary do not understand the true significance of their Messiah-child's destiny. Luke represents their reaction as one of joy and anticipation mixed with perplexity and amazement. Cf. 2 : 48–50.

33. His father is replaced in some manuscripts by 'Joseph', doubtless out of deference to the virgin conception. But Matthew (1 : 16) and Luke recognize Joseph's fatherhood both legally and, probably following Semitic thought patterns, realistically. The case for Jesus' messiahship rests solidly on his Davidic heritage, and nothing is made of Mary's possible descent from the tribe of Levi (1 : 36; see on 20 : 41–44; cf. Heb. 7 : 14*b*; Machen, pp. 128ff.). This is not, in their thinking, inconsistent with the fact that Joseph is not Jesus' natural father. The Levirate marriage (cf. 20 : 28) offers a partial parallel: a son by the wife of a deceased brother is viewed as the brother's son.

36f. Possibly Anna belonged to an order of widows with specifically religious functions in the temple. See on 20 : 46f.; cf. 1 Tim. 5 : 3–16. Her long widowhood is a mark of honour, and as 'a prophetess' she is accorded a recognition rare in Jewish history. Only 'seven prophetesses have prophesied to Israel . . . Sarah, Miriam, Deborah, Hannah, Abigail, Huldah, and Esther' (*Meg.* 14a).

THE INAUGURATION OF MESSIAH'S MISSION 2 : 41–4 : 30

Here are placed a series of episodes in which the mission of Jesus is inaugurated and his messianic character set forth. At the age of twelve the Lord senses his unique character and mission (2 : 41–52). God specifically confirms this at his baptism. Following the witness of John (3 : 1–20) and of the baptism (3 : 21f.), the genealogy (3 : 23–38) and the temptation (4 : 1–13) give a further testimony to the person of Messiah. There is a continuing emphasis on the fact that Messiah is 'Son of God'. The last episode, like the first one, gives Christ's own witness to his messianic role and forecasts his rejection by his own people (4 : 14–30). Throughout the section the nature of Jesus' messiahship is progressively revealed.

THE WITNESS IN THE TEMPLE **2: 41–52**

Structure. The only canonical account of Jesus' boyhood is his discussions with the 'teachers' in the temple. As a transitional narrative it furthers Luke's purpose of giving a comprehensive and
connected story (1 : 3). But its significance lies in its witness to
the developing wisdom and messianic consciousness of Christ
and the recognition of these qualities by others (47, 52, 49). Within
Luke's scheme, therefore, this narrative belongs with the succeeding episodes rather than with the foregoing 'infancy Gospel'. See
above, pp. 30f.

Background. At thirteen years of age a Jewish boy entered into the
full responsibilities of adulthood. During the prior year the father
was required to acquaint him with the duties and regulations
which he was soon to assume. Thus Jesus, when he was 'twelve
years old', made his initial visit to Jerusalem to the same feast at
which, on a future springtime, he was to be the sacrificed 'paschal
lamb' (1 C. 5 : 7).

Teaching. Jesus appears in the role of a learner, first hearing and
then asking questions of the rabbis in the manner of the time.
Their astonishment at his wisdom is paired with the amazement
of his parents at finding him in the temple. Jesus' surprised reply
is, 'I must be about my Father's business (*AV*),' or, more probably, 'I must be in my Father's house.' The subtle distinction
between Mary's query, 'your father', and the Lord's reply, 'my
Father', points to the kernel of the narrative, the relationship of
Messiah to God. Cf. 8 : 19ff.

41–42. The Law prescribed that Jewish males should attend
three religious festivals each year: Passover, Pentecost, and Tabernacles (Dt. 16 : 16). At the beginning of the Christian era, however, it had become customary for those living at a distance to
come only at the Passover, the feast celebrating Israel's deliverance from death in Egypt (Exod. 12 : 21ff.). Some rabbinical
teaching required women to attend this feast as well.

43–45. parents: see on 2 : 33. On pilgrimages to Jerusalem,
villagers travelled in large companies or caravans in which the
women and younger children preceded the men. After the journey
began, they would not meet again until the previously agreed

rendezvous had been reached. Under these circumstances, it is understandable that Joseph and Mary would assume that Jesus was with the other parent or **their kinsfolk**

46. After three days: probably the third day after beginning the return trip. They came back to Jerusalem the second day and found Jesus on the following day.

temple: see the special note at 19 : 45–20 : 18. During the feast days and Sabbaths, the temple Sanhedrin did not conduct hearings and judgments. But on these days they did sit within the temple area and informally receive questions and state their traditions (*Sanh.* 88b). In some such gathering of teachers (see on 3 : 12; cf. Ac. 22 : 3) Jesus sat absorbed. As a young disciple he enacts a prelude to a future scene in which, on these same temple steps, he will be teaching *his* disciples (cf. 19 : 47; 20 : 1ff.; Mk 12 : 41ff.).

47. amazed: intended not just as a tribute to Jesus' intelligence but as a witness to his relationship to God. Luke often uses the word to express the reaction to the present working of the divine power of the coming age. The same 'Holy Spirit' power, later to be manifested in Jesus' ministry, even now is at work. Jesus interprets the Scripture not from the knowledge gained in rabbinic training but from the 'wisdom' given by God.

49. my Father's house: cf. Job 18 : 19 LXX; Plummer; E. R. Smothers, *HTR* 45, 1952, 67ff.

50. did not understand: Mary reacts here as she did to the shepherd's story. Although realizing her son's miraculous birth and his messianic destiny, she remains ignorant of the true nature of his mission and of his designation, Son of God. Had not Elizabeth also conceived miraculously? Are not all Israel's kings 'Son of God' in a special way (2 Sam. 7 : 14; Ps. 2 : 7)? If Messiah is to be a great political leader, why is Jesus so absorbed with the scholars of the temple? Perhaps these questions and many more cause the perplexity which colours Luke's portrait of Mary.

52. Destined to be exalted as the 'Wisdom of God', Jesus now grows 'in wisdom'. See on 11 : 49–51.

THE WITNESS OF JOHN THE BAPTIST 3 : 1–20

Josephus records the following of John. It is in general accord with Luke's account.

Herod slew (John the Baptist), who was a good man, and commanded the Jews to exercise virtue, both as to righteousness toward
one another, and piety toward God, and so to come to baptism;
. . . Herod, who feared lest the great influence that John had over
the people might put it into his power and inclination to raise a
rebellion, thought it best, by putting him to death, to prevent any
mischief he might cause, and not bring himself into difficulties, by
sparing a man who might make him repent of it when it should be
too late. Accordingly he was sent a prisoner, out of Herod's
suspicious temper, to Machaerus, the castle I before mentioned,
and was there put to death (*Ant.* 18, 5, 2).

Structure. The story moves swiftly. It covers the setting (1f.), the
nature of John's mission (3–6), the emphasis of his message (7–14),
the crucial 'messianic' question (15–18), and the imprisonment
which ends his brief career (19f.).

Background. For a Gentile to become a Jew there were three
requirements, baptism, circumcision (for males), and sacrifice.
Baptism, a self-administered immersion, even without circumcision fully sufficed to make one a true Israelite. It was a regener-
ative rite, a new birth. A proselyte was regarded as risen from the
dead. Cf. *Yeb.* 22a, 46b; Daube, pp. 109f. There may be some
connection between proselyte baptism and the baptism of John.
But the Baptist is distinguished not only because his baptism
was not self-administered but also because he baptized Jews.
That is, he places Jews in the category of Gentiles. Physical relation to Abraham is of no avail. Circumcision, the sign of the
covenant, is of no avail. One must reaffirm the covenant by
repentance and baptism. Unless one repents, one will have no
share in the coming kingdom (8f.). Significantly, Luke records
that it is the social outcasts, the grafting politicians, and their
soldier-police who express serious concern. The religious leaders,
Abraham's children *par excellence*, do not respond. See on 7 : 18–35;
18 : 9–14; cf. 20 : 4; Mt. 3 : 7.

Teaching. John gives essentially the same instruction to all: forsake
your sin and conduct your life in a manifestation of neighbour-
love (10–14). The sin of all groups is not the profession they follow
but the attitude in which they live their lives. This points to the

meaning of John's baptism. It was a manifestation of a repentant
heart. Those who sought baptism as an admission ticket, John
condemned (7f.).

The function of the Baptist's ministry was threefold. He prepared Messiah's way by arousing a spirit of repentance and expectation (3ff.). He witnessed to the nature of Messiah's mission
(6, 16f.). In baptizing Jesus he was the occasion for the inauguration of Messiah's ministry (21f.). The last is the focal point of
Luke's presentation. If Luke wishes to distinguish it from the
present episode, Jesus' baptism is the third attestation of his
messiahship. The first is the emerging consciousness of the child
(2 : 41–52). The second is the Baptist's witness to one 'mightier
than I' (16). The baptism is the witness of God himself to his
beloved Son.

1. fifteenth year: probably it is reckoned from Tiberius'
accession to the throne (AD 14) rather than from his association
with Augustus in ruling the provinces (AD 12). If so, the preaching
of John (and baptism of Jesus?) occurs in AD 28–29 or AD 27–28.
Two of Herod the Great's sons, Herod Antipas and Herod Philip,
continued as tetrarchs or 'princes' (*NEB*) during Jesus' ministry.
After AD 6 Judea was under direct Roman supervision.

governor: more specifically, 'prefect', according to a Latin inscription found at Caesarea (Palestine) in 1961: [PON]TIUS
PILATUS [PRAE]FECTUS JUDAE[AE].

Lysanias: this has been dismissed as a mistaken reference to an
earlier 'King Lysanias'. But an inscription in Abilene, probably
dating from AD 15–30, mentions 'Lysanias the tetrarch'. Cf.
Ramsay, pp. 297–300; Creed, pp. 307ff. The synchronisms of this
verse follow the practice of Greek historians and 'cannot be
challenged for accuracy' (Sherwin-White, p. 166). See on 2 : 1. Cf.
Bruce, p. 15. For other secular interests in Luke cf. Cadbury,
pp. 240ff.

2. Annas was deposed by the Romans in AD 14, but the Jews
regarded him as the rightful high priest. During the term of his
son-in-law, Caiaphas, Annas probably continued to exercise the
power of office (cf. Jn 18 : 13).

word of God came: prophetic idiom; e.g., Isa. 38 : 4; Jer. 13 : 3.
wilderness: see on 1 : 80.

3. Baptism is not just something that is done: it is preached
(cf. Ac. 10 : 37).

the Jordan: the gateway to the 'promised land', ending the
Exodus journey. Probably this symbolism is in mind. John exhorts
the Jews to enter anew into the ancient covenant and, thereby,
to inherit the 'promised land' into which Messiah will bring them.
Whether the idea of 'the baptism of the Exodus generation' was
present in first-century Judaism (or only later) does not affect the
matter. Cf. J. Jeremias, *ZNTW* 28, 1929, 312–20.

4. The DSS apply the passage (Isa. 40 : 3) to their community.
Cf. 1*QS* 8 : 13f.; 9 : 19f. There the 'way of the Lord' is prepared
by the study of the Law and separation from the world. Cf. Hill,
pp. 91f.

his paths: i.e. of Jesus. Isaiah has 'of our God'. The alteration
is an expression of the Evangelist's Christology. Cf. Stendahl,
pp. 48, 201.

5f. The addition of Isa. 40 : 4f. is important for Luke's theme.
He wants to emphasize the 'salvation of God'. See on 2 : 26; cf.
Mt. 3 : 3; Mk 1 : 2f. The Isaiah passage begins a section in which
the Exodus is a basic motif. Its immediate reference is to the
Babylonian exile. The application to John's eschatological message by the New Testament arises from the conviction that these
earlier 'redemptions' prefigure the future exodus of Israel from
the realm of death to the kingdom of God. The Baptist is the
herald or 'voice' of this messianic deliverance. Unlike Matthew
(3 : 2), Luke (4 : 43) begins the proclamation of the kingdom of
God with the mission of Jesus. For Luke the 'proclamation' of the
kingdom is nothing less than its 'presence'. Only Jesus will effect
this. See on 10 : 9; 16 : 16.

7. Multitudes is a deliberate generalization of 'Pharisees and
Sadducees' (Mt. 3 : 7). For Luke, John's rebuke includes the
whole nation. Since the Pharisees do not reject the Baptist out of
hand, H. Braun (*TR* 28, 1962, 105) doubts that he was (then)
identified with the Essenes or Qumran. See on 1 : 80.

brood of vipers: a similar characterization is found in the DSS
(1*QH* 3 : 17). Cf. Mansoor, p. 115n.

8. Repentance was prerequisite to baptism also in the Qumran
community. Cf. 1*QS* 5 : 13f.; see on 1 : 77f.

9. trees: i.e. Israel or those in Israel (see on 13 : 6). In the Old
Testament the 'vine' also frequently symbolizes the nation (e.g.,
Hos. 10 : 1; Jer. 2 : 21). Cf. 20 : 9ff.

11. let him share: in contrast to Qumran (and to modern

Socialism) the Christian 'sharing' ethic is voluntary. Cf. Ac. 5 : 4; 1 *QS* 1 : 12.

12. Tax collectors: see on 5 : 29; 19 : 8.

Teacher (*didaskalos*): an inscription on a first-century tomb in Jerusalem has confirmed that the title was equivalent to rabbi. Cf. Jn 1 : 38; H. Shanks, *JQR* 53, 1963, 343f. Whether it is a technical term for 'theologian' is uncertain. See on 2 : 46; 5 : 5.

14. Soldiers refer, in all probability, to Jews. They may be either police assigned to protect the tax-collectors or soldiers of the Jewish puppet ruler. See on 7 : 1–10.

rob: i.e. by bribes or threats. Cf. Jeremias, *Jerusalem*, pp. 125f.

16. Holy Spirit and fire: some think that the phrase is Essene and identifies John with that background. The DSS give only uncertain support to that interpretation (cf. Cross. p. 204n). 'Fire' is absent in Mark and probably is a Christian *pesher*-ing to the Pentecostal fulfilment. Cf. Ac. 1 : 5; 2 : 3, 19. See on 12 : 49–53; above, pp. 7ff. The DSS do state that in the last day God will purify man 'and clean his flesh by a holy spirit from all ungodly acts' (1 *QS* 4 : 21). Messiah is given no role in this, but in *Test. Levi* 18 : 11 it is intimately associated with his work. Cf. Isa. 44 : 3; Ezek. 36 : 26f.

'Fire' (as judgment) is usually regarded as the original word, and 'holy spirit' as a Christian re-interpretation (cf. Taylor, *Mark*, p. 157). But this overlooks the fact that the word is addressed to the faithful ('you') who are delivered from the destructive judgment fire. The objection that some of the Baptist's followers were ignorant of the Holy Spirit is irrelevant. The evidence cited, Ac. 19 : 1–7, probably refers to Christians in any case (cf. Haenchen, Bruce).

sandals: to carry (Mt. 3 : 11) and to take off the master's sandals were characteristic services of a slave. Some rabbis regarded the latter duty as too degrading even for a Hebrew slave. But a disciple might show his respect by such a service (*Mek.* Exod. 21 : 2). If this thought lies behind the present passage, John is saying that he is unworthy to be Messiah's slave. But he will show his discipleship by a service not even required of a slave. Cf. Daube, pp. 266f.

16f. John distinguishes himself from Messiah in two ways. He preaches a coming judgment; Messiah will execute it. He baptizes with 'water', Messiah with 'Holy Spirit and fire'. The refer-

ence to Pentecost is coupled to the destructive Gehenna fire of
verse 17. This is one of several passages in which Luke couples the
present and the future manifestations of the kingdom. See on
17:20–37. Both are eschatological (see above, pp. 13ff., 48ff.)
and both are judgments. The first purges and redeems, the last
judgment will destroy. That fire, like that in Mk 9:43 and
Isa. 34:10, refers to 'a fierce fire which cannot be extinguished
rather than to an endless fire which will never go out' (Plummer).
See on 12:5; cf. Edsman, p. 142; E. E. Ellis, *NTS* 12, 1965–6,
27–30.

20. prison: John 'prepares the way' of Jesus and of the Church
not only by his baptism and preaching but also by his sufferings.
Cf. G. Braumann, *ZNTW* 54, 1963, 126. The verse appears to
conclude the episode (cf. 1:80; 2:40, 52). Therefore, the Baptist
is not mentioned in 3:21f.

THE WITNESS OF JESUS' BAPTISM **3:21–22**

Background. Both the nation and the king of Israel were viewed in
ancient Jewish thought as a 'corporate personality'. That is, the
nation existed as an entity, embodied in the king as an extension
of the king's personality (cf. Johnson, pp. 2f.; Shedd, pp. 29ff.).
Prophecies concerning righteous Israel or 'the righteous king'
pointed forward to messianic times and to Messiah, King David's
greater son. In him Israel manifested its corporate existence. From
this background the New Testament speaks of the Church as 'the
body of Christ' and interprets 'royal' Psalms of Messiah (e.g.,
Ps. 2:7; Ac. 13:33; cf. *Suk.* 52a). The present passage applies
to Jesus the corporate figures of the king (Ps. 2:7) and the
Servant (Isa. 42:1). See on 9:33–35. Similarly, the dove that
descends upon Jesus signified for Judaism the congregation of
Israel (*SBK* 1, 123).

Teaching. The climax of John the Baptist's ministry does not lie
at its end but in its midst, at the baptism of Jesus. For Luke the
baptism is God's witness to Jesus as the Christ. And it is the divine
inauguration of Jesus into his messianic mission. To Messiah shall
be the gathering of the people. In Messiah the true Israel has its
origin and being. The figures of the 'Son' and the 'dove' heighten
this messianic theme.

21. baptized. The act of baptism is subordinated to the subsequent imparting of the Holy Spirit. Cf. Jn 1 : 33f.

heaven opened: this is not poetic description (so Ps. 78 : 23) but indicates that the event was understood as a vision. Cf. Ezek. 1 : 1; Ac. 7 : 56; 10 : 11; *Test Levi* 2 : 5f.; *Apocryphon of John* 47 : 30; W. C. van Unnik, HA, pp. 269–80.

22. The **dove** does not symbolize the Holy Spirit; it *is* the Holy Spirit. In contrast to Matthew and Mark, Luke speaks of its 'bodily form'. Evidently he views it as a theophany (cf. Gen. 18 : 2; 19 : 1; Jg. 6 : 13ff.) or a symbolic vision of God (Exod. 3 : 2; Isa. 6 : 1ff.). But in Luke virtually any supernatural appearance is a vision (cf. 24 : 23; Ac. 26 : 19; Mt. 17 : 9). For the participant it is indistinguishable from a 'nature' event (Ac. 12 : 9; cf. 2 C. 12 : 1f.).

A voice is reminiscent of 'the voice from the open heaven' in *Test. Levi* 18 : 6 (*CAP* II, 314). There it refers to the priestly Messiah, and some have interpreted the present passage as a priestly consecration. But the same images are used in Judaism of the messianic king. And the New Testament ordinarily puts the Lord's priestly consecration at his death and resurrection. Cf. H. Braun, *TR* 28, 1962, 107. See on 4 : 18; 13 : 32; 24 : 33–53.

Son: the designation, son of God, is used in the Old Testament of angels (Job 1 : 6), the nation (Exod. 4 : 22), and the king (2 Sam. 7 : 14). Later Judaism used the term for Messiah (4 Ezra 7 : 28), and this is the connotation here. It emphasizes Christ's divine authority rather than his divine nature. However, 'beloved Son' (= 'only son'; G. Shrenk, *TDNT* II, 740n), may go beyond a messianic significance. 'Jesus taught his disciples that he himself stood in a unique relation of sonship to God, and that this sonship was to find the essential pattern of its obedience in the fulfilment of the destiny of the Isaianic Servant' (Fuller, pp. 8ff.). See on 20 : 13; 22 : 70.

well pleased: Leaney and others (cf. Williams, pp. 45ff.) favour the reading of Codex D: 'Thou art my son, today I have begotten thee.' It is from the Septuagint version of Ps. 2 : 7. The best manuscripts appear to combine Ps. 2 : 7 with Isa. 42 : 1. Both texts were used in Judaism of Messiah, sometimes in combination. Cf. *Midrash* Ps. 2 : 7 (§9); Jeremias, *Servant*, p. 71.

THE WITNESS OF JESUS' GENEALOGY **3: 23-38**

Background. The numerous genealogical lists in the Old Testament testify to their importance in ancient Israel. In the first century the historian Josephus (*c. Apion.* 1 : 7) describes the care with which such records were kept. One example well illustrates their significance. The authorities required a priest to trace his fiancée's descent through four generations of mothers to see that nothing disqualified her from being a priest's wife (*Kid.* 4 : 4 = 76a).

The different genealogies of Matthew and Luke have been given several explanations. (1) Matthew lists the royal heirs and Luke the natural descent of Joseph. (2) Matthew follows Joseph's line, Luke follows Mary's. (3) Joseph has an adoptive relation to one line and his physical descent from the other. There is insufficient evidence to reach a firm conclusion. Cf. Johnson, *Genealogies*, pp. 229-52.

Teaching. The reason for another variation in the Lukan genealogy is clearer. Jesus not only is the heir of David and seed of Abraham (Mt. 1 : 1); he also is the second or 'eschatological' Adam and the 'son of God'. Elsewhere Adam is viewed as a type of Messiah, the one who restores the Paradise that Adam lost. See on 23 : 43; cf. Rom. 5 : 12ff.; 1 C. 15 : 45; Heb. 2 : 6ff. Unlike Matthew, Luke does not place the genealogy among the birth narratives but among the series of episodes attesting the messiahship of Jesus. It seems, therefore, that this messianic motif is the primary reason for listing Messiah's descent from Adam, the son of God (3 : 38).

23. about thirty: a person's age frequently was given in multiples of five. Therefore, Luke's chronology is only very general. Cf. H. J. Cadbury, *JBL* 82, 1963, 275f. It may be an allusion to the time of mature manhood or to the minimum age for public teaching. Cf. Num. 4 : 3; 8 : 23; Jn 8 : 57.

THE WITNESS OF THE TEMPTATION **4: 1-13**

Structure. In a style he uses elsewhere, Luke follows an introductory summary (1-2*a*) with a detailed exposition (2*b*-13). Cf. 1 : 57-66, 67ff.; 4 : 16-22, 23ff. The latter is the core of the episode. The transition between them is not chronological and the temptations, therefore, may form both a part and the climax of the 'forty days'. The order of the second and third temptations is reversed in Matthew. It may be that Luke changed the sequence in order to climax the temptations in the temple at Jerusalem.

Teaching. Both Jesus and Satan presuppose the messiahship of Jesus (3), the authority of Scripture to reveal the will of God (4, 10ff.), and the lordship of Satan over the present age (6). The temptations are designed to make Jesus 'prove' his messiahship and, thereby, pervert it. The Devil pictures the messiahship as an opportunity for self-aggrandizement and self-glory. But Jesus counters him by an awareness of the true nature of his mission. And to Satan's twisted hermeneutic Jesus brings a 'Spirit led' (1) interpretation of the Scripture.

1. from the Jordan: the connection of the temptation with the baptism is not incidental. For the meaning of the temptation is grounded in the baptismal anointing of the 'Holy Spirit'. Although the Devil is the agent, Jesus is 'led by the Spirit' into this testing. According to the book of Hebrews (2 : 17f.; 4 : 15) the temptations of Jesus fit him for his present priestly role in heaven. See on 3 : 21.

2. forty days in the wilderness: a conscious reflection upon the Exodus experience. Israel, filled with manna, rebels and doubts God. Jesus, fasting, refused to tempt or doubt God. Cf. Ac. 7 : 36, 39; Heb. 3 : 8f.

3. the devil: as is the case elsewhere in the New Testament, the fountainhead of evil is presented as an extra-natural, personal power. Although he has only authority that is granted by God, the Devil is in powerful, deliberate, and designed opposition to God's redemptive purpose. Cf. 2 C. 4 : 4.

If you are: a concession intended by Luke to show Satan's recognition of the messiahship of Jesus.

Son of God: probably a conscious reflection upon the Adam-Christ typology in the preceding episode. See on 3 : 22, 23–38. Jesus is the new Adam, the forerunner of all Christians in temptation and victory. Cf. A. Feuillet, *Bib.* 40, 1959, 628ff. But see Gerhardsson, *Testing*, p. 25: an Israel-Christ typology; cf. Dt. 8 : 5.

command this stone: on requests for a sign see on 11 : 29–36.

bread: later Jesus, a prophet like Moses (Ac. 3 : 22), will give 'manna' to the people (9 : 13ff.; cf. Jn 6 : 48ff.). But he will not pervert a messianic sign to test God or to satisfy his own hunger.

Proper desires fulfilled in an improper context become sinful.
They must be related to the whole will of God which here has led
Messiah, like Israel of old, to suffer hunger in the wilderness
(Dt. 8 : 3).

4. It is written: the word of divine authority and, therefore,
the word of finality.

Man: perhaps 'Son of man'. See on 6 : 5.

live: see on 9 : 24; 12 : 13–34.

5–8. Like the first temptation the purpose is to induce Christ
to secure a legitimate end through illegitimate means. If Jesus
will subordinate his messianic rule to Satan's lordship, his kingdom can be gained without conflict with the powers of evil, without rejection, without a cross. But Satan's offer involves both a
subversion of Messiah's proper role and an attack upon his
allegiance to God. To accept the offer would not be to displace
Satan's lordship but, like Adam, to fall into bondage to it. Jesus
chooses to resist and to fight the satanic powers in the power of
the Spirit. And he will win. Cf. 10 : 18f.; Jn 12 : 31.

in a moment of time: a phrase found only in Luke. It implies
that the experience, like the opened heaven (see on 3 : 21), was
understood to be different from a 'nature' event.

9–12. A late Jewish midrash (*Pesikta R* 36 = 162a) states that
the Messiah would 'stand on the roof of the holy place'. Sometimes the passage was cited in connection with the present
quotation, 'he will give his angels charge of you' (Ps. 91 : 11). If
the tradition reaches back to the first century, it is suggestive
for the meaning of the third temptation. Jesus is tempted to gain
messianic recognition by a bizarre act rather than by a cross and,
in addition, to 'prove' his baptismal anointing. Thus, the final
temptation combines elements of the first two.

13. every temptation: i.e. every kind of (*panta*) temptation.
The three recorded illustrate their nature and Christ's reaction
to them.

departed: see on 22 : 3.

THE MANIFESTATION AT NAZARETH **4 : 14–30**

Structure. Used as a transitional piece, this passage concludes the
present (Jerusalem–Judea) section and introduces the succeeding
(Galilean) 'acts of Messiah'. The episode is placed at this juncture

in the Gospel for a thematic purpose. Chronologically, it can be located only very generally in the Galilean mission. It presupposes a previous ministry that has brought considerable fame to Jesus (15, 23). Probably, with Augustine, one should identify this visit with that of Mt. 13 : 54 and Mk 6 : 1. But Luke employs a different source and changes the Markan setting.

Background. Documents describing an ancient synagogue service date from some time after the first century. But probably they reflect in large measure the practices of the New Testament period. Cf. Schürer, II, ii, 52ff.; *SBK* IV, 153ff. The service included the recitation of the *shema* (Dt. 6 : 4-9; 11 : 13-21; Num. 15 : 37-41), a prayer, a reading from the law, a reading from the prophets, and a benediction.

The law was read in stated sections and completed over a three-year cycle. The reading from the prophets, with certain exceptions, also seems to have followed an assigned cycle of lessons (Guilding, pp. 20ff.). It occurred only at the main Sabbath service each week. Three verses (for the law, one verse) were read in Hebrew and then were translated by an interpreter into the common Aramaic dialect. Afterwards the reader could give an exposition of the passage. While any member of the congregation might serve this function, precedence was given to priests and Levites. Probably the same courtesy would be accorded a visiting 'rabbi' such as Jesus (cf. Ac. 13 : 15).

Teaching. The rejection of Messiah, alluded to earlier (2 : 34f.), is the keynote of this 'inaugural' address of the Galilean mission. It is a rejection not merely of Jesus' 'kingdom of God' message nor of the Servant-Messiah concept but of his person as well. The request for a 'sign' (23) is evidence of their unbelief and, therefore, of their rejection of him. In the face of it Jesus sounds a warning of God's rejection of them. It is a tragic story, and Nazareth is a preview of what is to happen later in all areas and among all classes of Jews (cf. 9 : 52f.). It is here also that Jesus first hints that the benefits of the gospel will be given to the Gentiles (26f.).

14f. The summary provides a transition to the scene of the Galilean mission. Cf. 4 : 1.

16. brought up: i.e. from a very small child. Cf. van Unnik, pp. 33f.; Ac. 22 : 3.

his custom: synagogue attendance was expected of every devout
Jew. In mind here may be the use of the synagogue service as a
place of teaching. The practice was followed also in the post-
resurrection mission of the Church. Cf. 4 : 44; 6 : 6; 13 : 10; Jn
18 : 20; Ac. 17 : 1f.
stood up to read: and then sat down to give the exposition.

17. given to him: probably indicating that the passage was
one assigned for the day.

18. The speaker in Isaiah (61 : 1f.; 58 : 6), with whom Jesus
identifies himself, is 'the servant of the Lord' (and not the prophet). See on 5 : 24; 9 : 35.
anointed: at his baptism. Cf. Ac. 10 : 37f. According to W. H.
Brownlee (*NTS* 3, 1956–7, 205f.) the reference to Isa. 61 : 1
identifies Jesus as the priestly Messiah. But see on 3 : 21.
good news: Jesus brings redemption through a message, not a
social or political reform; through a word, not a war. The **poor,
captives, blind, oppressed,** represent the righteous remnant
in the nation. See on 6 : 20–22; cf. 7 : 22. A rabbinic comment on
the Isaiah passage reads, 'Whoever mourns for Zion will be
privileged to behold her joy' (*B.B.* 60b).

19. the acceptable year: see above, p. 14.

21. The Lord's appropriation of this Scripture to himself
apprised the audience, at least, that he was a prophet (4 : 24).
Probably it carried messianic connotations.
today: see on 23 : 43.

22. Joseph's son: the awe inspired by his **words** was mixed
with scepticism because of his origin. Since Joseph appears nowhere in Jesus' ministry or in the post-resurrection community,
it is usually assumed, probably correctly, that he had died. The
reference here may mean only that Jesus was known as 'Jesus
Barjoseph', Jesus, Son-of-Joseph (cf. Jn 1 : 45). But it is possible
that Joseph was still living or had died only recently. Cf. Jn 6 : 42;
Mt. 13 : 55; Mk 6 : 3. But see E. Stauffer, *NES*, pp. 119–28.

23. do here: Jesus states what the crowd is murmuring. The
request for a 'sign' is broached by Satan (4 : 3), echoed by hostile
churchmen (11 : 16), and still scornfully made at the crucifixion
(22 : 64; 23 : 8, 35ff.). However, signs were not for the sceptic
but for the believer: 'your faith has made you whole'. The proverb
'you profess, now produce' did not reflect faith but only curiosity.
See on 9 : 9; 11 : 29–36.

you did at Capernaum: the original perspective of Isaiah's prophecy probably was deliverance from political oppression. Its messianic fulfilment has a much vaster scope. It is a personal and cosmic deliverance from the powers of sin and of death. Demonic possession and sickness are visible manifestations of these powers. Therefore, the 'signs' of Jesus' ministry are pre-eminently exorcism and healing. Cf. 4 : 40f.; Mt. 8 : 16f.

24. Truly (*amēn*): translated in Lk. 9 : 27; 12 : 44; 21 : 3 by *alēthōs*. Jesus' use of the term is unique. Most likely it is a formula for introducing a prophetic oracle. It is a substitute for 'thus saith the Lord', perhaps to avoid using the divine name. Cf. Manson, *Teaching*, p. 207; J. Jeremias, *SS*, p. 90. 'The six Amen sayings in Luke' (cf. J. C. O'Neill, *JTS* N.S. 10, 1959, 1–9) are adopted selectively and may have a theological significance. Usually they introduce words of assurance and refer to the manifestation of the kingdom of God at Jesus' resurrection or at the *parousia*. Cf. 12 : 37; 18 : 17, 29; 21 : 32; 23 : 43.

25–27. The 'Elijah and Elisha' saying appears only in Luke (cf. Jas 5 : 17). It emphasizes the true meaning of the rejection at Nazareth: God will pass over a rebellious Israel and give his blessings to Gentiles.

shut up: cf. Sir. 48 : 3; ps-Philo, *Ant. Bib.* 48 : 1; Rev. 11 : 6.

and six months: from the end of the 'latter rain' in April to the beginning of the 'former rain' in October three years later. Cf. E. F. F. Bishop, *ET* 61, 1950, 126f.

29. out of the city: foreshadowing the day of his crucifixion. Executions were not carried out within the walls. Cf. Lev. 24 : 14; Ac. 7 : 58. By their action they excommunicate Jesus and, in effect, make him a Gentile.

30. passing through: because 'his hour had not yet come', Jesus was divinely protected from harm. Cf. Jn 7 : 30, 45; Dan. 6 : 22. Contrast Jn 8 : 59.

ACTS OF MESSIAH: THE NATURE OF HIS AUTHORITY **4 : 31–6 : 11**

Structure. Twenty-four episodes make up the Galilean ministry. In them the acts of Jesus are so presented as to illustrate the nature of his messiahship and the character of his messianic kingdom. Luke appears to arrange his material into four sections, each with six episodes. The healings in Capernaum, presupposed in the Nazareth episode above, constitute the first of the 'acts of Messiah'. The succeeding sections begin with the choosing of the twelve (6 : 12), the 'kingdom of God' mission (8 : 1), and the mission of the twelve (9 : 1).

The initial section of episodes is the first of several blocks of Markan material. Only the miraculous catch of fish (5 : 1–11) is not from Mark. The second section (6 : 12–7 : 50) is largely from the common Matthean material, i.e., the 'Q' traditions. Of the three exceptions, the choosing of the twelve is paralleled in Mark but is from Luke's special materials (L). Likewise the widow of Nain episode (7 : 11–17) and the anointing story (7 : 36–50) are found only in Luke. Apart from the introduction (8 : 1–3), the third (8 : 1–56) and fourth (9 : 1–50) sections use Mark and Q. Excepting 8 : 19–21, they follow the Markan order as well. See above, pp. 25f., 30f. Cf. Ellis, *CIB*; Schramm, p. 186.

Teaching. In the first section Messiah's authority is a continuing theme. Jesus does not speak as the scribes (4 : 32; cf. Mk 1 : 22). He exercises power over the demonic spirits, over sickness, and over nature (4 : 36; 5 : 6). He removes the leper's curse and forgives sin, disregards the traditions and declares himself to be 'Lord of the Sabbath' (5 : 13, 24; 6 : 1, 5). The 'signs' are clear: Jesus does works that only God can do. He supersedes all authorities before him and sets forth to Israel a new and startling meaning of Messiah's person and role.

Jesus' 'new teaching' is not accepted. The first three episodes are set within the context of rising popularity. The last three accent the rise of opposition as the implications of the 'signs' for the person of Jesus and for Jewish traditions become apparent.

HEALINGS IN CAPERNAUM 4 : 31–44

Background. The 'ordained' or learned rabbis, in distinction from ordinary teachers and scribes, had authority to enunciate new teaching and interpretations of the Law and to command evil spirits. Cf. Daube, pp. 205ff.; *Suk.* 28a.

Teaching. 'A Sabbath in Capernaum' consists of three incidents: the exorcism in the synagogue (33–37), the healing of Peter's mother-in-law (38f.), and the healing of the multitudes (40f.).

The theme is the 'authoritative word' of Jesus, both in his teaching and, particularly, in his exorcisms (cf. 24 : 19; Ac. 1 : 1).

According to Jewish tradition demonic power was to be crushed
in the messianic age (see on 11 : 22; cf. *SBK* IV, 527; *Test. Zebulun*
9 : 8). It may be, therefore, that exorcism as such was regarded as
a witness to Jesus' messiahship. Luke makes this explicit. The
demons give verbal witness to Jesus: 'You are the Son of God'
(41, cf. 34). The ultimate meaning of the ministry in Capernaum
is not the healings or the edification of the people. It is who
and what these actions reveal. This significance is lost upon the
people. They accept Jesus, but it is largely the surface acceptance
of emotional appeal.

32. teaching or *didachē*: both his acts of healing and his authoritative and new interpretations of Scripture. Little or no distinction is made here between Jesus' public teaching and his preaching or *kērygma* (4 : 43f.). The 'preaching of the kingdom, consists
of words and deeds. Its evident 'authority' raises a question that
is to follow Jesus throughout his ministry.

Unlike Mark (1 : 22) the contrast of Jesus' teaching to that of
the scribes is not made explicit. Luke points rather to the cry of
the demons.

33. synagogue: see on 7 : 5.
unclean: sometimes the demon is identified by the effect that it
causes. If so, the possessed person may be 'filthy in person and
speech' (Leaney; cf. 11 : 14). More likely, this is only a general
description of all demonic spirits. Cf. 9 : 39, 42; Mk 9 : 25.

34f. The ultimate purpose of Messiah's mission is to 'destroy'
the kingdom of Satan. See on 8 : 32; 10 : 18f.; cf. 2 Pet. 2 : 4.
us ... him: on the oscillation between the plural and the singular
cf. 8 : 30f.
Holy One of God: a designation of one 'consecrated' to God
(cf. Ps. 106 : 16). Here it has messianic connotations. Cf. 1 : 35;
2 Kg. 4 : 9.
rebuked: a conventional expression, not 'threatening' but exercising authoritative control over evil power. Cf. Zech. 3 : 2; *Jubil.*
10 : 5–9; 1QM 14 : 10 (gāʿar); Bultmann, p. 223. See on 4 : 38f.

36. amazed: by the manner as well as the fact of the exorcism.
The ordinary exorcist used 'incantations, charms, and much
superstitious ceremonial' (Plummer).

38f. high fever: the words probably reflect Luke's medical interest. The 'rebuking' seems to personify an impersonal evil, but it may rather reflect the conviction that behind all sickness is the working of Satan. See on 5 : 20; 8 : 24; 13 : 11, 16; cf. 1 C. 15 : 26. On *epitimein* cf. H. C. Kee, *NTS* 14 (1967–8), 232–46; *JBL* 92 (1973), 418.

40. when the sun was setting: i.e. the moment the Sabbath was over, in the short twilight period between sunset and darkness. **hands:** transmitting healing power. See on 5 : 13. But Jesus also healed by a word (e.g., 7 : 10, 17 : 14).

41. Son of God: see on 3 : 22.

not to speak: possibly because demonic utterance was considered unholy (Manson) or, more probably, because Jesus did not want his messiahship to be disclosed at this time or in this fashion. It is a part of the consistent refusal of Jesus to be identified publicly as 'Messiah'. In Jesus' day the term carried many false implications. See on 5 : 24; 8 : 28.

43. must preach: see on 4 : 32. It is not a matter of personal option or wish but the manifestation of a mission to which he has been ordained and 'sent'.

44. Judea: i.e. all Palestine (cf. 1 : 5; 23 : 5) with the possible exception of Samaria. So. Pliny, *Natural History* 5, 15 (70), who also includes Peraea.

THE SIGN OF THE FISH **5 : 1–11**

Structure. Luke chooses a story in which the call of the disciples is incorporated incidentally into his 'signs' motif (cf. 5 : 27–39). It is a substitute for a similar story in Mark (1 : 16–20). Like the earlier Nazareth episode it presupposes that Jesus had achieved considerable popularity. Also, a standing acquaintance with Peter, James, and John is assumed. Probably they already are regarded as disciples (cf. Jn 1 : 40ff.).

A similar miracle in Jn 21 : 1–14 may reflect consciously upon the present incident. The confession of Peter at 9 : 20 also is related. The three episodes otherwise are quite distinct, but each witnesses to the importance of Peter's role in the Gospel tradition. Originally they may have belonged to a collection of stories on this theme.

Teaching. The thrust of the narrative is the fear of Peter and the reply of Jesus. Implicit in Peter's cry, 'Lord' (8), is the messianic

confession that only later comes to conscious expression. Likewise, Christ's response is the prelude to Peter's later commissions.
Cf. 9 : 20; 22 : 32; Jn 21 : 1ff.; Mt. 16 : 16ff.

1f. lake of Gennesaret: i.e. of Galilee. The early morning
scene contrasts the quiet ritual of the fishermen with the excitement of the crowd to hear 'the word of God', that is, the message
of the kingdom (4 : 43).

3. boat: an open craft some twenty to thirty feet in length. It
provided a platform free from the congestion of the crowd.
According to the custom the speaker 'sat down' and the audience
stood.

5f. Master: the word is Lukan and is found only on the lips of
those who submit to the authority of Jesus. O. Glombitza (*ZNTW*
49, 1958, 275–8) thinks that the term distinguishes Jesus from a
'teacher' (*didaskalos*) of a theological school. Cf. 2 : 46; but see
on 3 : 12; 11 : 45; 14 : 27.
at your word: the attitude is more a sceptical obedience than a
response of expectant faith.

8–10. Peter's doubts about Jesus give way to doubts about himself. The acted parable of the catch of fish reveals the remedy for
Peter's lack of spiritual qualifications. To Peter's first protest the
Lord answers with a miracle. To the second he replies: 'You will
be catching men.' The power of Messiah overcomes the impossi-
bilities of each situation. What Jesus commands, he empowers to
perform.

10. Simon: probably a shortened form of Simeon. Cf. 2 Pet.
1 : 1 *NEB*. Luke emphasizes the role of Peter; James and John
appear only as companions. Cf. 8 : 51; 9 : 28.
Do not be afraid: like the angel of Luke 1 : 13, 30, Jesus is the
mediator of the divine power and presence.
catching men: as 'partners' now with Jesus. Cf. Wuellner, pp.
166–207, 217.

11. they left everything: their response to Jesus' assurance.
Probably the verse should not be pressed to mean a complete and
immediate abandonment of their trade, but it gives clear indication where the priorities of their lives now lie. See on 14 : 27;
cf. Mk 3 : 14.

THE HEALING OF A LEPER 5 : 12–16

Again Luke's stress is upon the sign rather than upon the person
involved. Contrast Mk 1 : 40, 43, 45. It may be that Jesus normally healed in private to avoid drawing excessive attention to this
aspect of his work. Nevertheless, the 'sign' value, which was of
great importance in the public healings, was not entirely lost.
The instruction to fulfil the regulation of Moses (Lev. 13–14) was
not just to satisfy the religious authorities: it was 'for a witness to
them' (*AV*) that prophetic power was at work in Israel (Manson;
2 Kg. 5 : 8).

13. touched him: this action or, conversely, Jesus being
touched by a person is frequent in the Gospels. Cf. 7 : 14; 13 : 13;
18 : 15; 22 : 51; Ac. 5 : 15. The practice seems to have its origin
in the Elijah-Elisha healings and to identify the healer as a
prophet in whose body lies supernatural healing power (cf. 8 : 46;
1 Kg. 17 : 21; 2 Kg. 4 : 34; 13 : 21). The ritual is mentioned at
Qumran but not in rabbinic healings. Cf. DSS *Gen. Apocryphon*
20 : 21–29; Daube, pp. 233–6; Jas 5 : 14.

14. tell no one: i.e. the public. Mark (1 : 45) gives the reason.

15. to hear and to be healed: elsewhere the people merely
desire to be fed and be healed (cf. Jn 6 : 26).

HEALING: A SIGN OF DIVINE FORGIVENESS 5 : 17–26

Structure. The literary form is frequent in the Gospels. Jesus per-
forms a revolutionary action; a protest ensued; Jesus silences the
remonstrants. This literary form gives concise and dramatic expression to the teachings of Jesus in his conflicts with the Pharisees.
Such an apologetic was particularly necessary for the early
Church, situated as it was in a hostile Jewish environment. Cf.
Daube, pp. 170ff.; 5 : 27–32; 6 : 1–5; 11 : 14–20, 37–41; 13 : 10–
17; see on 7 : 36–50.

Teaching. The Scribes rightly see in Jesus' offer of forgiveness far
more than a prophet's role (cf. 2 Sam. 12 : 13). To their challenge,
who but God 'is able' (*dynatai*) to forgive, Jesus answers: the Son
of man 'has authority' (*exousian*) to forgive. His word has effectual
power because it has lawful authority. The implications of the
churchmen are not denied. Indeed, Luke's description hints that

the title, Son of man, as well as the word of forgiveness involve divine prerogatives. At least, the presence of divine power is suggested in the effect of Jesus' actions on the people: 'they glorified God and were filled with awe.' See on 1 : 17; 8 : 37.

17. teachers of the law: used in the rabbinic writings of those who give 'halacha', i.e., authoritative interpretations of Scripture. This specific designation is Lukan and is important for his setting and theme. Cf. *SBK*; see on 11 : 37, 45.

power of the Lord: perhaps equivalent to the Spirit of the Lord. Cf. 1 : 35; 4 : 18; Ac. 10 : 38. Jesus is the instrument of God and works in perfect accord with the Father. Cf. Jn 5 : 17ff.

20. 'Your sins are forgiven': is interpreted variously. (1) Christ is making a connection between the paralytic's sickness and his sin (Geldenhuys; cf. Jn 5 : 14). (2) He assumes the popular view of such a connection (cf. Jn 9 : 2f.). (3) He affirms the generic although not necessarily personal, relationship between sickness and sin and thereby points to the true 'sign'-ificance of his healing. The last explanation is the most likely.

Both the Jewish and the apostolic writings recognize the close relationship of sin and sickness, healing and forgiveness. Sickness is caused, immediately or ultimately by an 'evil spirit', sometimes sent by God as a punishment for sin. Cf. Jn 5 : 14; 1 C. 11 : 29f.; DSS *Gen. Apocryphon* 20 : 16–29; 1 Sam. 16 : 14. See on 13 : 11, 16. Sickness is a form of death, and healing is a temporary repelling of the powers of death. According to the rabbis no sick man is healed until his sins are forgiven (*Ned.* 41a; cf. Jas 5 : 15). That men may know that he can deliver from sin Christ says, 'Rise' (24). That is, he delivers the man from sin's visible effects (cf. Rom. 6 : 23; 1 C. 11 : 29f.; Jas 1 : 15; Cullmann, pp. 167f.).

21. question (*dialogizesthai*): see on 6 : 8.

blasphemies: this is the first intimation of the charge for which the Jews will crucify Jesus (Mk 14 : 64). The nature of the Messiah's mission is bound up in the nature of his person. To reject the one involves the rejection of the other.

24. Son of man: the origin of the term and its use in the Gospels has been the subject of much discussion. Cf. A. J. B. Higgins, *NTE*, 119–35; M. Black, pp. 310–30; in *BJRL* 45, 1962–3, 305–18; but see J. A. Fitzmyer, *CBQ* 30 (1968), 424–8. Some scholars seek the background of the Son of man conception in

a 'heavenly man redemption myth', a view advanced a couple of
generations ago (cf. Manson, *Jesus*, pp. 7–11). The myth concerns
a pre-existent heavenly figure who descends and redeems the
world. It supposedly affected the use of the term Son of man in pre-
Christian Jewish writings (Dan. 7 : 13; *Enoch* 37–71) and in earliest
Christianity. But there is no evidence that such a myth existed as
early as the first century. Cf. Colpe, pp. 201f.; Wilson, pp. 220–6.
Also, the use of the title in the *Similitudes of Enoch* (*Enoch* 37–71) does
not fit the theory very well. First, the absence of this apocryphal
writing from the DSS raises a question about its date since every
other section of Enoch appears there. Even if it is pre-Christian,
T. W. Manson (*Studies*, pp. 130–42) has shown that its description
of the Son of man is not necessarily that of a pre-existent, heavenly
being.

The background of the term in all likelihood is to be found
directly in the Old Testament. Son of man is used there for man
in general, for a prophet (Ezek. 2 : 1f.), and for a corporate or
representative figure of mankind (Ps. 8 : 4) or of the people of
God (Ps. 80 : 17; Dan. 7 : 13). Probably it had no one specific
religious connotation in pre-Christian Judaism, and there is no
certain use of it as a title. It is likely that Jesus appropriated the
term precisely because it was ambiguous to his hearers, as Hill
(pp. 162ff.), E. Schweizer (*NTS* 9, 1962–3, 259ff.) and O. Cullmann (*Christology*, p. 154) have suggested. This enabled him to
mould it into a term of new and original significance.

'Son of man' is a favourite self-designation of Jesus. His use of
this expression reflects a practice throughout his ministry not to
associate himself publicly with the term 'Messiah'. See on 9 : 21.
At his trial he identifies the title with the exalted figure in Dan.
7 : 13. But more often he uses it of his present mission and sufferings (e.g., 9 : 22, 58). That is, in the Son of man sayings Jesus
combines the Danielic 'Son of man' with his role of the 'Suffering
Servant'. Both are corporate figures for the nation Israel as it is
embodied in its 'head'. Cf. Manson, *Studies*, pp. 142–5; Cullmann,
Christology, pp. 160–4. On a broader scale the same type of representation is involved in the image of Messiah as the second man,
the eschatological Adam, who embodies a new humanity (see on
3 : 23–38; cf. J. Jeremias, *TDNT* I, 141f.; Ellis, pp. 96f.). See on
4 : 4; 12 : 8; above, p. 11.

Some argue that the term 'Son of man' was only later ascribed to Jesus by his followers. But this fails to explain why the Evangelists restrict the title to the words of Jesus. The term is hardly ever used elsewhere in the New Testament (Ac. 7 : 56; Rev. 1 : 13; 14 : 14; cf. Eus. 2, 23, 13), and it is in the earliest strata of the Gospel traditions. There is no very strong reason to think that the Son of man sayings were only imputed to Jesus. If some of the sayings interpolated the term (Mt. 16 : 28; cf. Mk 9 : 1) or substituted it for an original 'I' (Mt. 16 : 13; cf. Mk 8 : 27), or if some originated in oracles of early Christian prophets (cf. Bornkamm, p. 231), this is best explained as a development of Jesus' own pre-resurrection usage. Cf. Jeremias, *Theology*, pp. 264–268.

authority to forgive: probably referring to the role of the Suffering Servant. Cf. Isa. 53 : 4–12; Mt. 8 : 16f.

26. awe (*phobou*): see on 8 : 37.

THE TAX COLLECTORS' BANQUET: SIGN OF THE NEW AGE **5 : 27–39**

Structure. See on 5 : 17–26. Since the 'separatist' Pharisees most likely were not present at the party, the disputations (30–39) represent subsequent encounters and reactions to the revolutionary action of Jesus.

Teaching. The call of a tax collector clarifies further the nature of Messiah's mission. Jesus offends the Pharisees in two ways: he associates with the wrong people, and his convivial attitudes are wholly unbecoming to religious persons. Even the 'disciples of John' the Baptist fast!

Jesus replies that his mission concerns 'wrong' people (31f.), and it is a new order that will not fit old patterns (36ff.). Therefore, his actions are quite appropriate. His purpose is not to dispense religion but to inaugurate a new age.

27. Levi: identified more commonly by the (Christian?) name Matthew, the son of Alphaeus (cf. 6 : 15; Mt. 9 : 9; Plummer). It is less likely that he is the brother of James (Mk 2 : 14; 3 : 18; cf. Taylor).

29. tax collectors: scorned not only for their graft-ridden occupation but for their collaboration with the Roman occupiers. They levied taxes on goods entering and leaving the country as well as on the local populace. If verse 28 implies that Levi re-

signed his post, the 'great feast' may have been not only 'for
Jesus' but also a farewell dinner for his colleagues. See on 3 : 14;
19 : 1–10.

30. Pharisees: i.e. separated ones: the expected critics in this
case since they were devotees of ceremonial cleanness. 'Over
against the Pharisaic idea of salvation by segregation, Jesus sets
up the new principle of salvation by association' (Manson). See
on 11 : 37, 45.

31f. Like the preceding episode, this passage points to the inter-
locked ethical-physical nature of messianic redemption. Jesus
addresses the whole man.

sinners: the Pharisees' term for people who did not keep the
ceremonial regulations laid down by the rabbis.

righteous: see on 15 : 7.

33. fast: required by the law only on the Day of Atonement.
The Pharisees practised frequent fasting (cf. 18 : 12). In this they
were followed by the disciples of the Baptist, who apparently
remained a well-defined group even after John's arrest.

35. bridegroom: an image that the Church continued to apply
to Jesus. It is found only here in Luke. Cf. Mt. 25 : 1ff.; Jn 3 : 28f.;
Eph. 5 : 23.

taken away: implying rejection and violent death. Cf. 23 : 18;
Ac. 8 : 33; J. Jeremias, *TDNT* I, 185f.

will fast: fasting was a regular practice in the early Church.
Cf. Mt. 6 : 16ff.; Ac. 13 : 2ff. See on 22 : 14–23.

36ff. The two parables illustrate the dichotomy between Christianity and traditional Judaism. To mix the 'new' with the 'old'
will ruin both. Each has its place, but the new is more than the
old revised. In the context of the pre-resurrection mission the
issue was fasting. Luke's readers doubtless applied the Saviour's
words to other issues (cf. Gal. 5 : 2ff.).

39. The added note of rejection, found only in Luke, sums up
the episode and underlines the Evangelist's understanding of it.

MESSIAH: LORD OF THE SABBATH **6 : 1–11**

Structure. See on 5 : 17–26; 7 : 36–50. The sixth and last episode
of this series records two sabbath controversies. Together they
reiterate two themes running through the section: 'the Son of
man is Lord' (5), but he is a Lord rejected (11). Like the

preceding section (4 : 29f.), this one also ends on a threatening
note: 'they were filled with fury' (11).

Background. In the rabbinic tradition reaping and healing were
strictly forbidden on the sabbath. But the rules were suspended
when life was in danger. Cf. *Shab.* 132a; *Yoma* 8 : 6; *SBK* 1, 622ff.
The rabbis regarded the action of David (3) to be such an exception. And perhaps Jesus, from a quite different perspective,
applied the rule to his disciples (cf. Manson).

Teaching. The grain-gathering (1-5) and the healing (6-10)
present similar assertions of Christ's authority. His violation of
accepted traditions rests on two considerations. In Jesus' eyes any
refusal to do good is to do evil (Manson). In the context of his
mission all soul-life stands under imminent threat of death and,
therefore, under demand for decision (cf. 13 : 3; 9 : 23ff., 59f.).
No longer is there any neutral ground, no longer any do-nothing
alternative. To refuse to 'save life' is to 'destroy it'. The Lord's
action reveals his interpretation of his mission. It is redemptive
and it is urgent, a matter of life or death.

   1. 'second first' (margin): the text is doubtful. If original, it
may refer to the second sabbath after Passover.
disciples: since they are the violators, Jesus' word in verse 5
includes them.
plucked and ate: probably as part of a meal during a preaching
tour (4 : 44). Mission takes precedence over ritual. See on 10 : 38-
42; cf. Jn 5 : 16f.
   4. bread of the Presence: i.e. 'consecrated loaves' (*NEB*).
The bread was kept in the Holy Place for use in the temple ritual.
Cf. 1 : 5-25; Lev. 24 : 5-9. By this comparison Jesus seems to
place sabbath observance in the category of ceremonial rather
than of moral law (cf. Rom. 14 : 5).
   5. Son of man: Mk 2 : 27 adds, 'the sabbath was made for
man'. In the language that Jesus spoke 'man' and 'son of man'
may be represented by the same word. To his hearers the ambiguous repetition of the term remained unexplained. Cf. Jn
12 : 34; see on 5 : 24. Mark elucidates the Lord's meaning by his
translation: the sabbath was made for God's people; and their
'head', in whom they are incorporated, is Lord of the sabbath.
Cf. T. W. Manson, *CN*, pp. 145f.

Codex D adds here an interesting, though perhaps spurious, saying of Jesus to a man working on the sabbath: 'Man, if you know what you are doing, you are blessed; but if you do not know, you are cursed and a transgressor of the law' (cf. Rom. 14 : 22f.). Westcott and Hort (p. 59) suggest the same source for it as for the story of the woman taken in adultery. See on 21 : 37f.

7. watched: narrowly, with sinister intent (Plummer).

8. thoughts (*dialogismous*): the word often is associated with evil or false 'reasonings'. Cf. 2 : 35; 5 : 21f.; 9 : 46; Rom. 1 : 21; 1 C. 3 : 20.

9. sabbath: see on 14 : 5f. The sabbath was a 'ritual anticipation of the advent of the messianic age'. Jesus' acts, therefore, may set forth a veiled messianic claim. (E. C. Hoskyns, *MC*, pp. 74ff.)

ACTS OF MESSIAH: THE NATURE OF HIS MISSION 6 : 12–7 : 50

In the six episodes of this section Luke abandons the Markan scheme and shifts his emphasis from the character and authority of Jesus' person to the nature of his mission. Of course, the two are not mutually exclusive, and at least one of the episodes (7 : 11–17) might be more appropriate to the earlier section. Nevertheless, the focus of interest clearly turns to the 'kingdom'. Only once earlier in Luke (4 : 43) does the phrase 'kingdom of God' occur. In this and the two following sections it occurs seven times.

The choosing of the Twelve (6 : 12–16) signifies for Luke, as undoubtedly it did for Christ, the reconstitution of Israel. That is, the apostles constitute the 'twelve-tribe' framework upon which the Israel of the new age is to be formed (cf. Creed; K. H. Rengstorf, *TDNT* II, 325). The second episode, the great sermon (6 : 17–49), sets forth the promises and principles of the impending kingdom of God. In the four subsequent stories further characteristics of the messianic kingdom are seen. The kingdom is received by faith. Thus its benefits extend even to Gentiles and prostitutes who have faith (7 : 1–10, 36–50). The kingdom means nothing less than deliverance from death itself (7 : 11–17). Although John the Baptist (7 : 18–35) is the apex of the old age, the new age so far surpasses the old that the 'least in the kingdom is greater than he' (7 : 28).

Two motifs recur through the section. They are the character and the recipients of the coming age. The messianic kingdom brings deliverance from sorrow, sickness, death, and sin, and its firstfruits are realized in the mission of Jesus (6: 21ff.; 7 : 10, 15f., 22, 48). In turn, the kingdom demands love, forgiveness, and faith. In those receiving Jesus this is evident (6 : 27, 37; 7 : 9, 47, 50). The ostracized and non-privileged groups—the poor, the Gentiles, the afflicted, the immoral—welcome the message of the kingdom (6 : 20ff.; 7 : 9, 22, 47). The rich, the satisfied, and the 'religious' reject God's redemptive purpose (7 : 30). Cf. 6 : 24ff.; 7 : 9; Mt. 21 : 31f. The note of rejection is like that in the earlier sections (4 : 29; 6 : 11). Those who reject John the Baptist also reject Jesus; the neutralism of Simon the Pharisee is in sharp contrast to the faith of the prostitute (7 : 33f., 36–50).

CHOOSING THE TWELVE 6 : 12–16

12f. to pray: more than the other Evangelists, Luke stresses the importance of prayer in the Lord's ministry. The Baptism, the choosing of the Twelve, the confession of Peter, the transfiguration, the betrayal—all are preceded by Christ in prayer (cf. 11 : 1). **twelve apostles:** see on 6 : 17; 9 : 1; above, p. 109.

14ff. In all of the apostolic lists—three groups of four—Peter is first and Judas last.

Zealot: apparently Simon earlier was a member of this extremist political-action group. See on 22 : 49.

Judas of James (Jn 14 : 22; Ac. 1 : 13) is Thaddaeus in Matthew (10 : 3) and Mark (3 : 18). This suggests that Luke follows a different source. The double name is not uncommon, e.g., Saul and Paul, Levi and Matthew. Peter is Christ's designation of Simon (cf. Mt. 16 : 18; Jn 1 : 42).

Bartholomew: traditionally identified with Nathanael (Jn 1 : 45; cf. Plummer).

Matthew: see on 5 : 27.

Iscariot: possibly 'man of Kiryoth', a town in Transjordan or Judea (cf. Schlatter, *Matthäus*, p. 327). More likely it means 'false one' assuming that the name relates to the betrayal. Cf. B. Gärtner, *SEA* 21, 1956, 50–81; C. C. Torrey, *HTR* 36, 1943, 51–62. O. Cullmann (*State*, p. 15; *RHPR* 42, 1962, 133–40) suggests 'zealot' or 'revolutionary'.

THE GREAT SERMON 6 : 17–49

Structure. Both this passage and the 'Sermon on the Mount' (Mt.
5–7) begin with Beatitudes, end with the parable of the builders,
and display the same general sequence and content. They include
the setting (17–19), the promises and principles of the kingdom
of God (20–26, 27–38), and the meaning of discipleship (39–49).
Arranging their materials topically, Matthew and Luke freely
incorporate appropriate sayings of Jesus spoken at various times.
For example, Matthew, but not Luke, puts the Lord's Prayer in
the Sermon (11 : 2–4; Mt. 6 : 9–13). And Luke includes in the
Sermon a teaching that Matthew places elsewhere (6 : 40; Mt.
10 : 24).

However supplemented, the Sermon probably is not just a
collection of scattered sayings. As a new 'law' it accords with other
symbolic acts of the Lord. Cf. 4 : 16ff.; 5 : 17ff.; 9 : 1ff.; 10 : 1ff.;
22 : 7ff. The Evangelists present the Sermon as such an act.
For this reason Luke places it here rather than among the 'Teachings of Messiah' (9 : 51–19 : 44). By placing the appointment of
the twelve apostles just before the Sermon, Luke may preserve a
symbolic sequence enacted by Jesus himself.

Background. According to some Jewish traditions Messiah was
expected to be an interpreter of the Torah, the Old Testament
law. He was to bring 'a new Torah', or to make 'all of the words
of the Torah clear' (cf. *SBK* IV, 1–22; Davies, *Sermon*, pp. 183–90,
433ff.). This background (or Jesus' own similar conviction) is most
evident in Matthew (5 : 17, 21ff.) where Jesus comes 'to fulfil'
the law and deliberately contrasts his teaching to the 'traditions
of the elders'. But the presentation of the Sermon as a messianic
'law' is present also in Luke (especially, 6 : 27–38). For a detailed
study of the background, the work of W. D. Davies (*Sermon*) is of
first importance.

Teaching. J. Jeremias (*Sermon*, pp. 30–5), in a very lucid essay, explains the Sermon as an early Christian catechism. He rightly
emphasizes that the commands of Jesus presuppose the gospel.
They are not a way of salvation. Rather they are addressed to
persons who already by faith have become sons of the kingdom.

They are invitations to manifest one's faith in one's conduct by the power of the Spirit.

But the 'law' character of the Sermon remains valid and important. The followers of Jesus—from the first twelve—always are a mixed group. Not all who say 'Lord, Lord' or come to catechism truly *are* sons of the kingdom. The commands of the Sermon are not only invitations: they are a test. To be sure, no one fulfils Jesus' demands. But throughout the Sermon the kingdom ethic stands as a present imperative for the followers of Jesus. One thus reveals one's relationship to the coming reign of God. The 'beatitudes' and 'woes' are not blessings or cursings *upon* those groups but are insights into their true condition (cf. Leaney). The fact of impending judgment is the all-important consideration. To one group the kingdom will come as salvation, to the other as a destroying flood. By their present conduct and attitudes the disciples show to which group they belong (35).

17. came down with them: A Farrer (pp. 309ff.; *SG*, p. 76) finds here a priestly symbolism as well as an allusion to the giving of the law by Moses, and, certainly, an attractive parallelism can be drawn. Like Aaron (Exod. 19 : 24), the Apostles accompany Jesus, the new Moses, into the mountain and are constituted a levitical ministry of the New Covenant. Since the New Covenant knows no special priestly class, the role must apply to all the disciples. However, there is a strong objection to a 'levitical' interpretation of New Testament ministry. Although allusions to levitical practice may be present (Daube, pp. 239f.), priesthood in the New Testament belongs to Jesus Christ alone (Schweizer, p. 173; cf. pp. 171–7). This priesthood, which the whole 'body of Christ' shares, does not arise from Aaron but from Melchizedek. See the special note at 1 : 26–38.

level place: apart from any symbolism, it is a more specific designation than Mt. 5 : 1. Three groups are represented: apostles, disciples, a great multitude.

18f. As earlier, the healings and exorcisms are signs of the kingdom.

touch: see on 5 : 13.

power: see on 5 : 17.

20–26. The 'woes', not found in Matthew, are the four blessings stated conversely. They, too, are directed to the disciples (cf. *'their'* in 6 : 23, 26). The lengthening of the fourth beatitude

creates an emphatic climax. Cf. Exod. 20 : 13-17; Daube, pp.
196ff.; see on 6 : 27-38.

The beatitudes, which are shorter than in Matthew, set the
theme of the Sermon. It is the contrast between this age and the
coming 'kingdom of God'. To be rejected now, 'for the Son of
Man's sake' (*AV*), signifies that one belongs to the kingdom. On
the other hand, for a disciple to be acceptable to the present age is
a warning that he really may belong to it and will share its judgment when the kingdom of God arrives. For the true disciple the
coming of the kingdom will mean fulfilment and blessedness.
For those who only profess to belong, as for the world, it will
mean condemnation.

20. poor: equivalent to 'poor in spirit' (Mt. 5 : 3). From
parallels in the DSS it means either 'the faint-hearted' (E. Best,
NTS 7, 1960-1, 256f.; cf. 1*QM* 14 : 7) or, more likely, the ones
counting worldly goods as nothing, 'the voluntarily poor' (K.
Schubert, *SSNT*, p. 122). The Qumran sect probably called
themselves by this title. Cf. 1*QpHab* 12 : 3. See on 8 : 14.

20-22. Poor, hunger, cast out describe one type of person,
a person dissatisfied with and rejected by the present age. The
elaborations of Matthew—'poor in spirit', 'hunger for righteousness'—make explicit that a religious and not an economic status
is primarily in view. Cf. Ps. 37 : 14. But there are economic
implications. See below, p. 163; on 8 : 14; cf. 2 C. 11 : 27.
name: i.e. as followers of Jesus, e.g., 'Christians', 'Nazarenes'.
Son of man: see on 5 : 24.

22, 24. Blessed . . . woe: for the antithesis elsewhere cf. Isa.
3 : 10f.; Ec. 10 : 16f.; *Yoma* 87a; C. H. Dodd, *MB*, pp. 404-10.

23. joy: see on 8 : 13.
prophets: K. Schubert (*SSNT*, pp. 123f.) makes the attractive
suggestion that in Matthew the reference is to Essene (Qumran)
prophets in Jesus' audience. And there is evidence of such prophetic activity in first-century Judaism (cf. Jos. *Ant.* 15, 10, 5;
War 6, 5, 3). However, the probable reference of Jesus is to Old
Testament prophets. The significant new fact is that the Lord
puts his followers in the role of the prophets. Matthew's (5 : 12)
addition, 'before you', makes the identification explicit. There
is an allusion to contemporary prophets in the passage, but
probably they are early Christians. See on 11 : 49-51.

23-25. The **reward** of the righteous originates and presently

exists 'in heaven' = 'with God' (Dalman, *Words*, pp. 206ff.) or
'in God' (see on 19 : 38). But it is to be received in the coming age,
at the manifestation of the kingdom on the earth. Cf. 14 : 14;
12 : 33–40; 2 Tim. 4 : 8. Fulfilment in this age is its own reward
or 'consolation'. In the coming age conditions will be reversed
(see below, pp. 187, 200; cf. Mt. 6 : 2, 5, 16). See on 6 : 35.

26. The rejection of the true prophets (and acceptance of the
false) was itself prophetic of the world's attitude toward the true
sons of the kingdom (cf. Mt. 23 : 29ff.). Jesus' followers are to
apply this test to themselves. Cf. Fäscher, pp. 182f.

27–38. In part the series of 'fours' continues (6 : 27f., 32–35,
37f.; cf. Prov. 30 : 15ff.; Am. 1–2). The last member of the series
forms an extended climax in 6 : 35, 38.

27. Love your enemies: in contrast to the members of the
Qumran community who are commanded to 'hate all the sons
of darkness' (1*QS* 1 : 10; 9 : 21f.; but contrast 1*QS* 10 : 18ff.).
Elsewhere love is identified as the core of the Old Testament law
(e.g., 10 : 27f.). Here it is the basic imperative for all who would
enter the kingdom. Although it is outgoing rather than possessive,
this love is not sentimentalism or philanthropic benevolence. Its
essential nature, its 'grace-ious' (*charis*) character, is revealed in
a person's attitude toward those who misuse him (27–30). The
world has 'tit-for-tat' love: 'what credit (*charis*) is that to you?'
(32). The love Jesus commands is nothing less than divine love;
and in manifesting it the children of the kingdom show themselves to be 'the sons of the Most High' (35). Cf. Mt. 5 : 45;
13 : 38.

The effect of Christian love in a person is in exact proportion
to his practice of it (37f.). The measure in which he shows grace
he will receive grace, now and in the judgment. Thus, in the
midst of grace, and dependent upon it, there is a principle of
justice. Cf. Rom. 2 : 6ff.; 2 C. 5 : 10. These verses are not just an
admonition. More significantly, they direct one towards a growing transformation into the image of a true son of God.

29. The injunctions, like the whole section, refer to the personal
conduct of those who have entered the new age. For the State,
i.e. for this age, the principle of justice remains the norm. See on
16 : 18. Probably Jesus and the prophets and teachers who transmit his teaching have real situations in view. They concern the
disciple's confession and mission, the highway robbery of a mis-

sionary or the ritual slap on the cheek given a Christian 'heretic'
in the synagogue. But the principle goes beyond this. It means
not mere passivity in the face of evil but rather the moral response
of love towards evil (or needy) persons. This principle of love
fixes the nature and limits of one's response (Geldenhuys) although
it does not exclude self-defence in the face of assault. See on 22 : 49.

30. give. Christ is not advocating perfunctory offerings to the
poor. He enjoins a moral concern that will express itself in a spirit
of self-denial in every encounter of life, and that will do this for
the sake of the kingdom of God (9 : 57ff.; 12 : 32f.).

31. do: 'The Golden Rule' activates the principle of neighbour
love (Lev. 19 : 18). It is stated in negative form by the rabbi
Hillel (*c.* 10 BC): 'What is hateful to you do not to your neighbour:
that is the whole Torah, while the rest is commentary' (*Shab.*
31a; *SBT*, p. 140). In his positive formulation the Lord puts the
matter in a new and deeper perspective.

32f., 35. love . . . do good: parallel to 6 : 27f. (W. C. van
Unnik, *NoT* 8(1966), 298). Contrast Mt. 5 : 44; cf. 2 *Clem.* 13 : 4;
1 Mac. 11 : 33.

35. reward. 'New Testament reward is very closely related to
the service of God, being in itself a form of communion with God'
(B. Reicke, *TC*, pp. 205, 195–206). It is not a recompense for
good deeds, to be claimed as due (17 : 7–10). Indeed, it may be
given in advance of any 'work' because its character is completely
gracious (Tit. 3 : 4–7). In this passage it may consist in the 'fruit'
of Christian service itself (cf. Jn 4 : 36). Thus, to be merciful (36)
is, according to Matthew (5 : 48), to be perfect. Both signify con-
formity to the gracious character of God.

Future recompense in the coming kingdom of God is viewed
in terms of degrees of service (cf. 19 : 17, 19; 22 : 29f.). But service
for the sake of reward must clearly recognize the reward as God's
smile and the motive as love for God. Collecting merit badges
violates the meaning of Christian service. 'Reward is a necessary
part of Christian theology, considering the fact that God is a
person. . . . What is good, according to the Christian faith, is what
God proclaims to be good, not any abstract idea of "good" . . .'
(B. Reicke, *TC*, p. 206).

be sons: i.e. reflect God's nature. The promise is spoken to
disciples for whom God already is 'your Father'. Jesus invites
them to actualize in their ethic the meaning of their relation to

God: 'become what you are!' H. W. Montefiore (*NTS* 3, 1956–7, 39) infers from this and similar verses (11 : 2, 13) a universal fatherhood of God. But all such verses almost certainly refer to the disciples of Jesus. At most, God is spoken of as the Father of Israel. Jesus does not view men as children of God by nature. Rather 'sonship' is God's gracious gift that is shown by repentance, by faith toward Jesus, and by good works. Cf. the perceptive remarks of T. W. Manson, *Teaching*, especially pp. 91–4; Kümmel, *Man*, p. 35f. See on 8 : 21; 11 : 2; 15 : 12; 20 : 36.

37. Judge not: probably defined in the parallel phrase, 'condemn not'. In the immediate context it refers to the censorious attitude of the Pharisees and other religious people toward the 'worldly' and the morally lax (5 : 33; 18 : 11ff.). Judgment, i.e. condemnation, is God's prerogative (cf. 9 : 54; Rom. 12 : 19; Jas 4 : 11ff.). But admonition and moral discrimination, as well as the pronouncement of God's judgment upon evil, is not only permitted but required of the follower of Christ (cf. Ac. 13 : 44ff.; Rom. 1 : 32; 1 C. 5 : 11ff.).
forgive: cf. 11 : 4.

38. will be put: i.e. by God. See on 16 : 9. See on 6 : 27–38 for the literary form.

39–49. The closing admonitions set forth principles that should govern the life of a follower of Jesus. First, it is a maxim that a person becomes like his teacher (40). If he learns from Christ, he will not, like some Pharisees, become a blind leader of the blind. To become a true leader requires, therefore, that he reform his own life rather than judge the lives of others (39–42). Cf. Mt. 15 : 14. Secondly, character determines conduct and, on the other hand, what a man does reflects what he is. The true disciple is the obedient disciple who 'hears my words and does them' (47). Only he will 'stand' in the day of judgment (43–49).

39f. Matthew (15 : 14; 10 : 24) may give these sayings in their original context. His text illumines their use here.

41f. This imagery also is used by the rabbis. Cf. *SBK* 1, 446, on Mt. 7 : 3.

47ff. This word-picture of a flash flood in Palestine is described more vividly in Mt. 7 : 24ff. Luke's key word (which Matthew lacks) is 'foundation'. Probably there is an allusion to Christians who have promoted false teachings. Cf. 1 : 4; 6 : 46; 1 C. 3 : 11–15; Creed.

THE FAITH OF A GENTILE ARMY CAPTAIN 7 : 1–10

Structure. Although Matthew (8 : 5–13) and Luke presumably employ a common source they present this story with considerable variation. Probably Matthew telescopes the narrative and, in Semitic fashion, corporately identifies the representatives with the centurion or 'army captain' (Moffatt). Cf. Mt. 9 : 18–26 with Mk 5 : 21–43; Mt. 21 : 18–22 with Mk 11 : 12–24. Luke retains the more detailed account in order to bring into fuller focus the personality of the captain and, perhaps, to enhance the parallel with the story of the first Gentile Christian (Ac. 10). The healing itself falls completely into the background.

Background. The Gentile army captain commanded native troops since Galilee was not part of a Roman province until AD 44 (Sherwin-White, p. 124). Such forces served Herod Antipas for police and tax-enforcement purposes. Because Capernaum was a border town, customs guards also were present (see on 3 : 14). Probably he was a 'God fearer' (5), that is, one who accepted the Jewish God but declined to become a Jewish proselyte. Cf. Ac. 10 : 2; 16 : 14.

Teaching. To the estimate of the Jews that 'he is worthy' (4), the army captain answers 'I am not worthy' (6f.). He thereby expresses both his humility and his great faith. His complete confidence in the power of Jesus' 'word' is prophetic of the future mission of the Church. To the Jews Christ came personally and was rejected, to the Gentiles he came only by his 'word' mediated through disciples (Manson). The believing faith of this Gentile is in stark contrast to the doubting curiosity in Israel (9). Cf. Rom. 9 : 30ff.; Gal. 3 : 7f.

3. sent . . . elders: presumably because he was a Gentile. Elders here are just civic leaders. Cf. Schürer, II, i, 150f. See on 20 : 1.

5. synagogue: the present-day ruin is from the third century, but it may be on the same site and probably conforms to the general plan of the synagogue in which Jesus preached. Cf. H. G. May, *BA*, pp. 231ff.

6. not worthy: perhaps because he was a Gentile. More probably, it reflects his high estimate of Jesus.

7. say the word: cf. Mk 7 : 29f., where the healing of another Gentile is done from a distance.

8. and I say: Jesus' power within his sphere of authority is at least equal to an army captain's power in his sphere of authority.

RESURRECTING A WIDOW'S SON 7 : 11–17

Structure. The story is found only in Luke. Apart from its own witness to the nature of Messiah's mission, it is the prologue necessary for understanding the following episode.

Teaching. Attention here is directed to Jesus, his compassion and his power. In contrast to the previous episode the faith of the woman plays no role. For the first time, significantly, Luke calls Jesus 'the Lord' (*kyrios*; cf. Ac. 2 : 36; Cullmann, *Christology*, pp. 206f.). Messiah's mission now is revealed as one that will deliver Israel not from the Romans but from the captivity of death (cf. Eph. 4 : 8 *AV*; Heb. 2 : 14f.).

Although this is obvious to Luke's readers, it is not fully grasped by those witnessing the miracle. The verbal allusion (15) to Elijah's resurrection of the 'only son' of a 'widow' points to the reaction of the people. (Cf. 1 Kg. 17 : 23; cf. 2 Kg. 4 : 32ff.). They see in Jesus 'a great prophet' or, at most, Elijah *redivivus* (cf. 9 : 8, 19). The incident at Nain both illumined and, in the popular mind, obscured the messianic character of Jesus' mission. In the context of the popular misunderstanding of Jesus' mission the rising doubts of John the Baptist (7 : 18–35) can be better appreciated.

11. Nain: located a few miles south of Nazareth overlooking the valley of Jezreel.

12. This was the saddest kind of funeral, for the **mother** was left alone and the family line was cut off.

14. touched: see on 5 : 13.

16. Fear: see on 8 : 37.

God has visited: probably a confession of Jesus as a prophet and not as the Messiah (cf. Manson).

17. Judea: see on 4 : 44.

JESUS AND THE BAPTIST 7: 18–35

Structure. The episode consists of three parts: the Baptist's question
(18–23), his role in redemptive history (24–28), and the meaning
of his rejection by the nation (29–35). The story appears also in
Matthew. Luke's addition of verses 29, 30 both serves as a transition and underlines his 'rejection' theme.

Background. Luke presupposes the tradition, found in the Gospels
of Matthew (3 : 14, 17) and John (1 : 32ff.), that the Baptist
earlier had affirmed the messiahship of Jesus. John the Baptist
understood Messiah's role to be an immediate redemption and
judgment of the nation. See on 3 : 16f. Yet Jesus had not 'baptized with the Spirit' or executed judgment. According to reports
given John (18), Jesus was only a teacher and a miracle worker.
Was Jesus after all only another prophet, or perhaps 'Elijah'?
The nature of Jesus' ministry and not the despair of imprisonment
causes John's growing doubt.

Teaching. The Lord's answer to John (22f.) clarifies the meaning
of his own mission. He interprets his present messianic work in
terms of the Servant of the Lord. See on 4 : 18; cf. Isa. 29 : 18f.;
35 : 5f.; 42 : 6f.; 61 : 1. The Messiah's role of judge will find its
fulfilment only in the future. See above, pp. 14f.
    The tribute to John also serves to identify his vocation. John
is the 'messenger' (27) of the new age, 'the Elijah' promised by
God (Mal. 3 : 1; 4 : 5; cf. Klausner, pp. 215ff., 455f.). Yet his
place in redemptive history belongs to the time of promise, the
pre-messianic era. Therefore, the least in the kingdom has a
'greater' status because he belongs to the 'greater' time of fulfilment (28). In the preaching and acts of Jesus the time of fulfilment now is being realized. See on 3 : 5f.; 16 : 16.
    John is a sign not only in his witness but in the response given
to it (32ff.). By rejecting the Baptist the 'churchmen and theologians' (30) forecast their rejection of Messiah. Both John and
Jesus call for repentance in the face of messianic judgment (cf.
13 : 1ff.). Both are believed by the outcasts but rejected by the
leaders of Israel. See on 3 : 20.
    19. Are you he: i.e. the Messiah. Some commentators interpret

the question as a sign of growing faith rather than a loss of previous certitude. (1) The Baptist would not have continued his separate group if he had recognized Jesus as Messiah (5 : 33; cf. 11 : 1). Nor (2) would Jesus have called the 'least in the kingdom' greater than John. Of course, Jesus speaks in terms of the Baptist's mission (see above). The first objection has more weight. But it is not at all clear that *John* continued his group: he was in prison (Mk 1 : 14). This episode shows that he did direct his followers to Jesus and that their reports (18) contributed to his doubts. The clue to the meaning of John's question is the Nain episode (see on 7 : 11–17).

who is to come: i.e. the Coming One (Moffatt): virtually a messianic title in several New Testament passages. It seems to have its origin in the Old Testament and later Judaism. Cf. 13 : 35; Jn 11 : 27; Heb. 10 : 37; Ps. 118 : 26. It may have been associated with a divine, 'glorious' Messiah (cf. *SBK* IV, 858, 860 on Ca. 2 : 8; E. Hill, *SE*, pp. 194ff.)

27. messenger: see on 1 : 17, 76; 20 : 21.
way: see on 20 : 21.

29. justified God: i.e. accepted his judgments as right.

30. Pharisees and lawyers: see on 11 : 37, 45.
for themselves: some manuscripts lack this phrase. It modifies 'reject' and means that they reject on their own responsibility God's redemptive purpose.

32. like children: who obstinately refuse to play 'whether the game be wedding or funeral' (Miller).

33. has a demon: see on 11 : 15.

34. eating: see on 5 : 33.
Son of man: see on 5 : 24.

35. Children of God's **'wisdom'** probably are contrasted with children of 'this generation' (31f.). They are not Jesus and the Baptist (U. Wilckens, *TDNT* VII, 516) but rather those who 'justify God' (29) by accepting their message. On this interpretation 'wisdom' is the Holy Spirit's action in the work and words of Jesus. However, the verse may be a word of Jesus (Ringgren, p. 124) or, more likely, an added comment of Luke's source (Davies, p. 156) in which wisdom is identified with Messiah. See on 11 : 49–51. A Feuillet (*RB* 62, 1955, 195f.) finds the background for Jesus' wisdom sayings in Jewish literature.

THE CHURCHMAN AND THE PROSTITUTE **7: 36–50**

Structure. In the earliest organization of stories about Jesus, alterations of setting apparently occurred in two directions. Sometimes composite stories were shortened and the original setting removed. The more concise form then was attached to or collected with other narratives. For example, Luke retains the original occasion of the Lord's Prayer (11 : 1). But then, for thematic purposes, he appends a parable and sayings whose original settings probably were different (11 : 5–8, 9–13). On the other hand Matthew (6 : 9–13; 7 : 7–11) has removed the setting of both the Lord's Prayer and the prayer sayings. He places both 'stripped' forms within the framework of his Sermon on the Mount.

Less frequently two stories were joined by dovetailing them into one composite unit. See on 14 : 1–24; 19 : 11–27. The present passage raises such a question. Were the anointing by the woman and the dinner with Simon originally two independent stories? A number of parallels between the anointing here and the one at Bethany (Mk 14 : 3–9) have caused some scholars to identify them. But the differences are too great to trace them to one tradition. Also such acts of devotion apparently were not unusual. Probably this story, like the similar incident in 14 : 1–6, was a unity from the beginning. In fact, the composite form of the present passage is very likely the more original literary type (cf. 8 : 40–56; C. H. Dodd, *BJRL* 37, 1954, 60). But a skilful hand has shaped its present form. The setting and the characters are sketched with brevity and naked clarity. Nowhere in Luke is the art of a descriptive writer more evident.

The literary form of the dialogue between Jesus and Simon is termed 'Socratic interrogation'. It consists in a question by the opponent (39) and a counter-question (42) that forced an answer from the opponent (43). By the answer given, the opponent then is refuted (47). Originating in Hellenistic rhetoric, the method was used by the rabbis and by the Evangelists in organizing their materials. It doubtless was employed by the Lord himself. By it Jesus was able to turn a hostile inquiry into an invitation to learning. Cf. 20 : 1–8; 6 : 6–11; Daube, pp. 151–7, 219f.; see also on 5 : 17–26.

Teaching. As the parable of the 'two debtors' (40–43) shows, the devotion of the woman is in gratitude for the forgiveness she has received. In contrast to the woman's devotion Simon's minimal hospitality (44–47) is revealing: the character of one's heart is made evident by one's works. That love is the fruit of a forgiven and regenerate heart is a common New Testament maxim (cf. 1 Jn 4 : 7ff.). The woman, Jesus implies, is not now the kind of person Simon had known.

Luke may place the episode here as an illustration of verse 35. In any case he presents Jesus as more than a 'prophet'. Above all he is one who 'forgives sins' and who receives, regardless of class all who have 'faith' (48ff.).

36. For the customs cf. *SBK* IV, 611–39, 615. Uninvited persons would come in to beg or snatch leftovers.

37. A woman . . . a sinner: this probably denotes a prostitute (*SBK*). But it may mean only the wife of an irreligious person (Schlatter; cf. 5 : 31f.). The traditional identification of this woman with Mary Magdalene is without basis.

39f. Simon's immediate question is answered and then by-passed: Jesus *does* know and, therefore, is 'a prophet'. Some manu-scripts have 'the prophet'. See on 9 : 35; the special note at 1 : 26–38.

41. A Roman denarius was equivalent to an Attic drachma. See on 15 : 8.

46. The cheap olive 'oil' is in contrast to the more valuable 'ointment' (*myron*).

47. loved: i.e. showed thankfulness. Cf. H. G. Wood, *ET* 66, 1954–5, 319f. According to some commentators 'love' is the *ground* for forgiveness, but this violates the context (7 : 41ff.) and is con-trary to New Testament teaching in general. 'For (*hoti*) she loved' is rather the evidence of her prior forgiveness. Cf. 13 : 2; Manson; Moule, p. 147. Thus *NEB*: 'Her great love proves that her many sins have been forgiven.'

ACTS OF MESSIAH: THE PROCLAMATION OF HIS KINGDOM 8: 1–56

Luke always presents the Lord as a sojourner 'on the move'. This is true earlier in the Galilean mission and is characteristic of the 'Central Division' (9 : 51–19 : 44). Cf. 4 : 44; 6 : 1; 7 : 11; 9 : 58. Some commentators regard the 'tour' of 8 : 1ff. as the beginning

of Christ's 'journeying' and, therefore, more decisive for Luke's
plan than the turning toward Jerusalem at 9: 51. However, this
view overlooks not only the earlier journeys but also the fact that
the break at 9: 51 has theological implications which go beyond
a mere change of place (Conzelmann, pp. 46, 63, 65).

It is probable that the tour is preparatory for the mission of the
Twelve that begins the following section (9: 1–50). The kingdom
message is to be broadcast far and wide both by the Lord and
by his disciples. Whether Luke regards the introduction (8: 1–3)
as a separate episode, and whether the raising of the girl and
healing of the woman (8: 40–56) are to be regarded as one
episode, is not entirely clear. But the divisions given below seem
to be more probable.

Luke places the teachings of Jesus in the Central Division of the
Gospel (9: 51–19: 44). (The Great Sermon (6: 17–49) and the
parable of the soils (8: 1–18) are only apparent exceptions. The
former is essentially a symbolic act, the giving of the messianic
law. The latter is intended to summarize the results of Jesus'
mission.) The Galilean mission is presented in terms of Jesus'
actions. The word of God, i.e., the kingdom message (8: 11ff.,
21), finds its initial expression in the authoritative and creative
word of Messiah. The new creation, like the old, comes into being
by a word (cf. Gen. 1). Jesus speaks to the wind, the demons, the
dead—and they obey! By his touch the sick find new life (8: 24,
32, 44, 54). Earlier such acts were presented as signs pointing to
Jesus' messianic character (cf. 4: 40f.; 5: 8; 7: 49). In the context of the 'kingdom of God' mission attention shifts to the meaning of Christ's *message*: the kingdom will deliver men from death
and evil and even restore to nature its intended order.

Concurrently the *way* in which men can enter the kingdom
also is a continuing motif. Only those who hear the word and
'keep' it are true sons of the kingdom, true 'brothers' of Messiah
(8: 15, 21). 'Faith' is the response through which the benefits of
the kingdom are given (8: 25, 48, 50; cf. 8: 13). But in each
episode faith is lacking or is mixed with unfaith: the unproductive
soils, the sceptical brothers, the fearful disciples, the rejecting
Gerasenes, the doubtful Peter, the jeering mourners (8: 12ff., 20,
25, 37, 45, 53). The note of rejection is dominant, but in the midst
of it—some have faith! Such was the destiny of Jesus' kingdom
message in Galilee. Such, Luke implies, is its destiny in the world.

SOWING THE SEED OF THE KINGDOM 8: 1–18

Structure. Used as an introduction to the whole section, Lk. 8 : 1–3
serves the Evangelist especially as the context for the following
parable. Luke began the previous section (6 : 12ff.) with the
establishment of the messianic kingdom. He now presents the
wider proclamation of the dawning reign of God through
the preaching of Jesus and 'the Twelve'. In this framework
the Parable of the Four Soils (4–15) finds its meaning both
for the mission of Jesus and for the mission of the early Church.

Teaching. Why did the preaching of Jesus and of the early Church
get so little response from the people of Israel? Indeed, why did
the kingdom message find a true and lasting response only in a
minority of Gentile hearers? The parable answers this question
with the doctrine of the remnant (cf. Rom. 9 : 27). For most
people the Devil, temptation, cares, and riches are effective de-
terrents to the gospel message. The parable tells a story of rejection. In turn, this rejection becomes a ground for teaching in
parables. The parable is a sign that the rejectors are themselves
rejected by God (10). Jesus, like the New Testament generally,
sees in the negative response of the Jews the hidden purpose of
God (cf. Rom. 9–11). The conclusion (16–18) applies the parable
as a warning to everyone to 'take heed how you hear'. The unbelieving Jewish nation which 'has not' the truth of God shall lose
even what it 'thinks' that it has.

2. The **women** are important for Luke's scheme. Like the
Apostles, they also are witnesses in Galilee as well as at the
crucifixion and resurrection (23 : 49; 24 : 10; cf. Ac. 1 : 14, 21f.).
It is uncertain whether they and the Apostles are set over against
Mary and Jesus' brothers (8 : 19–21). The fact that they are
identified by name suggests that they were important in the
Palestinian church. Their 'service' (*diēkonoun*, 8 : 3) to Jesus and
the Twelve may be a prototype of the 'deaconess' (*diakonos*)
found later in the Church. Cf. Rom. 16 : 1; cf. Lk. 2 : 36ff.;
10 : 39; Ac. 9 : 39; 1 Tim. 5 : 9.

and infirmities: perhaps 'even infirmities', identifying the effects
of the evil spirits from which the persons were 'healed'. More
likely they are different afflictions. The 'healing' apparently includes exorcism (*exelēluthei*). See on 13 : 11, 16; cf. 9 : 42.

Magdalene: i.e. from Magdala, a Galilean village.
seven demons: see on 8:30.

8. ears to hear may mean 'listen, this is important'. Morĕ
probably Christ is calling for right understanding of the deeper
meaning. See on 8:11–15. Cf. 8:18 and Mk 13:14: 'Let the
reader understand.'

10. secrets: i.e. the true nature of the kingdom. In the Gospels
it occurs only here (and in the parallels). Cf. 1 C. 4:1; Col. 1:26f.
1 Tim. 3:16; 1 Pet. 1:10ff.

'so that' (*hina*): Christ teaches in parables (1) *in order* to conceal
the 'secrets of the kingdom', i.e. its true character, from some
hearers. Or, at least, (2) this is the *result*. In either case it is a
teaching method that conceals rather than reveals the way to life.
The parable is a sign of judgment.

Doubting that Christ would deliberately conceal the gospel
message, several scholars (e.g., Black, pp. 212f.; Manson, *Teaching*,
pp. 76ff.) argue that the Aramaic word underlying *hina* should be
translated as a relative pronoun: '*who* seeing see not.' But this
will hardly suffice for the parallel in Mk 4:12. Cf. Jn 12:36ff.;
Ac. 28:24ff.; E. Stauffer, *TDNT* III, 327–30. That the parable
is followed by an explanation shows that, even in the post-
resurrection situation, its meaning was not self-evident. How
much more would this be so in the pre-resurrection mission.

It is difficult to avoid the conclusion that Christ connects parabolic teaching (and particularly the Parable of the Four Soils)
with the citation from Isa. 6:9ff. precisely because he views the
arcane parables as a judgment upon unbelief. J. Jeremias (*Parables*, pp. 17f.) thinks that the saying originally applied to all of
Jesus' preaching with the qualification, 'unless (*mēpote*) they turn
and God will forgive them' (Mk 4:12, following the Targum).
Cf. Mk 4:34; 8:17f. It is clear, in any case, that God's rejection
is viewed as a response to man's prior rejection.

While the parables are an enigma to the curious, they do benefit
sincere seekers. These persons, as yet unready, will receive full
understanding through the teaching of the apostles (cf. Ac. 2:42;
4:2; Mk 4:33). Those who do perceive their truth do so only
partially and because 'it is given' not because they are better or
more clever than other men. See on 9:18–27.

11–15. Since the important work of A. Jülicher (1899) allegorical meanings in the parables of Jesus usually have been denied.

Accordingly, the allegorical interpretation in these verses is thought to be an appendix of, e.g., an early Christian teacher. This probably goes too far. If Jesus' parables concealed their message from the hearers, as is argued above, then Jesus must have given private explanations of them. Since allegorical meanings appear in Old Testament and rabbinic parables, Jesus' explanations also very likely included them. Cf. M. Black, *BJRL* 42, 1959–60, 274–8. As Jeremias observes (*Parables*, pp. 77ff.), the interpretation here has been shaped by Luke and, probably, by his predecessors. But it does not follow that the parable originally had no allegorical intention. The 'mind of Jesus' given to Luke's readers only elaborates and re-applies an original explanation of Jesus himself. 'The parable and the interpretation fit each other as hand fits glove. If the parable . . . is from Jesus, then so is the interpretation' (B. Gerhardsson, *NTS* 14, 1967–8, 192). See above, pp. 7ff.; on 13 : 6; 14 : 24; cf. Cranfield, pp. 158–61; R. E. Brown, *NoT* 5, 1962, 40–5.

The interpretation of the parable concentrates upon the losses, in keeping with Luke's 'rejection' motif. The four types of soil are the hardened, the superficial, the double-minded, and right hearers. Only the last produces the fruit of witnessing and obedience (8 : 16–18, 19–21; cf. Miller).

12. word: cf. 8 : 21.

13. believe: probably an adaptation to the terminology of the post-resurrection mission. See on 18 : 14.

13, 15. temptation: i.e. trial. Instead of a specific 'tribulation or persecution' (Mk 4 : 17; cf. Ac. 8 : 1; 11 : 19; 14 : 22) this is a more generalized rendering. It points to the need for 'patience', i.e. steadfast endurance manifested in the context of trial (cf. 21 : 19; Rom. 5 : 3). See on 22 : 14–23. Cf. L. Cerfaux, *RB* 64, 1957, 481–91.

joy: it is the Christian's fate to suffer; it is his privilege to suffer with joyfulness (cf. 6 : 22f.; Ac. 13 : 50ff.).

14. riches: regarded by Jesus to be a great temptation and, therefore, a hindrance to entering the kingdom. See on 12 : 13–34; 16 : 14; 18 : 18–34. However, poverty as such is not a virtue, as it seems to have been at Qumran. See on 6 : 20.

16. light: see special note at 11 : 33–36.

17f. See on 12 : 2; 19 : 26.

JESUS' TRUE FAMILY **8 : 19–21**

Jesus' brothers, sceptical of his claims, did not believe in him until after the resurrection. In this context it is very possible, as Conzelmann (p. 48) suggests, that they want to 'see' some miracles (cf. 4 : 23; 9 : 9; Jn 7 : 5). The story teaches that one belongs to Jesus solely through call and discipleship. Possibly in the early Church it was used against a tendency to exalt Mary or Jesus' brother, James (cf. Gal. 2 : 12). But for Luke's theme the implicit meaning is that the Jews, Messiah's brothers, have no priority in the kingdom of God because of their physical descent. Also, the same family renunciation for the sake of the kingdom, which Christ later requires of his followers, he first makes himself. See on 2 : 6f.; cf. 9 : 58ff.; 11 : 27f.; 14 : 26.

21. My mother: cf. 1*QH* 9 : 34ff. In the Qumran community also the family of God replaces one's natural family.

CALMING THE STORM **8 : 22–25**

The funnel-type ravines around the lake of Galilee make it especially subject to sudden squalls. Attention turns again to the person of Christ, whose authority and transcendent faith are contrasted with the weakness and fearfulness of the disciples. For Jesus the issue is simply one of 'faith'. Reminiscent of the miraculous catch of fish, the apostles' question, 'Who then is this?', soon will become a confession (9 : 20; cf. 5 : 8ff.). See on 8 : 31, 33.

23. asleep: after a long day (cf. Mk 4 : 35).

24. Master: see on 5 : 5f.
rebuked: see on 4 : 38f. On the 'living' character of nature in Semitic thought cf. H. W. Robinson, pp. 12–16. The extent of Jesus' authority measures the extent of his purpose. The messianic kingdom will mean a redemption and renewal of nature as well as of men. Cf. Rom. 8 : 20ff.

25. afraid: see on 5 : 10.

HEALING A GENTILE DEMONIAC **8 : 26–39**

The exorcism (28–33) and the reaction of the populace and of the healed man (34–39) form the two parts of the episode. In the first the nature and power of the messianic redemption is revealed (see on 4 : 31–44). The second part represents the

Gentiles, like the Jews, as rejectors of Jesus' message. However, the cause here is not religious hostility but fear of the presence of divine power.

The work of Jesus is the work of God. Commanded to tell what *God* had done, the healed man proclaimed 'throughout the whole city' what *Jesus* had done. But Jesus returns to Galilee. The mission to the Gentiles belongs to the future, to the post-resurrection 'time of the Church'. Then they will accept the kingdom message (cf. Ac. 13 : 46f.; 15 : 12ff.). See on 24 : 47.

26. Gerasenes: referring to inhabitants of a town on or near the lake, probably the modern Kersa on the eastern shore. A mile south of Kersa there is a 'steep bank' (33), now some forty yards back from the shore. Mt. 8 :28 has 'Gadarenes'. Cranfield (p. 176) supposes that the original reference to Kersa was confused with the distant city of Gerasa (= modern Jerash). Therefore, the reference was changed to Gadara (Mt. 8 : 28), a town six miles inland, but perhaps with territory extending to the lake. 'Gergesenes', another correction, also may be traceable to Kersa. Cf. J. Soutar, *HDCG*, 1, 643f.

28. cried out: i.e. the demon. See on 4 : 31–44. For a recent interpretation of demonic powers in the New Testament cf. Schlier, pp. 11–52. The ancient world was well aware that mental disorder also could arise from organic or psychological causes. Cf. Herodotus, *History* 2, 173; 6, 84. But Luke will not, as Hippocrates does (*On the Sacred Disease*), ascribe all such afflictions to natural causes. For a similar scepticism about miracles cf. Cicero, *de divinatione* 2 : 28; van der Loos, pp. 7f.

torment: by forcing them to come out or by the threat of judgment that the person of Messiah presents.

30. many demons: indicating the severity of the possession. McCasland (pp. 57ff.) gives a parallel from modern missionary annals.

31, 33. abyss in Semitic cosmology is an abbreviated form of a mythopoeic term, the 'watery deep', i.e. a vast cosmic sea under the earth. It symbolizes the chaos in opposition to which the world was fashioned (Gen. 1 : 2) and by which it is ever threatened. From this threat Jesus brings deliverance to man and to the whole created order (Rom. 8 : 19ff.).

Here and in Revelation (9 : 11; 17 : 8; 20 : 1, 3) the term signifies the realm in which the devil and demons, who embody

and direct the forces of destruction, normally are confined until
the day of judgment. (Cf. 2 Pet. 2 : 4; in Rom. 10 : 7 the symbolism is used of Christ's conquest of this 'underworld' through
his death.) The demons beg not to be sent into the 'abyss'. However, in keeping with their destructive nature they impel the
possessed swine into the sea, that is, the abyss. Thus the demons
are returned to their proper confinement apart from the world
of men. And Christ, by his act, foreshadows the coming conquest
of the kingdom of God over the demonic realm. Cf. Heb. 2 : 14;
Johnson, pp. 56ff., 108ff.

The essence of the story lies just in the fact of Messiah's action.
He manifests his authority where the demonic powers exert theirs,
in the realm of history and nature. As it is in the Old Testament,
the ancient 'chaos myth' is broken, i.e. 'demythologized'. It becomes only 'an extended figure of speech' illustrating the meaning
of one aspect of messianic redemption (cf. Childs, p. 70). Messiah
opposes the demonic powers at work in man and in nature in
order to redeem man-in-nature, man as a totality and as a part
of the created cosmos. See the special note at 24 : 1–12; cf.
A. Oepke, *TDNT* 1, 391 on Ac. 3 : 21.

32. gave them leave: the action contributes to a continuing
Lukan theme. Messiah's present mission is not to destroy the
demonic powers but to deliver man from their influence. See
above, p. 14.

35. Contrast the effect of Jesus with the effect of the demons
(27) upon this man's personality.

37. fear: at the manifestation of divine presence and power.
Cf. 1 : 12; 2 : 9; 5 : 8ff., 26; 9 : 34.

39. declare: contrast 5 : 14; 8 : 56.

HEALING A WOMAN'S HAEMORRHAGE **8 : 43–48**

Structure and Teaching. In the pre-Gospel tradition this story and
the resurrection of the child were kept together (see on 7 : 36–50).
Probably there was a purpose beyond mere historical continuity.
The account is reminiscent of the raising of Lazarus where Jesus
purposely delays his journey (Jn 11 : 6). Here, as there, the
Saviour acts in the calm assurance of faith and in the confidence
of a life lived in the purpose and power of God. Jesus was never
in a hurry.

The woman's 'faith' receives its due reward, apparently apart
from any conscious intent of Jesus. As the episode introducing this
section shows, the healing is not to be understood as a mechanical
or magical result but as the confirming evidence of grace given
to the woman (cf. 8 : 10).

43. In condensing the account 'Luke the physician' chooses to
omit Mark's (5 : 26) derogatory reference to his profession.

44. touched: see on 5 : 13.

fringe: i.e. 'the tassel of his robe' (Moffatt) which perhaps
signified Jesus' consecration to God (Manson; Num. 15 : 38–41).

48. faith: the *trust* in expectation that produces an *act* in expectation. See on 17 : 19; cf. 8 : 15.

49. Teacher: see on 3 : 12.

RAISING AN ELDER'S DAUGHTER **8 : 40–42, 49–56**

The faith of this synagogue president illustrates that the religious
leaders were not always hostile to the message of Jesus. Out of
his anguish and need he comes to Jesus. In contrast to the
Gerasenes this man's 'fear' results from the presence of the power
of death (8 : 37, 50).

Christ also reveals his attitude toward death in his encounters
with it—the widow's son, Lazarus, Gethsemane (7 : 14; 22 : 42ff.;
Jn 11 : 11ff.). Like its younger brother, sickness, death is an enemy.
But it must yield to the powers of the messianic kingdom present
in Jesus. In the presence of Christ death becomes a 'sleeping' (52).
'Finis' is transformed into prelude. Until the *parousia* its sting
remains, but its ultimate threat is broken. If we 'believe', we need
not live in dread: 'fear not!' (50). Cf. 1 C. 15 : 26, 54f.

41. ruler: i.e. synagogue president (cf. *SBK* IV, 145). He is to
be distinguished from a civic official and from a Sanhedrin member (see on 20 : 1).

54. 'Get up, my child' (*NEB*): as though awaking the girl from
natural sleep (Leaney). See on 5 : 13.

55. spirit: i.e. breath or life-principle. See on 9 : 24. 'No story
in the gospels shows the reserve of the writers better, or better
illustrates the candour with which they leave open the facts to a
naturalistic interpretation, while making clear the evangelists'
own complete conviction' (Leaney).

ACTS OF MESSIAH: THE CONFIRMATION AND REJECTION OF
HIS MISSION 9: 1–50

Structure. This is the last of the four sections devoted to the Galilean mission. It is largely traditional, derived from (overlapping) Markan and Q traditions. Cf. Schramm, pp. 26–9, 128–41; E. E. Ellis, 'The Composition of Luke 9 and the Sources of its Christology', *CIB*. In it appear alternating notes of exaltation (9: 6, 17, 20, 32, 43) and rejection (9: 9, 22, 44). See on 9: 37–45. The confession of Peter, the passion predictions, the transfiguration, and 'the meaning of greatness' converge in the three synoptic Gospels to form a crucial turning point in the Lord's Ministry. In them the Galilean mission is brought to its culmination. Ahead is Jerusalem and the cross.

Teaching. Jesus' messiahship is now revealed to the apostles and, being revealed, is found to be a totally unexpected kind of messiahship. To Herod's question, 'Who is this?', two answers are given. From Jesus' preaching and miracles the people conclude that he is a resurrected 'John the Baptist' or an ancient 'prophet' or 'Elijah', the forerunner of Messiah (9: 7f., 19; see on 1: 17). The true answer comes to explicit expression in Peter's confession, 'You are God's Messiah' (*NEB*). It is followed by the witness of God himself: 'This is my Son' (9: 20, 35). The other episodes further define and clarify this answer. Jesus announces a kingdom that delivers from death and is characterized by humility and service (9: 6, 24, 46–50). He is the new Moses who gives 'manna' to the people, and the suffering 'Son of man' whom God will glorify (9: 17, 22, 26, 44).

Messiah's person is to be understood in terms of his 'kingdom of God' mission. The failure of the proclamation of the twelve is the failure of the people to apprehend its messianic implications (9: 7–9, 19). Their experience confirms the earlier rejection of Jesus by the religious leaders. This, plus the recognition of Jesus' messianic role by the apostles, indicates to Jesus that the purpose of the Galilean mission has been accomplished. He must now reveal to his apostles that 'the Son of man must suffer'. But they still are unable to comprehend either the nature of his messiahship or of the kingdom of God (9: 40f., 45f., 49).

Arguing that Jesus' messiahship was not recognized during his lifetime, a number of scholars (e.g., Bultmann, p. 278) have interpreted the transfiguration as a misplaced post-resurrection vision. Similarly, the mission of the twelve is understood as a charge of the risen Lord and the feeding of the five thousand as a later communion sermon. These conjectures depend upon a reconstruction of Jesus' person and mission completely at variance with the Gospel picture. While there is a creativity in the formation of the Gospel tradition, there are a number of historical and literary grounds for supposing that it manifested itself in quite a different fashion. See above, p. 9. Cf. C. H. Dodd, *SG*, p. 25; Taylor, *Mark*, pp. 374f., 387.

THE MISSION OF THE TWELVE 9 : 1–9

A Special Note on the Apostles and the Twelve

The Gospel of Luke uses the term 'the apostles' six times (Matthew once, Mark twice), 'the twelve' six times (Matthew four, Mark ten) and 'the eleven' twice. Unlike Matthew, neither Luke nor Acts uses the phrase 'twelve apostles' or 'twelve disciples'. In Acts (1 : 26; 2 : 14; 6 : 2) 'eleven apostles' occurs once, 'the eleven' once, and 'the twelve' once.

There is a widespread opinion that Luke equates the apostles with the twelve and that this equation is important for his theology. This is surprising, since Luke himself speaks of 'the apostles Barnabas and Paul' (Ac. 14 : 4, 14). The usual explanation, that this passage represents a pre-Lukan tradition, is plausible enough in itself. But it becomes doubtful when Ac. 14 is then said to contradict a specific and thematic Lukan understanding of the apostolate. Luke 'the theologian' does not hesitate elsewhere to select and shape traditions to fit his themes, and it is difficult to suppose that he failed to do so here.

Quite apart from Ac. 14, a number of passages clearly show that Luke does not equate the apostles with the twelve. (1) In Lk. 24 : 9f. the term 'apostles' is almost certainly inclusive of 'the eleven and all the rest' (cf. 24 : 13: *autōn*). Equally, in Ac. 1 : 2f., 8, 'the apostles whom he had chosen' and to whom 'he presented himself alive' in order that they should be his 'witnesses' are none other than the 'witnesses chosen by God' who 'ate and drank with him' in Ac. 10 : 41; cf. 13 : 31. Yet these references must refer to Lk. 24. There the appearances are to the Emmaus disciples

(30f.), Peter (34) and 'the eleven and those with them' (33, 36),
explicitly including Cleopas (18) who remains implicitly *in scena*
through the rest of the chapter. Indeed, Lk. 24 presents no
appearance exclusively to the eleven and does not mention the
twelve. (2) In addition, Matthias can *replace* Judas 'in *this* ministry
and apostleship' (Ac. 1 : 25 : *tēs diakonia tautēs kai apostolēs*), i.e., of
the twelve, only if it is presupposed that the circle of apostles
is broader than the twelve and includes those mentioned in
Ac. 1 : 8 (cf. Lk. 24 : 47f.). (3) Even though the twelve are the
first to be named 'apostles' (6 : 13), the Evangelist designates
them also as disciples (9 : 12, 16; 22 : 14, 39), parallels their
'apostolic' work to that of the seventy (9 : 2; 10 : 1, 9; cf. Mk
6 : 7–13) and, unlike Matthew, fails to specify twelve apostles at
the Last Supper or twelve thrones in the judgment of Israel
(22 : 14, 30). This indicates that he has no interest in identifying
the term 'apostles' especially, much less solely with the twelve.
(4) Like the other speakers in Ac. 15, James of Jerusalem is to be
regarded as an apostle, unless one supposes that Luke could make
a non-apostle the spokesman for a conference of 'the apostles and
the elders'.

In Luke-Acts the twelve are qualified by apostleship but, if the
above reasoning is sound, apostleship is in no way qualified by
or limited to the twelve. The phrase 'eleven apostles' (Ac. 1 : 26),
like 'twelve disciples' (Mt. 10 : 1; cf. 8 : 20f.: *heteros*), does not
express a limitation on the number of the apostles but rather
defines a particular group within the larger whole. 'The apostles'
may, of course, like the Matthean phrase 'the disciples', refer to
the twelve (or the eleven). But it is the context and not the term
itself that determines the reference.

What, then, is Luke's understanding of 'the apostles' and of
'the twelve'? It is, one must confess, easier to show the flaws in a
received opinion than to provide a more acceptable alternative.
But it may be worth while to begin by looking at certain aspects
of Lukan usage. *Apostolos* is used relatively more in Luke than in
Mark, 'the twelve' relatively less. It may be going too far to say,
with K. Lake (*BC* v, 46) that in the New Testament *apostolos* 'is a
Pauline-Lukan word'. But in Luke-Acts it is clearly underscored.
The phrase 'the twelve', on the other hand, is introduced editori-
ally only once or twice (8 : 1; cf. 9 : 12). More often, in comparison with Mark, it is lacking (19 : 37; 22 : 21), omitted (9 : 47),

or altered to 'disciples' (8 : 9) or 'apostles' (22 : 14). Primarily the changes are due to Luke's use of a non-Markan source. But granting the Evangelist's knowledge of Mark, they still show that Luke has a lessened interest in, or an interest in lessening, the significance of the twelve in Jesus' ministry. Like Mark, he describes the twelve as those who are 'named apostles', are 'with Jesus' and are 'sent out' (6 : 13; 8 : 1; 9 : 1). But he speaks of others in the same way (8 : 1f.; 10 : 1; Ac. 1 : 21f.).

In Acts, too, the Evangelist ascribes to others all of the functions ascribed to the twelve: witnesses to Jesus' resurrection (Ac. 1 : 22; 2 : 14; 3 : 15; cf. 1 : 8; 22 : 14f.; 26 : 16f.; 10 : 41; cf. Lk. 24 : 30, 43) or to his exaltation (Ac. 5 : 30ff.; cf. 22 : 20; 7 : 56), advisers to the Church (Ac. 6 : 1; cf. 15 : 19), appointers to ministerial tasks (Ac. 6 : 3; cf. 13 : 3; 14 : 23; 15 : 25ff.), imparters of the Holy Spirit (Ac. 8 : 14–17; cf. 9 : 17; 19 : 6). After Ac. 6 he does not mention the twelve as a group at all. As J. Fitzmyer has noted (*SL*, p. 247), the problem in Acts is why Luke gives attention to the reconstitution of the twelve (Ac. 1 : 15–26) only then to allow them virtually to disappear. We have contended above that it is not because Luke used 'apostles' as an equivalent term for the twelve. The answer seems to lie rather in the diminished importance of the twelve in the Lukan church at the time in which Luke was writing.

It is virtually certain that the twelve were set apart by Jesus during his earthly ministry (see on 9 : 1). It is probable, furthermore, that they were a symbolic representation of the nation: in them 'Jesus made visible to everyone His claim upon Israel, and He did so in such a way that it was evident that He did not merely claim a select group but the whole people in all its divisions' (K. H. Rengstorf, *TDNT* II, 326). It is uncertain whether, in choosing the twelve, Jesus knew of Qumran's leadership-group of twelve men + three priests or, less likely, nine men + three priests (cf. 1*QS* 8 : 1; B. Reicke, *SSNT*, pp. 151f.). But like Qumran, he speaks of his followers as 'sons of light' (16 : 8; cf. 1*QS* 3 : 24) and apparently regards his community to be the faithful Israel of the new covenant (22 : 28ff.; cf. *CD* 19 : 33ff.; 1*QS* 34 *bis* 2 : 5f.; Ringgren, *Qumran*, pp. 137, 200–4).

Luke accepts the representative role of the twelve and underscores it in Acts by the replacement of Judas and by the witness of the twelve to the 'house of Israel' (cf. 8 : 1; Ac. 1 : 21f.; 2 : 14,

36). In this he follows his traditions about the mission of Jesus
and the mother church in Jerusalem. More significantly for his
own point of view, however, Luke often subsumes the twelve
under the broader umbrella of 'apostles'. Why is this so?

Luke's church is a diaspora-community living a generation after
the resurrection. It is still substantially Jewish and stands only at
the beginning of the Gentile mission; but it has had to face the
reality of the failure of the national mission to the Jews (cf.
Jervell, pp. 56–64, 175; E. E. Ellis, *Int.* 28, 1974, 94–8). It was
founded and nurtured primarily by Paul and other apostles, not
by the twelve. For these reasons, among others, the Evangelist,
without denying an important place to the twelve, allows them
to merge somewhat into a broader background. Like Paul, Luke
sets the Church on the foundation of 'apostles and prophets'
(11 : 49; Eph. 2 : 20; 3 : 5; cf. 1 C. 12 : 28). And among them,
as the last half of Acts reveals, he gives most attention to the
figure that he and his diaspora-Church knew best, the apostle and
prophet Paul. Cf. Ac. 13 : 1; E. E. Ellis, 'The Role of the Christian
Prophet in Acts', *AHG*, pp. 62–6.

Structure. The earlier prophecy of Christ to Peter (5 : 10) now finds
a partial fulfilment. Later the Lord will give a wider commission
to include the Gentile world. However, during his pre-resurrection
ministry the mission is confined to the Jews (cf. 24 : 46ff.; Ac.
1 : 8; Mt. 10 : 5f.). The mission of the Twelve is a natural extension of Jesus' own mission tour. Like the earlier story at Lk.
8 : 1–18, it forms the setting for the episodes that follow and
reveals the reaction of the Jewish nation to the 'kingdom of God'
mission.

Teaching. Herod's attitude, about which the early Church was well
informed (cf. 8 : 3; Ac. 13 : 1), testifies to the fame both of Jesus
and of the mission of the Twelve. More significantly, it typifies
the attitude of the nation. Herod is disturbed and curious. He
wants 'to see' Jesus. But in their speculations the people and
Herod do not raise the question of messiahship. At most they
think that Jesus is 'Elijah' or a prophet. 'Seeing they see not'
(see on 8 : 10).

1. the twelve: a technical term for the inner circle of apostles
(9 : 10). The number is symbolic of a renewed Israel (see above,

pp. 109f.). The word 'apostle' has a technical connotation in the rabbinical usage which probably is present in the New Testament. Meaning 'sent one', it has its roots in the Hebrew word *šāliah* and involves both the idea of mission and of authorization and responsibility. However, it is the sender or commissioner who is most important. His 'power and authority' are manifested in the apostle. There are similarities to the modern law of agency. Within the scope of his mission the apostle is the 'embodiment' of the sender. His 'ambassadorial' actions are those of the one he represents. Therefore, to insult or reject Jesus' apostle is to reject Jesus (cf. 10 : 16; 2 Sam. 10 : 1ff.). Although used in a wider sense (e.g., Ac. 14 : 14; Heb. 3 : 1), for Luke apostle also refers to the twelve. The word has special reference to their function as eye-witnesses of the resurrection and as authorized bearers of the tradition of Jesus (Ac. 1 : 21ff.). Cf. Cullmann, pp. 59–99; K. H. Rengstorf, *TDNT* I, 420–43; II, 325ff.; Taylor, *Mark*, pp. 619–27; Schweizer, pp. 69f. (5h).

The view that the twelve represent only a post-resurrection phenomenon, suggested by Schleiermacher (p. 88) and Wellhausen (p. 139) and affirmed by Bultmann (p. 345) and others, is conveniently summarized by W. Schneemelcher (*ANT* 2, pp. 25–31). However, it depends upon inferences, drawn in considerable measure from a preformed image of Jesus' ministry. That is, a selectively extracted Synoptic picture of Jesus and his work becomes a measure for what in the Synoptic traditions truly reflects the ministry of Jesus. But does the resulting hermeneutical circle lie within an orbit that is historically probable? Supporting the view that the twelve were a constituted group in the pre-resurrection mission are the early stage of the traditions and the coherence of the Gospels' presentation: (1) Both Mark (3 : 14f.; 6 : 7) and Q attest to Jesus' setting apart of twelve disciples (9 : 1–6; cf. Schramm, pp. 26–9; E. E. Ellis, *CIB*; Mt. 19 : 28). Both probably associate the (subsequent) designation of the twelve as apostles with their 'sending out' (*apostellein*) by Jesus (9 : 1f., 10; Mk 3 : 14; 6 : 7, 30; cf. Mt. 10 : 1f., 5; Haenchen, p. 125). (2) The designation of Judas as 'one of the twelve,' found in traditions of Mark, Luke, and John, makes sense only if this circle existed during Jesus' ministry (cf. Jeremias, *Theology*, pp. 233f.). (3) Traditions referring to 'the eleven' likewise 'would have been pointless if the *dōdeka* had not been accepted as a group

originating in the period prior to the death of Jesus' (K. H.
Rengstorf, *TDNT* ii, 326; cf. B. Rigaux, 'Der Zwölf', in Ristow,
pp. 468–86).

2. to preach: including a call to repentance as well as exorcism
and healing (cf. 13 : 1ff.; Mk 1 : 14; 6 : 12). Each activity witnesses to the nature and demands of the kingdom. Luke, however,
stresses the healing ministry.

3–5. The missionary charge in the mission of the Seventy
(10 : 3–12) agrees with the more elaborate Matthean version.
The charge may have become a standardized 'form' in the early
Church. The essential meaning is not to go without preparation
but to *rely* on God and not on one's own resources.

3. The minor disagreements (e.g., Mk 6 : 8 permits one staff
to be taken) do not affect the meaning. Does the command to
'take nothing' signify a special protection from want and evil
during the period of Jesus' ministry (Conzelmann), or does it
merely reflect a missionary custom (Manson) or strategy (Daube)?
Perhaps both are true. The Essenes, another Jewish religious
group of the time, 'enter the houses of men whom they have never
seen before as though they were their most intimate friends.
Consequently they carry nothing whatever with them on their
journeys except arms as a protection against brigands' (Jos.,
War, 2, 8, 4). In any case the Lord's instructions later are
changed: the persecuted 'Church militant' and the Gentile mission will require a bag and a sword (see on 22 : 49; cf. Mt.
10 : 16ff.).

5. Upon re-entering Palestine religious Jews would 'shake off
the dust' of unclean Gentiles. Here it signifies an abandonment to
judgment (cf. 10 : 12).

7f. The comparison with John suggests that the message of the
'kingdom of God' mission was similar to the earlier preaching of
the Baptist.
Elijah: see on 1 : 17; 9 : 28–36, 54; 19 : 38.
prophets: see on 7 : 11–17, 39f.

9. Herod's wish to 'see' Jesus is not an expression of faith but
only of curiosity (23 : 8) or malice (13 : 31). Like the Baptist,
Christ answers such curiosity not with a miracle but with a call to
repentance (11 : 29ff.). For Luke only those approaching Jesus
in faith 'see' his miracles in their true significance. Only those
entering the kingdom of God really 'see' Jesus (9 : 27; cf. 13 : 35;

Jn 11 : 40). Belief must precede 'proof'. Peter, who believes, receives a sign; those who want a sign simply are commanded to repent. As is the case in the Fourth Gospel, the curious Herods of whatever name find in Jesus only an enigma. They search for a 'sign' until curiosity itself becomes a sign—of judgment! Cf. 4 : 23; Jn 6 : 30; 12 : 37, 40.

FEEDING THE FIVE THOUSAND 9 : 10–17

Structure. In all four Gospels this miracle marks the climax of Jesus' Galilean mission. It is spring (cf. Mk 6 : 39; Jn 6 : 4) and the cross is still a year or more away. Outwardly the mission tour of the apostles has been well received. The reaction of Herod (9 : 7–9) is only a cloud on the horizon. Yet Jesus' withdrawal from Herod's territory to 'Bethsaida' seems purposely to avoid an immediate encounter with that petty ruler. The experience of the Baptist is fresh in mind and Jesus' 'time' has not yet come.

Teaching. The meaning of the miracle is indicated to Luke's readers by its setting in the 'kingdom of God' mission (11). The healings and resurrections reveal the kingdom as the victor over death. The feeding of the five thousand is the positive side of the coin: the kingdom of God provides the nourishment of life.

Luke does not *say* that the bread multiplied. The Gospel miracles, like Jesus' messianic sayings, are not intended to force belief. The oblique presentation leaves room for the sceptical interpretation of the Pharisees or the side-show curiosity of the crowds, even as it invites a believing acceptance of the miracle in its true significance for Jesus' person and mission.

10. Bethsaida: a main city of Philip's tetrarchy. It lay on the north end of the lake of Galilee across the Jordan from Herod's jurisdiction.

12. lonely place: away from the city proper (9 : 12). The ministry at this time may be the basis for the later 'woe' against the city (10 : 13).

14. fifty: the division is reminiscent of the action of Moses in Exod. 18 : 21. There, as here, the count has reference to the men. The Exodus symbolism is more explicit at Qumran (cf. 1QS 2 : 21f.; 1QSa 1 : 14f.; 2 : 1).

16. loaves: Jesus' act would remind a Jew of the miracle of the

manna. John's gospel, which stresses Christ's identification with
the 'prophet like unto Moses', makes this connection explicit:
Jesus provides 'manna' that gives eternal sustenance (Exod.
16: 15f.; Dt. 18: 15; Jn 6: 14, 31; cf. 2 Kg. 4: 42–44).

blessed and broke . . . and gave: a typical Jewish blessing of
the time was 'Blessed art thou, O Lord our God, king of the
universe, who bringest forth bread from the earth' (*SBK*1, 685;
Ber. 6: 1). As the Fourth Gospel makes quite clear, the 'living
bread' of the kingdom is nothing less than Jesus himself. Thus the
early Church saw in the feeding miracle a prototype of the Last
Supper and of its own Eucharistic meals (22: 19; Jn 6: 48ff.;
cf. 24: 30). This was possible because Jesus, by such symbolic
acts, already had identified his disciples as the company of the
'new Exodus', the nucleus of the messianic community.

17. twelve baskets: one from each apostle, symbolizing perhaps the continuing miraculous sustenance of the new Israel of
God. They represent the visible part of the miracle. Probably it
was the bread left over and thrown away. At banquets it was
customary to use bread as 'pushers' and to wipe the hands. To
discard such bread was not wholly wasteful since it had served a
useful function. Cf. 16: 21; Daube, p. 37.

THE MEANING OF PETER'S CONFESSION **9 : 18–27**

Structure. Matthew and Mark locate Peter's confession in the area
of Caesarea Philippi. Luke, who at this point skips over a considerable portion of Mark (6: 45–8: 26), omits the geographical
setting. Probably it is because he wishes to connect the confession
to the feeding miracle (cf. Jn 6: 14, 68f.). The episode has three
parts, the inquiries (18f.), the confession (20–22), and the admonitions (23–27).

Teaching. The popular speculations reveal that Jesus had made
no direct claims to be Messiah (19). In contrast to the people in
general, Peter infers the true messianic significance of Jesus' acts.
He thereby fulfils the Lord's earlier prophecy: 'to you it has been
given' (8: 10; cf. 5: 10; Mt. 16: 17). Nevertheless, Peter and his
colleagues see only one side of the coin: Jesus is Lord over sickness
and demons and nature. Until the end the apostles fail to understand that Messiah must 'be killed and on the third day be raised'

and that the kingdom of God does not mean a political revolution but a revolution in the order of nature itself. In their eyes Jesus' 'pessimism' is unwarranted: swords are available. If some end up on a Roman cross, the cause will surely triumph. But their failure to understand also is in the providence of God. See on 18 : 34; cf. 17 : 25; 19 : 11; 22 : 37f., 49; 24 : 5f., 25f.

The requirement to enter the kingdom is utter and ultimate commitment to the way of Jesus (23–27). The suffering Messiah means also a suffering messianic community. In its original context to 'take up his cross' meant only one thing, to die with Jesus in Jerusalem. No one did. And Peter, who here represents the apostles in their messianic confession, there represents them in their failure (22 : 33, 56ff.). See on 12 : 41–48; cf. 18 : 28. Yet in spite of the impossible requirement 'some' before their death shall experience 'the kingdom of God'.

18f. praying: see on 6 : 12.

Elijah: see on 1 : 17; 9 : 28–36.

21. tell no one: a messianic claim through an apostle would be equivalent to an assertion by Jesus himself. Also, in the light of God's ordained purpose (22) it would be in vain and would be taken as Jesus' intention to be a political deliverer. See on 4 : 41; cf. Jn 6 : 15; Ac. 5 : 36f.

22. The Son of man is joined to the figure of the suffering Servant (Isa. 53; see on 5 : 24). The Servant was associated with Messiah by the Judaism of Christ's day (see on 20 : 17; cf. Stenning, on Isa. 52 : 1). But apparently the suffering was not interpreted of the Messiah personally but of the people of Israel (Manson).

must (*dei*) **suffer:** the beginning of a recurrent note in Luke. It expresses the finality of divine necessity. In contrast to fatalism or philosophical determinism, New Testament determinism is an ordering of events by a personal God for a redemptive purpose. Cf. W. Grundmann, *TDNT* II, 24; see on 24 : 26.

Elders, chief priests, and scribes: when used together, refer to the Jewish ruling body, the Sanhedrin. See on 20 : 1.

23. deny himself: i.e. abandon his allegiance to his natural life, ambitions, and interests, regarding them as irrelevant. To 'follow' Christ a person must become apostate from his egocentric self.

daily: Luke's interpretative addition. It shows that the words of the Lord have an abiding and existential significance. One still may go to Jerusalem and there in corporate identification 'be crucified with Christ'. One still may 'fill up his afflictions' in a life of obedience under trial (Rom. 6 : 3ff.; Gal. 2 : 20; Col. 1 : 24).

follow: see on 14 : 27.

24. life: one's dying natural 'life' (*psychē*) can be preserved to eternal life only as it is engrafted, by a death to self, into the resurrection life of Christ. Cf. Jn 12 : 25; Rom. 6 : 5f.; Col. 3 : 1–4; E. E. Ellis, *NBD*, pp. 735–39. See on 8 : 55.

25. See on 12 : 13–34.

27. see the kingdom of God: the suggested fulfilments of this prophecy range from the transfiguration to the *parousia* (cf. Plummer). In recent New Testament research the verse often has been interpreted as Jesus' expectation of the last judgment, the *parousia*, in the first century. Cf. 21 : 27, 32. However, two elements in the context make this interpretation doubtful, the foregoing warnings and the very pointed connection with the transfiguration (23ff., 28). The warnings contrast those now 'ashamed' of Jesus (26a) with those who 'see' the kingdom of God before their death (27). The 'before' (*heōs*) clause probably implies that the latter will die later (cf. 13 : 35; 21 : 32; 22 : 16, 18). That is, 'some', i.e. the faithful, will experience the kingdom in the context of losing their lives for Christ. Unbelievers will 'see' the kingdom only in the 'glory' of the *parousia*. See on 2 : 26; 9 : 9; 10 : 1–20; cf. 10 : 23; 13 : 35; 21 : 27; Jn 3 : 3; 14 : 19. For Luke the presence of the kingdom always is 'in power'; therefore, the redundant clause of Mk 9 : 1 is omitted.

Elsewhere Luke can change an original *parousia* reference into Christ's present exaltation (cf. 22 : 69; Mk 14 : 62). But this passage is only another instance of Luke's counter-positioning of the present (26a, 27) and future (26b, 28–36) manifestations of the kingdom of God. The distinction is present also in Matthew and Mark and is rooted in the teaching of Jesus himself. See on 17 : 20–37; above, pp. 13ff.; E. E. Ellis, *NTS* 12, 1965–6, 30–5. The connection with the transfiguration, implicit in the order of the episodes, creates a second reference to the *parousia*. For the transfiguration reveals privately what will be publicly manifested at the last day, the 'glory' (26b, 32) of Jesus' 'power and *parousia*'. Cf. 2 Pet. 1 : 16f.; Mk 9 : 1; Ac. 7 : 55f.; 22 : 11; see on 17 : 22; 24 : 4.

JESUS TRANSFIGURED 9 : 28-36

Background. Ancient Israel expressed its messianic hope in several figures (cf. E. Hill, *SE*, pp. 190–98). They included the Mosaic prophet (see on 9 : 35), the conquering king (see on 3 : 22), the humble servant (see on 4 : 18; 19 : 28–44), the corporate Son of man (see on 5 : 24), and the eschatological coming of God himself (Mal. 3 : 1; cf. Ps. 50 : 3; see on 1 : 68f.; 2 : 11; 7 : 19; 22 : 70). Jesus incorporates a number of these images into the self-disclosure of his messiahship. The narrative may have been composed in the context of a Christian (synagogue) *midrash* or commentary on Exod. 24 or 34 (cf. E. Schweizer, *TDNT* viii, 369).

Teaching. The Lord's immediate response to Peter's confession impresses on his disciples that Messiah must suffer. His delayed response ('about eight days') reveals that, after and through suffering, Messiah will enter into his glory (cf. 24 : 26).

The transfiguration is a prophetic preview of both the future glory and the true nature of Jesus' messiahship. Two elements make up the primary motif in the transfiguration story, the revelation of the Son of man (Dan. 7 : 13) and the vision of God at Mount Sinai. Cf. M. Sabbe, *CBG* 4, 1958, 467–84, cited in *NTA* 3, 1957–8, 235. The first draws upon parallels with the visions of Daniel (10 : 8f., 5f., 16). It appears in such items as the altered countenance, the sleep, the Son of man's 'glory', and the coming of 'Elijah' (cf. Rev. 1 : 13f., 17f.; see on 1 : 17). Allusions to Mount Sinai are seen (also) in the altered countenance, the 'booths', the overshadowing 'cloud', and the presence of Moses (Exod. 13 : 20f.; 33 : 9ff.; 34 : 29; cf. Daube, pp. 30ff.).

Doubtless the disciples interpreted their experience as a foretaste of an immediate *parousia*, i.e. the glorious and public revelation of the kingdom of God (19 : 11). Only after Easter did they recognize that the transfiguration glory also pointed to the resurrection/exaltation of the Lord (cf. Rev. 1 : 12ff.; Ac. 7 : 55f.). However, this application of the event was not improper. For the resurrection/exaltation of Messiah was, so to speak, the first stage of the *parousia* glory (1 C. 15 : 23). Cf. Riesenfeld, *Jesus*, pp. 292–302.

28. eight days: probably a symbolic alteration of Mk 9 : 2. It represents an entering into a 'new age' reality. See on 24 : 13; cf. *2 Enoch* 33 : 1f.

pray: see on 6 : 12.

30. two men: cf. 24 : 4; Ac. 1 : 10.

31. departure: i.e. 'exodus'. It probably includes the whole of
Messiah's redemptive work: death, resurrection, and ascension.
The 'exodus' typology is clearly in view. Jesus is the new Moses
who establishes a new Israel, gives a new covenant, and through
his death and resurrection delivers God's people from the 'Egypt'
of sin and death. See on 6 : 17–49; above, p. 109.

32. glory in the New Testament characteristically refers to the
reality of the 'new age'. This reality is consummated in Jesus
personally at his resurrection (e.g., 24 : 26; Heb. 2 : 9f.; 1 Pet.
1 : 21). It is revealed in his followers and in the natural order at
the open and public glory of the *parousia* (e.g., 9 : 26; Rom.
8 : 18ff.; 2 C. 4 : 17; 1 Pet. 4 : 14; 5 : 4).

33–35. In the feast of 'booths' the Jews commemorated God's
immediate presence and protection during their forty years in the
wilderness (cf. Daube, p. 30f.). This presence was to be renewed
in the end-time. The overshadowing 'cloud' of God's *Shekinah*
confirms Peter's apprehension of the divine presence. But God
rebukes the apostle's equation of Jesus with Moses and Elijah:
'This is my son, my Chosen, listen to him!' See on 3 : 22; 23 : 35.
At his baptism God confirmed to Jesus his messiahship. Following
Peter's confession God confirms this truth to the apostles.

35. Chosen: i.e. 'Elect' cf. 1*QpHab* 9 : 12 (Hab. 2 : 8).

listen to him: probably a reference to the eschatological prophet
of Dt. 18 : 15 LXX (cf. Ac. 3 : 22; 7 : 37; Jn 6 : 14). If so, Jesus
is here identified with the royal 'Son' (Ps. 2 : 7), the chosen
Servant (Isa. 42 : 1), and the prophet like Moses. Jesus himself,
by word and deed, defined his mission and his messiahship in terms
of these figures. Cf. Bruce, *Exegesis*, pp. 74f. See on 7 : 39f.; cf.
4 *Qtest* 5ff.

HEALING AN EPILEPTIC BOY **9 : 37–45**

Structure. The mission of the Twelve is followed by the unbelieving
curiosity of Herod (9 : 7). After Peter's confession Jesus immediately warns that he will be rejected (9 : 22). In the midst of the
transfiguration-glory sleepy Peter wants to build 'three' booths
(9 : 33). In the present episode the manifestation of the 'majesty
of God' is abruptly interrupted by the second warning of betrayal

and death (43f.; contrast Mk 9 : 30). The oscillation between the
confirmation and rejection of Jesus' messiahship is a continuing
theme through the section. Luke purposely moulds his narrative
to this end. Thereby he heightens the drama of the story and
drives home its truth: although Jesus' messiahship is amply
attested and his mission superficially popular, the actual verdict
is negative. The climax of the Galilean mission points to the cross.
Even his closest followers find such a fate for Messiah to be unthinkable. But this also is in the plan of God: for the meaning of
the prophecies 'was concealed from them' (45). See on 24 : 13–32.
Cf. Flender, pp. 30f.

The setting of the episode follows a pattern found earlier and
may reflect an habitual practice of Jesus. Following a night of
prayer on the mountain, the 'next day' Jesus descends to a waiting
crowd to teach and heal (37). Cf. 6 : 12, 17; 19 : 37; 22 : 39; Mk
6 : 46ff.; Jn 8 : 1f. The 'mountain' thus comes to have a symbolic
significance in the Gospels as a place of revelation and communion
with God. Conzelmann (pp. 44f., 57) rightly points to this
although his explanation of it is doubtful.

Teaching. Luke omits the reference to the faith of the boy's father
and stresses rather the disciples' lack of faith (41; contrast Mk
9 : 23f.). This point is reinforced by the marvelling but unbelieving
crowd (43). Faith is a prime requisite for entering the kingdom of
God. The notable lack of it, even in the face of many 'signs',
signifies to Jesus that the Galilean mission is nearing its end. The
journey to Jerusalem and the cross lies on the horizon.

39. a spirit: i.e. a demon (42). Demonic possession or oppression affects the afflicted person in various ways. See on 4 : 33; 8 : 28,
30; 13 : 11, 16. Here it causes or aggravates epileptic seizures.

41. faithless: a rebuke to the disciples (Cranfield) or, less
likely, a general reference to all (Taylor, *Mark*).

42. rebuked: see on 4 : 38f.

44f. delivered: i.e. 'betrayed' (Moffatt). See on 9 : 22; 18 : 31–
34. Jesus did not explain his words, and they 'were afraid to ask
him'. Since the saying contradicted their total concept of Messiah,
their lack of understanding was natural. And yet, as Luke makes
clear, it was not merely 'natural' (45). The fear of the disciples
suggests that the passion predictions may have been dramatic
oracular utterances upon which Jesus did not elaborate.

THE MEANING OF GREATNESS IN THE KINGDOM OF GOD **9 : 46–50**

These two incidents set forth the apostles' idea of greatness and thereby reveal their basic misunderstanding of the kingdom of God. Jesus points out that true greatness means humble service rather than precedence (46–48) and is expressed in the quality of the servant's purpose, not his official status (49–50).

The teaching reveals the meaning of the cross, and it shows also the meaning of the disciples' inability to grasp the fact of the cross (9 : 44f.). For Jesus, 'the rejected stone', came not to be served but to serve (cf. 20 : 17; Mk 10 : 45). That Jesus should have to repeat this lesson is understandable. In view of the continuing fascination for status and hierarchy among his followers the teaching had an abiding relevance (22 : 26f.; cf. Jas 2 : 3).

With these stories Luke brings the Galilean mission to its end observing that, even among those recognizing Jesus as Messiah, the nature of his mission and of his kingdom remains something of an enigma.

46ff. The stories may have been used in the Church as a missionary maxim. That is, tolerance wins converts (50) and humility is an instrument for evangelism (Daube, pp. 350f.; cf. 1 Pet. 3 : 1; 1 C. 7 : 16). But for Luke this motif is quite secondary.

47. a child: 'The service of love is tested by its operation toward the most insignificant' (Creed).

49. in your name: i.e. your authority. Jesus' fame as an exorcist would attract others to use his 'name' especially in the light of the mission of the Twelve. Cf. 10 : 17; Mk 9 : 39ff.; Ac. 19 : 13.

50. To remain neutral or independent when commitment is called for is equivalent to rejection (9 : 57–62; 11 : 23; cf. Ac. 17 : 30). But Jesus apparently regards this man as a prospective follower who, like the apostles earlier, is in a stage of transition (cf. Jn 1 : 39; Mk 1 : 16ff.; Ac. 18 : 25; 19 : 4).

THE TEACHING OF MESSIAH 9 : 51–19 : 44

THE LITERARY PROBLEM

The central division of Luke is built upon the framework of Jesus' journey from Galilee to Jerusalem. In the closing phase of the Galilean mission the necessity for the journey is disclosed. The recognition of Jesus' messiahship in Peter's confession and in the transfiguration brings with it an added revelation. Jesus is a suffering Messiah who must accomplish an 'exodus' in Jerusalem (9 : 22, 31, 44). This fact, as well as the journey itself, is common to the Gospels of Matthew, Mark, and Luke. Luke's distinction is to use the journey as a scaffolding upon which to present a different aspect of the Lord's ministry. But it is *only* a scaffolding and one should not expect the *content* of the central division to follow the Galilean mission chronologically or, necessarily, to have any chronological sequence at all.

The Galilean mission in Luke is presented in successive 'Acts of Messiah'. On a few occasions an extended teaching of Jesus is given, but even then the dominant feature continues to be the symbolic act that the teaching reflects. For example, the Great Sermon constitutes a part of Messiah's inauguration of the new Israel; the parable of the soils summarizes the fortunes of the 'kingdom of God mission' (6 : 17–49; 8 : 1–18).

The central division, on the other hand, is concerned predominantly with the teachings of Jesus. Cf. A. M. Farrer, *SG*, pp. 66ff., 74. Besides short proverbs more than twenty parables occur, distributed through every chapter. In the Galilean mission the Lord's acts are presented as a messianic witness. Here they primarily serve only as an introduction and a context for his teachings. Cf. 11 : 1, 14; 12 : 13. Compare 13 : 10 with 6 : 1ff.; 14 : 1ff.; with 7 : 36ff.; 14 : 25ff. with 9 : 18ff. See on 13 : 10–21; 17 : 12. The teachings include a variety of subjects, e.g., prayer (11 : 1ff.; 18 : 1ff.), repentance (13 : 1ff.), forgiveness (17 : 1ff.), discipleship (17 : 7ff.; 14 : 25ff.), and especially the kingdom of God (see above, pp. 12ff.). The pronouncement of judgment, in which Jesus is the warning prophet, is a continuing theme. Cf. 12 : 1ff., 35ff.; 13 : 22ff.; 14 : 15ff.; 16 : 14ff.

Professor B. Reicke has observed that the teaching matter in the central division alternates between the instruction of disciples and discussion with opponents. Each area would be important for the early Church, the former for those in congregational responsibilities and the latter for missionaries and others in contact with Jewish adversaries. 'The fact that the traditions are supposed to have been developed in the Church, and with regard to her interests, does not preclude our assuming that the Lord did act or speak in a corresponding way' (*SE*, p. 216). J. Schneider (*SS*, p. 221) comes to a similar conclusion. These chapters are teachings of Jesus that contain clear predictions of how the future Church, especially the leaders, should live and work. The theology of the Church grew out of the words of Jesus.

This leads to a broader question, the arrangement of the materials. One naturally would expect to find in the several journey references a clue for the ordering of the material. W. Grundmann (*ZNTW* 50, 1959, 252–70) has taken this approach. He divides the narrative into three journey reports (9 : 51– 10 : 42; 13 : 22–35; 17 : 11–19), each followed by a teaching section. Although his scheme is open to a number of objections, it rightly sees that Luke's central division is not a travelogue. That is, the journey references form a part of a thematic structure and are not markers in a running chronological account. For example, the Lord is no nearer Jerusalem in 17 :11 than in 9 : 51ff.

C. F. Evans (*SG*, pp. 37–53) also views the structure thematically. He notes that in the Gospels Jesus is 'the new Moses' and that the word 'received up' (9 : 51) is the title of an apocryphal book about the death and 'assumption' of Moses. From this clue Evans draws an extended parallel between Luke's plan of the 'Teachings of Messiah' and the 'Teachings of Moses' in Deuteronomy. A number of the parallels are striking. Whether they are sufficient, or sufficiently precise, to establish this ingenious theory is questionable.

It may be that the geographical references, for example, in 17 : 11, pertain only to the individual episode in which they appear (Schlatter, pp. 219f., 389f.). If so, Luke utilizes them and adds introductory comment to maintain a 'journeying' context. He inserts the phrases, for example, 'as they went on their way', 'as he drew near to Jericho' (10 : 38; 18 : 35). Cf. 9 : 57; 13 : 22; 14 : 25.) The reader keeps in mind, thereby, that in the progress of the ministry Jesus now is on his way to the cross. The journey references also give the *teachings* their proper perspective. They are the teachings of a messiah whom the Jewish nation has rejected (10 : 13ff.; 11 : 29ff., 47ff.; 13 : 34f.) and who is appointed by God to suffer in Jerusalem (12 : 50; 13 : 33; 18 : 31ff.).

H. Conzelmann's (pp. 61ff.) interest in the geographical element leads him to regard the journey itself as the motif that Luke is developing. This approach however, has a number of difficulties. For example, Conzelmann (pp. 66f., 69f.) must assume Luke's ignorance of the very geographical element that the Evangelist supposedly is concerned to stress. Luke even uses unaltered a number of episodes whose geographical setting is obviously incompatible with the scheme of the journey (p. 62n). Yet Conzelmann (pp. 98–136) shows that elsewhere Luke is quite capable of shaping the material to his thematic purpose. There is, therefore, an inner inconsistency in Conzelmann's argument. In any case, it is doubtful that the journey references will bear the weight which Conzelmann desires to place upon them (see, e.g., on 13 : 32f.). There seems to be implicit in his approach the traditional (and erroneous) view that the Gospel is intended to be a running chronological account of Jesus' ministry. If one relegates the (Markan) journey scaffolding to its rightful subordinate place, the real thrust of the central division is more clearly seen.

The Purpose of the Central Division

In the progress of Jesus' mission the central division of Luke is a transition piece. It is the counterpart to the earlier section in which the story moves from Jerusalem to Galilee (2 : 41–4 : 30). But Luke's primary intention is to present a theme not a chronicle, to present Jesus the teacher not Jesus the traveller. Throughout the ministry from 4 : 42 onward Jesus is presented always without a home, always on a mission, always on the move. Therefore, it is improper in any case to call Luke's central division 'The Travel Narrative'. Cf. Schlatter, p. 331; W. C. Robinson, Jr., *JBL* 79, 1960, 29f.; J. Blinzler, *SS* pp. 27–33, 41; P. Schubert, *NS*, p. 184.

This explains the freedom with which Luke incorporates episodes from various times in the Lord's ministry without regard to their chronological sequence. For example, 10 : 38–42 finds Jesus apparently on the outskirts of Jerusalem. Cf. Jn. 12 : 1–3. In 13 : 31ff. he is again in Galilee (or Perea); yet this episode closes with a lament found in Matthew (23 : 37–39) among the

Jerusalem sayings. A number of episodes have an indicated setting
in or near Jerusalem. In some instances, at least, Luke could
hardly have been unaware of that fact. (It suggests a 'Jerusalem
ministry' greater than that revealed by the Synoptic Gospels and
draws attention again to the plan of the Fourth Gospel.) See on
10 : 25–37; 13 : 1–9, 34f.; 18 : 10, 18; below, p. 228. Luke also
scatters through the section sayings collected by Matthew in the
Sermon on the Mount. In a few cases he may be giving their
original setting (11 : 1ff.). But in most he, no less than Matthew,
locates the passage to suit his thematic design (14 : 34f.; 16 : 18).

The audience in these chapters supports this view of the central
division. In the 'Galilean' mission the disciples are identified as
hearers only twice (6 : 20; 9 : 43). In 9 : 51–19 : 44 they are frequently mentioned. Sometimes this represents an editorial change
of audience (see on 12 : 41). On the whole, however, the references
only emphasize the setting of the sources and, probably, of the
pre-resurrection mission. Nevertheless, by the explicit designation
of the disciples and by the selection of appropriate episodes Luke
distinguishes the public Galilean mission (4 : 31–9 : 50) from the
'teachings' of the central division. The distinction is not as sharp
or complete as it is in the Gospel of John (1–12 and 13–17), but
the pattern is noticeably similar. It is entirely possible that Luke
is drawing upon two Gospel 'forms' known to him, Markan and
Johannine.

Only after the Lukan narrative rejoins Mark at 18 : 15 does a
semblance of chronological sequence reappear and the journey
actually progress toward Jerusalem. This editorial arrangement is
not 'erroneous' unless one insists on judging Luke as a 19th-
century historian. See above, pp. 6f. Nor is it arbitrary: the
Evangelist shapes his materials for a particular literary purpose.
Probably the bulk of Jesus' teachings did come in the latter stages
of his ministry. And, of course, there is a very general chronological scheme common to all Gospel writers (cf. O. Piper, *JBL* 78,
1959, 115–24). But for Luke all this is quite secondary, almost as
though it were taken for granted.

THE PLAN OF THE CENTRAL DIVISION

Like the earlier messianic 'acts', the messianic 'teachings' appear
as a series of episodes. Likewise, the episodes seem to fall into six

sections of six episodes each. The first three sections are introduced
by the journey reference in 9 : 51ff., and a similar editorial preface
is found at the beginning of the second half of the central division
(13 : 22; cf. 8 : 1). The first section (9 : 51–10 : 42) is in the context
of journeying (as far as Bethany). Correspondingly, the return to
the Markan framework in the last section (18 : 15–19 : 44) signals
the resumption of the actual movement, via Jericho, to Jerusalem.
Cf. the summary at Mk 10 : 1. The second section (11 : 1–12 : 34)
begins a number of 'set' teaching-pieces (cf. Grundmann). The
limits of the third and fifth sections (12 : 35–13 : 21; 16 : 14–18 : 14)
are not so obvious, although the composite summary at 16 : 14–18
is striking enough. It may well be that the division of the episodes
should be 6–12–12–6 with two long teaching sections enclosed
within two shorter journey sections. However, if the sixfold
arrangement of the first division of the Gospel is valid, a similar
partition of the central division would not be unexpected. In any
case it offers a convenient structure that probably is not far from
the Evangelist's intention.

The Meaning and Reception of the Kingdom Message
9 : 51–10 : 42

The section opens in Galilee with Jesus firmly set to go to Jerusalem. It closes on the outskirts of that city. Although the journey
context is explicit (9 : 56f.; 10 : 1, 38), it remains in the background. Each episode focuses upon a 'teaching word' of Jesus
about the kingdom of God or, in an equivalent expression, the life
of the coming age. The kingdom message proclaims the messianic
peace and Messiah's victory over the powers of Satan and of
death (10 : 1–20). It is a message of deliverance and not of judgment (9 : 55), but those rejecting it stand liable to severe judgment
in the future (10 : 13ff.). For this reason, to hear and obey the
proclamation of the impending reign of God takes priority over
every other concern of life (9 : 57–62; 10 : 38–42).

This is the 'hour' when all knowledge of the Father and the life
that it brings is mediated through the message of the Son. A
person discerns that message only as it is graciously revealed to
him (10 : 21–24). Therefore, all efforts at self-justification fall
short of obtaining the life of the coming age (10 : 25–37). Indeed,
there is a radical reversal of priorities in the bestowal of this bless-

ing. The wise and 'religious' do not find the way to life. It is rather the inconsequential and the rejects of this world—the simple-minded, Samaritans, women—who reveal that they are heirs of the kingdom (10 : 21, 25–37, 42).

REJECTION IN SAMARIA **9 : 51–56**

Background. The Samaritans, descendants of Gentile settlers and Israelites, had been a thorn in the side of the Jews for centuries. Cf. 2 Kg. 17 : 24–41; Ezr 4 : 3ff.; Neh. 4 : 1ff. In Jewish eyes they were racially half-breeds and religiously apostates. They were publicly cursed in the synagogues and made the object of a daily prayer—that they might not enter eternal life (Oesterley, p. 162). Their centre of worship in Samaria was a countertype and rival to the temple in Jerusalem (Jn 4 : 20). Therefore, Galilean pilgrims, crossing Samaria on their way to Jerusalem, were subjected to harassment and sometimes to overt violence (Jos. *Ant.* 20, 6, 1).

Teaching. Jesus was no ordinary pilgrim, and his rejection by the Samaritans has a special meaning for Luke. It points first of all to the Lord's steadfast purpose to go to Jerusalem. This is the only stated reason for the Samaritans' attitude. Secondly, there may be an intended parallel between the rejection by the Jews of Nazareth (4 : 28f.), the Gentiles at Gerasa (8 : 37), the Samaritans here, and the people and leaders of Jerusalem later (13 : 34; 23 : 1ff., 18). Jesus goes to the cross rejected by all. However, the parallel is a limited one. Only the Jews reject Jesus because of his messianic claims. Also, the Samaritans (and Gentiles) lie outside the scope of the 'kingdom of God' mission during Jesus' pre-resurrection ministry. Later, when there is a mission to Samaria, they will receive the message (Ac. 8 : 4ff.; 13 : 46ff.; cf. Cullmann, pp. 185–92).

The central thought of the episode appears to be not the Samaritan question but the nature of Jesus' messiahship (Grundmann). The words, 'as Elijah did', probably are not original; but they correctly interpret the meaning of the disciples' question (54, margin). Cf. 2 Kg. 1 : 10–14. Even on the road to the cross James and John, the sons of thunder (Mk 3 : 17), still regard Jesus as an Elijah-type messiah. The disciples' misunderstanding persists to

the end (cf. 22 : 38, 49). The Lord, however, knows that his
present mission is not as judge but as saviour. He is going to
Jerusalem to die.

51. Received up (*analēmpseōs*) probably refers to the whole
sequence of salvation events culminating in Messiah's ascension.
It may correspond to the term, 'glorified', in John's Gospel (Jn
13 : 31; cf. Schlatter, p. 269). B. Reicke (*SE*, p. 211) suggests that
there is an allusion also to the Jerusalem 'pilgrimage' (*ma'ªlāh*)
found to the titles of Pss 120ff. Cf. 2 Kg. 2 : 9–11.
set his face: cf. Isa. 50 : 7 LXX.

54. The allusion to Elijah has an interesting counterpart in the
episode at Nazareth (4 : 25; cf. 1 : 17). It also reveals an impressive faith on the part of the disciples. If Jesus so authorizes, fire
will fall. The disciples were not naive children and they were not
joking. This remarkable saying very likely is an incidental attestation to the miraculous works which must have been performed
previously by them 'in Jesus' name' (9 : 1; cf. 10 : 17; Mt.
14 : 28f.).

55. 'You do not know . . .' (margin): this apparently is a
copyist's addition. Cf. 19 : 10; Jn 3 : 17. It is a clarification of what
already is implicit in the text.

THE DEMAND OF DISCIPLESHIP 9 : 57–62

Structure. Of the three incidents making up the episode, the first
two are found also in Matthew (8 : 18–22). There they are located
in the Galilean mission. In Luke no locale is given. If 'you go and
proclaim the kingdom' (60) is not Luke's interpretative addition
(cf. Mt. 8 : 22), the incident occurs after the time Jesus begins to
send out the disciples (cf. 9 : 1ff.; 10 : 1). The setting merely conforms to the broader picture of Jesus the wanderer going in the
way toward Jerusalem. In the lengthening shadow of the cross the
demand of the kingdom finds added urgency.

Nothing is said of the identity of these candidates for discipleship or of the subsequent outcome of their encounter with the
Lord. The reader's entire attention is directed to the utter commitment involved in discipleship and the immediacy of its demand.
This literary form makes an appropriate 'charge' to candidates for
baptism or for the ministry. Originally it may have been tailored
to this purpose.

Teaching. The first and third candidates volunteer. Jesus probes their intent with the pointed reminder that there is no easy road to discipleship (cf. 9 : 23ff.; 14 : 25–35). The second man is called by Jesus. The stringent demand laid upon him is a positive counterpart to the warning given the others. Jesus will have no summertime soldiers, no fair-weather disciples.

The whole point of discipleship is that one should become like one's master (6 : 40), and Jesus requires no more than he himself has given. He is the penniless and ever-working one who has sacrificed family and home for the sake of the kingdom (9 : 58; 8 : 19–21). Whoever joins the fellowship of Jesus must also join the mission of Jesus. The issue is not the particular sacrifice that Jesus asks one to make but rather the principle involved. The claims of Messiah must have priority in the life of a Christian.

The mention of 'the kingdom of God' in 9 : 62 and the probable Lukan addition of the phrase in 9 : 60 point to the meaning implicit in the whole episode. To follow Jesus means to proclaim the kingdom. The requirements are not 'entrance tests' so much as a call for self-evaluation to all who call themselves followers of Jesus.

59f. bury: in rabbinical teaching the burial of deceased relatives was a sacred duty and a work of love. It imparted benefits both in this life and in the world to come (*Peah* 1 : 1; cf. *SBK* IV, 578–92). Because the presence of a corpse defiled one, it precluded the performance of any religious duty. An unburied relative anywhere apparently was equivalent to the presence of the corpse in the room (cf. *Ber.* 18a). In the light of these facts this man's desire appears to be both edifying and necessary. Why does the Lord react so negatively?

The answer of Jesus accords with his attitude elsewhere toward the traditional ceremonial laws. This duty, like fasting and Sabbath observance, must yield priority to the pressing mission of the kingdom. Cf. 5 : 33ff.; 6 : 6ff.; Jn 5 : 16f. If discipleship requires one to forsake living parents, how much more should it require this in regard to the deceased. It is not a question of the need for physical burial. The issue is one of personal sentiment and religious duty. The 'dead' are available to perform both those functions.

60. the dead: those who have not hearkened to the kingdom message and whose soul-life, therefore stands under the death

claims of the old age. In Judaism the term was used of the ungodly. In the New Testament it is applied more specifically to all
who do not share the resurrection life which Jesus imparts (*SBK*;
Jn 5 : 25; see on 9 : 24; cf. Daube, pp. 109f.). Perhaps the
usage of Jesus, as well as the fact of his resurrection, is the background of Paul's similar use of the term (Rom. 6 : 13; Eph. 2 : 1).

61f. These verses, like 9 : 60*b*, occur only in Luke. Elijah, who
granted a similar request, was thought by some to have reappeared
in Jesus. But it is uncertain whether Luke here intends to contrast
the prophet's mission with that of the Lord (9 : 19; 1 Kg. 19 : 20).
fit: well qualified or properly suited. Service for the kingdom
requires an undivided loyalty. Cf. 2 Tim. 2 : 4.

THE MISSION OF THE SEVENTY **10 : 1–20**

Structure. The episode falls into three parts, the instructions (1–12),
the woes upon the rejecting towns (13–16), and the victory and
meaning of the mission (17–20). The mission is an expansion of
the corps of 'advance messengers' (9 : 51f.) and a parallel to the
earlier mission of the Twelve (9 : 1ff.). The first part incorporates,
in a more or less standardized form, mission instructions which
were utilized in later post-resurrection missions of the Church.
The Lord's 'woe', found in a different setting in Matthew, is
inserted by Luke for purposes of his theme. It implies that the
mission was rejected (see on 9 : 1–9). The return of the Seventy
(17–20) is the core of the episode. It reveals in the midst of the
mission's rejection the nature of its victory.

Background. With significant qualifications (22 : 35f.; Ac. 1 : 8; cf.
Mt. 10 : 5) the instructions of Jesus for the pre-resurrection missions became an operating procedure for the early Church. Going
out in twos, missionaries lodged in a hospitable 'house' and went
out to 'heal' and preach the 'kingdom'. After a decisive rejection
they travelled on (e.g., Ac. 13 : 51; 17 : 5ff.; 18 : 6f.). A similar
pattern is evident in other Jewish religious groups. See on
9 : 3.

Teaching. The parallel with the mission of the Twelve suggests that
the Seventy also were viewed as representatives of the new, i.e.
the eschatological Israel, empowered by the spirit of the new

Moses. See above, p. 109. Perhaps there is also a prefigurement
of the later mission to the 'seventy' Gentile nations.

The setting of the mission is the messianic salvation, i.e. the
eschatological consummation, already in process. The 'harvest'
even now is being gathered (2), time is pressing (4), and rejections
final and damning (11, 13–16). The messianic peace is bestowed
(5), and the powers of the coming age are manifest in driving
back the powers of death and the Devil (9, 17f.). Not only in the
work of Jesus himself (cf. Kümmel, pp. 113f., 139f.) but also in
the works of his disciples the kingdom of God is being actualized.
So, re Matthew (10 : 1–8), Strecker, p. 195.

The lordship of Satan and of death yields to the in-breaking
powers of the new age. Yet, as King Belshazzar's guests continued
to feast unaware that his kingdom had fallen and his doom had
been sealed, so the present age is unaware that Satan's reign is
broken. It sees only a writing on the wall, and it cannot read
what it sees. For Luke the mission of the Seventy is the continuing
task of the Church. As Jesus' empowered representatives Christians
have a twofold task. First, they are to make the kingdom present
in healing, in exorcism, in the bestowal of the messianic peace.
As it was in the days of the pre-resurrection mission, this presence
is sporadic, partial, veiled. It is a writing on the wall occurring
only as the Spirit actualizes it. It is only a token, a minute foretaste of the universal revelation of the kingdom at the glorious
parousia of Jesus. Thus, secondly, Christians, like the Seventy,
must explain the writing on the wall. The present manifestation
of the powers of the new age proclaims that Jesus is Lord (17) and
that the public revelation of the kingdom of God is impending
(12). Cf. Jn 5 : 25, 28f.

1. Seventy: some manuscripts read seventy-two, correspond-
ing to the Septuagint enumeration of the nations in Gen. 10.
Which number is original 'cannot be determined with confidence'
(B.M. Metzger, *NTS* 5, 1958–9, 306).

The number had a weighty pedigree in Old Testament and late
Jewish tradition. There were seventy Gentile nations (Gen. 10),
seventy Israelites going into Egypt as the seed of the future people
of God (Exod. 1 : 5), seventy elders who accompanied Moses upon
the holy mount and who received a portion of his prophetic spirit
(Exod. 24 : 1; Num. 11 : 25). A similar number (plus the high
priest) composed the Sanhedrin, the ruling representatives of the

nation Israel (*SBK*). It is highly probable that in the present context the number is symbolic and theologically significant. Perhaps selected by Luke (see on 9 : 28), it is quite as likely that the numbering of the 'thirty five pairs' was an acted parable of Jesus himself.

1. sent: see on 9 : 1.

2. harvest: found only here in Luke. It signifies elsewhere in Jesus' parables the judgment, 'the close of the age' (Mt. 13 : 39; cf. Rev. 14 : 15; Jn 4 : 35).

the Lord of the Harvest: i.e. God, who prepares and sends the labourers. Those whose task is to 'pray' are then themselves 'sent'. But this Lord of the harvest is none other than Jesus who himself sends forth the disciples and upon their return is addressed as 'Lord' (10 : 17; see on 2 : 11).

3. lambs: i.e. helpless and dependent upon the protection of the Great Shepherd (Grundmann).

4. 'No purse or pack, and travel barefoot' (*NEB*). This corresponds to the specifications in 22 : 35 (cf. 9 : 3). The Lord replaces the usual ceremonial 'salute' (*aspasmos*; see on 1 : 41) with a new greeting filled with new meaning (Schlatter).

5. Peace: an ancient Semitic greeting. It now means God's messianic peace, the kingdom of God. See on 2 : 14, 29; cf. 19 : 42; Ac. 10 : 36; cf. Jn 14 : 27; 20 : 21f. This peace is more a benediction than a greeting. It is a gracious bestowal of power that will be retained by the recipient if he is a 'son of peace', i.e. a son of the kingdom (cf. Mt. 13 : 38).

7. wages: Paul uses the saying in 1 C. 9 : 14; 1 Tim. 5 : 18. The principle evidently violated the rabbinic rule that Scripture must be taught gratuitously (cf. Daube, pp. 395f.).

9, 11. 'The kingdom of God has come close to you' (*NEB*): the only instance in Luke in which Jesus uses the phrase. It is the local nearness of a present reality not the chronological nearness of a future reality. Cf. Mk 12 : 34; M. Black, *ET* 63, 1951–2, 289f. See above, pp. 12ff. Note the parallels between 10 : 9, 17 and 11 : 20; the exorcisms of the disciples signify no less than those of Jesus.

12f. Sodom and **Tyre** represent the most wicked Gentile cities. Israel's rejection of Jesus' message implies a greater hardness and therefore forecasts a severer judgment.

Woe: i.e. 'alas' (*NEB*): see on 6 : 17-49.

15. Hades: with one exception (16 : 23) the word in the New Testament has its Old Testament meaning, Sheol. It means simply death or the realm of death (see on 9 : 24; cf. Mt. 16 : 18; Ac. 2 : 27). Jesus predicts the future humbling or death of the city. Cf. Isa. 14 : 11, 14f. Today the deserted site of Capernaum bears its eloquent, silent testimony to his prophecy.

16. hears you hears me: see on 9 : 1.

17. Lord: see on 5 : 1–11.

name: both identified and conveyed the authority of the person as, e.g., 'in the name of the law'. The user, thereby, designated himself to be standing in the sphere of the person's power (cf. 9 : 49; Ac. 19 : 13f.; 1 C. 5 : 4; 2 Th. 3 : 6).

18f. saw: i.e. 'was observing' (*etheōroun*). The victory cry of the disciples is confirmed and interpreted by Jesus. The defeat of Satan by Messiah, expected by the rabbis in the last times (cf. *SBK*, II, 2, 167f.), is occurring in the works of Jesus and his disciples. See on 11 : 22; cf. Kümmel, pp. 113f. Is Jesus recounting a vision similar perhaps to one later experienced by John the Prophet (Rev. 12 : 8f.)? Cf. 1 *Enoch* 55 : 4.

19. serpents: symbolic of (or equivalent to) demons in ancient Jewish thought.

20. not rejoice: an implicit warning. See on 9 : 9; 11 : 29–36; cf. 4 : 3ff.; Mt. 7 : 22.

written in heaven: cf. Exod. 32 : 32f.; Dan. 10 : 21; 12 : 1; Rev. 20 : 15; 1*QH* 16 : 10 (Holm-Nielsen, p. 238); *Jubilees* 5 : 13f.; 23 : 32; Dalman, *Words*, p. 209. See on 6 : 23–25.

WHO RECEIVES THE KINGDOM? **10 : 21–24**

Structure. Matthew (11 : 25ff.; 13 : 16f.) locates the episode in a different context. It consists of a prayer (21), an exalted messianic affirmation (22), and a beatitude (23f.). The saying is to be understood in the framework of the 'hour' in which the kingdom powers are manifest to the disciples (see on 9 : 27). Therefore, it is placed appropriately after the mission of the Seventy and forms a counterbalance to the rejection of that mission by the cities.

Teaching. Each part of the episode answers the question, 'Who perceives, and hence receives, the kingdom?' In God's good pleasure the meaning of the kingdom message is to the 'babes revealed' and from the 'wise' concealed (see on 6 : 20–26). The knowledge of the Father is now mediated solely through the Son, his name, his word, and his work. In sum, this is the *eschaton*, the time of messianic salvation which the 'prophets' foretold and anticipated. Those who 'see' this are indeed 'blessed'. Each saying underlines the fact that nobody discerns the true character of Jesus' mission by his own 'desire' but only because it is 'revealed' to him.

21. hour: like 'season' or 'today', a technical eschatological expression and not a chronological yardstick. It is the 'hour' of 'these things', i.e. of the manifestation of the powers of the new age (10 : 17, 19). Cf. Cullmann, *Time*, pp. 43f.; 12 : 56; 19 : 44; 21 : 24; 22 : 53; 23 : 43; Jn. 4 : 23; 5 : 25; 2 C. 6 : 2; Heb. 3 : 7ff.

rejoiced (*agalliaō*): used most frequently in the New Testament of the joys of messianic redemption (cf. 1 : 14, 47; Ac. 2 : 26; Jn 8 : 56; 1 Pet. 4 : 13).

thank: the thanksgiving prayer is a form common to the Old Testament and occurs also in the Qumran hymns (e.g., Ps. 138 : 1; 1*QH* 7 : 26; 11 : 27). In a pattern noted earlier, the thanksgiving concerns the reversal of priorities in the coming age (see on 6 : 23–25).

Father: see on 11 : 2.

wise: the scribes, i.e. theologians, or perhaps anyone having only 'the wisdom of this world' (cf. 1 C. 1 : 18ff.).

well-pleasing (margin) (*eudokia*): used most often in the New Testament to root the 'why' of salvation in the gracious willing of God. See on 2 : 14; 12 : 32; cf. Eph. 1 : 5, 9.

22. delivered: denotes the transmission of a teaching or tradition. Jesus' teaching is received not from the fathers but from the Father (Grundmann). Having his teaching, the apostles also are independent of the traditions of the elders (cf. Cullmann, pp. 59–75).

no one knows: an adequate conception of the Father comes only through the revelation given through the Son (cf. Schlatter). 'Knowledge' is used in the Johannine (and Old Testament) sense of personal relationship; cf. 1 Sam. 3 : 7; Jn 17 : 3. On the relation to the term as it is used of Qumran see W. D. Davies, *HTR* 46, 1953, 113–39.

the Son: used in this absolute sense frequently in John's Gospel

but only once elsewhere in the Synoptics (Mk 13 : 32). The title
is applied by the Old Testament and the rabbis to the nation
and the king. Doubtless it is related here to the messianic designation given to Jesus at his baptism and at his transfiguration (see
on 3 : 21f.; 9 : 28–36). But the Father–Son association appears to
go beyond a messianic designation. It posits a unique, subjective,
and reciprocal relation between Jesus and God which finds fuller
expression in the Fourth Gospel and reaches definitive form in the
doctrine of the Incarnation. See on 22 : 70.

23. Blessed Another isolated beatitude occurs in 11 : 28; cf.
7 : 23; 12 : 37; Ac. 20 : 35.
see: see on 8 : 10; 9 : 9, 27; cf. Jn 8 : 56; 1 Pet. 1 : 10ff.

WHO INHERITS ETERNAL LIFE? **10 : 25–37**

Structure. The episode consists of two 'question and answer' pairs.
The first (25–28) strikes an optimistic note. The sequel (29–37),
which for Luke is the core of the passage, reveals why the 'great
commandment' did not enable one to 'inherit eternal life'. It was
not truly kept and, in the context of Jewish legalism, could not be.
See on 18 : 9–14; cf. Gal. 3 : 12; Rom. 10 : 5.

The Jerusalem temple debates in Mark include a question,
omitted in Luke, concerning the greatest commandment (Mt.
22 : 34ff.; Mk 12 : 28ff.). The first question of this episode is very
similar. Judging from the setting of the parable (30), Luke's story
also has a Jerusalem locale. If one allows for some literary re-
phrasing, it is possible that Luke relates the same incident. On the
other hand, the importance of this issue in first-century Judaism
makes it probable that such questions arose repeatedly in Jesus'
ministry (cf. *SBK* on Mt. 19 : 16; 22 : 36).

Probably originating as a Scripture discussion between Jesus
and a theologian, the episode was transmitted from the beginning
as a set piece of exposition (Gerhardsson, *Samaritan*, p. 28) in
which the parable served as a commentary on the cited texts
(27f.; cf. Derrett, pp. 222, 228).

Teaching. The answer of verse 27 refers to Scripture passages probably already recognized as an epitome of the law (Dt. 6 : 5; Lev.
19 : 18). The following parable points out Judaism's failure to
fulfil this law and, therefore, to obtain the life of the kingdom of

God. It answers a person who would 'justify himself' (29). And
its teaching is the implicit foundation upon which Paul will build
his thesis of righteousness through faith (cf. Ellis, pp. 118f.).

Not only does Jewish legalism fail but the despised Samaritan,
who is anathema to all that Jewish legalism represents, is nearer
than the Jew to a true fulfilment of the law. The subtle shift from
'Who is my neighbour?' (29) to 'Who was neighbour?' (36) underlines this point. 'Neighbour' is not an object that one defines but a
relationship into which one enters. The root of the law—love of
God and neighbour—goes beyond law. For the law stands fulfilled
when one shows 'mercy' (37). Cf. Mic. 6 : 8. On the other hand,
the law is broken when one, like the priest and Levite, gives self-
security or 'the rules' priority over the duty to love. The man's
question is answered implicitly: anyone needing aid is the proper
object of neighbour-love. At the same time the theologian is shown,
quite tactfully, that he is asking the wrong question. Doubtless
there is more than 'Good Samaritan theology' in the New Testament. (And the story often is confused with boy-scout philan-
thropy.) But this parable stands pre-eminent as the Lord's answer
to *all* attempts at self-justification, to all efforts to enter the
kingdom through formula obedience, to all legalisms—Jewish or
Churchly. See on 7 : 47.

25. lawyer: i.e. a theologian (see on 11 : 45). Apart from Luke
the term is found in the Gospels only in Mt. 22 : 35.

25-28. On the literary form see on 7 : 36-50.

Teacher: see on 3 : 12.

life (*zōē*): regularly used in the New Testament of the life of the
coming kingdom age (18 : 18, 24; cf. *SBK* on Mt. 19 : 16; see on
9 : 24). Inquiries about 'the greatest commandment' and 'inherit-
ing eternal life' ask the same question, namely, 'how do I attain
the kingdom of God?'

read: understand or possibly 'recite', referring to the daily recitation of the Shema, the basic Jewish creed (Grundmann; cf. Mk
12 : 29f.; Ac. 8 : 30).

27. Rabbinic Judaism regularly sought to reduce the Law to the
greatest or 'all embracing' commandment (*SBK* on Mt. 22 : 40).
The citations, Dt. 6 : 5 and Lev. 19 : 18, apparently do not occur
elsewhere in contemporary literature as the summation of the
Law although their essence appears in the *Test. Iss.* 5 : 2; *Test.
Dan* 5 : 3. Cf. Cranfield; Philo, *de spec. leg.* 2, 63.

28f. live (*zaō*): see on 20 : 38. The reference is to Lev. 18 : 5.
Cf. Rom. 10 : 5; Gal. 3 : 12.
justify himself: see on 18 : 9–14, 18–34.

30. Jericho: deep in the Jordan valley some seventeen miles
east of Jerusalem. It was the residence of about half of the priestly
orders.

31f. a priest . . . a Levite: who periodically went to Jerusalem
to serve in the temple (*SBK*; see on 1 : 5–25). The description
(31f.) is as realistic as the dangers of that lonely, robber-infested
road (Jos. *War*, 4, 8, 3). Their twofold witness (Dt. 19 : 15)
certified the unmerciful character of official Jewish religion. Carefully observant of religious duties in Jerusalem, they omit the
'love of God' (11 : 42). Is it from fear? Or religious rules prohibit-
ing contact with a corpse (Lev. 21 : 1; *Naz.* 7 : 1)? Or the conviction that one need not show mercy to a 'sinner' (Sir. 12 : 4–6)?
It is irrelevant. The story stresses one thing: the religious ones,
seeing the victim's need, passed by.

33. Samaritan: see on 9 : 51–56. The irony of the story is that
a foreigner, not included in the Jewish definition of neighbour, is
the one who showed himself neighbour to the unfortunate Jew.
Of all Jews the Jerusalem priesthood was especially bitter toward
the Samaritans because their 'heresy' involved a question of
priestly succession.

35. two denarii: see on 7 : 41.
36f. neighbour . . . showed . . . do: alluding back to the
cited texts (27f.).

THE PRIORITY OF HEARING THE WORD OF GOD 10 : 38–42

Structure. Presumably, the setting of the story is Bethany (Jn 11;
12 : 1f.), a village on the outskirts of Jerusalem. Probably the
account is from Luke's Jerusalem traditions. From this (Johannine?) source or from personal knowledge, Luke likely would
know where Mary and Martha lived. See above, pp. 28ff.; cf.
10 : 41f. with Jn 6 : 27. But his readers do not know, and he does
not enlighten them. The journey locale is secondary.

Teaching. Jesus, still on the move, is a guest in the home. More
importantly, he is 'the Lord', teaching the 'word' of life to a family in
which this same word later will be dramatically actualized (Jn 11).

The patristic Church interpreted the passage to show the superiority of the contemplative over the 'active' life. Similarly, some modern commentators think that the story illustrates, from Jesus' own example, the relative value of two kinds of ministry, 'liturgy' and 'diaconate'. The apostles' choice in Acts (6 : 4) concurs with Christ's attitude here (cf. Gerhardsson, pp. 239ff.; B. Reicke, *SE*, pp. 212f.). However, Jesus rebukes Martha for diverting Mary from his word to less essential tasks. The issue is not two kinds of Christian service but religious busyness which distracts the Christian—preacher or layman—from the word of Christ upon which all effective service rests. Mary chose 'the best dish' (42, Moffatt) because she saw the priority of the word of the kingdom to all worldly concerns.

Martha's concern was to be a proper hostess, Mary's to be a proper disciple. Jesus' concern, as ever, was to serve and fulfil his mission, not to have his rights as a guest. To Martha—and, Luke implies, to all her daughters—the Lord offers a gentle rebuke: don't let ordinary dinners spoil your appetite for the real dinner.

39. Probably the story reflects a dinner scene (cf. Schlatter). As was the custom, Jesus reclined on his side at the table. Mary, away from the table, 'sat at the Lord's feet' (cf. Ac. 22 : 3). The picture is that of a rabbi instructing his pupil (*SBK*). The extraordinary feature is that the pupil is a woman. Judaism did not forbid women to be instructed in the Torah (*Ned.* 35b; *SBT*, p. 107n). But it was very unusual for a rabbi to lower himself to this. In the social system of the time women were a 'rejected' group, and Luke pays considerable attention to the acceptance which Jesus accords them. See on 8 : 2.

42. 'few . . . only one' (margin): a few things for my meal, really one for your need. Some important manuscripts read 'one thing is needful'. A minor group reads 'a few things are needful'. The reading of the *RSV* margin is the best attested, but it possibly represents a conflation of the other two.

Teachings of Messiah: The Kingdom and the Power
11 : 1–12 : 34

Throughout the central division of Luke the Lord's teachings are addressed to men standing before the kingdom of God. The audience in the following section alternates back and forth be-

tween the disciples and opponents of Jesus. The episodes present
the kingdom primarily as a present reality in the mission of Jesus
and/or of the Church. Prior to the *parousia* the kingdom is
actualized only in the eschatological, miraculous works of the
Spirit. Therefore, the two elements, 'spirit' and 'kingdom', form
one theme virtually throughout the section. Disciples who are
taught to pray 'thy kingdom come' realize in the pentecostal gift
of the Spirit a (partial) fulfilment of their prayer (11 : 1–13). The
same working of the Spirit in Jesus' healings and exorcisms
(11 : 14–28) is the real sign of the impending kingdom. It is 'the
greater thing' that is present in his pre-resurrection ministry
(11 : 29–36). But the leaders of Israel dissuade and divert the
people from this reality. Thus they take from them the 'key of
knowledge' and become liable to God's judgment (11 : 37–54).

The post-resurrection ministry of Jesus is mediated, via the
Spirit, through his witnessing disciples. In their task they face two
dangers. By apostasy they may irrevocably alienate the Holy Spirit
who witnesses through them (12 : 1–12). By concern for material
security they may be diverted from their proper task of 'seeking
the kingdom' (12 : 13–34).

Within the general theme there are alternate notes of blessing
and admonition, appropriate to Luke's Christian readers. The
kingdom blessing is assured to those who ask persistently (11 : 13)
and who keep the word of God (11 : 28). God very personally cares
for every need (12 : 29ff.) and enables them to give a faithful
witness (12 : 12). Therefore, Christians are not to be anxious or
fearful of men or of life (12 : 4, 7, 22, 32). There is also a recurrent
and persistent note of judgment. It is directed to those who
experience the kingdom powers but do not obey the kingdom
message (11 : 24ff.), to a rejecting generation (11 : 29), wicked
religious leaders (11 : 42ff.), hypocritical followers (12 : 1ff.), and
to all who live for the present life only (12 : 21).

THE MEANING OF CHRISTIAN PRAYER 11 : 1–13

Structure. Whether Matthew (6 : 9–13) has an expanded version of
the Lord's Prayer or Luke an abbreviated one is not certain. But
the former is more probable. Both forms contain interpretative
alterations. Matthew inserts the prayer in the Sermon on the
Mount to illustrate the contrast between Christian prayer and the

'religious' prayer of hypocrites and pagans. Luke probably gives the original context. Hearing Jesus pray, a disciple asks him to teach them a proper prayer to offer. Cf. Jeremias, *Prayer*, pp. 6–15; Mk 2 : 18 with Lk. 5 : 33.

Background. Presumably, John the Baptist gave his disciples a distinctive prayer. The synagogues, probably even in the first century, had an official prayer that, in later form, became the 'Eighteen Benedictions' (cf. *SBK.*) Jesus' model has five petitions (in Matthew, seven). It is addressed to disciples who stand before the impending kingdom of God.

Teaching. The address, 'Father', and the requests that God's 'name be honoured' (Phillips), that his 'reign begin' (Moffatt), that he forgive our sins and not 'bring us to the test' (*NEB*, cf. 22 : 40) are the component parts of the prayer. Each points to the eschatological situation in which the mission of Jesus is conducted and the fulfilment toward which it is directed. That is, the locus of the prayer is the time of salvation, the kingdom of God, the new creation in which men will stand in a new relation to one another and to God. For this the follower of Jesus is to 'ask', 'seek', 'knock' (11 : 9)—and not in vain! The kingdom already is manifest in the works of the Spirit through Jesus (11 : 20). In the light of Pentecost Luke interprets the 'good things' that Jesus promised as the gift of 'the Holy Spirit'. This gift is nothing less than the manifestation of forgiveness and resurrection life, of the kingdom of God in the present dying age.

2, 13. Father (*abba*): i.e. 'papa', 'daddy'. See on 6 : 35; 10 : 22; cf. G. Kittel, *TDNT* i, 6. It suggests an intimate affection without cheap familiarity (T. W. Manson, *BJRL* 38, 1955–6, 438). As an address for personal prayer it appears to have originated with Jesus. Cf. *Ta.* 23b; Grundmann; J. Jeremias, *SS*, pp. 86–9; *Prayer*, pp. 17–21.

According to the rabbis 'any benediction which omits the mention of the Name . . . or . . . the Kingdom is no benediction' (*Ber.* 40b). The name 'Father' is both a christological sign of Messiah's unique relation to God and an eschatological sign to his followers of their sonship (Jn 17 : 6, 26; Grundmann).

2–4. The longer form of the Lord's Prayer in Matthew also is found here in some manuscripts. The changes represent a tendency to conform Luke's text to the liturgical usage of the churches. A few late manuscripts replace 'thy kingdom come' with 'thy Holy Spirit come upon us and cleanse us'. B. H. Streeter (p. 277) argued that this is a Lukan interpretation of Matthew's more original phrase. A. R. C. Leaney (pp. 60f., 68) ventures that 'the form may be derived from the Lord himself'. But the emphasis upon the Holy Spirit is a marked tendency of Lukan elaborations elsewhere. In any case the manuscript evidence is too scanty to regard this reading as original. See on 3 : 16.

3f. daily (*epiousion*)**:** perhaps 'day by day'. Cf. Black, pp. 203-7. However, the context of the prayer favours 'bread for the morrow' (margin), i.e. the morrow of the kingdom of God (cf. Origen. *On Prayer*, 27 : 13; Jeremias, *Prayer*, pp. 23ff.). If so, the appeal, 'the morrow's bread continue giving us each day', refers to the 'kingdom of God' powers now being mediated from the exalted Jesus. Luke's interpretation shifts the emphasis from the future to the present manifestation of the kingdom. It has affinities with the Gospel of John (4 : 32; 6 : 35) and, like John, reflects upon the 'manna' of the Christian's 'wilderness' journey. Cf. K. Stendahl, *PC*, p. 778; *SEA*, 22-23, 1957-8, 81f.; *MM*, pp. 242f.; T. W. Manson, *BJRL* 38, 1955-6, 111; R. F. Cyster, *Theology* 64, 1961, 378f.

bread: probably the messianic feast was originally in mind (cf. 14 : 15; 22 : 30).

for we forgive: not the ground upon which God bestows forgiveness but that upon which man can receive it (Manson; cf. Mt. 5 : 23f.; 6 : 12, 14).

into temptation: i.e. of God (Exod. 17 : 7 LXX; Ac. 5 : 9; 1 C. 10 : 9; Heb. 3 : 9) and/or a severe testing (*peirasmos*) by Satan resulting in one's destruction. Thus the explanatory addition in Mt. 6 : 13 follows: 'but save us from the evil one' (*NEB*). R. E. Brown (*TS* 22, 1961, 205) thinks that originally it referred to the final battle between God and Satan. Cf. Rev. 3 : 10. But, if so, again Luke has shifted the eschatological reference (11 : 3); see on 8 : 13; 22 : 40; cf. 1 C. 10 : 13; 2 Pet. 2 : 9; *SBK* on Mt. 6 : 13; K. G. Kuhn, *SSNT*, pp. 108-13.

5-13. The scene is a Palestinian village hut. To get bread at midnight would arouse the whole, sleeping family. The request is outrageous. 'Which of you' would ask such a thing (5)? Yet persistence is rewarded (cf. 18 : 1ff.). How much more rewarded is persistent prayer for the gifts of the new age, i.e. the Holy Spirit.

13. evil: i.e. imperfect in motive and act. Innate human sinfulness is for Jesus a basic presupposition. See on 13 : 1–9; 18 : 9–14.

Holy Spirit: Matthew has 'good things'. In rabbinical writings this term signifies the gifts of the messianic age to come (Jeremias, *Parables*, p. 145). Given Luke's emphasis upon the Holy Spirit, it is more likely that he *pesher*-s the original 'good things' to the post-Pentecost reality. Cf. Ac. 2 : 38; 19 : 2–6; Rom. 8 : 15f.; 10 : 15. See above, pp. 7ff., 10. S. S. Smalley suggests that 'Spirit, Kingdom and Prayer in Luke–Acts' (*NoT* 15, 1973, 64) are 'closely related at important moments in the progress of the salvation history'. Cf. 1 : 13; 3 : 21f.; 11 : 9; 12 : 32; 24 : 49ff.

EXORCISM: SIGN OF THE NEW AGE **11 : 14–28**

For the literary form see on 5 : 17–26. Jesus' exorcisms raise two questions that represent the general reaction of his opponents. Some attribute his power not to God but to Satan. Others reject exorcism as a sign. They want a 'sign from heaven'. This and the following episodes give Jesus' answer to these attitudes.

The allusion of the contest between Moses and Pharaoh's magicians points to the true meaning of Christ's exorcisms. They are 'by the finger of God' and signal that the messianic war has begun. The Prince of Light is the 'stronger one', who by his exorcisms 'overcomes' the power of darkness (21f.). Therefore, this is a time for decision. Anyone who fails to commit himself to Jesus' 'kingdom of God' mission 'is against me'. By implication he is like Pharaoh's magicians who according to Jewish tradition served the demonic powers. Cf. *Sanh.* 67b; *Exod. R.* 18 : 7.

Luke appends two further sayings (24–28) that explain this sober warning. First, the experience of the kingdom powers demands a firm commitment to the kingdom message, i.e. 'the Word of God'. The person who fails to respond to this demand is like a man freed from one demon only later to fall victim to a host of them (cf. Heb. 6 : 4ff.). Second, the real blessedness is not the passing joy of a mother whose son is a famous healer but the abiding joy of those who 'hear' his kingdom message and 'keep' it.

14f. dumb (*kōphon*): see on 4 : 33. The same affliction may originate from a divine (1 : 20), natural (Mk 7 : 32), or demonic source.

15. some: i.e. the churchmen and theologians. Cf. Mt. 12 : 24; Mk 3 : 22.

by Beelzebul: i.e. Satan. In effect they accuse Jesus of being possessed by a demon. Cf. 8 : 33; Jn 10 : 20. Because a prophet's words or acts are so startling or bizarre, they sometimes may create an impression that he is mentally unbalanced. Cf. 2 Kg. 9 : 11; Ac. 2 : 13; 26 : 24; 1 C. 14 : 23; Jos. *War* 6, 5, 3. The fact is, of course, that he communicates a reality to which the 'normal' world is deaf and blind (cf. Jn 9 : 39ff.).

16. See on 9 : 9. Cf. Jn 6 : 26, 30.

19. your sons: cf. Jos. *Ant.* 8, 2, 5. They condemned in Jesus what they practised themselves.

20. by the finger of God: Mt. 12 : 28 has 'spirit of God'. Luke doubtless is giving the more original wording (see on 11 : 13). In all likelihood it is Jesus' own phrase by which he defines his mission in terms of the Exodus (Exod. 8 : 19), as he does elsewhere. See on 6 : 17–49; 9 : 10–17. The eschatological presence of the Spirit is the presence of the kingdom. See on 10 : 1–20; cf. Barrett, p. 144n.

has come (*ephthasen*): see on 10 : 9, 11; above, pp. 13ff.

22. one stronger: a (probably) pre-Christian writing prophesied similarly concerning a coming messianic priest: 'Beliar (= Beelzebul) shall be bound by him, and he shall give power to his children to tread upon the evil spirits' (*Test. Levi* 18 : 12). See on 4 : 31–44; 10 : 18f.; 11 : 29–36; cf. Rev. 20 : 2; Isa. 53 : 12.

26. other spirits: see on 8 : 30.

28. Blessed: see on 10 : 23.

THE REAL 'SIGN' IN JESUS' MINISTRY **11 : 29–36**

Closely bound to the foregoing piece, this episode answers the second question raised there (11 : 16) and accents the same conclusion. The sign of Jesus' messiahship, like the sign of Jonah, is the message he brings and the power in which it is manifested (cf. 7 : 21ff.; Jn 2 : 18ff.). The passage falls into two parts, one directed to opponents and the other to disciples. The 'sign' character of Jesus' mission is a proclamation of 'judgment' upon an evil

and rejecting generation (29–32; cf. 11 : 23). Also, it is an admonition to his disciples to 'be careful' that they rightly receive and
manifest the light of the kingdom message (33–36; cf. 11 : 28).

'Signs' are not in themselves evil. Indeed, they are to be
expected and, when given, to be received (cf. 1 : 36; 2 : 12;
7 : 20ff.). If the 'request for signs is regarded in the Gospel tradition as of diabolical origin' (Barrett, p. 91), it is because the request
usually arises from curiosity or to entrap Jesus (4 : 3ff., 23; cf.
9 : 9).

The 'greater' thing present in Jesus is the Holy Spirit as the
power and presence of the inbreaking new age. This is the true
and adequate 'sign'. Those who accepted the divine character of
lesser manifestations of the Spirit in Solomon and Jonah will
condemn the 'generation' rejecting his unique and climatic work
in Jesus.

A Special Note on Light and Darkness **11 : 33–36**

These terms are used virtually universally for the contrast of joy
and sorrow, good and evil. Occasionally in the Old Testament
light denotes the coming messianic salvation and the ethical
change that God's word effects in men. Cf. Isa. 49 : 6; 60 : 18ff.;
Ps. 119 : 130. The ideas are present also in the Qumran writings
(cf. H. Conzelmann, *TDNT* vii, 431f.). The elect are the 'children
of light' who are guided and helped by an angel or 'prince of
lights' and opposed by an angel of darkness (1QS 3 : 17ff.; CD
5 : 18; cf. Dan. 10 : 13; R. E. Brown, *SSNT*, pp. 187ff.). According to this sect the children of God are enlightened by God's law
and the revelation of God's mystery (1QS 11 : 2f., 5; 1QH 4 : 6).
They walk in 'the ways of light' (1QS 3 : 20), and have as their
goal to stand 'in the glow of the Perfect Light . . . where no
darkness is' (1QH 18 : 29; cf. Jn 1 : 5ff.).

The Old Testament and such groups as the Qumran Community are the primary background of the New Testament's use
of these concepts. The 'power of darkness' (22 : 53) both in
Qumran and in the New Testament is a created evil spirit. Unlike
Qumran, in the New Testament the 'prince of lights', i.e. the
leader and guide of the 'sons of light' (16 : 8), is not an angel but
is God himself or Messiah. Cf. 2 : 32; 2 C. 6 : 14f.; Jas 1 : 17. Both
Jesus and other bearers of the gospel message are 'lights' (Jn

12 : 46; Ac. 13 : 47). To receive their kingdom message is to be enlightened to the Christian mystery (Eph. 3 : 9; Heb. 10 : 32), to pass from darkness into light (Col. 1 : 12f.; 1 Pet. 2 : 9), to become through faith children of light. Apparently the Holy Spirit is viewed as the present mediator of this light. Thus to walk in Christ or in the Spirit or in the light means the same thing. Cf. 2 C. 3 : 17f.; 4 : 6; Gal. 5 : 16; Col. 2 : 6 *AV*; Eph. 5 : 8; 1 Jn 1 : 7. To walk in the light is the test of true discipleship. For some temporary believers are enlightened, and experience the powers of the new age only to fall away, sometimes subverted by Satan disguised as 'an angel of light. (8 :12; 2 C. 11 : 14; Heb. 6 : 4).

These concepts and images have a bearing on the present passage. The warning in the previous episode continues (11 : 24ff.). The 'generation' that fails to appreciate the 'greater thing' in Jesus' ministry will be condemned. It will include some who, like the men of Qumran, profess to have been 'enlightened' (35). Whether in a useful lamp or a 'sound eye' or in salvation, the test of a true enlightenment is the effect it produces. Some of Jesus' hearers and disciples are deceived. Luke regards this warning to be no less appropriate for his Christian readers. See on 16 : 1–13.

29f. The form of the saying is a prophetic oracle. Matthew (12 : 40) compares Jonah's deliverance from death to the Lord's resurrection. Luke places the 'sign' emphasis fully upon the warning of judgment and the eschatological presence of the Spirit. But cf. 16 : 31.

sign of Jonah: probably connected with verse 31f., i.e. with the *parousia*. As Jonah did, Jesus will return from the dead to execute judgment. See on 13 : 34; cf. J. Jeremias, *TDNT* III, 408ff.; A. Votgle, *SS*, pp. 267ff., 272f.

generation: see on 21 : 32.

31f. wisdom: see on 11 : 49–51.

something greater (*pleion*): the neuter form rules out a reference to Jesus; probably it refers to the Spirit in his eschatological function. See on 10 : 1–20.

arise . . . with (*meta*): Jesus may anticipate the death of his generation before the time of the last judgment. Contrast 21 : 10 (*epi*); Ps. 93(94) : 16 LXX (*epi*); but see Jeremias, *Nations*, p. 50; Black, p. 134, who takes it as a Semitic idiom: 'dispute with'.

32. repented: see on 13 : 3.

33–36. Luke appends several independent sayings that have been collected under the catchword 'light'. Cf. 12 : 35; see on 16 : 1–13.

ALAS FOR THE CHURCHMEN AND THEOLOGIANS II : 37–54

Structure. Luke's fourth 'dinner episode' follows a pattern noted earlier (see on 5 : 17–26). The story proper (37–41, 53f.) is peculiar to Luke. It is supplemented by sayings from 'Q' (42–52) that interpret and reinforce the teaching at the dinner.

Teaching. Foregoing the ceremonial washing was like omitting the blessing. It arched the eybrows of the Pharisee. By his calculated action Jesus sets the stage for the question he desires to answer. What really makes a man religiously clean? It is not the externals, 'the cup and the platter', that are important but rather the inward man's actions, 'justice and the love of God' (41). Cf. Mk 7 : 14ff.; Ps. 51 : 17ff.; Rengstorf. The sin that brings Christ's startling rebuke is hypocrisy. Outwardly religious, the Pharisees at heart are full of greed 'and wickedness'. In short order they verify Jesus' charge, 'laying snares to catch him with his own words' (54, *NEB*).

The six woes (Matthew 23 has seven) reveal the appalling condition of many religious leaders of the time. The churchmen observe only the forms of religion and itch for the praise of men. By their example they succeed only in defiling men who, not aware of their deceit, emulate them (cf. Mt. 23 : 15). Equally guilty are the religious lawyers or theologians. By false interpretations of Scripture they create intolerable religious burdens. They honour the dead prophets but 'kill and persecute' the 'prophets and apostles' now among them. Luke climaxes the series with the most damning indictment: their perverse influence has led the people to reject Jesus' message and, thereby, has deprived them of the 'knowledge' of salvation (52). Cf. Mt. 23 : 13; Mt. 16 : 19.

Jesus had in mind the leaders of a rejecting Judaism, and this doubtless is Luke's primary intent. But there is also an implicit reference to Christians. For the early Church was not without leaders who for the sake of traditional dogma (or novel theory) perverted the gospel message. See on 1 : 4; 12 : 41–48; 20 : 45– 21 : 4; cf. Ac. 15 : 1, 10.

37, 43. Pharisees ('separated ones'): i.e. churchmen. They
were an influential politico-religious party that advocated a
segregated Jewish culture, looked for a political Messiah, and
stressed strict adherence to rabbinical interpretations of the Old
Testament. See on 11 : 45.

39f. fools: i.e. 'foolish men' or 'Have you no sense?' (Phillips).
The rabbis also recognized the inadequacy of external religion
(*SBK*). Thus, the Pharisees cannot but assent to Jesus' pointed
question.

39, 41. those things: perhaps the contents 'within' the dinner
cups, contents that the Pharisees have gained through 'extortion'.
Cf. Geldenhuys; Grundmann; 19 : 8.

42. woe or 'Alas': denotes a grieving giving up to judgment
(cf. Arndt). The threefold repetition (42–44, 45–52) may indicate
an emphatic finality (cf. Rev. 8 : 13).

44, 52. Each series of woes builds to a climax. The worst
offence of both groups is to divert the people from the truth of
God in the message of Jesus. Cf. 1*QH* 4 : 11 ('drink of knowledge').

45, 52f. lawyers, scribes, and 'doctors of the law' are virtually
equivalent terms referring to theologians, i.e., experts in the Torah
or religious law. Most of them were Pharisees. See on 5 : 17;
10 : 25; 20 : 46f. The more general term, Pharisee, designated the
practical religionist or 'churchman'. Cf. Jeremias, *Jerusalem*, pp.
246–67 for the role of the Pharisees in Jewish society.

A Special Note on the Christian Prophet **11 : 49–51**

This oracle occurs with minor variations in Mt. 23 : 34–36. It
appears here as a quotation introduced by the formula, 'the
Wisdom of God said'. Usually the phrase is taken to mean 'God
in his wisdom said' (Creed) or to refer to the title of a lost apocryphal book (Bultmann). It may be, however, that the meaning of
this strange expression is to be found elsewhere.

In the literature of later Judaism Wisdom and Spirit became
virtual personifications of God in action in the world. The two
terms are identified in the Wisdom of Solomon (cf. *CAP* on Wis.
9 : 17). Apparently they are viewed as 'aspects in Yahweh, hypo-
statized as his forms of revelation' (Ringgren, p. 168). W. D.
Davies (pp. 155–8) has shown that in the early Church Paul
identified the exalted Jesus with the Wisdom of God. But he

doubts that this equation was made by Jesus in his pre-resurrection ministry. However, in Lk. 11 : 31 Jesus contrasts the Holy Spirit's eschatological role in his mission with the natural wisdom of Solomon. And probably the (divine) wisdom in Lk. 7 : 35 also refers to the eschatological mission and message of Jesus. Elsewhere in Luke–Acts wisdom is identified with the Holy Spirit or with a gift of the Spirit (see on 21 : 14f.).

Paul similarly identifies the 'wisdom of God' with the Spirit-imparted message of the kingdom of God as well as with Christ, the chief actor in God's drama of salvation. For Paul wisdom also is an eschatological gift of the Spirit. Cf. 1 C. 1–2; 12 : 8; Eph. 1 : 17; 3 : 10; cf. Schlatter, *Matthäus*, p. 419; Rev. 5 : 12; U. Wilckens, *TDNT* VII 515f., 523.

The above observations show that in early Christian usage the phrase, 'the Wisdom of God said,' may not have been much different from 'the Holy Spirit says' or 'the Lord says'. The latter formulas were used by early Christian prophets when interpreting Old Testament passages and citing their own revelations (Ac. 21 : 11; 2 C. 6 : 17; Rev. 1 : 8; cf. Heb. 3 : 7).

The present saying occurs in Matthew as a prophecy of Jesus concerning his own followers. When compared with similar passages, the impression is confirmed that the reference of the prophecy is not to former prophets but to early Christians. They are those 'crucified', 'scourged in your synagogues', and 'persecuted from city to city' Cf. 12 : 11; Mt. 10 : 17, 23, 41f.; Ac. 26 : 11; 1 Th. 2 : 14; Rev. 18 : 20–24. Luke's text also implies this when it classifies the victims as 'prophets and apostles' (cf. 1 Th. 2 : 15; Tatian, *Diatessaron* 41 : 1). This is true even though the order is unusual (cf. Eph. 2 : 20; 3 : 5).

Assuming Matthew and Luke derive this saying from a common Q tradition, there can be little doubt that the formula, 'the Wisdom of God said', was in the source. Luke's addition of it is incomprehensible. But Matthew's omission of it is quite understandable if the saying was received as a word of the Lord. The Christian reference of the prophecy and the introductory formula both argue that the passage was not an Old Testament or Jewish testimony to Messiah (Harris, p. 62) or simply one among many sayings of Jesus. Rather, in its present form it arose in a Christian context and probably is to be traced to a Christian prophet or group of prophets.

Christian prophets are not very prominent in the New Testament. Yet there is evidence that they constituted a distinct order in the early Church, an order that remained significant into the second century. Cf. Ellis, pp. 107–12; 'The Role of the Christian Prophet in Acts', *AHG*, pp. 62–7. Eus 3, 37, 1; K. Aland, *JTS* n.s. 12, 1961, 39–49; J. G. Davies, *JTS* n.s. 14, 1963, 105f. Their gift was second only to apostleship, and it is not improbable that they exercised a correspondingly important function in the life of the Church (1 C. 12 : 28f.; Mt. 10 : 41f.). One of their number, John the Prophet, transmitted oracles of the risen Jesus to churches in Asia (Rev. 1 : 9ff.; 22 : 6, 9). Also, some Old Testament *testimonia* in the New Testament appear to have been shaped and cited originally by Christian prophets. (In the light of Eph. 3 : 5f.; 1 C. 13 : 2; and Col. 1 : 26f. it is just possible that the prophetic writings in Rom. 16 : 25f., through which are 'made known' to the Gentiles the 'mystery' which before was 'kept secret' but is 'now' 'disclosed', refer to Christian writings or elaborations of Old Testament texts. Cf. 1 Pet. 1 : 10f.; Rev. 10 : 7, 11.) All in all, it is not unlikely that the Christian prophet played a much greater literary role in the earliest Church than hitherto has been suspected.

The present passage seems to be best understood as an oracle from the exalted Jesus, or, more likely, a saying from his pre-resurrection ministry '*pesher*-ed' and given detailed application by a Christian prophet to the judgment on 'this generation' in the siege and destruction of Jerusalem (AD 66–70). Such an interpretation explains not only the structure and reference of the saying but also its authoritative status in the Gospel tradition. Moreover, it accords with Luke's considerable interest elsewhere in the phenomenon of contemporary prophecy. See above, p. 28; on 13 : 34f.; 21 : 20–24; cf. Ac. 2 : 17f.; 11 : 28; 15 : 32; 19 : 6; 21 : 9f. Finally, this view of the passage is especially relevant for understanding Matthew's (23 : 35) phrase, 'Zechariah son of Barachiah'.

Usually commentators identify Zechariah as the son of Jehoiada whom Matthew and (?) the Targum on Lam. 2 : 20 (cf. Mc-Namara, pp. 160–3) confused with the author-prophet (2 Chr. 24 : 21; Zech. 1 : 1; cf. Leaney). Thus, Abel-Zechariah, an obvious chronological bracket, encompasses all the righteous victims in the Old Testament from Genesis (4 : 10) to 2 Chronicles, the book placed last in the Hebrew Bible. But it is strange that Jesus (or the

'Q' tradition) should limit the guilt to 'canonical' murders, especially since he singles out John the Baptist elsewhere as a prophet-martyr and predicts a similar fate for himself and his disciples (cf. Mt. 17: 12; Mk 10: 39). A better solution, which fits the Christian reference of the prophecy and also concurs with Matthew's identification, is yet another 'Zechariah son of Barischiah' (or Baris) who was murdered in the temple courts AD 67–68 (Jos. *Wars*, 4, 5, 4; so, Wellhausen, pp. 118–23; E. Meyer, I, 234ff.; Grundmann; cf. Creed). The crimes against the righteous continue right down to the final destruction that God brings upon the rejecting generation in AD 70.

This understanding of Luke's quotation does not necessarily mean that it is less 'authentic'. Granting the prophet's credentials, the saying is as genuine a word of the Lord as a *verbatim* saying from the pre-resurrection ministry. For 'authenticity' has to do with the authority by which a word of Jesus comes to us, not with the ability of scientific historians to give the word a certain ratio of historical probability. Furthermore, this text tells us that the sayings of Jesus sometimes were moulded in a fashion similar to quotations from the Old Testament (cf. Ellis, pp. 139–47). And it gives us a glimpse into the role of the Christian prophet in the formation and transmission of the Gospel tradition. See above, pp. 7ff.; Bultmann, pp. 127f.

A WORD TO WITNESSES AND MARTYRS **12: 1–12**

Structure. The first verse serves as a transition from the previous episode and a general, although vague, setting for the present one. The picture is one of popularity mixed with clandestine opposition. Apart from verse 10 the rest of the passage is in Matthew (10: 26–33) within 'the mission of the Twelve'. Luke has a different headline: Christian witnesses must guard against pharisaical hypocrisy.

Teaching. The sayings are directed to the Church's mission after the resurrection, and Luke so applies them. The passage is remarkably similar to 21: 12–19. As he does there, Jesus anticipates a future time when the veiled 'messianic secret' will be publicly revealed, proclaimed, and known. Then it will be the fate of his followers to suffer for his sake. It will be their mandate to 'acknow-

ledge' him without hypocrisy. Above all they must not deny him.
Cf. 9 : 26; 22 : 61; Rev. 2 : 10, 13. Jesus no longer will be with
them, but God's personal care will be as minute and individual as
the 'hairs' of their heads (cf. 21 : 18). And the Christ-sent Holy
Spirit will enable them to give a faithful and effective confession
(Ac. 2 : 33; Jn 14 : 26; 15 : 26f.).
The theme alternates between encouragement (6–8, 11f.) and
adomonition (1, 4f., 9f.), but the latter is the dominant note. The
awfulness of hypocrisy in a follower of Jesus is seen in its outcome
under trial: apostasy. Without a proper 'fear' of God a person
becomes captive to the fear of men. Thus he is led to say the words
of finality, 'Jesus be cursed' (1 C. 12 : 3). He thereby utterly
denies the Holy Spirit within him and 'blasphemes' the only one
who can mediate God's forgiveness. For this there is no remedy.

1. leaven: i.e. 'yeast' (Phillips): here an influence that cor-
rupts others. Cf. 1 C. 5 : 6.

2. covered . . . revealed: (1) the dynamic effect even of a
secret telling of the gospel or (2) the public nature of the post-
resurrection witness to Jesus' messiahship contrasted with its veiled
proclamation during the pre-resurrection ministry. Cf. 8 : 10, 17;
9 : 21, 36; Ac. 2 : 14; 4 : 31.

4. friends: confidants as well as disciples, and those who will
suffer for his sake. Cf. Jn 15 : 13ff.

5. fear him: not Satan but God who can raise our mortal
bodies from the death power of Satan (Rom. 8 : 11; Heb. 2 : 14)
or give us over 'body and soul' to death in hell. Destruction in hell
is viewed in Matthew (23 : 33) and Mark (9 : 43ff.) as God's
judgment on sin. This also is the meaning here. Cf. *SBK* on Mt.
10 : 28; cf. Mt. 5 : 29f.; Rev. 20 : 12–15; Plummer.
hell (*gehenna*) occurs in a number of Jesus' sayings. It always refers
to the judgment at the last day. The name derives from the 'valley
of Hinnom' (*gē-hinnōm*) on the south and west sides of Jerusalem.
Long used for idolatrous practices, after the reform of Josiah it was
turned into a rubbish dump 'where their worm does not die and
the fire is not quenched' (Mk 9 : 48; cf. Isa. 66 : 24; 2 Kg. 16 : 3;
23 : 10). Thus it came to symbolize eternal punishment, though
not necessarily eternal suffering 'since while the fire is continuous
(through the ever-smouldering rubbish) what is thrown there is
destroyed' (Leaney). Cf. 1*QH* 3 : 19–36. See on 3 : 16f.

6. sparrows: a part of the diet of the poor. Cf. *LAE*, pp. 272ff.

8. Son of man: see on 5 : 24. The mysterious distinction here between 'me' and the Son of man reserves the latter title to Messiah's role in the last judgment (cf. 9 : 26; Mk 14 : 62). This is not to identify Son of man with a third figure but to preserve a certain ambiguity (cf. Kümmel, pp. 45ff.). It is in accord with the refusal of Jesus elsewhere to make open claims to the messianic office (see on 9 : 18–27). In him the eschatological future has become present, but it is a presence that is now 'covered' and 'hidden'. To make it 'known' will be the task of his post-resurrection mission through the Church (cf. 12 : 2). Strangely enough, the Church will do this almost altogether with other terms and images.

10. against the Holy Spirit: in Mark (3 : 29f.) and Matthew (12 : 32) the 'unpardonable sin' is to attribute to demons the Holy Spirit's manifestation in Jesus' mission. In Luke the application is to the Spirit's manifestation in the witnessing Church. C. K. Barrett (p. 106) adopts the patristic interpretation: blasphemy against the Son of man is the forgivable opposition of non-Christians; blasphemy against the Holy Spirit is the unforgivable apostasy of Christians. See special note on 11 : 33–36.

An alternative interpretation is less probable. That is, the Jewish nation (or individuals) which rejects Jesus, the Son of man, is given a second chance after Pentecost. If it again rejects, it sins against the Holy Spirit (in the disciples) and seals its own destruction. Cf. Ac. 2 : 39–41; 3 : 26; 28 : 25ff.; cf. Manson; Conzelmann, pp. 179f.; but see on 19 : 41–44. See on 11 : 14–28; 22 : 57; cf. 2 Pet. 2 : 20.

Yet another form of this saying appears in the apocryphal *Gospel of Thomas* (44): 'Whoever shall blaspheme the Father shall be forgiven, but whoever shall blaspheme the Holy Spirit shall not be forgiven, neither on earth nor in heaven.'

11. rulers and the authorities: probably Gentiles. The phrase apparently is Luke's elaboration and may allude to the experience of Paul. Cf. 21 : 12; Ac. 9 : 15; 24 : 10; 26 : 1. It relates to the post-resurrection mission to the Gentiles and may represent an alteration in wording to that situation (cf. Mt. 10 : 5, 18). However, the rationale for the Gentile mission originates in the teaching of Jesus even though his own (pre-resurrection) ministry was restricted to Jews. Cf. Jeremias, *Nations*, pp. 55–73. See on 21 : 12.

12. will teach: see on 21 : 14f.

GOALS IN LIFE: TO HAVE OR TO LIVE? 12: 13–34

Structure. The request for a ruling on an inheritance becomes the
occasion for a maxim on the true relation between 'living' and
'possessing' (15). The maxim then is illustrated by the parable
(16–20) and, in its positive form (23), applied to the disciples in
the appended sayings (22–34). The whole is brought to a climax
with the admonition that the disciples fix both desire and energy
upon the one true value in life, the kingdom of God. Compare the
similar literary pattern in 10 : 25–37; 13 : 1–9. See below, p. 179.

Teaching. The Lord refuses to fill the traditional rabbinic role of
judge because his mission concerns a more important question,
the question of life itself. Jesus points his hearers (and Luke his
readers) to the importance of priorities in the quest for 'life'. The
foolishness of the rich man lay more in his attitude to life than in
his specific actions. He built his life on great expectations only to
find sudden and bitter disillusionment at the very moment of their
fulfilment. Concentrating on 'my . . my . . . my . . . my . . . my'
(17ff.), he discovered too late that all, even his own being, was a
short-term loan from God. 'This very night you must surrender
your life' (*NEB*). Thinking he was an owner, he found that he
himself was owned. Life does not consist in possessing. Life consists in living, and in losing that one loses all.

For the 'disciples' worldliness presents itself more often in an
anxious attitude than in the overt materialism of the rich man.
'Food and . . . clothing' (22) are not trifles, and the force of Jesus'
saying can be appreciated only when the cupboard *is* bare, or the
coat *is* ragged, or some other life essential *is* missing. Jesus' word is
no Sunday-school motto. It is a hard saying: he speaks to those
who 'hunger now' (6 : 21). Yet life's essentials must not be life's
mission or determine life's attitude: 'seek not . . . nor be of
anxious mind' (29).

The Lord's reasoning is twofold. First, the crows and wild-
flowers testify to God's provision for the most inconsequential
creation-life. To ape the 'seeking' attitude of the pagan 'nations'
shows 'little faith' in God's obviously much greater concern for
his children's need (24–30). Second, the follower of Jesus has been
made aware of a higher goal, the kingdom of God, toward which
his 'seeking' should be directed (31–34). Only in the light of the

kingdom do other life-needs find a proper perspective and fulfilment. For the threat to man's being, which motivates his ceaseless
seeking for material security, is met only in this 'treasure that does
not fail'. See on 18 : 18–34.

13. Teacher: i.e. rabbi. See on 3 : 12.

14. judge: see on 2 : 46. The request is not rejected because he
is an outsider (1 C. 5 : 12f.; 6 : 4) or because his motive is wrong
(cf. 10 : 25f.; 18 : 22f.). It is rather a question of mission. Jesus is
not a social reformer nor an arbiter of personal disputes. For his
society he has only one word: 'repent and follow me' (cf. 9 : 59f.;
13 : 1ff.; see on 20 : 19–26). Even for his followers he enunciates
ethical principles more often than he gives rules for specific situations (cf. 9 : 46ff.).

15. beware . . .: 'Guard against every form of greed' (Arndt.)
life (*zōē*): cf. 4 : 4; 12 : 22f.; see on 9 : 24.

16. a parable: not to show the sinfulness of greed but the
futility of it.

16–20. For a similar attitude and result cf. 1 *Enoch* 97 : 8–10.

20. is required: literally, 'they are requiring'. See on 16 : 9.

21. Like verse 15, the context is an abiding earthly situation in
which one's world ends at death. Decision for the kingdom is in
the face of this threat of death rather than of the imminent end
of the age. This is true also in the second part of the passage (22–
34). The different perspective is not to be understood as Luke's
re-interpretation of a saying of Jesus about the end of the age.
When complemented by the following episode (12 : 35–48), it gives
a true reflection of the two-fold aspect of Jesus' own message. That
is, the demand of the kingdom is equally relevant for those who
die before the last judgment and for those who are living at that
unknown hour.

22. Life (*psychē*) and **body** are parallel terms, the 'self' viewed
from different perspectives. Cf. 1 : 46f.; 12 : 19. See on 9 : 24.
anxious: cf. 9 : 3, 23ff.

32. Fear not: according to W. Pesch (*Bib.* 41, 1960, 33f., 38)
the saying originally was Jesus' word to disciples threatened by
his death and the resultant scattering persecutions' Luke univer-
salized the saying to apply to the daily life of all Christians. See
on 9 : 18–27. This is possible but it is also likely that Luke has a
specific and current crisis in view. See on 12 : 1–12; above, pp.
57ff.

little flock: but with a great destiny. God's reversal of men's status in the age to come is a continuing theme. See p. 187. There may be an allusion to the 'poor of the flock' in Zech. 11 : 11 cf. 13 : 7 *AV.* See F. F. Bruce, *BJRL* 43, 1960–1, 346. See on 19 : 28–44.

your Father: see on 6 : 35; 11 : 2.

33. heavens: see on 6 : 23–25; cf. 12 : 21.

TEACHINGS OF MESSIAH: THE KINGDOM AND THE JUDGMENT
12 : 35–13 : 21

Structure. Although this section is closely related to the preceding one, a number of differences are noticeable. Apart from the last episode, the opponents disappear. The first three episodes are addressed to disciples, the last three to 'multitudes' or synagogue audiences. The present manifestation of the kingdom, so prominent in the previous section, gives way to an almost constant reference to its future revelation in judgment. Instead of the earlier 'king-dom-spirit' motif, judgment becomes the dominant note.

Parables occur in five of the six episodes. They follow a definite Lukan literary pattern in which an introductory saying, question, or incident is illustrated or applied by a concluding parable. E.g., 12 : 35, 36ff.; 12 : 41, 42ff.; 12 : 54–57, 58f.; 13 : 1–5, 6ff.; 13 : 10–17, 18ff.; cf. 11 : 1–4, 5ff.; 11 : 14–20, 21ff.; 12 : 13–15, 16ff. Some parables retain their original or pre-Lukan setting. Others (e.g., 13 : 18–21) appear to be appended by Luke to underline his theme. Parable 'pairs' also frequently occur.

Teaching. At the coming judgment each disciple will be judged according to his faithfulness during Jesus' absence (12 : 35–40, 41–48). Indeed, the fire of the Spirit-carried message already is exercising a judgment among men, sharply dividing them according to their attitude toward the word of Jesus (12 : 49–53). This sign of the Spirit warns of an approaching final judgment (12 : 54–59). In the face of it men have two alternatives, repentance or death (13 : 1–9). In spite of the testing of 'the present time' and the reality of impending judgment, the faithful disciple can find assurance in the knowledge of the inevitable victory of the king-dom of God (13 : 10–21). On this note of encouragement Luke concludes the section.

A WORD TO SERVANTS OF THE ABSENT LORD 12 : 35–40

Structure. Verses 35–38 are peculiar to Luke. Otherwise this and most of the following episode (12 : 41–46) are parallel to Matthew's (24 : 43–51) eschatological discourse. This fact may (or may not) point to the original setting of the sayings, that is, in or near Jerusalem shortly before the crucifixion (cf. 19 : 11–27).

Teaching. The episode addresses Christians generally and stresses the blessedness of the wakeful servant. In the parallel story (12 : 41–48), addressed to Church leaders, the issue is not 'wakefulness' but 'faithfulness'; the note of punishment for unfaithfulness becomes dominant.

Jesus knows that he must leave his disciples. The time of his return remains uncertain (cf. 12 : 38, 46). In this context he gives two parables admonishing his followers to be 'ready' (40, 47) for the returning 'Son of man'. In the parables the master's return is unexpected, like a light switched on in a dark room (cf. 17 : 24). There is no getting ready. So, also speculation about the 'time' or the 'delay' in Jesus' return is of no purpose. A Christian must just take care that when that hour strikes, it finds him faithful. See on 17 : 20.

35. . . . girded: i.e. 'Be ready for action with belts fastened' (*NEB*).
lamps: cf. Mt. 25 : 1ff.
37. awake: cf. 1 Th. 5 : 6; Eph. 5 : 14. The exhortation to wakefulness is a theme of some importance in the New Testament. Such sayings of Jesus may have been used in the instruction of converts. Cf. C. H. Dodd, *NTE*, pp. 106–18; Lövestam, *Wakefulness*, pp. 133–9.
truly: see on 4 : 24.
serve: in Jn 13 : 5 Jesus washes the feet of his disciples. Probably he there enacts a messianic symbolism that is implicit in this parable. The master's 'service' is not true to life and is an allegorical shaping of the story to the application which Christ will give it. Cf. the similar tendency in 12 : 46 ('unfaithful'), 13 : 25ff., 16 : 31.
39. thief: cf. 21 : 34; 1 Th. 5 : 2; 2 Pet. 3 : 10; Rev. 3 : 3; 16 : 15. See on 12 : 21. Cf. Mk 13 : 34–37.
40. Son of man: see on 5 : 24. The parable discloses that the

'coming' of the Son of man is nothing else than the 'returning' of the 'Lord' (35 *AV*; *kurios*), that is, Jesus himself. Cf. 12 : 36, 41ff.

A WARNING TO UNFAITHFUL CHURCHMEN 12 : 41-48

Luke apparently is addressing a situation in which some Christian leaders have become corrupt and despotic, 'lords over God's heritage' (1 Pet. 5 : 2f.). By inserting verse 41 and changing 'servant' to 'steward' (42) he distinguishes and emphasizes the additional responsibility resting upon Christian leaders. They must not only share the alertness of all Christians (12 : 35-40). Above all they must give a faithful performance of the special trust committed to them. If they misuse their trust they will be punished.

'Peter' (41) probably represents the apostles or, to Luke's readers, all Christian elders. These 'stewards' have the potential both of greater reward and of greater judgment (44, 46). The (Evangelist's?) commentary (47f.) on the parable underlines the punishment awaiting the unfaithful steward. This is not merely the Lukan 'judgment' motif (see above, pp. 14f.). It also reflects the actual danger facing the Christian ministry in his time. And his time is the time of the absent Lord, the Church any time and anywhere. See on 17 : 1-10; 20 : 45-21 : 4.

41f. Contrast Mt. 24 : 44f. The alterations apparently change the setting in order to apply the Lord's words to Luke's special situation. See on 18 : 35. The change of audience is an appropriate re-application of the intention of Jesus. Like the crowds (or opponents) in the pre-resurrection mission, the Church and its leadership also are a mixed multitude. Cf. Jeremias, *Parables*, pp. 99, 42. No less than Jesus' first hearers 'Christians' also stand under the judgment of the returning Son of man. And some of them will be put 'with the unfaithful' (46).
Peter: also introduced elsewhere by Luke as the representative disciple (8 : 45; cf. Mk 5 : 31; Cullmann, *Peter*, pp. 23-32). For the practice of answering a question with a question cf. 10 : 26; 18 : 19.

44. Truly (*alēthōs*): see on 4 : 24.
45. delayed: Jesus anticipates an absence of sufficient length for this attitude to evolve. The servants' sin is not in calculating a long absence but in using this as an occasion for unfaithfulness. Cf.

Mt. 25 : 5; Heb. 10 : 36ff.; 1*QPHab* 7 : 9ff. (on Hab. 2 : 3f.).
Similarly, the risen Jesus' warning, 'I come quickly' (cf. 18 : 7f.;
Rev. 3 : 11; 22 : 7), is not a chronological marker but a pointer
to the suddenness of the coming judgment.

46. unfaithful: see on 8 : 12f.

47. In contrast to the punishment in the parable (46) the
application appears to include those who in the end are saved 'as
by fire' (1 C. 3 : 15). The severity of punishment varies in relation
to one's knowledge and position of responsibility (47f.; cf. *SBK*;
Jas 3 : 1).

48. they: i.e. God. See on 14 : 24; 16 : 9. 'Men' is an incorrect
interpolation.

SIGN OF THIS TIME: DIVISION 12 : 49–53

Structure. The episode consists of two oracles (49f., 51f.) concluded
by a commentary based upon Mic. 7 : 6 (53).

Teaching. Christians, Luke implies, can understand their life in the
world only in the context of this prophecy of the Lord. Although
Jesus' followers have the messianic peace, 'peace on earth' does
not exist (see on 10 : 5f.; 19 : 38). The time of the Church is a time
when the Spirit of the absent Lord, like a burning fire, will
accomplish his work of judgment in the hearts of men. In the
mission of the Church, no less than in the pre-resurrection mission
of Jesus, the call for decision is a call for 'division'. And the
demand of the kingdom is such that this division will reach into
the most intimate personal relationships, into 'one house' (cf.
9 : 59; 14 : 26).

Jesus eagerly presses towards his 'baptism', the death-judgment
to which he is ordained. For he knows that out of it will be
kindled the holy 'fire' through which the kingdom of God will
find its consummation.

49. fire: perhaps parallel to 'baptism' (50) and a reference to
God's penal judgment, of which Jesus' death is the first instance
(G. Delling, *NoT* 2, 1958, 109ff.). More probably it is the eschatological outpouring of the Holy Spirit (Grundmann; Geldenhuys)
who will mediate the 'judging' message of the kingdom. While not
to be identified with the fire of the final judgment, it is closely
associated with it (cf. 3 : 16f.).

Jesus does not now cast 'upon the earth' the fire of Elijah or of Sodom. This awaits his glorious manifestation as the revealed Son of man (9 : 54; 17 : 29f.) Rather, he sends the Spirit who will be a fire both to cleanse and to judge (Ac. 5 : 5, 9; 11 : 9, 15f.; 15 : 8f.; cf. 1 C. 3 : 15; 11 : 30). The judging function of the law seems to be paralleled in some measure by the Spirit's mediation of the gospel message (Ac. 6 : 10; 7 : 51; 2 C. 2 : 16; cf. Jn 16 : 8; Rom. 7 : 9ff.).

Compare the similar aprocryphal sayings of Jesus: 'I cast a fire and watch it till it burns'; 'Who is near me is near the fire, who is far from me is far from the kingdom' (*Gospel of Thomas* 9, 82).

50. baptism: Messiah's immersion 'through the eternal Spirit' in the waters of death, ordained as a redemptive judgment for sin (Heb. 9 : 12ff.; cf. Mk 10 : 38, 45).

51. division: a clarification of the original word, 'sword' (Mt. 10 : 34). Cf. 22 : 36ff. 'Division' as much as the mighty works of Jesus (11 : 20) may be evidence of the presence of the kingdom of God. But this is true only if the cause of division is the gospel message. See above, pp. 13ff. Cf. M. Black, *ET* 81 (1969-70), 115-18.

52f. The commentary on the oracle is from Mic. 7 : 6. It apparently was applied elsewhere in Judaism to the time of distress preceding the messianic kingdom. Cf. *Enoch* 100 : 1f.; *Jubil.* 23 : 19; 1*QpMicah* in Barthélemy, p. 79.

henceforth (*apo nun*): see on 22 : 69.

SIGN OF THIS TIME: APPROACHING JUDGMENT 12 : 54-59

Structure. The episode combines two independent traditions (54ff., 57ff.). Apparently Luke appends the second one to explain the meaning of 'the present time' (56). The teaching of the 'paired' parables is disclosed in the last verse (59). See above, p. 179.

Teaching. This 'fateful hour' (56, *NEB*) is the time of an approaching final judgment. Its verdict will rest strictly on *quid pro quo*, 'eye for eye' justice. An obviously guilty party in a legal dispute will settle out of court if he is wise. So guilty man approaching the inevitable judgment of God should settle accounts with that Creditor. For the 'last copper' in that judgment, as the next episode will show (13 : 1-9), is nothing less than his life.

54f. west . . . south: the directions of the Mediterranean Sea and of the Negev desert. A similar weather parable appears at Mt. 16 : 2f.

hypocrites: play-actors who observe the religious forms but refuse to face the real religious issues. Cf. Mt. 15 : 7.

56. time: i.e. season (*kairos*): a word-play. See on 10 : 21.

58f. paid: for the concept of sin as debt cf. 11 : 4. Cf. the judgment context also in Mt. 5 : 21, 25f.

59. I tell you . . .: an application to the final judgment that is merged with the story in the parable. Thus, the saying has a double meaning. See on 14 : 24.

DEMAND OF THIS TIME: THE FRUIT OF REPENTANCE **13 : 1–9**

Structure. The literary pattern occurs frequently in this section. A saying of Jesus (1–5) is illustrated by a following parable (6–9). The two incidents occur in Jerusalem (1, 4), and it is probable that the Lord's admonitions were delivered before a Galilean (synagogue?) audience there. (Note the parallelisms: 'Galileans . . . you', 'offenders in Jerusalem . . . you'; 13 : 2f., 4f.). It is less certain that the warnings concern the future destruction of the city in AD 70 (Creed; cf. Kümmel, p. 48. See on 19 : 45–20 : 18; 21 : 20–24). Although the connected parable appears to point in that direction, the saying applies equally well to the final judgment before which all men stand. Indeed, the preaching of Jesus here is reminiscent of the Baptist (3 : 8f.).

Background. J. Blinzler (*NoT* 2, 1958, 32) places the massacre of the Galileans at the Passover preceding the crucifixion when, according to Jn 6 : 4, Jesus was absent from Jerusalem. This assumes a questionable chronological arrangement in the episodes of the Fourth Gospel. But it is probable that the incident did occur at the time of the Passover 'sacrifices' and in connection with an attempted revolt. The massacre is not reported in other sources. But Galileans were known to be fond of sedition (Jos. *Life* 17). And the severe reaction is characteristic of Roman rule in Palestine (cf. Jos. *Ant.* 17, 9, 3; 18, 4, 1f.).

Teaching. In the Gospels Jesus does not speak to the question of original sin. However, in this saying he assumes the universality of sin and of death as its consequence. In every death, whether an accident at 'Siloam' or an execution by Pilate, the funeral bell 'tolls for thee'. Hear its warning and 'repent'! Just as an unfruitful tree sooner or later is cut out of the orchard, so the judgment of God comes at length upon those who never bring forth the fruit of repentance (cf. 12 : 13–21). For Jesus the 'parable of the extra year' probably concerned God's final hour of patience toward an obstinate Jewish nation. See on 13 : 34f.; 19 : 41–44; 21 : 20–24. The warning concurs with those elsewhere in which the kingdom of God is given to the Gentiles (13 : 28f.; 20 : 16; cf. Mt. 21 : 43). Luke and his readers would properly apply the lesson to all who hear the gospel message.

1. told: as news. Presumably Jesus was not in Jerusalem at the time.

mingled: i.e. the two events occurred at the same time and place. It is a rhetorical expression. Cf. *Exod. R.* 19; *SBK* II, 193; J. Blinzler, *NoT* 2, 1958, 28f.

3. repent: see on 3 : 8; 15 : 7. 'The prevalence of sin in all men is, for Jesus, a self-evident element in his view of man, even if it is not dogmatically formulated' (Kümmel, *Man*, p. 19).

4. Siloam: perhaps near the pool of Siloam near the south wall of Jerusalem.

6. vineyard: sometimes a symbol of the nation Israel. If so here, the thought is that Israel is going to be culled (3 : 8f; cf. Isa 5 : 1–7). It may be, however, that the single tree represents the nation. Cf. Hos. 9 : 10; Jl 1 : 7; Rom. 11 : 17ff. Some allegorical elements appear in Jesus' parables but, like the subtle features of a painting, they are more in the nature of hints than of precise equations, more susceptible to feeling than analysis (cf. 20 : 16). See on 8 : 11–15.

8. this year also: judgment is past due, but God's mercy holds it in abeyance.

THE INEVITABLE VICTORY OF THE KINGDOM OF GOD 13 : 10–21

Structure. Both the 'synagogue' setting and the literary form are reminiscent of healings in the Galilean mission (see on 5 : 17–26). Why is this act of Messiah (10–17) abruptly introduced into the 'teachings' section? The attached parables and the conclusion of the story (17) suggest that Luke is not using the incident as a witness to Jesus' messiahship (see above, p. 146). It serves rather to illustrate the powers of the kingdom.

Teaching. In Jesus' mighty works the coming kingdom already was being manifested (10 : 1–20; 11 : 29–36). Although this caused division (12 : 49–53), the Lord 'reduced his opponents to shame' (Phillips), and 'the people rejoiced'. The point of the story is the victory of the impending kingdom over the opposition of men and 'Satan'. It is reinforced and developed by the appended pair of parables (19–21). A tiny 'seed' or a bit of yeast produces a very great effect. So, also, the minute manifestations of the kingdom powers—a healing here, a conversion there—will produce in the end a very great result.

In this result the true meaning of the 'Sabbath' will be fulfilled. From the beginning the Sabbath was prophetic of the consecration of creation to its good and proper end (cf. Heb. 4 : 4–10; Grundmann). This will be accomplished by the deliverance of God's creation from Satan's power. The Sabbath controversies related earlier point to Messiah's *authority* over the Sabbath (6 : 1–11). This story presents Messiah's teaching about the *meaning* of the Sabbath.

10. synagogues: a healing in this setting probably was a deliberate device of Jesus. The resulting opposition gives an occasion for a 'teaching word' (cf. Daube, p. 181; see on 4 : 16).

11–16. Luke projects a graphic word picture of each character: the woman, the president of the synagogue, the Lord. See on 7 : 36–50.

11. spirit of infirmity: apparently a purely physical effect caused by demonic power and not 'demon possession' of the personality. See on 4 : 33, 38f.; 8 : 2; cf. 2 C. 12 : 7; DSS *Gen. Apocryphon* 20 : 21–29. Cf. 7 : 21; 8 : 2 where persons are 'healed' of evil spirits. Demonic activity is equated with the activity of Satan.

13. hands: see on 4 : 40; 5 : 13.

14, 16. ought . . . ought: the synagogue president goes back to Sinai (Exod. 20 : 9), Jesus to creation (see above).

14f. ox: the Qumran sectarians were stricter Sabbatarians than the Pharisees. Their Sabbath rules applied even to a suffering animal or to a man whose life was endangered. Cf. K. Schubert, *SSNT*, pp. 127f.; see on 6 : 1–11; 14 : 5f.; cf. *SBK*.

15. hypocrites: see on 12 : 56.

16. daughter of Abraham: see on 19 : 9.

18ff. The parables do not teach a gradual growth of an earthly kingdom in the Church. The point is that insignificant 'seeds' will produce a very great effect. To judge from the earlier episodes of the section the *parousia* victory probably is the ultimate effect in view (cf. Kümmel, pp. 128f.). The parables occur separately in the apocryphal *Gospel of Thomas* (20, 96).

19. birds: This may be a hint that the kingdom will be given to the Gentiles. In the imagery of Dan. 4 : 20ff. birds represent the nations. See on 13 : 29; cf. Plummer.

TEACHINGS OF MESSIAH: WHO WILL ENTER THE KINGDOM?
13 : 22–16 : 13

Structure. Like the preceding section, the episodes frequently follow a prescribed literary pattern. To an incident or saying is appended a concluding, explanatory parable. The main point of the episode usually lies in the appended material. Cf. 14 : 15ff., 34f.; 15 : 11ff. Compare also the appended allegory in 13 : 25ff. In 13 : 34f. the conclusion is an oracle. And the form can be reversed: a parable is followed by a concluding, explanatory saying in 16 : 1–13.

Teaching. Both this and the following section contain selected episodes that answer the question, 'Who receives the kingdom of God?' Broadly put, the answer is, 'Not whom you think'. Jesus teaches that between this age and the next a principle of reversal is operative. Many now 'first' shall then be 'last'. Those now exalting themselves will be 'abased'. But those humbling themselves in repentance will, like the prodigal, be exalted. Cf. 13 : 30; 14 : 11, 24; 15 : 21f.; 1 : 51–53; 6 : 20–26.

Three of the episodes apply this motif pointedly to proud, religious Judaism. These churchmen are 'the rejected-seekers' (13 : 22–30), 'the excluded guests' (14 : 1–24). And theirs is 'the Godforsaken city' (13 : 31–35). Similarly, the unforgiving 'elder brother' represents the religious Jew who will not recognize God's acceptance of 'the repentant sinner' (15 : 1–32). The disciples of Jesus also are included in these warnings of rejection. 'Three-quarter discipleship' (14 : 25–35) will not suffice to inherit the kingdom. And disciples who do not show 'faithfulness' in this life cannot expect to enter the life of the age to come (16 : 1–13).

Parallel but subordinate to the rejection motif is the positive side of the coin. In contrast to religious Judaism the despised Gentiles and the rejects and prodigals of Israel will repent and find forgiveness. With all wholehearted and faithful disciples they will take their place in the kingdom of God. Cf. 13 : 29; 14 : 21, 23, 26; 15 : 32; 16 : 9.

THE REJECTED SEEKERS 13 : 22–30

Structure. The episode contains four parts, the initial question and answer (22–24), an appended prophetic allegory (25–27) and judgment scene oracle (28f.), a concluding saying (30). A number of parallel sayings occur in Matthew. But only the oracle and the conclusion are sufficiently alike to suggest an immediate common source. Cf. Mt. 7 : 13, 22f.; 25 : 11f.; 8 : 11f.

Teaching. The allegory and oracle (25–29) are a commentary on the rejected seekers (24). The setting is the messianic feast at the consummation of the age. Jesus is the host and the seekers call him Lord. They 'ate and drank' with him once, and listened to him preach. They have a right to be there. Yet they are 'thrust out'. Even more galling, Gentiles from 'east and west, north and south' take their place.

The episode teaches that the time of the joyous fulfilment of the kingdom, the messianic feast, also will be a time of judgment. And the judgment will reveal surprising reversals. Many 'first' in this age then will be 'last'. Originally Jesus' prophecies referred both to his opponents and to the Jewish masses who made no ultimate commitment to him. By his conclusion (30) Luke appears to broaden the application to all followers of Jesus who do not strive to enter 'the narrow door' (cf. 2 C. 13 : 5; 2 Pet. 1 : 10).

22. On the journey reference see above, pp. 147ff.

23. few: see on 14 : 25–35; cf. 1 C. 9 : 24ff. The Jewish theologians were divided on this question. Cf. *SBK.*

he said: characteristically, Jesus does not answer the question directly. Rather he directs the man (and the company) from curiosity about others to concern about himself. Many seekers will not 'enter' the kingdom of God. That is sufficient reason for one to 'strive' for this highest goal.

24. the narrow door: the picture of the 'two ways' is more explicitly formulated in Mt. 7 : 13f. It also is present in the Old Testament and late Jewish writings (Jer. 21 : 8; 4 Ezr. 7 : 3ff., 12f.). It is not a 'spatial' image, i.e. entering the gates of heaven. The contrast is between this age and the age to come ('strive' . . . 'will seek'). The time of division is the last judgment. Cf. Mt. 25 : 32f., 46.

25ff. When: i.e. at the end of the age. The curious mixture of parable and allegory is not unlike some parables in Mt. 25. It may be Christ's own allegorical shaping of the story or, perhaps, a Christian prophet's elaboration of his parable. See on 11 : 49–51; 12 : 37.

27. I tell you: see on 12 : 59; 13 : 35.

depart: the rejected seekers are identified with the enemies of the righteous in Ps. 6 : 8.

28. see: see on 13 : 35.

29. men: i.e. Gentiles. See on 12 : 11.

sit at table: The banquet scene continues from verse 25. Cf. Mt. 25 : 10ff.; Rev. 19 : 9. The Qumran sect had a similar anticipation of a messianic banquet. Cf. 1QSa 2 : 11–22.

30. The saying occurs in variant forms in Mk 10 : 31; Mt. 19 : 30; 20 : 16; cf. *Barnabas* 6 : 13.

THE GOD-FORSAKEN CITY **13 : 31–35**

Structure. The incident (31–33), found only in Luke, is followed by a lament (34f.) that recurs in Mt 23 : 37ff. The lament is the sequel to the prophecy concerning Jerusalem in verse 33. The passage clarifies the charge, 'workers of iniquity', made against Messiah's Jewish brothers in the last episode (13 : 27).

Teaching. Jesus will not be deterred by the threats of a third-rate politician. He asserts the priority of his mission: . . . and on the third day 'I reach my goal' (32, *NEB*). The goal is his consecration and enthronement into the messianic office (see below). Knowing that this is to be accomplished through his death, Jesus charts his path under divine necessity. He 'must' meet his appointment in 'Jerusalem'.

In condemning Jesus the obstinate city is true to her age-old character. She affirms with terrible finality the nation's rejection of Messiah. 'You always resist the Holy Spirit' (Ac. 7 : 51), Stephen will say of her. Her sin is not just in killing the 'prophet' Jesus. The oracle stresses the city's repeated rejection of God's messengers. Yet, in the midst of this stringent judgment Messiah's last word is not 'desolate'. One day Jerusalem will 'see' and say, 'Blessed'.

31. hour expresses an important though not necessarily a 'calendar' connection with the previous episode. See on 10 : 21. **here:** the territory of Herod Antipas, i.e. Galilee or Transjordan. Herod's attitude probably arose from fear of another John the Baptist; he disliked any kind of excitement in his realm (Jos. *Ant.* 18, 7, 2). See on 9 : 1–9.

32f. tell that fox: the reply suggests that Herod sent a direct message (cf. 9 : 9). 'Fox' has three possible connotations. It was a negative expression denoting any inconsequential person (*SBK*). It may have meant deceiver. This was the rabbis' opinion of Herod (Daube, p. 191). 'Destroyer' is a third, less likely, possibility (cf. Leaney).

today, tomorrow, and the third day: a Semitic idiom for a short indefinite period followed by an imminent and certain event. 'Today and tomorrow' means simply 'day by day' (Black, p. 206). Cf. Hos. 6 : 2; 1 C. 15 : 4; see on 18 : 33. Conzelmann's (pp. 63, 68) view is less likely. He thinks that for Luke the expression signifies a lengthy journey or the three stages in Jesus' ministry: Galilee, the Journey, Jerusalem (cf. pp. 65, 154n, 197).

third day: Luke's readers undoubtedly would call to mind the Lord's resurrection. This meaning is confirmed by the following word, 'finish'.

finish, i.e. 'be perfected' (*AV*; *teleioō*). The term is used in the Septuagint (e.g., Exod. 29; Lev. 8) of the consecration of priests. In Hebrews (2 : 10; 5 : 9) it refers to Jesus' consecration, through death and resurrection, to his high priestly work. Probably the cultic significance of the word also is present here. See on 24 : 50

go on my way (*poreuesthai*): probably the course of Jesus' whole ministry, and not just the journey to Jerusalem.

prophet: cf. Ac. 3 : 22; 7 : 37. This is the second passion prediction in the central section (cf. 12 : 50). To it Luke adds a third prophecy against Jerusalem (13 : 34f.; see on 23 : 28ff.). On the prophet as martyr cf. G. Friedrich, *TDNT*, vi, 834f.

34. How often. The lament presupposes a repeated ministry of Jesus in Jerusalem. Matthew's location of the passage suggests that it is the despairing conclusion of Jesus shortly before his crucifixion. But it also is possible that in its present form it is his post-resurrection oracle through a Christian prophet. (1) In Matthew it is the conclusion of, and may be an integral part of, such an oracle. (2) The words are reminiscent of the martyrdom of Stephen, who was 'sent' to the people of Jerusalem, who accused them of 'killing the prophets' and announced the desolation of their 'house'. For this he was 'stoned' (Ac. 6 : 3, 13f.; 7 : 47–58). See on 11 : 49–51; 12 : 10; cf. Grundmann. The 'I', then, would include his disciples (cf. Ac. 9 : 4). The tragedy of Jesus (like that of Jeremiah) is that one who loved the nation most deeply had the mission to pronounce its doom.

wings: cf. Ps. 57 : 1; *SBK*.

35. Both this and the preceding episode have Old Testament citations at their core (cf. 13 : 27). In Jer. 22 : 5 (alluded to here?) the 'house' of Israel was the palace; in Jesus' day the nation's centre was the 'temple house'. Thus the citation is applied to the temple (cf. 11 : 51 *AV*; 19 : 46; Ac. 7 : 47).

forsaken: i.e. 'desolate' (*AV*): probably a gloss derived from the Old Testament passage. But it is a proper interpretation. After Messiah's resurrection God's presence moves to a new temple, a 'house not made with hands'. Cf. Ac. 7 : 48; 1 C. 3 : 16f.; see on 19 : 41–44; 23 : 43.

The term occurs in the DSS where it means 'desecrated and polluted' (*4QFlor.* 1 : 5f., 12; cf. 1 Mac. 2 : 12). There also 'the expectation of a new temple is linked with a negative attitude to the existing sanctuary'. It will be a temple that the *Lord* shall make (Exod. 15 : 17), a house 'not made with hands' (D. Flusser, Y. Yadin, IEJ 9, 1959, 95ff., 102). See the special note at 19 : 45–20 : 18.

see: see on 9 : 9. Contrast Mt. 23 : 39 (*ap arti*).

Blessed . . . : from Ps. 118 : 26. According to some rabbinical tradition the Psalm was composed for David's coronation. It was to be recited again at the coming of Messiah (cf. *SBK* 1, 849f., 876). The passage was used in the 'throne of Elijah' ceremony, perhaps with a messianic significance (see on 1 : 57–80).

The prophecy does not refer to the 'triumphal entry' in Luke or in Matthew. In 19 : 38 (q.v.) the cry does not occur in Jerusalem and does not represent the sentiment of the city. The setting

in Mt. 23 : 39 is after the entry. It must be left an open question
whether the prophecy anticipates that Jerusalem will 'see' Jesus
in a future conversion or in a recognition of his Lordship, too late,
in the final judgment. See on 9 : 9, 27; cf. Rom. 11 : 25ff.; Phil.
2 : 10f.

he who comes: See on 7 : 19.

THE CHURCHMEN'S DINNER PARTY—AND A STORY OF EXCLUDED GUESTS 14 : 1–24

Structure. It is not impossible that this dinner episode was transmitted from the beginning as the events of one sabbath. More
probably, however, it is a Lukan 'symposium' that summarizes
Jesus' teachings at a number of such dinner parties. The first
part (1–6) forms the setting to which the other stories are attached.
Luke follows accepted convention in shaping the disparate
elements to a literary unity (cf. X. de Meeûs, *ETL* 37, 1961, 857–
70). The episode consists of a healing (1–6), two precepts (7–11,
12–14), and a concluding parable. As elsewhere, Luke uses the
final parable to apply the episode to his theme. See above, pp.
179, 187; on 7 : 36–50.

Background. It was customary to invite the 'visiting preacher' and
other guests to dinner after the synagogue service (cf. *SBK*). The
fact that the host is a 'ruler' suggests a Jerusalem setting for the
story (cf. Grundmann). The 'watching', the presence of the
theologians (3), and the sudden appearance of the sick man may
indicate that the occasion was staged by the opponents of Jesus.

Teaching. The contrast between the 'invited' guests and the unfortunate intruder provides the theme for the whole episode. The
churchmen display a thoroughly false standard of values. Not only
are they hard-hearted toward the sick man (3f.) but both guests
(7) and host (12) are status-seekers and social climbers. The principles (5, 10, 13) that Jesus enunciates were known and approved
by all. The sting of his words is their utter candour. He undresses
their concealed and half-forgotten motives and lays them naked
on the dinner table. Most embarrassing, he applies the principles
to the churchmen's relation to God.

At the last 'banquet' God will be host. There the proud

'climbers' of this age will be 'abased', and the humble-'poor' with
those befriending them will be 'exalted' (11, 14).

The 'parable of the excluded guests' is directed to this point
(16–24). As the long-invited guests reject the final invitation, so
religious Judaism rejects Jesus' urgent invitation to the messianic
banquet in 'the kingdom of God'. Like the excluded guests, the
churchmen will be replaced at the messianic feast by the social
and religious rejects, 'the poor and maimed' (21ff.).

1. sabbath: on the question of Sabbath healing and for a contrasting literary form see on 6: 1–11.

dine: Luke's sixth dinner episode. Cf. 5: 29; 7: 36; 9: 16; 10: 39;
11: 37; also, 22: 14; 24: 30. Probably the Zacchaeus story is not
to be counted (see on 19: 8).

ruler: a Sanhedrin member who belonged to the Pharisees or a
leader of the Pharisee party. Cf. 24: 20; Jn 3: 1; 7: 48ff. See on
20: 1; 22: 54–62.

3. lawyers: see on 11: 45.

4. let him go: i.e. 'sent him away' (*NEB*). The man was not
a guest. According to a rabbinic 'old wives' tale' dropsy was a
venereal disease, i.e. the result of immorality (cf. Grundmann).

5f. ass: important manuscripts read 'son'. See on 13: 14f.; cf.
BK 5: 6. Jesus argues *a fortiori*: 'how much more' should one
aid a suffering person. This method of argument followed a recognized rabbinical rule, and the theologians present had no ready
answer. For a member of the Qumran sect 'even if a beast drop
its young into a cistern or a pit, he is not to lift it out on the Sabbath' (*CD* 11: 16f. = 13: 22ff. in *CAP* II, 827).

7–11. The parable is based upon Prov. 25: 6f.: 'It is better to
be told, "Come up here", than to be put lower'.

8–10. A different form of the saying occurs in some manuscripts
at Mt. 20: 28. Cf. Black, pp. 171–5. On the guest meal in ancient
Judaism cf. *SBK* IV, 611–39.

11. The reference is to the last judgment. God's name is veiled
by the passive voice. See on 16: 9; cf. 18: 14; Mt. 23: 12.

13. lame, blind: see on 14: 21.

14. repaid: every act has its consequence, i.e. its 'reward' (and
its reward motive). One should act therefore, so as to elicit the
'reward' or response most worthwhile, God's approval in 'the
resurrection of the just'. See on 6: 20–26, 35.

resurrection of the just: some rabbis taught that only the righteous would be resurrected (cf. *SBK*). But this view should not be imputed to Luke, to Jesus, or to Paul. Cf. Ac. 24 : 15; Lk. 10 : 12; 11 : 31f.; Jn 5 : 28f.; Rom. 2 : 5ff.; 2 C. 5 : 10; 2 Tim. 4 : 1. For the New Testament the fact of a 'last judgment' presupposes a resurrection of saved and lost, although only the resurrection of the righteous, qualitatively considered, is a resurrection in the true sense. Cf. 1 C. 15 : 42, 50; Phil. 3 : 11; Heb. 11 : 35 *AV*.

15. eat: at the messianic banquet. It is contemporaneous with the judgment of the 'excluded guests'. See on 13 : 22–30; cf. 22 : 16; Rev. 19 : 9.

16–24. Mt. 22 : 1–10 relates a similar story. Whether it is an independent parable with the same theme or an altered form of this parable (i.e. merged with another parable) is uncertain. The use of the same parabolic theme to teach different truths is frequent in rabbinical writings (Oesterley, pp. 126ff.). See on 15 : 4–7; 19 : 11–27; cf. 12 : 35–40 with Mk 13 : 34–37; X. de Meeûs, *ETL* 37, 1961, 869f.

16. banquet: the question (15) shows that the banquet concerns the great feast that was expected to inaugurate the kingdom of God.

17. To require repeated invitations was a status symbol in Jerusalem society (cf. Manson).

18ff. excuses: cf. 9 : 57–62.

20. come: 'come at all' or, less likely, 'come on time'. On the latter interpretation the parable means, 'Accept Jesus' invitation to the kingdom feast now, or it will be too late'. Cf. E. Linnemann, *ZNTW* 51, 1960, 246–55. See on 13 : 22–30.

21. maimed: the physically blemished were barred from full participation in Jewish worship (Lev. 21 : 17–23). This rule was stressed in the Qumran community (cf. 1*QSa* 2 : 5ff.; *CD* 13 : 4–7).

23. compel: i.e. 'constrain' (*RV*). The intent is to persuade. The man sent a servant not a policeman.

24. you: i.e. the audience of Jesus. The exclusion has less meaning in the parable proper since the guests did not intend to come. The climax is an allegorical reference to the messianic banquet. It is a common literary pattern to end a parable with an application by Jesus. Often the application is fused ambiguously to the parable. Sometimes the pattern is original with Jesus (e.g., 12 : 59; 16 : 31). Sometimes it is appended by the Evangelist or his source (e.g., 14 : 11). Cf. G. Lindeskog, *ST* 4, 1950, 151–65. For this practice elsewhere see on 12 : 46ff.; cf. 15 : 7, 10; 16 : 8f.; 18 : 8, 14; 19 : 26.

THREE-QUARTER DISCIPLESHIP—AND A STORY OF POLLUTED SALT 14 : 25–35

Structure. The first (25–27) and last parts of the passage have partial parallels in Mt. 10 : 37f.; 5 : 13. The coupled-parable (28–33) occurs only here. The conclusion of the first two sayings (27, 33) is illustrated by the final salt parable (34f.).

Teaching. Jesus now extends to the 'multitudes' warnings earlier given the apostles and others (see on 9 : 18–27, 57–62). The passage reflects a period in Jesus' ministry when the shadow of the cross began to loom large. As no prudent man would build a 'tower' or go to 'war' without estimating the 'cost', so no one should assume the responsibilities of discipleship lightly. The lukewarm disciple, like the lukewarm guest (14 : 18ff.) in the end will find himself rejected, thrown out like worthless, polluted salt (cf. Mt. 5 : 13). Jesus' purpose (and Luke's) is not to dissuade the prospective disciple but to awaken the half-hearted follower to the disastrous consequences of his kind of discipleship.

26. hate: hate one's own greater desire for any natural affection (Leaney) or, more likely, utterly subordinate anything, even one's own being, to one's commitment to Jesus. Cf. 16 : 13.

27. bear his own cross: imitate Jesus' own utter commitment in one's discipleship. See on 9 : 23; cf. Phil. 3 : 10. Perhaps it also refers to the literal consequence of following Jesus. But the task is not a rebellion against Rome (as the original audience may have thought) but a witness under persecution. See on 12 : 1–12. **come after:** to follow as a servant in contrast to 'coming to' Jesus for instruction or succour. Cf. 9 : 12; 14 : 26; Mt. 17 : 14f. The terminology may derive from Jesus' role as rabbi or teacher. Cf. Davies, *Sermon*, pp. 422f.; see on 3 : 12.

32. ask terms: see on 12 : 54–59.

THE REPENTANT SINNER: SOURCE OF THE JOY OF GOD 15 : 1–32

Structure. Like the earlier symposium (14 : 1–24) this episode presents several stories under one theme. The arrangement—the

seeking shepherd, the weeping woman, the loving father—possibly
may be drawn from the picture of God's love for Israel in Jer.
31 : 10–20 (cf. H. B. Kossen, *NoT* 1, 1956, 75–80). However, the
coupled parable and other elements of Luke's literary style suggest a different background. Probably the stories of the 'lost sheep'
and 'lost coin' formed one unit (1–10). To this the Evangelist
appended the 'parable of the two sons' to reinforce the theme and
bring it to a climax (see above, pp. 179, 187).

Teaching. The preceding section stressed the urgency of repentance
12 : 54ff.; 13 : 1ff.). This passage reveals its meaning. Repentance
brings joy to the heart of God (3–10) and renewed fellowship
between God and man (11–32). The parables answer a frequent
complaint of the Pharisees that Jesus associates with the wrong
people. 'What man of you', Jesus asks, 'would not rejoice at the
rescue of a lost sheep, or coin, or son? Can you not perceive and
share God's joy at the rescue of a lost man?'

The thrust of the episode is in the last parable. In it the father's
love represents God's attitude toward both religious Judaism (the
elder son) and the non-religious Jew (the prodigal). The meaning
for Luke's readers is simply that God loves the world—the common, mixed-up, moral-immoral, devil-may-care world. Jesus'
mission expresses that love. His joy with 'that gang' is not an
approval of their ethic—it *is* low (13, 15f.). Nor is it a social-work
humanitarianism. His joy is that sinners respond to his message
and, penitent, are brought back into fellowship with God.

Like the elder brother, religious Judaism has a rightful claim to
legitimacy. Also like him it shows its incapacity to forgive on the
basis of mere repentance. The tax collectors may be received only
if they adopt the Pharisaic ethic. They are not sought out with
love (4). Jesus teaches that God requires only simple, genuine
repentance. Those who want God's forgiveness also must forgive
and commune on that basis (17 : 3ff.; 11 : 4).

   1. tax collectors and sinners: see on 5 : 29, 31f.

   2. receives sinners: not to share their evil but to rejoice with
them at their deliverance. See on 15 : 10; cf. 5 : 29; 7 : 34, 47ff.;
19 : 6ff.

   4–7. Only these verses have a synoptic parallel (Mt. 18 : 12–14;
cf. *Gospel of Thomas* 107). This probably is not an instance of two
parables using a similar theme. See on 14 : 16–24. The parallel

derives from one parable that, it appears, Matthew altered and gave a different setting and application.

7. joy: see on 15 : 10.

repents: i.e. turns in true sorrow from sin to God (15 : 21; cf. 18 : 9–14).

righteous: (1) in the Old Testament sense (cf. 1 : 6); (2) in fellowship with God and, therefore, without need of an initial act of repentance (Conzelmann, p. 277f.); (3) an *ad hominem* argument assuming the Pharisees' claim of righteousness. See on 5 : 27–39; 7 : 36–50; 18 : 9.

8. silver coin: a drachma. It was about 60 grains weight and was a (subsistence) day's wage for a labourer. Cf. Mt. 20 : 2; Rostovtzeff, I, 471; Jeremias, *Jerusalem*, pp. 91n, 111, 121f.; see on 15 : 29.

10. joy before the angels: parallel to 'joy in heaven' (15 : 7). It refers to God's joy in company with the angels. Mutual rejoicing at a happy outcome is one theme of the parable (cf. A. F. Walls, *NoT* 3, 1959, 314ff.).

11f. two sons: cf. Mt. 21 : 28ff. Both are essential to the story and it is a mistake to view 15 : 25ff. as a later appendix. The younger son's 'share' would be about one-third of the estate. Cf. Leaney; *SBK*.

12, 21. Father: H. F. D. Sparks (*SG*, p. 250n) rightly notes that the father in the parable is not God. And it is a mistake to allegorize the parable to find a 'universal fatherhood of God'. But the parable does mean that God's love for the lost in Israel is like the father's concern for the prodigal. In the Christian community Luke's readers quite properly would understand this concern to extend to the Gentiles. See on 6 : 35; 11 : 2.

15. feed swine: an accursed lot for a Jew.
pods: to eat them signified the ultimate poverty.

21. against heaven: i.e. against God: see on 6 : 23–25; 16 : 9. Ultimately all sin is sin against God.

24, 32. dead: see on 9 : 60.

29. a kid: worth about one drachma or denarius; cf. j*Ber*. 6, 8(44b). See above on 15 : 8.

30, 32. Note the contrast between 'this son of yours' and 'this your brother'.

31. Son: the marked degree of sympathy for the elder brother, i.e. the Pharisees, may indicate that the parable came fairly early in Jesus' ministry. He does not judge the Pharisees but entreats them to appreciate the meaning of his associations.

32. be glad: forgiveness brings communion and joy. Quite naturally the father gave a party. See on 15 : 10.

FAITHFULNESS: THE BADGE OF ACCEPTABLE DISCIPLESHIP 16 : 1–13

Structure. The story of the prodigal calls forth another parable in which a worldly-wise man makes a prudent use of money entrusted to him. The audience changes to the 'disciples'. Like the preceding piece, the episode is a composite. The 'parable of the clever manager' (1–8) is followed by an exhortation (9–13). In poetic-proverbial form the appended words explain and apply the lesson of the parable. Each part is distinct, but it is not unlikely that they already were joined in the pre-Lukan tradition. The words of exhortation appear to gather around the catchwords, 'mammon' and *adikia* (see on 16 : 9).

Teaching. In the story, a wasteful manager (1), having received notice of dismissal (2), turned his limited talents to an intelligent self-interest (4ff.). For this the Lord 'commended' the manager's astuteness. As the following verses show, the parable is not an example to follow but a 'real life' illustration from which a lesson can be learned. Like the rich man and the judge in following parables (16 : 19; 18 : 6), the manager is not 'dishonest' or unjust' (*AV*; see below) in any special sense. He is just a man who, like all the 'sons of this world', gives first priority to himself and his 'worldly' security.

The Lord exhorts his followers (9–13) to exercise a similar self-interest in securing their goal. They, 'the sons of light', define their purpose of existence no longer as temporal security but as 'eternal habitations', the kingdom of God. They render their service no longer as the self for mammon, but the self for God. In contrast to the 'worldly' manager they achieve their goal through 'faithful' stewardship of material possession, i.e. 'the unrighteous mammon'. Their conduct in these externals—faithful or worldly—indicates whether they in their hearts serve God or mammon. Therefore, it shows whether they will inherit the 'true riches', the kingdom of God. See on 6 : 17–49; 12 : 13–34.

4. houses (*oikous*): see on 16 : 9.

6f. A measure of 'oil' was about 10 gallons, a measure of 'wheat' about 10 bushels (cf. Arndt).

write fifty: the reduction represents the steward's profit in accord with the Palestinian customs of agency and usury. He forgoes his own profit in order to ingratiate himself with the debtors. Cf. J. D. M. Derrett, *NTS* 7, 1960–1, 198–219. J. A. Fitzmyer, *TS* 25, 1964, 34ff.

8. master: i.e. 'Lord' (*AV*): probably Jesus although, like 14 : 24, the verse may be deliberately ambiguous. Cf. 12 : 59; 16 : 31. Several factors favour a reference to Jesus. (1) It accords with the similar pattern of 18 : 6. (2) In Luke 'the Lord' used absolutely, almost always refers to Jesus or to God. (3) Verse 8*a* seems to be an adaptation to the literary form that ends a parable with a word of Jesus to his audience (see on 14 : 24). (4) If 'master' refers to the rich man so probably must the 'wiser' sons (8*b*). Cf. 'for', i.e. 'because' (*hoti*). But, in fact, Jesus is commending the manager or steward. Cf. Jeremias, *Parables*, p. 45; *contra*: cf. J. A. Fitzmyer, *TS* 25, 1964, 27f.

dishonest: i.e. unrighteous (*adikia*). The term or its cognate occurs in verses 8–11. Apparently it is a catchword on the basis of which verses 9–11 were joined to one another as well as to the parable (1–8). Like 'sons of light', *adikia* most probably is a technical theological expression. It is a Greek equivalent of ʿ*āwel*, a term used technically at Qumran for the principle and reality of evil in the end time.

Adikia occurs in three Lukan passages, all parables and all in eschatological contexts (13 : 27; 18 : 6). In 2 Th. 2 : 10, 12; 2 Tim. 2 : 19 the term is used in contrast to messianic truth. In Acts (8 : 23) one who seeks to buy the eschatological gift of the Spirit is accused of being 'in the bond of unrighteousness' (*adikias*), a bond which, Jesus declares in Luke 4 : 18, it is his mission to break. (The allusion to Isa. 58 : 6 is present in both passages; cf. 13 : 16.)

These and other considerations suggested by H. Kosmala (pp. 195–200, 367) show that *adikia* does not refer to individual ethics but to the universal character of 'this age'. 'Dishonest steward' and 'unjust judge' (18 : 6 *AV*) are misleading translations; these men are neither better nor worse than other 'sons of this world'. The description, *adikia*, means only that they belong to this age and order their lives according to its principles.

generation: i.e. society, class: see on 17 : 25; 21 : 32.

sons of light: see the special note at 11 : 33–36.

9. friends . . . they: probably God or the angels who, as God's agents, distribute punishment or reward. 'They' frequently is used in rabbinic literature to avoid mentioning the name of God. Cf. 12 : 20, 48. Less likely, the reference may be to the persons helped by the 'unrighteous mammon'. Instead of accusing (cf. 11 : 31f.), they will be friendly witnesses at the last judgment.

unrighteous mammon: not 'tainted money' (*SBK*) but 'worldly possessions', i.e. possessions characteristic of this 'unrighteous' age. See on 6 : 20–22; 16 : 8.

habitations (*skēnas*): only twice in Luke (cf. 9 : 33). Like 'house' and 'temple', the word is used elsewhere of the reality of the coming age that inheres in the corporate life of the resurrected Messiah. Probably it has that connotation here. See on 20 : 38; cf. Ac. 15 : 16; 2 C. 5 : 1; Heb. 8 : 2; 9 : 11.

11. true: a theological expression pertaining to the realities of the coming age. Occurring only here in Luke, the term has affinities with the thought of John (e.g., 6 : 32) and Hebrews (8 : 2; 9 : 24).

13. The only verse in the episode that occurs elsewhere (Mt. 6 : 24; cf. *Gospel of Thomas* 47). Luke or his source appropriately utilizes this 'Q' tradition, perhaps attracted by the word 'mammon'.

TEACHINGS OF MESSIAH: THE COMING OF THE KINGDOM
16 : 14–18 : 14

Structure. The teachings in this section for the most part continue themes that were present in the preceding section. Indeed, the text gives little indication that this is a separate block of material. It may be that Luke intends the twelve episodes (13 : 22–18 : 14) to be viewed as one unit.

Teaching.—The reversal motif continues (see above, p. 187). The rejected and oppressed of this age—Lazarus (16 : 14–31), the thankful foreigner (17 : 11–19), the persecuted Christians (18 : 1–8), the tax collector (18 : 9–14)—will be accepted and exalted in the coming kingdom. The persecutors and proud Pharisees will be condemned. False leaders in the Church will suffer the same judgment (17 : 1–10).

The kingdom cannot be earned. Repentance, faith, and for-
giving hearts characterize its recipients (17 : 3–6, 19; 18 : 13). But
since these are God's gifts (8 : 10), they do not give rise to pride
but evoke humility and thanksgiving (17 : 10, 16).

The section is characterized by two contrasting pictures of the
kingdom of God, its present manifestation and its future revelation
in judgment. This double perspective is clearly evident in 17 : 20–
37). But it is implicit in earlier episodes and is characteristic of
Luke's theology as a whole (see above, pp. 12–15; cf. 16 : 14–31).
Some episodes exhibit only one aspect or the other. For example
the destitute Lazarus and the persecuted Christians find deliverance only in the *future* revelation of the kingdom (16 : 22; 18 : 8).
The healing of the Samaritan and the justification of the tax
collector represent benefits that the kingdom conveys in its *present*
manifestation (17 : 15; 18 : 14). In the following section the twofold manifestation of the kingdom becomes important for the
Evangelist's understanding of the present kingship of Christ.

THE RICH MAN AND LAZARUS: THE STORY OF A STRANGE REVERSAL
16 : 14–31

Structure. The episode consists of a double-pronged saying (14–18)
followed by an explanatory double-pronged parable (19–31; see
above, p. 179). The first prong of the saying (14f.) is illustrated
by the first part of the parable (19–26, esp. 25). One's status in
this age is reversed in the next. Exaltation (rejection) by men
forecasts judgment (blessing) by God.

The second prongs also are parallel. The abiding witness of the
Old Testament message (16–18) is sufficient basis for believing the
'kingdom of God' message. No miraculous sign would be more
persuasive (27–31).

Background. The general theme of the parable is familiar to the
Lord's audience (see below). In this sense the rich man and
Lazarus is a 'true life story'. But it is not necessarily a 'true after-
life story'. Some have thought that Jesus tells the parable to reveal
what happens after death. However, the general currency of this
story-theme in Judaism does not support this view. And Jesus
himself expresses contrary views elsewhere about the future life
(see on 20 : 27–40). These facts indicate rather strongly that he

does not intend here to give a preview of life after death. On this almost all commentators agree (cf. Geldenhuys). It is probable, rather, that Jesus makes use of a well-known story to illuminate certain truths about the kingdom of God.

Teaching. Jesus teaches elsewhere that the reversal of one's status is characteristic of the coming messianic age (see above, p. 187). This motif is the apparent connecting link between the seemingly rag-bag collection of sayings appended to 16 : 14f. Before John the Baptist the kingdom of God was 'prophesied' (cf. Mt. 11 : 13), after him it is 'preached'. Not one 'dot' of the law can fail, yet in contradiction to the law, divorce and remarriage is adultery. These sharp distinctions mean that a new era has been entered. Although it abides as a 'pointer', the law stands fulfilled. It is superseded by a higher and prior demand under which all now stand (see below.)

Luke illustrates this truth with an appended parable (19–31). Like the rich fool (12 : 16) or the clever steward (16 : 1) or the stern judge (18 : 2), the rich man is a typical man of the world who finds his fulfilments in this age. The poor Lazarus looks on in misery. In the next life Lazarus reclines with Abraham while the rich man looks on in misery. See on 13 : 22–30; 14 : 1–24. The reversal is 'fixed', and the rich man's relation to 'Father' Abraham has no redemptive effect. Nor can the five brothers, by means of a miracle, be warned to 'repent'. The last verse (31) reveals the point of the parable. Those who reject Moses' witness to Jesus will not be persuaded by a 'sign'. They will not be convinced even by Jesus' resurrection from the dead.

14. Pharisees: the change of audience signals a change of theme (cf. 16 : 1; 17 : 1).

lovers of money: the Pharisees saw no conflict of interest between piety and possessions, God and mammon (16 : 13; cf. *SBK*). Of the Gospels Luke emphasizes most the 'holy poor' and the polluting tendencies of money (cf. S. E. Johnson, *SSNT*, p. 132).

15. exalted among men: see on 18 : 9–14; above, p. 187.

16. since then (*apo tote*): either from the appearance of the Baptist (Mt. 11 : 12; cf. Daube, pp. 285f.; Grundmann) or, more probably, from the end of the Baptist's ministry. The latter interpretation appears to be important for Luke's theme. Cf. Conzelmann, p. 20; Ac. 10 : 36f.; 13 : 24f. See on 3 : 5f.; 7 : 18–35; 24 : 33–53.

preached: see above, pp. 13f.

enters violently or 'presses' (*AV*; *biazetai*). The term is much debated and half a dozen interpretations are possible (cf. Daube, pp. 285ff.). (1) The demonic powers (or Jesus' opponents) 'oppress' it. (2) The Zealots seek to 'force' it to birth through violence. (3) The believing 'press' into it. The last interpretation is inviting: what before was expected now is encountered and eagerly entered (cf. 3 : 7, 10; see on 10 : 5). Yet this does not seem to conform with the parallel in Matthew (11 : 12) or with the rejection of Jesus' message stressed elsewhere by Luke. Cf. F. W. Danker, *JBL* 77, 1958, 235. Most probably the first interpretation is the correct one (cf. Kümmel, pp. 121ff.). The Pharisees fight against the kingdom and seek to keep men out of it. However, their efforts cannot prevail (16 : 17; see on 11 : 37–54).

17. dot: either (1) the smallest Hebrew letter, (2) a mark distinguishing similar letters or, less likely, (3) a style mark above a letter. The meaning in any case is 'the smallest bit'. The reference is to the law understood as a pointer to Jesus' message (31). Since the kingdom of God is the fulfilment of the law, no amount of hostility can prevail against it (cf. 16 : 16; Mt. 5 : 17).

17f. The Qumran sect also viewed itself as the harbinger of the messianic age. It is perhaps significant that it similarly combines an emphasis on the sanctity of the law with a prohibition of polygamy. In doing so it also cites Gen. 1 : 27. Cf. Mk 10 : 2–12, *CD* 4 : 20; Daube, pp. 298, 362–72.

18. The divorce saying concerns only the man (*contra* Mk 10 : 12) and lacks the 'except for fornication' clause (*contra* Mt. 5 : 32; 19 : 9; cf. 1 : 19). Matthew's exception may refer to marriage with a close relative or to unchastity of the bride or wife; cf. Hill, pp. 124f., 279ff. The usual Jewish restriction of divorce action to the man suggests that Mark interpreted the saying for a Gentile or diaspora audience. Their interpretations are not, then, contrary to the Lukan saying. They may be implicit in it.

The saying also rules out polygamy ('marries another'). Perhaps it points to God's original order in creation in which 'the pair' formed one being (cf. Gen. 1 : 27; Mk 10 : 5–9). That is, the messianic age is apparently viewed as a restored or consummated Eden in which God fulfils his original purpose in creation.

Cf. J. Jeremias, *TDNT* v, 769f.; *Barnabas* 6 : 9–13; but see on
20 : 35.

The divorce saying is not intended as a civil law, nor is it just
a higher morality (see on 6 : 29f.). It is a saying for the messianic
community. Those who now receive the kingdom message and its
powers must express increasingly in their personal lives the principles of the coming age.

A Special Note on Adultery

In the Old Testament adultery involved the sexual intercourse of
a married or engaged woman with someone other than her husband or fiancé. This violation of the seventh commandment was
punished by the execution of both parties (Exod. 20 : 14; Lev.
20 : 10ff.; Dt. 22 : 22–27). Similar injunctions and penalties were
contained in the Babylonian Code of Hammurabi (129) and,
optionally, in early Roman law (Dion. Hal. 2, 25, 6). Cf. Pedersen, I–II, 547–52. The severity of the punishment suggests that
ancient societies viewed adultery not just (privately) as a violation
of the spouse's right to exclusive sexual enjoyment of the partner
but also (socially) as a serious threat to the familial fabric of
society. The biblical understanding of the offence was given an
additional basis in Gen. 2 : 24: in marriage the two 'become one
flesh'. That is, a new 'corporate' reality comes into being, a
reality that both includes and transcends their individual persons
(cf. Pedersen, I–II, 62f., 270f.). As a sin against marriage, adultery,
then, apparently has the character of murder either in robbing the
husband of his selfhood (Piper, p. 150) or in destroying the cor-
poreity that is created by the sexual union. In any case it is from the
standpoint of Gen. 1–2 that Jesus speaks of the indissolubility of
marriage and of its lifelong permanence (cf. Mt. 19 : 4ff.; Mk
10 : 6–8; 1 C. 7 : 10f.).

In the New Testament the scope of adultery is broadened in
several respects. First, Jesus gives a radical and inward interpretation of the commandment: 'Everyone who looks at a woman
lustfully has already commited adultery with her in his heart' (Mt.
5 : 28). With God, he implies, it is not only one's acts that are
significant but also one's thoughts and intentions. Unlike Old
Testament practice but like the Qumran community of his own time
(*CD* 4 : 20f.), Jesus equates divorce and remarriage with adultery,

and by his application also excludes polygamy (see on 16:18). In this way he calls his followers to exemplify God's original order in creation (Mt. 19:4ff.; Gen. 1:27; 2:24), an order destined now to be restored (Mt. 19:28).

Second, the New Testament gives a different focus to the Old Testament depiction of idolatry as adultery against God (Jer. 3). St Paul writes that an immoral sexual union and the union 'with Christ' are mutually exclusive relationships and that, therefore, fornicators will not inherit the kingdom of God (1 C. 6:9–20). His rationale appears to be two-fold. First, because redemption is physical, the individual Christian's body belongs to Christ in a special way. Also, since Christians are members of Christ's corporate body, he and they are implicated when one of the members is involved in this sin (1 C. 5:6; cf. 12:27; Eph. 5:28–31). Second, sexual immorality 'implies not the mere possibility but the necessity of my being enslaved by an alien power. It occupies this relatively unique position because it can never take place "outside" me and "I" consequently cannot isolate myself from it' (Thielicke, I, 91; cf. pp. 631–47). For both Jesus and Paul the sexual union is not merely what one *does;* it effects a qualitative change in who one *is* (Mt. 15:19f.; 1 C. 6:16).

In this context one cannot justify adultery in terms of 'situation ethics'. Some violations of God's law, e.g., a theft to feed a starving person or a lie to save an innocent person, may occur within the framework of God's love. But 'there are certain conditions and attitudes with which the Holy Spirit cannot in any [situation] co-exist under the same roof in the same ego . . . The first is fornication (*porneia*)' (Thielicke, I, 87). However, adultery is never regarded as an unpardonable sin. This is evident both in Paul's writings (1 C. 6:11) and in Jesus' attitude, best expressed perhaps in the tradition found at Jn 7:53–8:11: 'Neither do I condemn you. Go and do not sin again' (8:11).

19–31. H. Gressmann traces the parable proper (19–26) to an Egyptian story. In it the sumptuous funeral of a rich man coincided with the bare burial of a poor man. An onlooker concluded that in death, as in life, the rich fare better. But the following scene in Hades showed the poor man in the rich man's apparel and the rich man in want.

With variations the rabbis adopt this theme in a number of stories to express the truth that one's status in life is reversed at death. Cf. Creed; Gressmann; Jeremias, *Parables*, pp. 182ff. The second part of the parable (27–31) also has a parallel in a rabbinic story of a woman suffering in Hades. In contrast to the present parable she sends a warning to her surviving husband and thereby brings about his repentance (Bultmann, pp. 212f.).

20, 31. Lazarus ('God helps'): some see a veiled reference to the brother of Mary and Martha (Jn. 11 : 47ff.; 12 : 9f.). But the arguments are not very compelling. Very likely the name is chosen for its symbolism. On names for the rich man, inserted by later scribes, cf. B. M. Metzger, *ET* 73, 1961–2, 202f.; J. A. Fitzmyer, *CBQ* 24, 1962, 175f.

21. what fell: see on 9 : 17.
licked: i.e. aggravated his misery.

22. by the angels: like the rest of the story, this reflects the current beliefs of many Jews. See on 20 : 27–40.

Abraham's bosom: either (1) a later expression equivalent to the phrase 'gathered to his people' (e.g., Gen. 15 : 15; 25 : 8), (2) an expectation to be received by Abraham at death (cf. 4 Mac. 13 : 17; *Kid.* 72b (?); *SBK*), or (3) a picture of the messianic banquet (cf. 13 : 28ff.).

buried: honoured to the last.

23, 26. Hades: distinct from 'Gehenna'. See on 10 : 15; 12 : 5. The picture here is unique in the New Testament. It is reminiscent of the poetic symbolism in Isa. 14 : 8–11. But it also presupposes, in part, a Greek view in which 'souls' go at death into the underworld for punishment. Some Jewish thought, especially that of the Pharisees, had assimilated this teaching. Cf. Stewart, pp. 142–6; *SBK* IV, 1017. See on 20 : 27–40. However, no Jewish writings view Paradise or Abraham to be a part of the 'underworld'. Therefore the 'gulf' apparently is between Hades and the heavenly realms (cf. Creed; *SBK*). The picture of judgment and reward immediately at death is contrary to the usual New Testament understanding. Cf. Mt. 10 : 15; Ac. 17 : 31; Jn. 5 : 28f.; 1 Th. 4 : 13ff.; 2 Tim. 4 : 8; Rev. 20 : 13. See on 23 : 43. Probably it should be understood simply as a part of the setting of the story.

25. lifetime (*zōē*): the word usually denotes immortal, resurrection life. See on 9 : 24; cf. 12 : 15.

31. should rise: an allusion to Jesus' own resurrection. See on 11 : 29f.; 24 : 13–32; cf. Jn 5 : 46; 9 : 28.

A WORD TO CHURCH LEADERS: THE ROLE OF THE SERVANT **17 : 1–10**

Structure. The two teaching-words on 'stumbling-blocks' (1f., margin) and forgiveness (3f.) have a parallel in Mt. 18 : 6f., 15; Mk 9 : 42. The faith saying (5f.) and the characteristic concluding illustration (7–10) related to it are apparently from Luke's special tradition. The Evangelist appends them as an appropriate counterpart to the 'impossible command' to forgive. See above, p. 179.

Teaching. Jesus anticipated the inevitable coming of false leaders among his followers after his departure (1). Luke experienced the fulfilment of that prophecy. With these collected sayings of the Lord the Evangelist exhorts the Church leaders to fulfil their proper role. They are to 'take heed' not to cause a weaker brother to stumble and fall away from the faith. Rather they must give a responsible rebuke to a sinning brother and a ready and continuing forgiveness to his word of repentance.

Such forgiveness is an impossible command. To forgive, no less than to receive forgiveness, requires faith. Such faith is not within man's power. It is the gift of the Lord. This thought underlies the plea, 'Increase our faith' (5). But if this faith is divine power, its presence in the least 'mustard seed' amount is sufficient to fulfil the demands made upon it (6). Further, if that which is 'commanded' is accomplished through a divine gift, the disciple can make no claims in return for his service. To be given faith is to be given responsibility, and the manifestation of faith in life is a 'duty' that is owed, not a personal achievement for which thanks are due (7–10).

1. 'stumbling-blocks' (margin): anything that causes an alienation of one's allegiance to Jesus. Cf. 17 : 23; 21 : 8; Rom. 14 : 13; Mk 9 : 43ff.
him: i.e. anyone. Perhaps the reference originally was to Judas, whose betrayal caused the other disciples to desert. Cf. 22 : 22; Mk 14 : 27ff. More likely, however, Jesus' warning is of a more general nature, as the plural, 'temptations', indicates. Cf. Mt. 7 : 15.
3. if he repents: see on 15 : 1–32
4. against you: applies to a personal offence, a command that Jesus earlier addressed to his messianic community of 'brothers'. Cf. Mt. 18 : 15, 21. The phrase is absent in 17 : 3 and in Mt.

18 : 15 (cf. *NEB*). There the necessity for 'rebuke' apparently rests on the Semitic concept of corporate responsibility: (1) an unjudged sin in the church is a sin of the church, or (2) toleration of it involves the church in the evil. Cf. 1 C 5 : 6ff.; Lev. 19 : 17.

4–6. seven times: i.e. without limit; cf. Mt. 18 : 21f. Christ has not commanded his followers to move a tree or hill (Mt. 21 : 21). His requirement is a harder miracle, to forgive.

5f. For similar but probably independent sayings cf. Mk. 11 : 22ff.; Mt. 17 : 20.

apostles: for Luke they probably represent all Church leaders. See on 12 : 41–48; cf. Ac. 20 : 28ff.

7. one of you: it is not unlikely that some of Jesus' followers were slave-holders (cf. 5 : 27ff.; 19 : 1ff.; 23 : 50).

a servant: his only 'hand' (Manson).

8. afterward: this reflects the general custom although some rabbis required the slave to be fed first (cf. *SBK*). Contrast 12 : 37.

10. our duty: cf. an ancient rabbinic saying. 'If thou hast learnt much Torah do not claim credit unto thyself, because for such purpose wast thou created' (*Aboth* 2 : 8).

HEALING TEN LEPERS: THE GRATEFUL SAMARITAN 17: 11–19

All the lepers show 'faith'-obedience and all are 'cleansed'. But only the foreigner' (18) is thankful for the grace received. The others, Jesus implies, think solely of the benefit received: they 'were filled' (Jn 6 : 26f. *AV*). Like the rich fool and the clever steward (12 : 16; 16 : 1), they see life's meaning solely in terms of this age.

The ungrateful 'nine' exemplify the general attitude of the Jewish people toward Jesus' mission; the 'Samaritan' is prophetic of the future response of non-Jews to the gospel (Ac. 8 : 5f.; 11 : 18). With this real-life parable Luke emphasizes once more that the grace of God and the powers of the new age can be experienced in two ways, in their true meaningfulness or in vain. See on 11 : 14–28.

11. As the order of the place names suggests, 'the borderlands of Samaria and Galilee' (*NEB*) may reflect the perspective of a Jerusalem narrator. The order also would be explained if the verse refers to an earlier northward journey of Jesus. If so, Luke

has moulded it to the context of the journey to Jerusalem. The
phrase 'to Jerusalem' probably is the addition of Luke.
between (*AV*: 'midst'; *dia meson*): it is a peculiar construction. Cf.
Moule, p. 55; Funk, p. 119. Conzelmann (pp. 68ff.) interprets
the phrase, 'going south between Samaria and Galilee'. This supposes that Luke mistakenly thought Galilee bordered Judea on
the south, with Samaria alongside on the west. This is more con-
jectural than the *NEB* reading, and it is incompatible with
Conzelmann's (pp. 18ff.) own view of Luke's strong geographical
interest. If Luke was Paul's companion, he must have had some
knowledge of the area (Ac. 21 : 15f.). A later 'Luke', who had an
interest in the geography, doubtless would have consulted informed Palestinian Christians. In fact, the Evangelist does reveal
first-hand knowledge of Palestine, as Harnack has shown (*Acts*,
pp. 71–87). Whatever symbolic geography there is in Luke, it need
not have arisen from the author's ignorance of the real situation.
The truth of the matter, however, is that Luke is not charting
any route, symbolic or otherwise. Conzelmann's interpretation
here arises from a misunderstanding of the role of the journey in
the central division. See above, pp. 147f.

12. ten lepers: this is the second healing narrative (cf.
13 : 10ff.) and the fourth healing incident in the 'teachings' division. Cf. 11 : 14; 14 : 4; 18 : 35. In each case the theme of the
episode is not the miraculous act but the teaching-word arising
from it.

14. Go: a test of faith; cf. 2 Kg. 5 : 10–15.

16. Samaritan: see on 9 : 51–56; 10 : 25–37.

19. faith: not a merit achieved but a grace manifested. Therefore it does not demand thanks but is thankful. See on 17 : 1–
10; 8 : 48; cf. 18 : 42.

A CAUTION TO ANXIOUS WAITERS: THE COMING OF THE KINGDOM . . .
AND OF THE KING 17 : 20-37

Structure. The episode consists of an oracle (20f.), peculiar to Luke,
followed by a series of apocalyptic sayings (22–37). Matthew places
the sayings in the Olivet Discourse (Mt. 24). By appending them
here Luke creates a thematic setting in which the present manifestation of 'the kingdom of God' is set in relation to the future
glorious revelation of 'the Son of man'. Cf. Noack, p. 47.

This alternating present/future perspective of the kingdom is found earlier. Cf. 3.16 (present) with 3.17 (future); 9.26*b* (future) with 9.27 (present); 11.2 (future) with 11.3, 13, 20 (present); 11.31f. (power present and judgment future); 12.37–46 (future reward and judgment) with 12.49, 52 (immediate judgment); 16.16 (present) with 16.19–31 (future reward and judgment). This feature has affinities with the Fourth Gospel (see above, pp. 12ff.). See on 23.42f.

Background. Luke addresses a Church that harboured two errors and a doubt concerning Messiah's *parousia*. (1) Jesus has already returned secretly (2 Th. 2 : 1f.; cf. Mk 13 : 6, 21; Acts 1 : 11). (2) Jesus will come very shortly at a calculable date (1 Th. 5 : 1f.; 2 Th. 2 : 3ff.). (3) Jesus is not coming (see on 18 : 1–8; cf. 12 : 45; 2 Pet. 3 : 4). From the stress laid upon the public character of the *parousia* the first error may well have been as serious a problem as the second (cf. Mt. 24 : 26ff.; Rev. 1 : 7). Like Paul before him, Luke seeks to correct these misunderstandings. (Perhaps it is not without significance that Ac. 16 : 16; 20 : 5f. ('we') places Luke in Macedonia where this problem was particularly acute.) Cf. Jos. *War* 6, 5, 4; Tacitus, *Hist.* 5, 13; Suetonius, *Vespasian* 4.

Teaching. Elsewhere (12 : 35–48; 19 : 11–27) Luke points out that Jesus anticipated a considerable and incalculable lapse of time before his return. Here he teaches, from selected words of Jesus, that the coming will be unexpected (26, 28). The kingdom appeared in the Lord's pre-resurrection mission without 'signs' for the curious (21). So also there will be no preliminary signs, 'see here, see there', to herald him as the revealed 'Son of man' (23f. *AV*). The appearance of the kingdom in Jesus' mission was evident to believers by his acts. How much more will his glorious and public *parousia* be self-validating.

The Lukan additions to the sayings (as compared with Matthew) strongly accentuate the warning elements to Christians (22, 25, 28f., 32f.). Because the Son of man is now 'rejected', his second appearing will be a time of judgment. There will be no time to get prepared; one must be prepared. The Pharisees, obsessed with 'signs', forfeited the kingdom. The disciples (22) are in danger of making the same fatal mistake. See on 12 : 35–48.

20. kingdom of God: see above, pp. 12ff.

signs to be observed (*AV*: 'observation'; *paratērēsis*): besides 'signs' the term may refer to cultic rites (cf. Gal. 4 : 10). The night of the Passover was the 'night of observation' (Exod. 12 : 42 Aquila) in which many expected the coming messianic redemption to occur. If Christians applied this interpretation to the time of the *parousia*, a twofold meaning may be present in this passage. See on 22 : 14–23; cf. *Mek. Exod.* 12 : 42; Grundmann; A. Strobel, *ZNTW* 51, 1960, 133f.; Jeremias, *Eucharistic Words*, pp. 137f.

21. in the midst of: the rare preposition, *entos*, may mean 'within' (*AV*) or 'among' (*NEB*). Jesus hardly would regard the kingdom to be 'within' the unbelieving Pharisees. Probably the phrase is parallel to 'upon you' in 11 : 20 (Conzelman, p. 107n). Thus, it refers to the presence of the kingdom in the eschatological powers manifested in Jesus' person and acts. See on 11 : 29–36; 16 : 14–31; cf. *Gospel of Thomas* 113. See the discussion of Kümmel (pp. 32–5); C. H. Roberts, *HTR* 41 (1948) 1–8.

22. one of the days of the Son of man: (1) perhaps past manifestations of Jesus' glory, e.g., the transfiguration (so, Grundmann; Leaney). More probably, (2) the plural is equivalent to 'days' in verse 26 and to the singular 'day' in verse 30. It may be a rabbinic idiom for the times of Messiah (*SBK*); or 'one' (*mian*) may mean 'first'. In this context the phrase would refer to the *parousia*. To 'see' the days of the Son of man, i.e. the *parousia*, is something different from 'seeing' the kingdom of God. See on 9 : 9, 27.
Son of man: see on 5 : 24.

22f., 25. In these oracles Jesus prophesies his rejection, followed by an absence of considerable length. In this interim his disciples will be in danger of being led astray.
this generation: a derogatory expression referring primarily to a class of people and only secondarily to a chronological period. It is an ethical rather than a physical generation. The people are the 'rejectors' of the end time, the children of this age (16 : 8). Luke universalizes the warning originally applied to those crucifying the Lord. All stand in danger of belonging to this generation: 'remember Lot's wife' (32). See on 9 : 23f. ('daily'); 21 : 32; cf. 1QS 3 : 14; M. Meinertz, *BZ* 1, 1957, 283–89; Brownlee, p. 13n.

23. Lo, here: see on 21 : 8.

34f. The setting is the hour before sunrise in which some sleep and others have arisen to prepare the day's bread. The time may be symbolic: Jesus' coming heralds a new day. Cf. 2 Pet. 1 : 19.

taken (*paralēmphthēsetai*): out of judgment and probably not 'taken away in judgment'. Cf. Mt. 24 : 31; 1 Th. 4 : 17; Jn 14 : 3.

37. **eagles:** proverbial symbol of judgment and not Roman standards conquering Jerusalem (21 : 20). In this context (and in Mt. 24 : 28) the proverb refers to the last judgment. Judgment will occur where it is required, i.e. universally. Cf. Hab. 1 : 8.

THE JUDGE AND THE WIDOW: JUSTICE ON JUDGMENT DAY **18 : 1–8**

Structure. Possibly this is a concluding parable to the above episode (Grundmann). But the introduction suggests that Luke treats it as a separate piece. Besides the introduction (1) the passage consists of a parable (2–5) with a double conclusion (6–8). Elsewhere a second conclusion to a parable may represent a Lukan appendix (11 : 8, 9ff.). Cf. 12 : 46, 47f.; 16 : 8, 9ff.; Jeremias, *Parables*, 1954 edition, p. 84; reversed in the case of Lk. 18 : 8*b* in his revised edition, p. 155. Here, also, the second conclusion (8*b*) may be Luke's application of the episode to the despair and apostasy caused by persecution. See on 17 : 20–37.

Background. Luke apparently is writing to a situation in which Christians under severe persecution are denying their faith. Even if 'cry day and night' is the Lord's conclusion, the second question (8*b*) probably is a later addition. Whether Luke's word or an independent saying of Jesus, Luke's use of it here suggests an appalling and current crisis (cf. 12 : 11).

For the early Church the 'delay' of the *parousia* was not a chronological problem but a 'life' problem. Nor was the fact that Christians were dying in itself the pressing concern. From the first this had a simple and effective answer (20 : 37f.; 1 Th. 4 : 13ff.). It was not delay *qua* delay but delay in the face of continuing death under persecution that caused hope to fade and apostasy to rise. 'Sunshine' delay poses no problems. But a thousand years go by in one short hour waiting for the lions. Cf. G. Braumann, *ZNTW* 54, 1963, 145.

Teaching. This prayer parable is similar to that of the 'friend at midnight (11 : 5–7). In the latter passage the prayer, 'thy kingdom come', is answered by the pentecostal gift of the Spirit

(11 : 2, 13). Here the 'cry' that God 'see justice done for his chosen' (Phillips) is answered by the coming of 'the Son of man'. A hardened and 'worldly' judge has little concern for poor and unimportant people. But out of exasperation even he will satisfy the just complaint of a persistent widow. How much more will God answer persistent prayer. How much more will he 'vindicate' his children who are suffering and dying at the hands of persecutors. Their prayer will not go unanswered. His just judgment will be certain and sudden. See on 12 : 35–40; cf. 17 : 26–30.

1. always to pray: i.e. for the coming redemption.

3, 5, 7, 8. vindicate: i.e. 'avenge' (*AV*): the key word binding together the parable and its application. The term means the vindication of a wronged person by the punishment of the wrong-doer. Cf. Ac. 7 : 24. Elsewhere the wronged person is God, here God's elect. Cf. 21 : 22; Heb. 10 : 29f. The thought is not emotional reaction but 'justice under law', God's law. The New Testament never regards vengeance as wrong as such but does regard it as God's prerogative (Rom. 12 : 19). As those who have received mercy, Christians are to show mercy and not to 'take justice into their own hands'. Nevertheless, justice is the basic principle in God's judgment of men (e.g., Rom. 3 : 25f.; 2 C. 5 : 10), and apart from that touchstone mercy loses its meaning.

6. unrighteous: i.e. 'worldly'. See on 16 : 8.

7. elect: i.e. chosen ones. Cf. 23 : 35.

cry: cf. Rev. 6 : 9f.; Gen. 4 : 10.

delay over them (*AV*: 'bear long with them'): the *AV* is preferable since the thought is 'to be patient with' (cf. Mt. 18 : 26). It is closely related to the foregoing clause and may mean, (1) 'will not God vindicate his elect who cry . . . and be patient with their complaint'; (2) '. . . and be patient with the wicked' (Grundmann; cf. 2 Pet. 3 : 9f.); (3) '. . . and he is longsuffering over them' (*RV*, cf. Rev. 6 : 11); (4) '. . . or can he just endure their plight?' (cf. H. Ljungvik, *NTS* 10, 1963–4, 293). The probabilities favour (1).

8. speedily (*en tachei*): i.e. suddenly, with the time left indefinite. Although God tarries, when he acts he will act swiftly as he did at the Flood and at Sodom. Cf. Plummer. Cf. 12 : 40, 46; Kümmel, p. 33; C. Spicq, *RB* 68 (1961), 81–5. Otherwise, Wilson, *Mission*, p. 73.

THE CHURCHMAN AND THE POLITICIAN: RIGHTEOUSNESS CLAIMED VS. RIGHTEOUSNESS GIVEN **18 : 9–14**

Structure. Luke introduces (9) and concludes (14*b*) the story in a manner designed to further his theme. The two preceding episodes have to do with a pending judgment (17 : 20–37) that will render strict justice (18 : 1–8). Who, then, will be found just? In answer Luke points to a parable that Jesus told the Jewish churchmen.

Background. In common with other Jerusalem placed stories Luke may have obtained this 'temple' parable from the traditions of the mother church. From its Pauline ring, however, one is tempted to think that he heard it first as a 'Jesus tradition' related by Paul. Cf. 1 C. 7 : 10; 9: 14; 2 Th. 2 : 15; 1 Tim. 5 : 18*b*.

Teaching. Because he was busy tabulating his 'score', the Pharisee overlooked the essential requirement, a right attitude. Confidence about God precludes confidence in God. This is the fatal misunderstanding of all 'merit' religion (cf. Grundmann). Believing that one has attained inevitably leads one to 'despise' those who have not. Thus the religionist, so very sincerely, cuts himself off from God and from the love of God. God can relate only to a person who, having lost his self-confidence, 'humbles himself' in repentance. Cf. 10 : 29; 13 : 2f., 30; 14 : 11; 16 : 15.

9. righteous: and therefore acceptable candidates for the kingdom. See on 15 : 7.

10. to pray: public prayers in the temple occurred twice daily, private prayer at any time. See on 1 : 5–25; cf. Ac. 3 : 1. **Pharisee:** see on 11 : 37, 45.

11. prayed thus: although dramatized, the Pharisee's attitude is not untypical. In the Talmud one rabbi was reported to be confident that his righteousness was sufficient to exempt his whole generation from judgment. If the saved numbered only 'a hundred, I and my son are among them; and if only two, they are I and my son' (*Suk.* 45b). Similarly, Paul could describe himself 'as to righteousness under the law, blameless' (Phil. 3 : 6). These were sincere convictions based upon a meticulous obedience to the law as they understood it.

In this context one can understand the shock and antagonism that Jesus' teaching would arouse. However, in the midst of the equally strong legalism at Qumran one encounters a concept of God-given righteousness not unlike that of the New Testament. 'My own righteousness is due to God . . . and from the fountain of his righteousness my sins will be expiated, from the fountain of his righteousness comes my justification' (1QS 11 : 2, 3, 5).

12. This Pharisee greatly exceeded the normal requirement to 'fast' once a year and give 'tithes' of certain types of income. Cf. *SBK*.

13. tax collector: see on 5 : 29.

14. justified: i.e. by God. By justifying himself the Pharisee rejects justification as a gift from God. Cf. Rom. 3 : 20-27. At Qumran justification was by grace alone but not, as it was for Paul, through faith alone. See on 18 : 11. Justification remained tied to the law. Of course, for Paul also it was not divorced from the law (Rom. 8 : 4). Unlike Qumran this parable bases justification on repentance alone. But see on 18 : 15-17, 18-34; cf. 24 : 47. Unlike Paul it says nothing about the role of faith as trust. That will be developed largely after Pentecost although it cannot be excluded from the perspective of the pre-resurrection mission Cf. 20 : 5; 22 : 67; Mk 1 : 15; 9 : 42.

every one . . . : perhaps an independent saying of Jesus that Luke attaches here. See on 14 : 24; cf. 14 : 11.

THE ROAD TO JERUSALEM: DISCIPLESHIP AND THE REJECTED KING 18 : 15-19 : 44

Structure. At this point Luke returns to the Markan outline. The journey, which from 11 : 1 has served only as a literary frame for the teachings, again takes on actual and geographical content. Jesus moves through Jericho to the gates of Jerusalem. In this transition to the scene of the crucifixion the narrative naturally plays a greater role. But the 'teachings of Jesus' continue to be the major thrust. The first three episodes are from Mark, the fourth and fifth peculiar to Luke. The last episode is mixed, but its essential character is created by Luke.

Teaching. Through the section run two concurrent themes, the recipients of the kingdom and the messiahship of Jesus. Who inherits the kingdom of God? Its recipients are all who accept it like trusting children (18 : 15–17). They are the committed souls who, like the disciples, leave all else for the sake of the kingdom (18 : 18–34). They are the outcasts who, like blind Bartimaeus, call upon the Lord in faith (18 : 35–43). They are the lost who, like Zacchaeus, repent and receive Jesus' message (19 : 1–10). They are all disciples who, like productive servants, are faithful and fruitful in the tasks given them (19 : 11–27). Those who do not meet these tests will not enter the kingom of God (cf. 18 : 17; 19 : 22). See above, pp. 187, 200f.

Bartimaeus and Zacchaeus seem to be intended contrasts to the rich ruler (18 : 18–34). The ruler's blindness remains, Bartimaeus finds sight and salvation (cf. Jn 9 : 39ff.). The rich churchman rejects the kingdom's demand, the rich politician repents and accepts it (cf. 18 : 9–14).

In the first episode receiving the kingdom may be equated with receiving Jesus. The nature of Jesus' messiaship is stressed increasingly as the section progresses. Jesus, the Son of man, truly is the longed-for Messiah, the Son of David, the Lord, the King. Cf. 18 : 38, 41; 19 : 8, 38. But he is a messiah rejected whose destiny is to enter his glory through suffering, death, and resurrection. Cf. 19 : 14, 42; 18 : 33.

JESUS AND THE CHILDREN: OF SUCH IS THE KINGDOM 18 : 15–17

The episode raises once more an earlier question. How does one inherit the kingdom of God? One must 'receive' the kingdom as the children received Jesus: readily, trustingly, personally. The attitude of the children is in sharp contrast to the curiosity of Herod (9 : 9), the critical religiosity of the churchmen (e.g., 11 : 37ff.), and the sceptical questioning of the theologians (e.g., 5 : 21; 20 : 2). Probably Luke deliberately contrasts the children with the Pharisee and the religious ruler in the preceding and following episodes. They want to merit the kingdom.

The faith of the coming children is primarily not an attitude, or obedience, 'toward something' but a relationship 'with someone'. Faith is never present for man in his aloneness. It always presupposes, creates, and exists in relationship—personal relationship with God in Christ.

15. touch: see on 2 : 28ff. For the different origin and meaning

of the healing touch (see on 5 : 13) and the 'laying on of hands'
(e.g., Ac. 6 : 6) see Daube, pp. 233ff., 237.

16. Let the children come: inconsistent with verse 15 unless
'infants' (*brephē*; contrast Mk 10 : 13) means merely 'child'. On
Jesus' relationship with children cf. 9 : 48; Mt. 18 : 10; Leaney,
pp. 57ff.

17. Truly: see on 4 : 24.

receive the kingdom: at its future coming (Kümmel, p.
126) or, less probably, in its present manifestation in Jesus'
person.

like a child: its trusting and dependent nature, not its virtuous
character.

THE CHURCHMAN AND THE DISCIPLES: HAVING ALL VS. LEAVING ALL
    18 : 18–34

Structure. The dialogue with the religious ruler (18–23) is followed
by a 'teaching word' on the relation of riches to discipleship
(24–27). The apostles, who have left 'their belongings' (*NEB*) for
the sake of the kingdom, are set in sharp contrast to the ruler
(28–30). By omitting Mark's (10 : 31f.) introduction, Luke appears to regard the passion prediction (31–34) as an appendix
and conclusion to the episode: Jesus also has forsaken all for the
sake of the kingdom. See on 9 : 57–62.

Teaching. In another context the ruler's question was asked by a
theologian (10 : 25). In both cases the inquirer is referred to the
law. This churchman's attitude, however, is quite different from
the theologian's. He has observed the law meticulously, but he
has found no assurance of eternal life. In a rare and significant
gesture Jesus invites him to discipleship. Suddenly, he discovers
'sadly' that for him life's first priority is not God's kingdom but his
riches.

Jesus always requires from one just that earthly security upon
which one would lean. Only in the context of abandonment to
Christ's demand can one's basic life motivation really be 'for the
sake of the kingdom of God'. Peter represents the true disciple
who answers, 'We have left our homes and followed you' (28).
Jesus likewise is the true leader whose demand does not exceed
his own commitment—unto death (31–34)

18, 24. ruler (*archōn*): perhaps indicating a Jerusalem setting; see on 14: 1–24; 20: 1.

eternal life: to inherit eternal life means to inherit 'the kingdom of God'. See on 10 : 25–37; cf. Jn 3 : 2f., 15f.

19. No one is good but God: Jesus is neither confessing to sinfulness nor covertly pointing to his deity. He expresses a recognized truth. Perhaps he hints that the goodness God exemplifies— and requires—involves much more than the young ruler has realized. The man's casual use of 'good' reveals the poverty of his moral perception.

20. commandments: see on 10 : 25–37.

22. Sell all: Jesus puts his finger on the one commandment, unmentioned before (20), that the young man failed to keep. He was covetous. See on 16 : 14; cf. 12 : 33f.

treasure in heaven: see on 6 : 23–25; 12 : 13–34.

27. possible with God: perhaps a hint that the young man later became a disciple. The camel-needle proverb (25) is to be taken very literally. Anyone's salvation is a miracle. This especially is evident in those smoking the pacifying opium of possessions and living in the bright promise of youth (cf. Mt. 19 : 20).

28. Peter: see on 9 : 18–27.

homes: literally, 'own possession', in comparison with those of the ruler.

29. Truly: see on 4 : 24.

30. receive: obedience has its reward although not a 'merited' one. One's motive should not be reward-centred but for 'the kingdom'. See on 14 : 14, 26; 17 : 1–10.

eternal (*aiōnios*) **life** properly belongs to the coming 'age' (*aiōn*). See above, p. 14; on 9 : 24; 20 : 27–40; 23 : 43.

31–34. It is the seventh prediction of the Passion. See on 9 : 22. Cf. 5 : 35; 9 : 22, 44; 12 : 50; 13 : 32; 17 : 25.

32. the Gentiles: the Romans' part in the crucifixion first appears here. Luke omits Mark's (10 : 33) reference to the Jews. But see on 22 : 63–23 : 25; cf. Ac. 2 : 23; 3 : 13.

33. third day: an idiom equivalent to 'after three days'. Cf. Mk 10 : 34; cf. Est. 4 : 16; 5 : 1; Gen. 42 : 17f.; Hos. 6 : 2 LXX.

34. understood none of these things: how was such a fate possible for Messiah? How could it have any bearing on Messiah's mission or on the fulfilment of the writings of the prophets (18 : 31)? The intent of Jesus' words was, of course, clear enough.

By adding this verse Luke emphasizes to his readers that God's
redemptive plan can be perceived only when it is revealed to one.
Cf. 24 : 26f., 45f.; Ac. 8 : 30f.; Schlatter; Grundmann.

JERICHO: THE FAITH OF A BLIND MAN 18 : 35–43

Structure. This is the third and last Markan episode in this section.
The conclusion (43*b*) and the address, 'Lord', are Lukan. The
only other significant change from Mark is the locale of the
healing (see below). General geographical areas have been indicated or implied earlier in the journey (e.g., 9 : 52; 13 : 1–5, 31;
17 : 11). But this is the first specific place name to be mentioned.
Jericho is seventeen miles from Jerusalem.

Like 13 : 10–21, the narrative at first appearance seems to be an
'act of Messiah'. Is it not out of place in the 'teachings' division of
Luke's Gospel? The present section again gives prominence to the
messiahship of Jesus, perhaps because it serves Luke as a transition
to the passion story. But the messianic confession (38) is not the
high point of the episode. Greater emphasis is placed upon the
persistence of the blind man's faith and the sequel to his healing:
he 'followed' Jesus.

Teaching. In contrast to the rich ruler's polite address (18 : 18) this
man comes to Jesus with a confession, 'Son of David'. He recognizes his blindness as an outcropping of death. The ruler's 'blindness', also deadly, is unrecognized. The ruler subordinates his
quest for the kingdom to the riches of this life. Bartimaeus (Mk
10 : 46) will permit no obstacle to turn aside his desperate plea.
In his determined cry and in the 'faith' in Jesus underlying it is the
quality of true discipleship.

35. drew near: Mark (10 : 46) places the incident as Jesus
'went out of Jericho'. The attempts to harmonize the two accounts
are as strained as they are numerous (cf. Plummer). The most
probable explanation is that Luke changes the locale. This allows
him to keep together the three Markan episodes (18 : 15–43). After
them he can use his own Jericho story and attach a related
parable to it (cf. 19 : 11). Luke knows Mark's text, but he is more
concerned with the thematic arrangement than with locale and
chronology. See above, pp. 6f.

Jericho: see on 10 : 30; 19 : 1–10.

38f. Son of David: which Messiah was expected to be (cf. 4 Ezr. 12 : 32; 4*Qpatr* 3f; 4*QFlor* 1 : 11). Perhaps the term was a messianic title in later Judaism (*Ps. Solomon* 17 : 23). If so, in the context of Jewish nationalism it was a dangerous title to apply within the hearing of the Roman occupiers. For shortly thereafter Jesus was crucified as 'King of the Jews'. Cf. 23 : 2, 38.

42. faith: see on 8 : 48; 17 : 19.

43. the people: Luke's conclusion. They recognize Jesus as the instrument of God. In the following chapters the attitude of the 'people' is frequently contrasted to that of the leaders. Cf. 19 : 47f.; 20 : 19; 22 : 2; 23 : 13ff., 27; Conzelmann, p. 164.

JERICHO: THE CONVERSION OF A RICH POLITICIAN **19 : 1–10**

Structure. Found only in Luke, this story continues to address the question, 'Who receives the kingdom?' The introduction (1–4), the encounter (5–7), Zacchaeus' conversion (8f.), and the conclusion (10) are brief and pointed. The clear initial setting fades away before the teaching emphasis. Probably the transition is to the home of Zacchaeus. There he 'stood' and made his confession (8).

Background. Besides itself having a considerable tax potential, Jericho was a customs point for goods entering Palestine from the east. As 'chief tax collector' Zacchaeus received a share of all revenues whether collected by himself or subordinate officials. In a word, he was 'rich'. No doubt he had heard of the Nazarene prophet who irritated churchmen by his association with unsavoury politicians. Perhaps he knew of Levi's conversion (5 : 27f.). Like Bartimaeus, his determination is noteworthy (18 : 39). His desire to 'see' Jesus is not the curiosity of Herod (9 : 9) or the sign-seeking scepticism of the crowds (11 : 16, 29). As the sequel shows, Zacchaeus was interested in and open to the message of Jesus.

Teaching. The New Testament teaches that the kingdom of God and the 'salvation' which it brings belong to the heirs of Abraham. In this regard Christianity is absolutely Jewish. But who is 'a son of Abraham' (9)? Natural descent or religious adherence to the law was the qualification required by contemporary Judaism. In the eyes of the Christians the religious leaders had distorted the Old Testament teaching. The true heir, that is, the true Jew, is one who shares the faith and does the works of Abraham. This concept is rooted in such sayings of Jesus as the 'teaching word' in this passage. Zacchaeus receives the kingdom message and with it the messianic 'salvation'. This shows that he is a son of Abraham.

1. Jericho: see on 10 : 30.

5. today: see on 19 : 9. Where Jesus is present, salvation is present. The selection of Zacchaeus is an act of sovereign grace as much as the physical healing in the preceding episode.

6f. Contrast the reaction of Zacchaeus with that of the crowds. Cf. 5 : 30; 15 : 2.

8. stood: presumably at or after dinner. Reference to the dinner seems almost deliberately to be suppressed. See on 14 : 1–24; 24 : 13–32.

half my goods: he is not fulfilling a rule, and Jesus has given no command (cf. 18 : 12, 22). It is a thankoffering expressive of a changed heart.

if I have (and I have): i.e. whenever I have.

defrauded (*sukophanteō*): extortion through intimidation. Cf. 3 : 13; 2 Sam. 12 : 6.

9. salvation: elsewhere in Luke only in the messianic prophecy of Zechariah (1 : 69, 71, 77). The saying views the messianic salvation to be present 'today'. See on 10 : 1–20; 23 : 43; cf. 2 : 11; Ac. 13 : 26f.; 2 C. 6 : 2.

a son of Abraham: cf. Rom. 2 : 28f.; Jn 8 : 39; see on 13 : 16; 24 : 21.

10. Son of man: see on 5 : 24.

TOWARD JERUSALEM: A STORY OF A REJECTED KING **19 : 11–27**

Structure. Luke's story is a double parable that carries out two motifs, the meaning of discipleship (13, 15–26) and the rejected king (12, 14, 27). The first continues a theme of the preceding episodes; the second introduces the following passage (19 : 28–44).

A very similar parable occurs at Mt. 25 : 14–30. Since there are considerable differences between them, it may be that Jesus employed the same theme on different occasions (see on 14 : 16–24). If so, this story, like the parable of the two sons, was double-pronged from the beginning (see on 15 : 11f.). But here Luke (or

his source) probably has merged two parables of Jesus to serve his
literary purpose. The double conclusion, for example, supports
this interpretation. See on 18 : 1–8. In any case it is unnecessary
to view the rejected-king motif as the interpolation of a Christian
writer after the resurrection. For Jesus knows what awaits him in
Jerusalem; nevertheless, he has identified himself with the coming,
judging Son of man. See on 5 : 24; 12 : 8; Kümmel, pp. 45ff.

Teaching. The disciples share the common Jewish view that
Messiah's is an earthly kingdom and that it is to 'appear' at
Jerusalem (cf. *SBK* II, 300; Ac. 1 : 6). As the company of Jesus
nears the holy city, their anticipation of the immediate appearance
of the kingdom of God is heightened (cf. 24 : 21; Mk 10 : 36f.).
Jesus counters this misunderstanding with a number of sayings
and with such parables as the 'Pounds' and the 'Rejected King'
(cf. 17 : 22f.; 18 : 1–8; 21 : 8ff.).

By coupling these two parables Luke answers the problem posed
in his introduction (11). Jesus is not coming, he is going (Manson).
Only upon his return from the 'far country' will his 'kingly power'
be manifest. That will be a time both of judgment and of reward.
Like the 'servants' of the absent king, the disciples of Jesus must
get ready for faithful waiting. The true servant is one who is productive (cf. 8 : 15). The fearful, unfruitful servant, no less than
the enemies, will be judged and rejected. The following episode
is a commentary on this parable. See on 12 : 35–48; 16 : 1–13.

11. As they heard: perhaps a contrast is intended between
Zacchaeus (19 : 8) and the servants in the parable. See on 16 : 1–13.
The verse is an editorial transition (cf. Jeremias, *Parables*, p. 99).
appear (*anaphainesthai*): in contrast to the more ambiguous 'coming' of the kingdom (17 : 20ff.; 11 : 20; cf. 22 : 18), the 'appearing'
refers specifically to the *parousia*. Cf. 2 Th 2 : 8; 2 Tim. 4 : 1;
S. Aalen, *NTS* 8, 1961–2, 221.

12. kingly power: before his birth an angelic prophecy de-
clared Jesus to be a future king. Luke now reintroduces this motif.
Cf. 1 : 33; 19 : 38; 22 : 29; 23 : 3, 11, 37f.

12, 14, 27. The story of the rejected king has a partial similarity
to the experience of Archelaus, son of Herod the Great. At the
death of his father (4 BC) he went to Rome to obtain the Palestinian kingdom Although the Jews sent a delegation opposing
him, Archelaus was given Judea. Jos. *Ant.* 17, 9, 3f.; 17, 11, 1;

cf. Leaney. For Jesus (and for Luke) the 'citizens' who reject the king, become his 'enemies' and face his judgment are the Jewish leaders who have rejected him.

13, 16. pound (*mna*)**:** = 100 drachmas (Arndt). See on 15 : 8; cf. 16 : 1off.

14. do not want: cf. 13 : 34.

17. ten cities: the reward of duty fulfilled is duty (cf. Grundmann).

20. another (*heteros*)**:** of a different kind or type. The three reporting servants may represent the three types of response from the ten servants (13).

26. I tell you: a phrase that frequently introduces a saying at the end of a parable. The rabbis made similar combinations of a proverb (cf. *SBK* 1, 661, on Mt. 13 : 12). The form very likely was used by Jesus himself. But the Evangelists sometimes supplement it by substituting or attaching, on their own, editorial sayings or independent words of the Lord. See on 18 : 14; 14 : 24; cf. 8 : 18; G. Lindeskog, *ST* 4, 1950, 153f.

TOWARD JERUSALEM: JESUS THE REJECTED KING **19 : 28–44**

Structure. The episode consists of an introduction (28), preparation for the messianic act (29–34), the acted parable and the response (35–40), the appended lament (41–44). It is a transition piece between Luke's central division (9 : 51–19 : 44) and the final group of episodes set in Jerusalem (19 : 45–24 : 53). Called the 'triumphal entry', the passage usually is connected to the following Jerusalem events. Two considerations compel a reappraisal of this judgment.

First, the story is partially based on Mark and retains its general synoptic setting, but Luke's alterations and additions give it a different frame of reference. The changes determine the literary form and the meaning of the story. The narrative is scarcely 'triumphal' in any Gospel. In Luke it is not even an 'entry'. Jesus is still 'on the way'. Matthew (21 : 1of.) climaxes the story by the entry, but Luke's climax is Jesus' lament (19 : 41–44). Conzelmann (p. 64) correctly argues, 'We cannot place the end of the central section at 19 : 11, for *engus* means precisely that they are not yet at their destination.' The verdict applies with equal force at 19 : 28 (cf. 19 : 29, 41). This episode is a 'real life' commentary on the foregoing parable and continues the themes of the present section (18 : 15–19 : 44).

Second, several parallels to this pasage appear in the closing episodes of the Galilean mission. For example, the recognition of Jesus' messiahship is accompanied by a misunderstanding of its nature. And confession of Jesus by the disciples is coupled with his rejection by the nation's leaders. See on 9 : 37–45; cf. 19 : 37ff., 41–44. From these observations there arises a reasonable presumption that Luke regarded this episode as the conclusion of the central division.

Background. The setting is the Bethany–Jerusalem road as, rounding the Mount of Olives, it comes into sight of Jerusalem. At that point the road begins the 'descent' to the city. It is about a mile south-east of the city wall.

Zechariah (9 : 9) prophesied that a future king of Israel would come to Jerusalem in humility, riding on a 'colt', the foal of an ass. The rabbinic writings regularly interpreted this prophecy of Messiah (cf. *SBK* I, 842ff.). 'Jesus by a conscious act associates himself with the prediction and shows thereby that he wishes to be a Messiah without pomp, but yet just in this lowly action the eschatological consummation is already revealing itself' (Kümmel, p. 117). Cf. F. F. Bruce, *BJRL* 43, 1960–1, 336–53.

Teaching. This acted parable is not different in kind from the Lord's announcement in Nazareth (4 : 21), his messianic acts (cf. 7 : 21f.), or his acceptance of a messianic title (18 : 39; cf. Mt. 21 : 9). It is just a further step in a progressive public disclosure of his messiahship. The process will culminate in a direct messianic confession at his trial (22 : 67–71). Then the 'secret' known to his disciples (9 : 20f.) will become public property (23 : 38). The significance of the act is not lost upon his disciples (37f.) or his opponents (39). Yet the meaning is sufficiently veiled to avoid the suspicions of the Roman officials. The rebuke of the Pharisees represents the real attitude of Jerusalem toward Jesus. He is not now Messiah triumphant but Messiah rejected, and Jerusalem does not stand before a coronation but before judgment. Jesus knows these things. Therefore, as the demonstration dies away and the city looms closer, he, like Jeremiah, utters his oracle of doom in tears (41–44).

The central division of Luke opened with Jesus' rejection in Samaria (9 : 53). It closes with his rejection at Jerusalem. During the following days the Lord will consummate his mission and enter into the glory of his messianic kingship. But he will do this in a manner unsuspected by anyone other than himself.

29. Bethphage: apparently located on the Mount of Olives, just east of the summit and about a mile east of Jerusalem.

Bethany: on the southeastern slopes of the Mount some two miles from the city. It was the home of Mary, Martha, and Lazarus (cf. 10 : 38ff.) and is still occupied (population *c.* 700).

30. colt: or 'male ass' (cf. Kümmel, p. 117; O. Michel, *NTS* 6, 1959–60, 81f.).

ever yet sat: cf. 23 : 53.

31. A disciple's possessions always are subject to a single word, 'The Lord has need of it.' Cf. Ac. 4 : 34–37.

32. as he had told them: cf. 22 : 13, 21, 34; Jn 14 : 29. Fulfilled prediction was a sign of a true prophet. Luke shows considerable interest in setting forth Jesus in this role. He knows the hidden thoughts of men (7 : 39f.; cf. Jn 1 : 47ff.; 4 : 18f.). He makes unerring predictions, and his teaching accords with Moses and the prophets (24 : 6, 26f.). See on 9 : 35; 13 : 32f.

35f. garments: cf. 2 Kg. 9 : 13.

38. Blessed . . . : some in the crowd may have given this salutation with Messiah's forerunner, Elijah, in mind (cf. 9 : 8; Daube, p. 23). But the immediate circle of disciples was hardly under this false impression. See on 13 : 35; 7 : 19.

King: By inserting this title instead of the original—and also messianic expression—'coming one' (Mk 11 : 9; see on 7 : 19) Luke, like Matthew, joins the hosanna of Ps. 118 : 26 with the prophecy of Zech. 9 : 9 (cf. Mt. 21 : 4f.). His interpolation also serves to tie this episode to the preceding 'parable of the rejected king'. For the background of the title cf. K. Berger, *NTS* 20 (1973–4), 1–44.

Peace . . . : also a Lukan addition. The messianic peace is realized now only **in heaven,** that is, in the realm to which the resurrected Jesus goes (see on 6 : 23–25). 'Peace on earth' (2 : 14) is rejected by Jerusalem (19 : 42) and must await the *parousia* for its fulfilment. Cf. 10 : 5f.

38f. Note the contrast between the praising disciples, the rejecting Pharisees, the weeping Jesus (19 : 38–41) and the weeping disciples, the violent mob, the judging Jesus in 23 : 21, 27ff.

40. stones would cry out: Jesus' identity as Messiah earlier was 'hidden' and forbidden to be revealed (9 : 21; 12 : 2). It must now out. For the passion is at hand and Jesus will be crucified on a messianic charge. Or perhaps the saying points to Israel's alternative to accepting Jesus as Messiah. The 'crying stones' then may be a subtle reference to Hab. 2 : 11 where they refer to the judgment of Israel. If so, this catchword leads Luke to append at this point an oracle on the destruction of Jerusalem. It is noteworthy that the Qumran commentary on Habakkuk takes the passage (Hab. 2 : 8) as a prophecy of the capitulation of Jerusalem (and her wicked priests) to the army of the Kittim (= Romans?). Cf. Kosmala, *op. cit.*, p. 346; 1*QpHab* 9 : 6ff.

41–44. What blind Bartimaeus accepts (18 : 41), the blind leaders of Jerusalem reject. They will not see and, at the same time, Jesus' messiahship is 'hidden' from them. See on 9 : 9; 11 : 29f.; cf. Jn 9 : 39. The plundering of Jerusalem was predicted at Qumran (see on 19 : 40). This oracle speaks of an utter destruction. Cf. Jos. *War* 6, 5, 3.

It is sometimes argued that the prophecy could not have originated in the pre-resurrection mission because Jesus anticipated the destruction of Jerusalem only as an eschatological, i.e. end of the world, event. Certainly, the destruction in Mark (13 : 2) is associated with the final end. But the chronological relation between the two events is hardly crystal clear. Luke (21 : 20–24) 'historicizes' the apocalyptic *description* in Mark, but it is doubtful that he is historicizing an *event* which in the original oracle referred to the end of the world. See on 21 : 20–24, 32.

Furthermore, it is not true to the perspective of the New Testament to put 'historical' and 'eschatological' events in mutually exclusive categories. The resurrection of Jesus, Pentecost, the presence of the messianic temple are all viewed as both historical and eschatological. The present passage apparently does not even accommodate the wording to the destruction of AD 70. The phraseology is largely that of the Septuagint (cf. Isa. 29 : 3; 37 : 33; Ezek. 4 : 1–3; Leaney). In sum, there are no good grounds to disallow the oracle to the pre-resurrection mission, although a *pesher*-ing of it by Christian prophets remains a possibility. See on 21 : 20–24.

THE CONSUMMATION OF MESSIAH'S MISSION 19 : 45-24 : 53

Structure. The concluding division of the Gospel follows the outline of Mark only very loosely. In a number of passages the
Evangelist draws upon 'Q' and other non-Markan traditions.
Even where Mark is followed, the material is refashioned and
stamped with Luke's own interpretation.

In the traditional interpretation of Mark, Jesus entered Jerusalem on Sunday, cleansed the temple on Monday, held the
temple debates and Mount Olivet discourse on Tuesday, was
anointed on Wednesday, gave the Last Supper on Thursday
evening, and was arrested, tried, and crucified by 9 a.m. Friday.
There is some reason to believe, however, that Mark has 'telescoped' the sequence of events. See below, p. 228; the special note
at 22 : 7-38; on 22 : 63-23 : 25.

In Luke this chronology is by-passed. Instead, there is a thematic collection of episodes. The 'last days' are divided into three
sections, each with six episodes. The section on 'Messiah and the
temple' (19 : 45-21 : 38) is concerned with the significance of the
temple in redemptive history. From the last supper to the trial
Luke depicts 'the meaning of Messiah's death' (22 : 1-23 : 25).
'The glorification of Jesus the Messiah' (23 : 26-24 : 53) concludes
the Gospel and fulfils the prophecies with which the story began.
Messiah is exalted, and in this event the 'age to come' is realized.
But the old age remains a very concrete reality for Messiah's
people, his Church, his body. The conclusion, therefore, is really
a beginning, a beginning which Luke also has been chosen to
interpret. But that story belongs to his second volume, the Acts of
the Apostles.

Teaching. The 'teachings' motif of the central division continues. Indeed, the break between the central and concluding divisions of
the Gospel is not very marked. And it may be recalled that the
'Exodus' goal with which the central division opens is accomplished only at the resurrection. There is, however, a change to a
Jerusalem setting and a return to the theme of the first division
of the Gospel, the meaning of Jesus' messiahship. Much more than
Mark, Luke places the figure of Jesus the teacher again and again
in the foreground. His sayings and his acted and spoken parables
reveal the theological meaning of these 'last days in Jerusalem' for

the total plan of redemptive history. These crucial hours mark the end of an epoch and the beginning of the new messianic age. And they move inexorably to that end, Luke reiterates, because the things concerning Messiah 'written in the law of Moses and the prophets and the psalms' must be fulfilled (cf. 24 : 44).

Messiah and the Temple 19 : 45–21 : 38

Structure. The section opens with the rejection of Jesus by the temple authorities (19 : 45–20 : 18). It closes with Jesus' prediction of the temple's destruction (21 : 5–38). Of the other four episodes three pertain to the 'temple debates', and one presents the Lord's judgment upon religious hypocrites (20 : 45–21 : 4).

The temple debates (as presented in Mark) consist of a legal question (20 : 19–26), a mocking question (20 : 27–40), a nonlegal interpretative problem (20 : 41–44), and a moral principle. (Luke either omits the last question or shifts it to his 'teachings' division: 10 : 25–37). This fourfold scheme also is found in the rabbis. It is probable that these 'debates' formed a thematic collection before they were incorporated into the Gospels. D. Daube (pp. 158–63; *NTS* 5 158–9, 180ff.) argues that the structure is based upon Jewish Passover-eve discussions. If so, the collection was formed, probably in Jerusalem, in the earliest decades after the resurrection. They represent Jesus' Scripture discussions, some perhaps given in a synagogue within the temple area.

In this connection T. W. Manson (*BJRL* 33, 1950–1, 271–82), following M. Goguel (II, 250f.), argues that Mark has 'telescoped' the events of the last days in Jerusalem. More probably, he thinks, the period is some six months and begins with Jesus' cleansing of the temple at the feast of tabernacles. For Mark this would be a reasonable literary expedient. And in Luke the considerable number of Jerusalem episodes does presuppose a longer Jerusalem ministry than traditionally has been allotted. See on 13 : 1–9, 34; 14 : 1–24; 18 : 9–14. The answer may lie along the lines that Manson has proposed.

In the temple and trial scenes the Pharisees disappear as a group. That is, they merge into the more significant opposition group, the Sanhedrin. The rejection of Jesus by this ruling body is a dominant note, and it is significant for the meaning of the temple episodes. Jesus comes to the temple of Israel to purge and renew it. Instead of accepting his messianic role the Sanhedrin insistently resist and reject him, Jesus, in turn, accepts the rejection as the purpose of God. He then pronounces God's judgment on religious Judaism and its temple.

THE CLEANSING OF THE TEMPLE—AND A STORY ABOUT ITS MEANING
19 : 45–20 : 18

Structure. The passage has three parts, the temple cleansing and the reaction to it (45–48), a challenge to Jesus' authority to act as he does (1–8), and a concluding parable revealing the meaning of his actions (9–18). Cf. 10 : 25–37. The narratives and their sequence are common to the first three Gospels, but Luke summarizes them and forms them into a single teaching unit. In contrast to Mark (11 : 15ff.) Luke views the cleansing only as a prologue. The thrust of the episode is the opposition of the religious authorities and the parable. The latter reveals the meaning of this opposition for redemptive history.

Background. The temple tax, required of all Jews, had to be paid in special Jewish coinage. At certain times money-changers set up counters for this purpose in the courtyards of the temple. In the same 'court of the Gentiles' the temple administration handled the sale of offerings and sacrifices. The high priest's family seems to have shared the profit of this trade. Cf. *Shek.* 1 : 3; *SBK* I, 850; II, 570f.; Jeremias, *Jerusalem*, p. 49. These practices and the profiteering involved in them created great resentment among the visiting pilgrims. Jesus' action and teachings against the traders doubtless contributed to his popularity among 'all the people'.

Teaching. The deputation of the Sanhedrin (1–8) no doubt challenges the right of an unordained rabbi to teach in the temple courts. But it is Jesus' action, pregnant with significance, that arouses their greatest enmity and fear (47). The question (2) probably is a probe for a messianic confession, a confession that the Lord is not ready to make. In a debating pattern used by the rabbis, Jesus parries the question (see on 7 : 36–50). Yet in a subtle way he answers it by relating his mission to John's proclamation. He implies that, like the Baptist, his authority is from God. And his message is more than that of a prophet (7 : 26f.). It is an eschatological message that heralds the turn of the ages and the coming of the reign of God. To those who have ears to hear, Jesus' words, as well as his act of cleansing the temple, have a messianic ring. This implication probably is not lost upon his enemies.

The meaning of the episode is made explicit for Luke's readers by the appended allegorical parable (9–18). Religious Judaism, tenants of God's 'vineyard' Israel, mistreated God's prophets and killed God's 'Son' and 'heir'. Therefore, God will 'destroy' religious Judaism (with its temple) and give the vineyard to 'others'.

A Special Note on Jesus and the Temple

The temple is significant in Luke's presentation of Messiah's mission. In the Holy Place an angel announces the birth of the Baptist (1 : 13). In the temple courts Simeon utters his prophecy, and Jesus himself first shows a consciousness of his coming work (2 : 27, 49). In this place Satan tempts him to reveal, prematurely and perversely, his messiahship (4 : 9). After 'cleansing' the temple, Jesus prophesies its destruction (21 : 6). Although continuing to use it, Jesus' followers declare that it is not really God's building. They regard the establishment of God's messianic temple to be quite independent of it. Cf. Ac. 7 : 48; 15 : 16; Ellis, pp. 90ff.; Lohmeyer, pp. 112ff. Luke's total picture reveals (1) that the mission of Jesus is mysteriously and intimately associated with the temple, and (2) that this association ends with strong words against the temple and its authorities.

The unbelieving Jews insistently alleged that Jesus and his followers purposed to destroy the temple. Luke defers mention of this charge until the trial of Stephen (Ac. 6 : 13f.). But Matthew and Mark include it in the process against Jesus. And John's Gospel (2 : 19) attributes it to a misunderstanding of a saying that Jesus made at the cleansing of the temple. The same misunderstanding is present at the trial of Stephen, although at that time an explicit and public prediction of the temple's destruction may be involved (see on 13 : 34).

All this indicates that the false witnesses at Jesus' trial did not invent their charge. Rather they misunderstood or twisted a saying about the temple that Jesus actually did make. This probability is strengthened by several facts. First, in contemporary Judaism some believed that God would raise up a new temple in the last days (see on 13 : 35). Also, in the earliest strata of New Testament tradition a concept of a 'new temple' already is present, a temple that inheres in the messianic community. Furthermore, this concept is built upon a number of Old Testament *testimonia*, one of which is cited in Luke's (20 : 17) account of the cleansing of the temple. Cf. 1 Pet. 2 : 6ff.; Ellis, pp. 87, 89ff.; 1*QS* 8 : 5ff.; 9 : 6; 1*QH* 6 : 26ff.

Obviously the cleansing is not viewed by Jesus or his opponents as a breach of the peace, and it goes beyond a prophet's reform. It is presented as a messianic act. This act declares the time of the messianic renewal to be present and Jesus to be the inaugurator of it (Zech. 14 : 21; Kümmel, p. 118). As Conzelmann (pp. 75–8) rightly points out, Luke pictures Jesus as one who asserts possession of the temple (19 : 47; 21 : 37). His presence represents, symbolically at least, a displacement of Jewish religious authority. But this enhances and by no means negates the meaning of the cleansing as an act of judgment. The present episode shows that the cleansing is the prologue not merely to possession but to ejection, an ejection that Jesus himself anticipates. Thus, the emphasis of the passage lies in the objection to Jesus' authority (1–8) and in his ejection as the 'rejected stone' (9–18, esp. 17). Jesus will become the 'cornerstone' of God's temple, but not of the temple of religious Judaism. With his departure that house is left to them. See on 23 : 45; cf. Ac. 4 : 1ff.; O. Cullmann, *NTS* 5, 1958–9, 164f., 172; Gärtner, *Temple*, pp. 105–22; K. Balzer, *HTR* 58, 1965, 270–7.

45. those who sold: not only the sale of sacrificial birds and animals but probably a broader commercial traffic also.

46. robbers: an allusion to Jer. 7 : 11.

48. The people (*laos*) support Jesus during the temple scene (19 : 45–21 : 38). Cf. 20 : 19, 26, 45; 21 : 38. See on 18 : 43.

1. chief priests, scribes, elders: representing the three elements of the Sanhedrin. See on 11 : 45. 'Elders' and 'principal men' (47) are equivalent terms that refer to the non-priestly members. 'Rulers' (23 : 13) designated priestly or non-priestly members and, outside Palestine at least, local civic officials. Cf. Ac. 4 : 5, 8; Schürer II, ii, 245f.; Jeremias, *Jerusalem*, pp. 165f., 197, 222–6. On the reading 'chief priests' cf. G. D. Kilpatrick *NES*, pp. 203–8; favouring 'priests' cf. Metzger, pp. 238f.

2. these things: his teaching and his actions. Cf. Leaney; Daube, pp. 217ff.

4. baptism of John: see on 3 : 1–20.

9–18. The parable is both a messianic claim and a passion prediction. In comparison with Mark (12 : 1–11) it is altered at a number of points. Verse 18 heightens the note of judgment (cf. Dan. 2 : 34, 44). Verse 15 alters the sequence to the actual experience of Jesus (contrast Mk 12 : 8: 'killed . . . and cast him out'). 'Beloved' son (13) may represent a similar accommodation, as Jeremias supposes (*Parables*, p. 73).

C. H. Dodd (pp. 125–32) gives the best reconstruction of the historical situation of the parable. Problems between an absentee landlord and defaulting tenants were common enough in ancient Palestine. But historical realism does not exclude the possibility of allegorical elements in the original story. See on 8 : 11–15. W. G. Kümmel (*TC*, pp. 125ff., 130f.) rightly recognizes that the messianic allegory is inherent in the parable. But he concludes that the parable, therefore, was created by the early Church. This view faces two difficulties. Very likely, no allegory originating after the resurrection would have stopped short at the murder. Nor would it have put the murder *in* the vineyard. The resurrection was too central and the excommunication of Jesus too vividly remembered for that (cf. Heb. 13 : 12). Also, in the light of the Qumran discoveries (e.g., 4*QFlor* 1 : 11) Kümmel's reservations about the pre-Christian messianic use of 'son' no longer apply. See on 22 : 70.

The parable, a part of Jesus' temple teachings, is his commentary on Isa. 5 : 1f. (9), a text that is supplemented by concluding references to Ps. 118 : 22(17) and Dan. 2 : 34 f., 44 f. (18). The whole accords with a synagogue commentary pattern (cf. *SBK*, IV, 173; E. E. Ellis, *MBR*, pp. 309–12).

9. people: but the churchmen are implicitly present (20 : 16f., 19). See on 18 : 43; cf. Mk. 11 : 27.

vineyard: see on 13 : 6; cf. Isa. 5 : 2–5.

12. yet a third: the 3 + 1 (= prophets + Jesus) formula was a familiar literary device. The fourth part of the series formed a dramatic climax. See on 6 : 27–38.

13. son: the unique status of the last emissary corresponds to the significance both of Jesus' mission and of his person. 'Son of God' probably first became a *title* for Messiah in the Church, but

it had long been descriptive of his role. See on 22 : 70. Characteristic of Jesus' presentation of his messiahship, the messianic
reference is veiled. The theologians and churchmen sense only
that the parable is 'against them' (19).

17. stone: a frequently used 'testimony' to Messiah from Ps.
118 : 22. In Palestinian Judaism the term was related to the messianic 'servant'. Cf. the Targum on Ps. 118 : 24; Zech. 3 : 8f.;
Walton III, 274 (Pss.), 114 (Zech.).
head of the corner: Judaism expected a glorification or renewal
of the temple in the days of Messiah. Cf. *SBK* I, 1003f.; see on
13 : 35.

RENDER TO CAESAR . . . AND TO GOD **20 : 19-26**

Background. A tribute was regularly levied by Rome upon her
provinces. Among the Jews it was very unpopular, especially
because it symbolized Israel's subjection. During Jesus' childhood
it had been the occasion of a serious revolt against the Romans
(cf. Jos. *War* 2, 8, 1; *Ant.* 18, 1, 1). See on 2 : 1f.

Teaching. The theologians and 'chief priests' recognize the threat
that Jesus poses for their traditions and power. The 'tax question'
is calculated either to alienate the people from Jesus or to bring
about his arrest. Jesus answers that one's obligation is not to God
or Caesar but to God and Caesar (Manson). Thus he makes very
clear that his kingdom is not in rivalry with Caesar's and, on the
other hand, that the rightful claims of God must not be com-
promised to the state.

Although Jesus effectively squashes any insinuation of treason
or heresy, his enemies have made their point. And the slander will
be repeated at his trial (23 : 2). With the nationalists now solidly
against him, the cross looms nearer.

19. people: see on 19 : 48.
21. the way: i.e. 'the way' of the kingdom of God (1 : 79;
3 : 4; Ac. 18 : 25f.; cf. *CD* 20 : 18; 1*QS* 3 : 10). It later becomes a
title for the early Church. Cf. Ac. 9 : 2; 19 : 9.
22-25. For the literary form see on 7 : 36-50.
25. render or 'give back': the coin obviously is Caesar's, and
all using it have an indebtedness to Caesar. Cf. also Rom 13 : 1-7;
1 Pet. 2 : 13-17. The Lord's answer represents his refusal to

tie his mission to current political issues. For the Evangelist it becomes an abiding principle for the Church's relation to the state.

THAT THE DEAD ARE RAISED **20 : 27–40**

Structure. The question of the Sadducees (27–33) remains substantially the same as it is in Mark. Jesus' answer (34–38) and the conclusion (39f.) contain a number of alterations. Luke omits the Lord's two rebukes and adds several explanatory phrases (34–35a, 36, 38b). Perhaps they represent a tradition independent of the second Gospel. The conclusion apparently is based upon the following Markan (12 : 32, 34) passage.

Background. In the time of Jesus Jewish views on the future life varied from group to group. Usually more resistant to the inroads of Hellenistic culture, the Pharisees in this matter were considerably, and rather early, influenced by Greek thought. The departure of the 'soul' to reward or punishment immediately at death was for them a widespread if not dominant belief. R. Meyer (pp. 12–15) detects remnants of an older viewpoint in some rabbinic sayings. In them the 'soul' remains near the grave after death (e.g., *Hag.* 15b; *Ber.* 18a; *Shab.* 13b). But even here the body/soul dualism already is presupposed. The Essenes (or some of them) shared this view, perhaps along with the Pharisees' doctrine of resurrection. Cf. *Jubilees* 23 : 31; Hippolytus, *Refut. Haer.* 9 : 27; see on 16 : 23, 26. The Sadducees believed in neither 'resurrection, neither angel nor spirit'. In their view soul and body perished together at death. Cf. Ac. 23 : 8; Jos. *War* 2, 8, 11–14; *Ant.* 18, 1, 3–5; *SBK* 1, 885f. on Mt. 22 : 23.

Like the Sadducees and the Old Testament Psalms (e.g., 6 : 5; 115 : 17), the Qumran writings also seem to regard the whole man as mortal, perishing at death. Cf. 1QS 11 : 22; 1QH 10 : 3; 12 : 25–31; Mansoor, pp. 84–9. But in addition there is the distinct hope that God fashioned the elect 'from the dust unto eternal foundation . . . to stand in array with the host of holy ones', and that they 'shall be roused to (destroy the sons of) wickedness' (1 QH 3 : 21f; 6 : 29f.) Similarly, M. Black translates 1QH 6 : 29f., 34 : 'all the sons of his truth shall arise . . . and all the sons of wickedness will cease to be. . . . And those that sleep in the dust shall raise up a standard and the worm among men lift up a sign' (Black, *Scrolls*, p. 142). Cf. 1 *QH* 4 : 21f.; 11 : 12; 18 : 25-29.

Taken together, these ideas apparently imply an immortality for the righteous via resurrection. This view is closer to New Testament thought than the teachings of either the Pharisees or Sadducees. Some other late Jewish apocalyptic writings also combine an interim 'sleep' with a future resurrection hope. However, they sometimes present it in the framework of a body/soul dualism. Cf. 2 *Baruch* 21 : 23f.; 23 : 5; 30 : 2; *Enoch* 91 : 10; 100: 5.

Teaching. The 'test case' posed by the Sadduccees presents the idea of resurrection as an absurdity. Doubtless the argument was effective against the common view that resurrection life was merely an extension of the good life of this age. Cf. *SBK* 1, 887ff. on Mt. 22 : 28; *Enoch* 10 : 17ff.; 1*QS* 4 : 7. By asserting a fundamental difference in sexual relationships in 'that age', Jesus dismisses their immediate question as irrelevant. Turning to the basic issue, he appeals to Moses to show 'that the dead are raised'.

Jesus' argument is one of inference. It proceeds from several assumptions common to him and the Sadducees. Moses called God the God of Abraham after Abraham was dead. But God is not the God of the dead. Therefore, Jesus concludes, Abraham's resurrection must be certain. For God can be related to the dead Abraham only if such a relationship can be actualized by his coming to life again. Further, what is true of Abraham must be true also of those who share his covenant relation with God. Cf. H. Odeberg, *TDNT* iii, 191.

Many commentators conclude that Jesus is asserting Abraham's immortality, i.e. that he is now individually living 'in heaven'. But this assumes a body/soul dualism that is, to say the least, uncharacteristic of the New Testament view of man (cf. Bultmann, *Theology* i, 209; Kümmel, *Man*, pp. 43-6, 83). In the context this interpretation is hardly possible because it would defeat the precise point of Jesus' argument. If Abraham is now personally 'living', no resurrection would be necessary for God to be 'his God'. The premiss of the argument is the Old Testament (and Sadducean) view of death. From this premiss, the nature of the 'living' God, and God's convenant with Abraham the Lord infers the necessity of a resurrection. The question between Jesus and the Sadducees is not Plato's but Job's, not 'if a man die is he still alive' but 'if a man

die shall he live again'. To this question Jesus gives a firm and
positive answer: the paths of glory lead *from* the grave.

29–33. Posing resurrection riddles was a favourite game of the
Sadducees and often an embarrassment to the Pharisees. For
example, will those resurrected require ritual cleansing (since they
were in contact with a corpse)? Cf. *Nid.* 70b; *Sanh.* 90b.

35. worthy: only the righteous are in view. See on
14 : 14.

neither marry: in sharp contrast to the expectation of the
Pharisees (cf. *SBK* 1, 888, on Mt. 22 : 28). It also is at variance
with 16 : 18 (q.v.). There indissoluble marriage seems to be the
rule for the messianic community. Presumably the rule applies
only for the interim until the *parousia*.

At 20 : 34 the Western text, which Grundmann thinks may be
original, has 'are begotten and beget'. That is to say, the sons of
this age find the ground and continuity of their existence in pro-
creation. In contrast, the life of the resurrection is rooted immediately and continually in the life of God (cf. 1 C. 15 : 44f.). Pro-
creation, which in the context of the Sadducees' question is the
primary purpose of marriage, is pointless and will cease. The
Western reading would accord better with the thought at 16 : 18.
Possibly it represents a Lukan alteration of Mark, made with that
passage in mind.

36. equal to angels: in that they cannot die and are 'sons of
God'. But they do not become angels, nor are they like them in all
respects (cf. Heb. 2 : 14–18). The DSS and other Jewish writings
also speak of the likeness of the redeemed to angels. Cf. 1*QH*
3 : 21ff.; 6 : 13. Cf. Black, *Scrolls*, pp. 139ff.; *Enoch* 104 : 4ff.;
SBK 1, 891.

sons of God: contrasted with the sons of this age (34). Cf. Mt.
5 : 9, 45; see on 15 : 12. Resurrection life itself signifies sonship
with God because it is a confirmation of God's covenant relationship. It has been manifested first in Messiah (Ac. 2 : 36; Rom.
1 : 4). But it is vouchsafed equally to all who share in the messianic
covenant. It may be that Jesus' confidence in his own resurrection
(as Messiah) rested ultimately in such Scriptures as this word of
God to Moses (37). See on 24 : 26.

37. the passage about the bush (Exod. 3): their Bible had
no chapters and verses. Cf. Rom. 11 : 2; Heb. 4 : 7. A 'proof'
from 'Moses', i.e. the Pentateuch, was of the highest authority for

the Sadducees. The rabbis had similar arguments for the resurrection. Cf. *Sanh.* 90b; *SBK* I, 893, on Mt. 22 : 32.
he calls (*legei*)**:** better, 'it says'. The word is an introductory formula (cf. Rom. 9 : 25) for the following citation (Exod. 3 : 15). God, not Moses, is the speaker. 'The Lord' is God's covenant name, associated with God's covenant promises.
38. all live . . .: 'For him all are alive' (*NEB*). Perhaps this means 'from God's perspective' or, proleptically, 'in the prospect of a sure resurrection'. See on 1 : 51–53; cf. 4 *Mac.* 7 : 19; 16 : 25. More probably Luke adds this phrase with his Christian readers specifically in view. They live 'in God' (cf. Ignatius, *To the Ephesians* 6 : 2). The life of the coming age has become present in the resurrection of Jesus Christ. It is not that the Christian 'enters' the hidden life with the Lord at death (Grundmann) but rather that the Christian's present (corporate) existence in Christ continues in spite of his (individual) death. What the Christian now shares corporately, 'in Christ', will be fulfilled individually at the *parousia*. This idea already has been developed by Paul. See on 6 : 23–25; 9 : 24; 23 : 43. Cf. Ac. 17 : 28; Col. 1 : 16; 3 : 3f.; E. E. Ellis, *NTS* 10, 1963–4, 275f.

DAVID'S GREATER SON **20 : 41–44**

Structure and Background. The rabbis recognized that Messiah was David's son (see on 18 : 38f.). Yet it also was affirmed that in Ps. 110 David referred to Messiah as 'Lord'. In a patriarchal order the younger is never so honoured by the elder. How are these conflicting scriptural propositions to be reconciled? It is very unlikely that Jesus (and certainly not Luke) means to deny that Messiah is David's son (cf. 1 : 32, 69). Luke places the saying after the question on the resurrection. This arrangement may suggest that it is intended to pose a dilemma similar to that raised by the Sadducees (20 : 33). If so, the answer is to be found along the same lines.

Teaching. The messianic age is not merely an extension of this age. It introduces a new order in which the traditions and customs and rules of this life are consummated and superseded. Therefore, Messiah is not in rivalry with Caesar (20 : 25). Nor is he merely David's successor. Though he is David's son, he is greater than David because he has a more exalted role. He is 'first' in a greater age. Cf. Ac. 3 : 15; 5 : 31; see on 7 : 18–35. Perhaps Jesus also hints that Messiah is a more exalted person, i.e. with a unique relation to God. But at most this meaning is secondary.

42. There is a complete absence of a messianic interpretation of Ps. 110 in the rabbinic writings of the early Christian centuries. P. Billerbeck suggests, probably correctly, that it is no accident but is in reaction to the Christian usage. After the third century the (pre-Christian) messianic interpretation is revived. Cf. *SBK* IV, 452–65.

David says: Jesus reflects the common view of his day concerning authorship of the Psalms. But in this case the recital by and/or reference to David is important for the teaching involved. Recent Old Testament studies are open toward such a background for the psalm. Cf. Johnson, pp. 120ff.

44. As is the case in similar questions posed by the rabbis, 'the answer implied is not that one notion is right and the other wrong but that both are right in different contexts' (Daube, p. 163). Cf. Cullmann, *Christology*, pp. 127–33.

THE CHURCHMEN AND THE WIDOW **20 : 45–21 : 4**

Structure. As he has done earlier (6 : 24f.; 18 : 9–14), Jesus condemns the hypocritical piety of the theologians (45–47) and the comfortable religiosity of the rich (1–4). The two scenes are taken from Mark. They are merged into one episode by altering the transition verse (21 : 1) and by using the 'widow' theme to bind them together.

Teaching. The contrast between the common people and the religious leaders, the poor and the rich, is more than a moral judgment on his society. The Lord speaks in the context of his mission, i.e. in the prospect of the coming kingdom of God. Hypocritically pious Judaism and its 'rich' adherents stand under impending judgment (see on 21 : 5–38). For the truly pious, as for this widow, the coming kingdom will mean deliverance from oppression and the fulfilment of their hope in God. Luke does not include this episode merely as a polemic against the Church's enemies. All of Jesus' judgments upon the religious Judaism of his day were, in the Gospels, not only read *in* the Church but *to* the Church. This is, therefore, a warning to the Church's own leaders who are in

danger of falling into the pattern of the Jewish churchmen. See
on 12 : 41–48; cf. Jas 2 : 2–7; 5 : 1–6.

46f. scribes: see on 11 : 45.
robes: resplendent academic and clerical garb (Daube, p. 125).
best seats: see on 14 : 1–24.
widows' houses: perhaps the property of widows who were
dedicated to the service of the temple (see on 2 : 36f.), property
possibly managed by the temple authorities. Cf. 19 : 46; Manson;
J. Jeremias (*Jerusalem*, p. 114) thinks that it refers to the hospitality
of these women, which the scribes exploited. Cf. 8 : 3; Ac. 16 : 15.

1. rich: see on 6 : 24ff.; 16 : 14.
treasury: i.e. boxes placed in the public eye in the women's court,
the area to which Israelite women (as well as men) were admitted.
Cf. 2 Kg. 12 : 9ff.

2. two copper coins: about one hundredth of a denarius.
See on 15 : 8.

3. Truly (*alēthōs*): see on 4 : 24.

THE SIGNS OF THE AGE . . . AND OF THE END **21 : 5–38**

A Special Note on the Eschatological Discourse

This discourse occurs in Matthew, Mark, and Luke. It has been
the subject of more scholarly debate than perhaps any other
passage in the Gospels. Two questions have dominated the discussion. What is the meaning of the connection made between the
destruction of Jerusalem and the *parousia*, i.e. the end of the world?
How much of the discourse represents pre-resurrection prophecies
of Jesus and how much is created or interpolated by Christian
writers?

The discourse (in Matthew and Mark) combines a question
about the destruction of Jerusalem with one about end of the
world. Not without reason, some scholars in the last century identified the two questions. For Jesus the destruction would signal the
end of the world. Since the end did not occur, one must recognize
that Jesus was in error about the time of the end and, perhaps,
about the fact itself. Others accepted this interpretation but sought
to shift the error from Jesus to the Church. The first critical question, therefore, gave rise to the second.

To salvage the trustworthiness of Jesus the 'little apocalypse'
theory was born. According to this theory a Jewish (-Christian)

handbill was the origin of the apocalyptic element of the discourse, i.e. the portion predicting the end of the world. It was first circulated either when Pilate put Roman ensigns in Jerusalem (? AD 26), when the emperor Caligula threatened to place his image in the temple (AD 40), or when Roman armies moved against the city (AD 66–70). Later, the prophecy was wrongly attributed to Jesus. Therefore, the theory concludes, Jesus is not implicated in the erroneous prediction and not to be associated with such apocalyptic speculation.

Although it is an ingenious reconstruction, the 'little apocalypse' has little to commend it critically. It originated more from worthy sentiment than from critical exegesis. When sought in the text, it forms no meaningful literary structure (cf. Beasley-Murray, pp. 18–21; Kümmel, pp. 98f.). The fundamental error, however, is the theory's tacit acceptance of the 'apocalyptic' interpretation of the discourse in the Gospels.

The 'little apocalypse' theory regards Luke's (21 : 20–24) 'anti-apocalyptic' saying as representing Jesus' original meaning. An hypothesis popularized by A. Schweitzer takes just the opposite point of view. Jesus was an apocalyptic preacher who made erroneous predictions about the end of the world. The Church toned them down (e.g., in 21 : 20–24) because of embarrassment over the delay in their fulfilment. Unfortunately, the 'toning down' occurs before there was time to get embarrassed. The 'delay' motif already is present in the earliest New Testament writings (2 Th. 2 : 3–5; Mk 13 : 10, 21, 33f.). And the interests of the theory appear to be the chief obstacle to deriving the motif from the intention of Jesus himself (see on 12 : 45). It is true that an increased emphasis upon the 'delay' appears in the later New Testament books, e.g., in Luke. But the reason is something more fundamental than embarrassment (see on 17 : 20–37; 18 : 1–8).

The 'apocalyptic' interpretation of Jesus finds support in Mt. 10 : 23. The saying predicts, at least at first reading, a *parousia* of the Son of man in the context of the earliest mission to the 'cities of Israel'. However, assuming the earliest date of Matthew, the Evangelist scarcely understood the saying in this way (cf. Mt. 10 : 18; 24 : 14). And in the intention of Jesus himself the Jewish mission was only the prerequisite for a later inclusion of the Gentiles (Jeremias, *Nations*, p. 73). The apocalyptic interpretation of Mt. 10 : 23, it appears, is not as certain as it might be. In any

case it is not sufficient ground upon which to build an eschatology
of Jesus, especially when it is contradicted by equally primitive
traditions. See on 9 : 27; 12 : 21; cf. 13 : 29.

Probably, the meaning of the eschatological discourse will find
no scholarly consensus in the near future. But interpretations pro-
ceeding from either 'apocalyptic' or 'anti-apocalyptic' reconstructions of the eschatology of Jesus are inadequate for the task. Future
discussion must take account of two elements in the teaching of
Jesus. He did announce a coming end of the world, and he did
reckon with a considerable and indefinite interval before the end.
See on 17 : 22f., 25; 21 : 32. Neither element can be denied to him
on critical grounds. And both are necessary for a proper understanding of the eschatological discourse.

Structure. The introductory question (5–7) is answered by four
appended sign-sayings. The first two are signs of the age, false
Messiahs and 'tumults' in the world (8–11) and persecution for
the Church (12–19). The last two are signs of the end, the destruction of the Jewish nation (20–24) and final catastrophic events
(25–33). An admonition and conclusion, peculiar to Luke, complete the episode (34ff., 37f.).

The time-span in all four sign-sayings has one point of termina-
tion, the end of the age. Thus, 'signs from heaven' will signal the
culmination of world history (11, 25). And perseverance then will
find its reward in 'redemption' (19, 28). The fulfilment of the 'times
of the Gentiles' (24) either is equated with the *parousia* or introduces the final distress preceding it (28, 32).

However, the time-span of the four sayings is not completely
parallel. For Luke the time of trial is nothing less than the time of
the Church (12–19). See on 22 : 40. Probably the first 'sign of the
age' (8–11) is equally extensive. Cf. Ac. 11 : 28; 16 : 26. The first
'sign of the end' (20–24) begins with the judgment on the Jewish
nation. The second (25–33) is more narrowly defined (see below).
The arrangement provides a kind of stair-step progression from
the death-resurrection (R) to the *parousia* (P) of Jesus:

```
                        R              P
     (8–11)        ———— ........ ————
     (12–19)       ———— ........ ————
     (20–24)          ———— ........ ————
     (25–33)                    ————
```

In all the Gospels the eschatological discourse is a collection of the Lord's sayings. It cannot be read as though it were one sermon (cf. Kümmel, pp. 97f.). The precise relation of Luke's account to Mk 13 and to the Evangelist's special sources is difficult to assess. The arrangement and general content are parallel to Mark. But only one segment (8–11) is clearly based upon the second Gospel. Some differences doubtless are due to Lukan alterations. But probably there were variant forms of the sign-sayings in the pre-canonical tradition. The structure of the discourse also may be pre-Markan.

Background. Twenty years after the resurrection of Jesus the Church already was threatened by a false apocalypticism. Claiming to be apostolic, it taught that Jesus had returned secretly and that the world's end was imminent (see on 17 : 20–37). Perhaps this false teaching was bound up with the crisis coming upon the Jewish nation. In any case the Evangelist recognizes it and answers it in the context of Jesus' prediction of the destruction of the temple. Although expanded by the traditioners and the Evangelist, the eschatological discourse probably originated as a paraenetic midrash or commentary on certain Old Testament texts, a midrash given privately by Jesus to his disciples (cf. Hartman, pp. 245–8).

Teaching. The Lord has taught his disciples that he will be 'taken away' (5 : 35). See on 12 : 35–48; 19 : 11–27; Kümmel, pp. 74–87. The prophecies here presuppose his absence and his future reappearance. In the interim his followers are to shun any self-styled announcers of his return. And they are to reject the usual apocalyptic interpretation of political distress. It is a sign of the age, not of the end. For the Church it is a time of persecution and 'testimony' not of final redemption (8–19).

Nevertheless, two end-signs may be anticipated. The 'desolation' of Jerusalem (20–24) publicly manifests the effective end of the old covenant and the old age, an end that has occurred in the death and resurrection of Jesus. That is, in the destruction of the temple in AD 70 'the sign of the torn veil' (23 : 45) finds its fulfilment, and the proclaimed presence of the new messianic temple finds its confirmation. Similarly, the second end-sign reveals that the glorious *parousia* is *near* (25–33). Here, 'the sign of the darkened sun' at Jesus' death (23 : 45) probably points to the actual dis-

ruption of the cosmic order at his *parousia*. At least the disasters
will be of such proportion as to produce mass despair. But in
them Christians will discern a hopeful sign: 'your redemption
is drawing near'.

   5. temple: see on 13 : 35; 19 : 41–44; the special note at
19 : 45–20 : 18. The temple consisted of a large (*c.* 400 × 500
yards) walled enclosure. Much of it was restricted to Jews. Within
the restricted area and dominating the whole complex was a
temple house. In front of the house the sacrifices were offered.
Within it were the sanctuaries, the Holy Place and the Holy of
Holies. Rebuilt after the return from the Babylonian exile (515
BC), the 'second temple' underwent a complete renovation from
c. 19 BC to AD 64. The new buildings were composed of massive
stone blocks. Those not plated with gold or silver were so white,
writes Josephus (*Ant.* 15, 11, 3; *War* 5, 5, 3–6), that at a distance
the whole appeared to be the snow cap of a mountain. Tacitus
(*Hist.* 5, 8, 1) describes it as a temple of immense wealth. At the
conquest of Titus Jerusalem was so completely destroyed that,
except for certain towers and wall-portions deliberately left, one
would scarcely have guessed that it had been inhabited. Cf. Jos.
War 7, 1, 1ff.

   7. Teacher: see on 3 : 12.
this: i.e. the destruction of the temple. In contrast to Matthew,
Luke does not apply the additional question to the end of the age.
By the oracle (20–24) his readers are prevented from identifying
the two events. Perhaps his alteration implies that such a mistaken
identification has been made. The question asks when; the answer
(8–36), much broader, tells the meaning of the destruction. Cf.
Cranfield, pp. 388, 393f.

   8. I am he (*egō eimi*) or 'I am here': this seems to be someone
claiming to be Jesus' representative who announces Jesus' (secret)
presence. Cf. Daube, p. 325.

   12. before all this: apparently to indicate that this saying
(12–19) is chronologically overlapping the preceding one.
synagogues: omitting 'councils' (Mk 13 : 9; cf. Mt. 10 : 17),
which Luke uses only for courts of the Jerusalem Sanhedrin. This
may suggest that Luke's church is Jewish-Christian—but in the
diaspora. Cf. 12 : 11.

   14f. The close relationship in Israelite tradition between
martyrdom and prophecy continues in early Christianity.

mouth and wisdom: the power of the Holy Spirit and perhaps a specific prophetic gift. The first person and the absence of the favourite Lukan term, 'Holy Spirit', shows that Luke does not follow Mark (13 : 11). He may have in hand a Christian prophet's oracle or (a variant form of) the tradition that Mark has used. Cf. Kümmel, p. 99n. See on 11 : 49–51; cf. 12 : 11f. In Ac. 4 : 8, 13; 6 : 3, 10 the promise of this verse finds a fulfilment in the Spirit-filled words of the apostles and of Stephen.

16–18. Although put to 'death' not a hair will 'perish'. Cf. 12 : 4, 7; 1 C. 15 : 16–18; Mt. 10 : 28 (*apolesai*).

19. endurance: i.e. under continuing trial. See on 8 : 13, 15; 18 : 1–8; 22 : 28. *Hypomonē* in faith is only possible in the face of *peirasmos*, and conversely *peirasmos* requires *hypomonē* (Brown, p. 48). **lives:** see on 9 : 24.

20–24. This passage is structurally too independent to be viewed as Luke's paraphrase of Mark. And the priority of Mark's wording appears more probable than that Mark and Luke are independent adaptations of an original oracle. C. H. Dodd (*JRS* 37, 1947, 52, 54) has shown that the Lukan passage is composed of the phraseology of Old Testament prophets and that the Evangelist probably has drawn upon 'oracles in the manner of the ancient prophets'. Cf. LXX: Isa. 3 : 25f.; 29 : 3; Jer. 20 : 4f.; 52 : 4; Dan. 9 : 26f.; Hos. 9 : 7; 14: 1; Zeph. 1 : 14f.; Schramm, pp. 178ff.

According to Eusebius (3, 5, 3), the fourth-century Church historian, Christians were warned to flee shortly before the destruction of Jerusalem by the oracle of a Christian prophet. This passage is itself probably not that oracle. But it may be another oracle of the same type. That is, Luke adopts a version of Jesus' 'abomination' oracle (Mk 13 : 14ff.) that has been restated for a generation that is experiencing its fulfilment. This type of *pesher*-ing probably has its origin in the activity of early Christian prophets. See the special note at 11 : 49–51.

It is not uncommon to regard this passage as an historicizing of Mark. That is, Luke's alteration turns the Jewish war into an ordinary event in history. The original oracle (in Mark) referred to it as an 'end of the world' event. But this interpretation of Mark is not tenable. First, as Conzelmann (p. 135n) has observed, how does one escape the final catastrophes by fleeing Judea (Mk 13 : 14)? Further, Daube (pp. 425ff., 432) has shown that Mark's mysterious phrase, 'let the reader understand', probably refers to a matter about which it is dangerous to speak openly. This could hardly apply to an 'end of the world' prediction. But in the context of Jewish nationalism it would be very true of a prediction of Jerusalem's destruction by the Romans. Cf. H. Conzelmann, *ZNTW* 50 (1959), 210–21.

The whole Gospel tradition interprets this prophecy of the destruction of Jerusalem in the continuing course of history. There are no very strong critical grounds to dissociate Jesus' original oracle from this meaning. See on 19 : 40, 41–44; 21 : 32.

22. vengeance: for Jerusalem's wilful and continuing apostasy from God and sins against the righteous. Cf. Ac. 7 : 51; Jer. 5 : 29. See on 18 : 3.

all that is written: part of the oracle. Perhaps it includes previously written Christian (as well as Old Testament) prophecies concerning Jerusalem's destruction. See on 13 : 34f.; 19 : 41–44; special note at 11 : 49–51; Mk 13 : 14; Zech. 14 : 2. Josephus (*War* 6, 9, 3), perhaps speaking hyperbolically, estimates that in the Jewish rebellion more than one million died and that one hundred thousand went into exile.

24. the times of the Gentiles: i.e. of the Gentile possession of Jerusalem. Cf. Rev. 11 : 2. The period may extend to the *parousia*. But it is also possible that Luke understands the final 'sign saying' (25–33) to follow the Gentile 'times'. If so, a future repossession by the Jews is anticipated.

25–33. The last 'sign saying' begins with the 'signs from heaven' that culminate the first saying (8–11). It concludes with an appended parable and oracle (29–33).

25–28. Anxiety before the events is conquered by the hope which their meaning inspires.

25. signs: in this passage and elsewhere Jesus teaches that the *parousia* will not be preceded by signs evident to the unbeliever (see on 17 : 20–37). Even the unwary and sleepy disciple will be caught unawares (34f.). This suggests that the apocalyptic language (25f.) should not be interpreted literally of awesome cosmic dissolution but figuratively of desperate political distress (Plummer). Probably, however, cosmic phenomena cannot be excluded from Luke's meaning (Grundmann). This common stock apocalyptic terminology is used in Jewish writings both of political upheaval and of the end of the age. Cf. Isa. 13 : 10; 34 : 4; Ezek. 32 : 7; Am. 8 : 9; 4 Ezra 13 : 30ff.; 1*QH* 3 : 29–39.

27. see: see on 9 : 9, 27.

cloud: cf. 9 : 34; Ac. 1 : 9–11.

31. kingdom of God is near: i.e. its *parousia* manifestation. See on 9 : 27; 17 : 20f.; 19 : 11.

32. Truly: see on 4 : 24.

this generation (*genea*): interpreted chronologically as Jesus' generation (Kümmel) or the generation of the end-signs (Conzelmann); non-chronologically as believers or unbelieving Jews (cf. Grundmann), or mankind (Leaney). The context seems to demand a chronological meaning. Within this framework it is scarcely realistic to interpret the Evangelist's meaning as Jesus' generation. For both Mark and Luke the generation of Jesus is past. Even if the desolation of Jerusalem foreshadows the *parousia*, Mark (13 : 21f.) still anticipates a further interval. Luke is perfectly aware that the *parousia* will not occur in Jesus' generation and is concerned to counter imminent apocalyptic expectations (see on 17 : 20–37).

In this context Luke (or Mark) would hardly use a saying that fostered speculation about an imminent end of the age, speculation that contradicted the reality that he was experiencing. Kümmel (p. 60) argues that the saying, in Jesus' mouth, referred to his generation. However, he admits that it cannot be so interpreted in the immediate (Markan) context. But how can one establish the meaning of a short isolated text without a context, and especially a meaning in contradiction to the only context available to us?

Since the turn of the century the point of view accepted by Kümmel has been widely held. But several facts call for a revision of it. First, it is opposed to the Evangelist's understanding of the phrase. Also there is some evidence that Jesus himself perhaps did not expect the end of the age in his generation (Linnemann, pp. 132–6; see on 11 : 31). Furthermore, the unexpectedness of the end and the anticipation of 'sleeping' disciples (see on 17 : 20–37; cf. Mk 13 : 32–37; Mt. 25 : 1–13), repeated emphases in the teaching of Jesus, are inconsistent with a 'calendar' appointment within a generation. More decisive, in the Qumran writings the term, 'last generation' (1*QpHab* 2 : 7; 7 : 2), apparently included several lifetimes. Their usage indicates that in the New Testament 'this (last) generation', like 'last hour' (1 Jn 2 : 18) or 'today', means only the last phase in the history of redemption. None of the terms are to be understood in a literal way. See on 17 : 25; 23 : 43. The public revelation of the kingdom *is* just around the corner, but its calendar time is left indeterminate.

'This generation' in this passage is the 'generation of the end-signs' (cf. Conzelmann, p. 105). It is identical with the 'generation of the end time' to which Jesus spoke and which extends from the pre-resurrection mission to the *parousia*. The fact that it covers several (or several dozen) lifetimes is quite irrelevant. Luke especially wishes to stress this point in his opposition to the false, apocalyptic interpretation of Jesus' saying. See above, pp. 13f.

34. take heed: see on 12 : 35–48.
cares of this life: cf. 8 : 14.
37f. This is the conclusion for the whole temple scene (19 : 45–21 : 38). To it some manuscripts append the story of the woman taken in adultery (cf. Jn 7 : 53–8 : 11).

THE MEANING OF MESSIAH'S DEATH 22 : 1–23 : 25

The setting in this section shifts from the temple to the city, from Jesus' judgments to Jesus under judgment. The section opens with the plot against Jesus (22 : 1–6) and closes with his arraignment and trial (22 : 63–23 : 25). The meaning of the plot and the Lord's own attitude toward his coming execution reveal the significance of his death. Jesus is a willing victim. He consecrates himself to death in the conviction that it is the will of God (22 : 39–46) and that it, like the passover of long ago, will deliver Israel from death to life (22 : 7–38).

Betrayed (22 : 47–53), denied (22 : 54–62), and 'delivered up', Jesus has no advocate. Nor does he take his own defence. Nevertheless, the trial discloses that he is innocent of any wrong. Luke is at pains to present his death as a religious act of cosmic proportion. The real battle is not with the law but with the churchmen and Satan (22 : 31, 40, 53). And the real issue is religious (22 : 70). It is a death 'at the feast'. It may be that Luke views the total process against Jesus as a sacrificial ritual (Conzelmann, p. 79). But this idea, if present, lies below the surface.

THE PLOT TO KILL JESUS 22 : 1–6

Since Jesus' temptation Satan himself has been under attack (cf. 10 : 18; see on 11 : 14–28). He now resumes the initiative,

determined as ever to thwart Messiah's mission. The mention of
the role of Satan draws attention to the parallel between this crisis
and the earlier temptation. In each Jesus is under sustained and
extreme pressure to desert or pervert his calling. In each he stands
abandoned and alone. In each a capitulation would effectively
destroy the meaning of his mission. In the temptation Satan en-
tices; in the passion he threatens. In both he tempts the Lord to
preserve his life (4 : 3f.; cf. 22 : 42), to yield to the appeal of a
political kingdom (4 : 5ff.; cf. 22 : 38, 49f.), to make a grandstand
bid for messiahship (4 : 9; cf. 22 : 64, 67).

1f. Passover: see the special note at 22 : 7–38.

feared: that the people would follow Jesus (to revolt?) or that
they would resent and resist his public arrest. Cf. Jn 11 : 48ff.

3. Satan: according to Conzelmann (p. 80) Luke regards Satan
as 'absent' during the pre-resurrection mission (4 : 13–22 : 3). His
return signals a new epoch of 'temptations' (cf. 22 : 35ff.). Probably Luke does implicitly associate with Satan the 'trials' which the
Lord predicts for his followers. But Satan appears in Acts (5 : 3;
13 : 10) only twice as tempter. Both passages stress the power of
the gospel over him rather than his threat to the Church. The
same is true of the pre-resurrection mission, where demonic activity is the activity of Satan (cf. 13 : 11 with 13 : 16). Cf. 10 : 18;
11 : 14–28; Eph. 6 : 12; see on 12 : 5. But Satan also is aggressive
and, in individuals, destructive during the mission of Jesus as well
as that of the Church (8 : 2; Ac. 5 : 3).

Judas: Satan tempts but the responsibility remains on Judas.
What were his motives in the betrayal of Jesus? Coveteousness
was involved and possibly a disillusionment with Christ's non-
political concept of messiahship (Ac. 1 : 18; cf. Jn 12 : 4f.). Some
suggest that Judas only wanted to force a showdown and, thereby,
an immediate establishment of the kingdom (cf. Manson). This
has a certain appeal, but it is not suggested by the texts.

4. captains: see on 22 : 52.

5. they were glad: Judas' defection provides the priests and
theologians with an opportunity to secure Jesus' arrest without
arousing the pilgrims sympathetic to him.

MESSIAH'S CONSECRATION TO DEATH: THE LAST SUPPER **22 : 7–38**
A Special Note on the Nature and Date of the Last Supper
In recent years the Last Supper has been the subject of considerable scholarly inquiry and debate. See E. Schweizer, *RGG* I, 10–22;
Jeremias, *Eucharistic Words*; Higgins; C. W. Dugmore, *TU* 79,
1961, 420f. Much of it has centred upon the relation of the Supper
to the passover meal. The passover lamb was sacrificed on the
14th day of Nisan (= March/April), the first month of the ecclesiastical year, and was eaten that night (cf. Exod. 12). 'Passover'
was followed by 'the feast of unleavened bread' (15–21 Nisan).
Since the Jewish day began at sundown, the evening passover meal
was coincident with the beginning of the second feast. The whole
eight-day festival sometimes was reckoned as one 'holy day' and
called by either title (see on 22 : 7).
   All the Gospels place the crucifixion on Friday (see on 23 : 54).
The Fourth Gospel (13 : 1; 18 : 28) puts the passover sacrifice and
meal on the same day. Matthew, Mark, and Luke date the passover earlier. Indeed, they identify the Last Supper before Jesus'
arrest with the passover meal, as J. Jeremias (*Eucharistic Words*)
has convincingly demonstrated. Jeremias concludes that John
alters the chronology to achieve a theological goal. By synchroniz-
ing the crucifixion with the passover sacrifice, John sets forth
Jesus as 'our paschal lamb' (cf. 1 C. 5 : 7).
   But perhaps both John and the synoptic Gospels not only are
theologically significant but also chronologically unaltered. In the
first century the Qumran sect, some Sadducees, and other groups
followed an unofficial calendar in which the passover meal always
occurred on Tuesday evening (14–15 Nisan). If John's Friday
passover (14–15 Nisan represents the official calendar, the other
Gospels indicate that Jesus celebrated the passover on the earlier,
unauthorized date. (Astronomy would, then, fix the year at AD
30 or, more likely, AD 33 (cf. H. E. W. Turner, *HC*, pp. 68–74;
Reicke, *Zeit*, pp. 136f.)).
   Several facts support this supposition, set forth by Mme A.
Jaubert (pp. 103–21; cf. *NTS* 14, 1967–8, 145–64). (1) The Last
Supper is dated on a Tuesday by a few Christian traditions. (2)
In the Fourth Gospel also it has some characteristics of a passover
meal. For example, it is eaten at night and includes a 'dipping'

ritual (Jn 13 : 26, 30). More important, (3) an 'earlier' Supper clarifies the account of the Passion. Jewish law forbade the trial and conclusion (i.e. execution) of a case on the same day. A trial on the eve of a sabbath or festival also was forbidden (*Sanh.* 32a, 35a). These laws, probably in force in the first century, pose a problem for the traditional view of a Thursday night Supper and a Friday morning crucifixion. In the light of their procedures elsewhere, the Evangelists or their predecessors may well have compressed the chronology (see above, pp. 6f.). That is, the Gospels have 'telescoped' into one night and morning proceedings against Jesus that actually lasted several days. Cf. M. Black, *NTE*, pp. 19–33; *contra*, J. Jeremias, *JTS* N.S. 10, 1959, 132f.; *Eucharistic Words*, pp. 24f.

A problem arises in relating this view of the Last Supper to the 'breaking of bread' in Acts (2 : 42, 46; 20 : 7ff.). The meals in Acts are generally similar to religious meals found elsewhere in Judaism. Cf. K. G. Kuhn, *SSNT*, pp. 84ff. O. Cullmann (*Worship*, pp. 14ff.) maintains, with some merit, that they originated in the post-resurrection meals of Jesus and his disciples (cf. 24 : 30). They were a joyful fellowship of 'the community of the resurrection' and an anticipation of renewed fellowship with Jesus in the coming kingdom of God. The Last Supper, however, associates this anticipation not with the meal but with a vow to fast.

Probably one must recognize two types of communion meals in the primitive Church in Jerusalem. There was the frequent 'breaking of bread' and the annual 'passover' meal. Only the latter was directly related to the Last Supper, and only in it was the *meal* a specific remembrance of Messiah's death. Christian worship outside Jerusalem merged the two meals (cf. 1 C. 11 : 20f., 23ff.). Thus, in the Lord's Supper the joyful fellowship meal became the 'Love Feast', and the passover meal became the 'Eucharist' or 'Communion'. The combined liturgy was frequently observed. But the annual feast, which originated at the Last Supper, in time disappeared except in the practice of isolated groups and in the strange references of Mark and Luke to the Lord's vow. See on 22 : 14–23.

Structure. The Last Supper is Luke's seventh dinner scene (see on 14 : 1). It includes the preparation (7–13), the passover meal and its interpretation (14–23), and appended 'teaching words' (24–38).

Luke interprets these 'teaching words' in the framework of the meaning of the supper.

Background. Residents of Jerusalem were under a religious obligation to provide rooms (in exchange for the lambskin) so that pilgrims might celebrate the passover within the city. The meal itself began after dark and followed a fixed ritual. Cf. *SBK* i, 988f.; iv, 41–76; Jeremias, *Eucharistic Words*, pp. 84ff. After the first cup of wine the passover story was related and Psalms 113, 114 sung. The second cup and main meal followed. After supper the third cup, 'the cup of blessing' (*Ber.* 51a; 1 C. 10 : 16), was taken and the second half of the passover *Hallel* or hymn was sung (Pss 115–18). The fourth cup of wine, 'taken to celebrate God's kingdom', concluded the liturgy (cf. Daube, p. 331).

The passover was a celebration of two events. It commemorated the deliverance from Egypt long ago (*Pes.* 10 : 5), and it anticipated the coming messianic deliverance. The latter part of the *Hallel* had special reference to the messianic kingdom. See on 19 : 38.

Teaching. Earlier Jesus predicted his death. In this episode he interprets it and consecrates himself to it. It was customary for the leader to interpret the elements of the passover meal. In an acted parable Jesus interprets the passover 'bread' and 'wine' of his coming death. He thereby declares his death to be the means by which the redemptive significane of the passover will be fulfilled. His shed 'blood' brings into being a new covenant and accomplishes a new Exodus, an Exodus from sin and death. See on 3 : 3.

Presumably the passover signified only deliverance. Nothing in the ritual warranted Messiah's interpretation of his body and blood as 'given for you'. These words speak not only of a new covenant but also of vicarious sacrifice. They can be explained only as an implicit reference to the suffering Servant who, as the covenant representative, 'poured out his soul to death and . . . bore the sins of many' (Isa. 53 : 12).

This concept is in mind when, departing from the Markan format, Luke makes the teaching words a part of his supper scene (24–38). They set forth Jesus, the serving Lord, as an example for his followers. Through the same servant role, and only through it,

they also are to receive a 'kingdom' and to rule (24–30). See on
12 : 35–48; 17 : 1–10. Peter's denial typifies the 'rejection by all'
to which the suffering Servant is destined (31–34). Cf. Isa. 53 : 3.
That Jesus is to be 'reckoned with transgressors' (37) forecasts a
similar rejection for his followers. The time of easy victory is past.
From 'now' on discipleship is to exact its cost, conflict with the
world and suffering for Jesus' sake (35–38). See on 9 : 23ff.;
10 : 1–20; 21 : 12, 19.

7. the day: or 'first day' (Mk 14 : 12). Possibly Luke thinks
in terms of a religious calendar in which the passover sacrifice
occurs in the middle of the festival week (cf. Goudoever, p. 180).
More likely, however, he uses a loose idiom in which the day of
passover was merged with the following feast. Cf. Jos. *Ant.* 2, 15, 1;
14, 2, 1; *SBK* II, 812ff.

8. Peter and John: cf. Ac. 3 : 1ff; 4 : 19; 8 : 14.
prepare: one had to slaughter and roast the lamb (see on 22 : 15)
and obtain the unleavened bread, bitter herbs, and wine necessary
for the meal.

10. The instructions apparently are intended to avoid detection
by the religious authorities. Perhaps this is because Jesus is already
under threat of arrest or, less likely, because he is preparing to
observe passover at an illegal time. See special note at 22 : 7–38;
cf. M. Black, *NTE*, pp 31f.

12. furnished: i.e. with couches. Slaves and the poor ordinarily sat at meals. For the passover supper 'even the poorest man
in Israel must not eat until he reclines' (*Pes.* 99b). This signified
the freedom obtained by the deliverance from Egypt.

13. as he had told them: see on 19 : 32.

14–23. Luke (or his source) divides the supper story into the
Lord's 'vow' of abstention from future passovers (15–18), his
interpretation of the bread and wine (19–20), and his prophecy of
the betrayal (21–23). Although the forms generally are Palestinian, Semitic, and early, the liturgical usage of the Church has
shaped in some measure the wording and ordering of all the
'Lord's Supper' narratives. Cf. K. G. Kuhn, *SSNT*, pp. 79f.

The double 'vow' followed by the double interpretation of
Messiah's death corresponds to the twofold perspective of the
passover (see above). In the Christian 'passover' the past reference
shifts from Egypt to Calvary, i.e. to the fulfilment of the redemption typified by the Exodus. Therefore, Jesus does not command

his disciples to repeat the passover but to repeat its interpretation 'in remembrance of me' (19–20). However, Jesus' death does not fulfil the future perspective of the passover. It does not bring the revelation of the kingdom of God but introduces the time of fasting and of trial (see on 22 : 28). By his 'vow' the Lord indicates that the disciples are to expect a long wait. But he also affirms that he is one with his followers in the fasting time (15–18). For 'messianic Jews', i.e. the Christians, the passover both in its past and future reference now belongs to the 'new age' reality inaugurated by Jesus the Messiah. Yet they, no less than 'blinded Israel', await with longing the fulfilment of the passover 'next year in Jerusalem', the new Jerusalem of the kingdom of God.

Several lines of evidence support the above interpretation. According to Mark's order Jesus' vow involves the fourth cup. In the ritual this cup is designated 'the fruit of the vine' (18) and is taken to celebrate God's kingdom. If the preceding *Hallel* or hymn ends the supper (Mk 14 : 26), it implies that Jesus reserves the fulfilment of the liturgy until the kingdom of God literally is revealed and celebrated (Daube, pp. 330f.). Furthermore, there is reason to believe that the first-century Palestinian Church spent the day of passover in a vicarious fasting for the Jews. (It was a practice of a third-century Christian group, the Quartodecimans, and probably had its roots in the early Palestinian Church. Cf. B. Lohse, p. 139; *RGG* v, 733; K. G. Kuhn, *SSNT*, pp. 91f.). The practice was not connected with a remembrance of the Lord's death but with an anticipation that the *parousia* would occur at passover-time (see on 17 : 20). Late in the night of 14–15 Nisan these Christians concluded their fast with the Lord's Supper.

The ordering of Luke's sayings (15–18, 19–20) probably reflects the liturgical practice of the Jerusalem Church. The first Jesus-word (15–18) has to do with fasting and points to the future reference of the passover, the *parousia*. The second (19–20) has to to with bread and wine and points to the past reference of the passover, the death of Jesus. Although Mark probably gives the correct chronological sequence, the two double-sayings of Luke are not a repetition of one original saying. (This has been one of the arguments against the genuineness of the longer text; see on 22 : 19*b*–20). Nor is it necessary to suppose, as K. G. Kuhn does (*SSNT*, p. 92), that the Jerusalem church created the words of institution (15–18) for their fasting tradition. If the passover character of the Last Supper is recognized, both the vow and the interpreted meal-elements are appropriate to the original setting (Jeremias, *Eucharistic Words*, pp. 207–37). Quite probably the Jerusalem church received its fasting tradition from the Lord on the night he was betrayed.

15. eat this passover: the idiom does not refer to the festival or the meal but to the lamb. Cf. C. K. Barrett, *JTS* 9, 1958, 305ff.

18. fruit of the vine: a more refined expression for wine and a formula used at the passover meal (*Ber.* 6 : 1 (= 35a); Dalman, p. 150). According to Jeremias (*Eucharistic Words*, p. 167n) the vow lies behind Christ's refusal of the wine-mixed narcotic on the cross (Mk 15 : 23). More likely, however, it pertains only to the passover celebration (cf. 22 : 15f.). It is not, then, an expectation of a soon 'appearing' of the kingdom of God (see on 19 : 11). Rather it points to Messiah's identification with his followers in the long 'fasting time' that is coming. See on 22 : 28.

until: i.e. until the coming messianic feast (see on 13 : 29; cf. 22 : 30) or, less probably, the resurrection/exaltation of Jesus (see on 9 : 27).

19b–20. This passage is the most discussed textual problem in Luke. Some modern translations (*RSV, NEB*), too hastily, have removed it from their texts. It is omitted by Codex D and a few Latin and Syrian manuscripts. And some Syrian texts rearrange the order: 16, 19, 20 (or 1 C. 11 : 23), 17, 18. The passage appears in all Greek manuscripts except Codex D and is in evidence as early as AD 150 (Justin, *Apology* 66; cf. Williams, p. 49). In the last century Hort (p. 63) accepted and popularized the shorter reading. In his opinion a later omission was very improbable, and the later addition (and rearrangement) was satisfactorily explained as a borrowing from 1 C. 11 : 23f. and Mk 14 : 23f. to eliminate the inverted cup → bread order.

The abrupt ending and the superfluous character of verse 19a have caused recent advocates of the shorter text also to eliminate it (19a) from the original tradition. It is taken to be an addition of Luke (H. Chadwick, *HTR* 50, 1957, 257f.) or of a later scribe (Bultmann, p. 286n), who did not perceive the verses 15–18 composed the complete formula with 'passover' (15) as the 'bread' word. Now it is quite understandable that Luke did not perceive this, especially since 'to eat the passover' did not mean 'bread' but the lamb. Hort's argument also is vulnerable. The addition of

verses 19*b*-20 to correct the cup → bread order necessarily would
have eliminated the first cup (17). Also, this order apparently
created no difficulty elsewhere (1 C. 10 : 16; *Didache* 9 : 2f.).

H. Schürmann, in an article (*Bib.* 32, 1951, 364-92, 522-41)
and later in a three-volume work, has thoroughly analysed this
passage. His results demonstrate the virtual impossibility that the
shorter text is original. First, several items in Luke's Last Supper
scene presuppose verses 19*b*-20. (1) The opening words of 22 : 21
('but behold') are strongly adversative and refer to the phrase, 'for
you'. (2) The sentence, 'I covenant to give you, as my Father has
covenanted to give me, a Kingdom' (29, Weymouth), builds upon
the previously mentioned 'new covenant'. (3) 'This cup' (42)
points the reader back to the 'cup' word in 22 : 20. (4) Verbal
peculiarities in 22 : 19*b*-20 make it unlikely that the verses are
drawn from 1 Corinthians 11 or Mark 14 (cf. Schürmann II, 8of.).
Second, the shorter text displays an unstable structure. It is difficult to suppose that verse 19*a* would be introduced without a
corresponding 'cup' word. And its inclusion is incompatible with
the parallelism of 22 : 15-18. Yet its removal against all textual
evidence makes 22 : 21 ('but behold') all the more incongruous.

The longer text also presents problems. Non-Lukan elements in
the style of 22 : 19*b*-20 pose no real objection since the formulas
are liturgical tradition. But one must account for the presence of
two cups and for the shortening of the original text. If the Last
Supper was a passover meal, the two cups are readily explained
(see above). The different intent of the latter saying (19-20) argues
against its being a repetition of verses 15-18. However, a Gentile
Christian scribe who did not know the passover ritual might not
discern the distinction. He, therefore, might have omitted 22 : 19*b*-
20 as a repetition. This is especially so if the scribe was accustomed
to a cup → bread order in his (Syrian?) liturgy.

On either view of the passage the abrupt ending of the shorter
text remains a problem. Some suggest that the omission, whether
Lukan or later, was meant to preserve secret the sacred formula of
institution. This is not convincing since verse 19*a* was not omitted
and such words were not avoided elsewhere. Cf. H. Chadwick,
HTR 50, 1957, 253ff. Schürmann (*Bib.* 32, 1951, 539ff.) rightly
associates the omission with liturgical usage. He supposes, perhaps
unnecessarily, that the omission occurred after the Lord's Supper
had been detached from a preceding 'Love Feast' (cf. 1 C.

11 : 20f.). Thus, the textual basis for the earlier, rejected practice
would be removed. It may be better, however, simply to ascribe
the truncated structure to a scribe who was liturgically unfamiliar
or unsympathetic with the bread → cup order and/or the passover tradition. In any case there is little reason to ascribe it to
Luke. The longer text in all probability is what the Evangelist
wrote.

19. This is my body: i.e. 'This means . . .' (Moffatt). The
elements are representative and are the preached word made
visible. The point is not the substance of the elements but their
use as a proclamation of a past event and of a Lord present in the
Body of believers. 'The Eucharist, therefore, is not a Passion play
like the Mass; Christ's death is preached (1 C. 11 : 26) not his
dying re-enacted' (M. Barth: cf. Higgins, *op. cit.*, p. 53).

22. determined: by the inviolable prophecies of Scripture (cf.
24 : 25f.). The destiny of Judas also is 'determined' (cf. Ac.
1 : 16ff.).

24–27. see on 9 : 46–50; 12 : 37.

28. The perfect tense indicates that the 'trials' abide throughout the mission of the Church. Cf. 22 : 36; Ac. 20 : 19; Conzelmann, pp. 81, 199. See on 5 : 35; 8 : 13; 12 : 1–12; 21 : 12, 19.

30. at my table: see on 13 : 22–30.
thrones: as he does at 22 : 14, Luke omits 'twelve' (cf. Mt.
19 : 28), apparently because of a broader understanding of the
apostolic leadership of the (present) eschatological Israel. See the
special note at 9 : 1–9.
Israel: i.e. the true Israel, the redeemed. Jesus asserts his royal
claim upon the nation that God will give to him. See on 22 : 69.

31f. Satan: see on 22 : 3. On the basis of Peter's coming denial
(34) Satan demands a right to have him (as well as Judas).
Against Satan's accusation Jesus makes priestly intercession on
behalf of Peter (cf. W. Foerster, *ZNTW* 46, 1955, 129–33).
you . . . you: the first (31) is plural, the second (32) singular.
Perhaps the plural refers to Peter and Judas. If it refers to all the
disciples, it is another example of Peter's representative role. Jesus
prays for Peter in order that he in turn, by his leadership, may
'strengthen' the others. See on 12 : 41; 22 : 54–62.

36. sword: although the term is usually regarded as a meta-
phor, the context indicates a literal meaning. Cf. 6 : 29; see on
9 : 3; 12 : 51; 22 : 49.

36ff. The necessity for suffering is attributed explicitly to Jesus' identification with the suffering Servant. Cf. Ac. 8 : 32f.; Isa. 53 : 12. Probably it is implicit in other passion predictions. **But now:** i.e. the future mission of the disciples (see on 22 : 3). **enough:** i.e. 'that's enough of that'.

MESSIAH'S CONSECRATION TO DEATH: THE PRAYER **22 : 39-46**

Structure. The scene moves to the Mount of Olives where Jesus and his disciples have their encampment ͵(21 : 37). Departing considerably from Mark, the story brackets Jesus' prayer with his admonition to the disciples: 'pray that you may not enter into temptation' (40, 45f.).

Teaching. The structure is instructive for Luke's meaning. The trials to which Christians are destined can be endured and overcome only through prayer. Eager to fight God's war with man's weapons (22 : 38, 49), the disciples fumble with the weapon that counts.

Socrates awaited death with indifference, if not anticipation. Jesus, like the Psalmist, found the prospect appalling. The difference lies in their opposite understanding of the meaning of death (cf. Cullmann, *Immortality*, pp. 19–27). For Jesus death is the consequence of sin (5 : 20). As a threat to one's being, it is—more awfully—a threat to one's relation to God: God is not the God of the dead (20 : 38). Through his resurrection Jesus becomes 'Lord of the dead', and thus the Christian is assured that even death cannot separate him from God's love and purpose in Christ (Rom. 8 : 38f.; 14 : 9). But this is not the lot of Jesus as he beseeches God to remove the cup of death. He, the sinless one, dies as a sinner, forsaken by man and God (Mk 15 : 34). And yet, in submission, he commits himself fully and freely to this 'hard' will of the Father.

40, 46. temptation: i.e. 'trial'. It is an abiding feature of the time of the end, the situation in which the Christian lives between the Cross and *parousia*. See on 18 : 1–8; cf. Conzelmann, pp. 81f. To 'enter into' temptation apparently means to succumb to its power and thereby be destroyed. See on 8 : 13; 11 : 3f.

41f. knelt: the usual position of prayer was standing (cf. Jn 17 : 1). Perhaps this reflects Jesus' humility and the urgency of the prayer (Grundmann).

Father: see on 10 : 22; 11 : 2.

43f. The verses are absent from a number of important manuscripts. In the opinion of Westcott and Hort (pp. 66f.) they are
not Lukan but, nevertheless, reflect a genuine extra-canonical
tradition. They were 'rescued from oblivion by the scribes of the
second century' in controversies with the Docetists. A. Harnack
argued for the presence of the verses in the original copy, and more
recent studies tend to agree with him (cf. Williams, pp. 6ff.).

45. for sorrow: i.e. 'worn out by grief' (*NEB*) or by distress.
Cf. MM, p. 382.

46. sleep: the passover union was broken if any of the partici-
pants fell asleep. This meaning may be involved in the original
situation. Cf. Mk 14 : 37-41; Daube, 332ff. More importantly,
Jesus sees in the attitude a lethargy toward the peril of temptation.
One who now sleeps soon will deny his Lord (22 : 62). Cf. 9 : 32.

THE BETRAYAL 22 : 47-53

Structure. The plot against Jesus mentioned earlier (22 : 1-6) now
begins to take its course. In contrast to Mark (and probably using
another tradition) Luke subordinates the action to the teaching
words of Jesus. His poignant question to Judas (47ff.), his rebuke
—in word and deed—to the disciple (51), and his interpretation
of the arrest (52f.) climax the three parts of the episode. All are
Lukan and reveal the meaning that the event has for Luke's
theme.

Teaching. Although Jesus is an innocent victim, treacherously
betrayed by one of his own, he renounces any appeal to the sword
(cf. 22 : 38). Messiah's kingship, Luke reiterates, is not one of
political power. Although responsible and guilty, his captors are
only willing tools in the hands of a more powerful 'power of
darkness'. Even Satan himself 'is only an instrument in God's
plan of which the Passion forms a part' (Conzelmann, p. 182;
22 : 22).

49. sword: according to Cullmann (*State*, pp. 31-4), Jesus
approved defensive sword-bearing but, unlike the Zealots (see on
6 : 14ff.), rejected such means to establish the kingdom of God
(22 : 36, 38). See on 6 : 29. *Contra:* P. S. Minear, *NoT* 7, 1964,
131ff.

51. touched: see on 5 : 13. For the names cf. Jn 18 : 10.

52. chief priests, captains, elders: a loose and variable idiom for the Sanhedrin or its deputations. The 'captains' were the temple custodians. See on 20 : 1; cf. G. Schrenk, *TDNT* III, 270ff.

53. hour: see on 10 : 21.

darkness: see the special note at 11 : 33-36.

THE DENIAL **22 : 54-62**

Structure. All the synoptic Gospels presuppose that Jesus had two hearings before the Jewish authorities, one in the small hours of the night and the other in the morning. (On the proceedings cf. Blinzler, pp. 81-163; Sherwin-White, pp. 45f.) In Mark and Matthew the messianic charge and confession occur at the night hearing. In Luke they occur at the morning session, and the night hearing is only implied by the setting (54).

This crucial incident may have occurred twice. And Luke's wide verbal variations from Mark do indicate that he has at hand non-Markan traditions. On the other hand Luke's thematic, episodic structure suggests that he has shifted Mark's order. The night scene is occupied solely with Peter's denial, and the legal proceedings are gathered into the following 'trial scene'. Mk 15 : 1 (*symboulion*; cf. Mk 3 : 6; Ac. 25 : 12) also seems to locate the official condemnation at the second hearing.

Background. The Sanhedrin, already at least two centuries old, consisted of seventy members plus the high priest (cf. Jos. *Ant.* 12, 3, 3; Leaney). Although it was the effective religio-political authority in Judaism, it required the assent of the Romans to execute a capital penalty (Jn 18 : 31; Jos. *Ant.* 20, 9, 1). See below, p. 261. The 'Sanhedrin' was the 'assembly in session' (22 : 66) as well as the organization. Its meeting place is not certain (cf. *Sanh.* 11 : 2). But it had been removed from the temple and probably was housed in a commercial building in the city (*Shab.* 15a; *Sanh.* 41a; *Yoma* 25a). The Sanhedrin could not, under its (later?) regulations, try a capital case at night (*Sanh.* 4 : 1 = 32a). And the rabbinical writings give no indication that it ever held its sessions in the high priest's house. Cf. *SBK* I, 998f., 1000; Jos. *Wars,* 5, 4, 2. Therefore, in the process against Jesus the first hearing probably was an informal interrogation, as Luke's account implies. Cf. 22 : 66.

Teaching. During the course of the first hearing Peter denies the Lord. The denial of Jesus leads to the denial of his discipleship (57f.). No phrase in the Gospels is more charged with feeling than the climax of the episode: 'The Lord looked at Peter, and Peter remembered' (61).

Peter was bolder than the others. They fled (Mk 14 : 50). In his more explicit denial he represents them in their failure and sin. But Peter's spirit is willing. His sin arises from fear, and in this it is quite distinct from that of Judas. Nevertheless, it has the same mark of apostasy. In Luke's mind the outcome is much more dependent on God's grace than on Peter's moral superiority to Judas. Jesus prayed for Peter; Judas, he gave up (22 : 22, 32). Judas is the 'other face' of every man which, left to its course, leads to destruction (Ac. 1 : 18ff.). Peter also represents that other face. But in him sin encounters grace and is purged.

57. denied: two meanings are implicit here: (1) to dispute, refuse to recognize, and (2) to abandon, deny solidarity with someone. The Church uses the term in the latter sense as the opposite of 'confession'. Thus, it indicates apostasy from the faith or from Christ (cf. 12 : 8f.; 2 Tim. 2 : 12). The theological meaning underscores the gravity of Peter's sin. But it also gives assurance to the penitent apostate that his is not an unforgivable sin. This story, then, is a counterbalance to the warning in 12 : 9. It would have been especially relevant at a time when the penitent apostate posed a problem for the Church. See above, p. 58. Cf. H. Riesenfeld, *CN*, pp. 213–19.

I do not know him: perhaps the formula of excommunication used in the synagogue (*SBK* 1, 469). Peter divorces himself from any relation to Jesus.

THE TRIAL: THE CONSUMMATION OF THE PLOT TO KILL JESUS
22 : 63–23 : 25

Structure. Luke's trial episode consists of the Sanhedrin hearing (63–71), the hearings before Pilate (1–5) and Herod (6–12), and the final hearing and surrender of Jesus to the Jews (13–25). Luke follows an independent tradition (and Q ? cf. 22 : 69 with Mt.

26 : 64) although he touches upon Mark at a few points. The
hearings are given no chronological sequence. However, 23 : 13
implies a recess before the convening of the 'judgment' session.
Probably one should think in terms of a couple of days. See the
special note at 22 : 7–38.

Background. The Sanhedrin condemned Jesus, but it did not have
authority to execute him. Cf. Jn. 18 : 31; j*Sanh.* 1 : 1; 7 : 2;
Blinzler, pp. 157–63; *contra:* Winter, pp. 75–90. To achieve their
end the churchmen may have substituted a political charge when
they came before Pilate, as they did later against Paul. Cf. Ac.
23 : 29; 24 : 5f.; H. J. Cadbury, *BC* v, 305f. More likely, they
placed multiple charges against Jesus, treason and religious blasphemy. The multiple charge, which was permitted in certain circumstances, gained the attention of the governor in the first
instance and the sympathy of the populace in the second. Cf.
20 : 20; Mk 15 : 3; Jn 18 : 33; 19 : 7; Sherwin-White, pp. 24–47;
Jos. *War* 2, 8, 1.

Teaching. In Jesus' consecration to death (22 : 7–38, 39–46) Luke
shows the divine necessity for Messiah's sufferings. This episode
interprets the historical unfolding of the *via dolorosa*. Each section
stresses the vehement determination of the religious leaders to
have Jesus killed. In the face of plain evidence of his innocence
their false accusations (2) conceal their own seditious sympathies
(18ff.). Although the condemnation of the Sanhedrin is implied
(71), Luke omits any explicit verdict of 'guilty' against Jesus.
Curious Herod, not getting his miracle, treated Jesus as a harmless
oddity. Pilate only 'delivered' him to the people. Together they
give a twofold witness—Jew and Gentile—to Jesus' innocence (cf.
Dt. 19 : 15).

Luke uses heavy strokes to picture the guilt of the Jewish
nation in Jesus' death. In contrast Pilate's threefold plea (14, 20,
22) depicts him almost as an advocate for Jesus. This serves Luke's
theme. In Luke's own day unbelieving Jews presumably continued
to assert, and Roman authorities to believe, that the Christian
Messiah was executed for sedition. On the contrary, Luke insists,
he was killed by religious leaders out of wicked hatred (cf. Ac.
2 : 23; 3 : 14f.). Even so, Pilate is not flattered. From political
expediency he yielded Roman justice to the will of a mob.

Jesus was abandoned by all; the 'world' rejected and crucified him. In the attitude of each person on that spring day, the Evangelist implies, every man in some measure can see himself reflected: unbelief in Jesus' message, hatred of the 'light', curious minds, indifference, expedience, and fear.

64. The 'blind man's bluff' game reveals the true role of Jesus: he is the rejected prophet. The later mockery of Herod's soldiers (23 : 11) shows the political cast of the trial. But it also furthers Luke's theme: Jesus is the rejected king. See on 19 : 28–44.

66. chief priests and scribes: see on 20 : 1.
their council: literally, their Sanhedrin. The term may refer to a specific building (Winter, pp. 20ff.).

67–70. In Mark (14 : 61) the high priest with *one* question identifies Messiah with the Son of God; Jesus gives *one* answer. By using another tradition (or by elaboration of Mark) Luke qualifies Jesus' acceptance of the 'Messiah' title and gives prominence to the titles, Son of man and Son of God. He may wish to make explicit the basic identity of the messianic titles (Conzelmann, p. 84). More probably, he wants to distinguish the political 'Messiah' from the non-political messianic terms (Grundmann). This distinction is implicit in Mark: 'Are you *Messiah*?' 'You will see the *Son of man*.' But Luke's fuller statement clarifies Jesus' intent: 'I am Messiah, but not the kind you think—or would believe in.'

69. from now on: (*apo tou nun*): i.e. from the 'hour' of the Lord's death-resurrection-exaltation. Cf. 12 : 52. Their hour and power (22 : 53) creates his hour and power (Grundmann). From the combined quotation in Mk 14 : 62 Luke omits the specific reference to Messiah's exaltation 'with the clouds' (Dan. 7 : 13) and elaborates the reference to his present exaltation (Ps. 110 : 1). Thus he emphasizes what in Mark is only implicit: Jesus' glorification does not await the *parousia*. It is effected and transcendently, hiddenly manifested from the time of his resurrection. The *parousia* is only its earthly, public manifestation. *Then* the Sanhedrin will 'see' it. See on 13 : 35. Luke's emphasis may show a concern to discourage false teaching that viewed redemption solely in terms of an end-of-the-world event. See above, pp. 12ff., 48f.; on 17 : 20f.; 21 : 5–38; 23 : 43.
Son of man: see on 5 : 24.
right hand: the verse is a combined reference to Dan. 7 : 13 ('Son of man') and Ps. 110 : 1 ('right hand'). O. Linton (*NTS* 7,

1960–1, 260f.) has noted that in early Christian exegesis Ps. 110 : 1 referred to a literal exaltation to heaven. Since Luke shared this view (Ac. 2 : 34), it may be the import of the reference to Ps. 110 : 1 here.

The probability that Ps. 110 figured in the condemnation of Jesus is heightened by the 'temple debate' on that passage (20 : 41–44). If at his trial Jesus applied to himself a literal fulfilment of Ps. 110 : 1 and Dan 7 : 13, the charge of blasphemy is readily understandable (cf. Mk 14 : 63f.). It may explain also why the charge is associated with the term 'Son of God' (cf. Rom. 1 : 4).

70. Son of God may have the connotation of deity, as it does at 1 : 35 (cf. Ac. 8 : 37). Elsewhere in Luke–Acts the designation, given to Jesus only by divine or demonic voices, has a messianic connotation. See on 3 : 22; 4 : 3, 41; 9 : 35. But the Lord's own references to his 'sonship' exceed a human, messianic function (cf. 2 : 49; 10 : 22; 20 : 13). From such traditions O. Cullmann (*Christology*, pp. 278ff.) infers that Jesus designated himself Son of God, thereby expressing a unique and exclusive oneness with God. The charge of blasphemy in Mk 14 : 64 partly supports Cullmann, for it would not apply to a messianic claim. Cf. E. Lövestam, *SEA* 26, 1961, 93–107. It is possible, however, that it arises from Jesus' promise to rebuild the temple or to his literal appropriation of Ps. 110 : 1 (22 : 69; see the special note at 19 : 45–20 : 18). Even so, the charge against Jesus still has important implications for his view of his person.

The term, Son of God, is not used by Jesus in the synoptic Gospels. The concept, as a designation for the coming messianic king, is already at hand in Judaism (from 2 Sam. 7 : 11–19; Ps. 2 : 7; cf. 4*QFlor* 1 : 11; 4*Q* Son of God). But there is no certain use of it as a title in a pre-Christian text. Probably the *title* originated in the Church. It is difficult to say whether it arose first as a messianic term or to indicate Jesus' unique oneness with God, a oneness that expressed itself in his claim to be the only way to God, to forgive sins and to create life out of death. See on 5 : 17–26; 10 : 21–24; cf. Jn 2 : 19ff. Perhaps it is a false dichotomy since Christians defined Messiah in terms of their experience of Jesus. Cf. Higgins, *Christology*, pp. 135–8.

In any case it is a mistake to seek a hellenstic derivation for the New Testament's use of the term, Son of God. In Greek usage the term was applied to almost any wonder-worker. Therefore, it would be quite contrary to the Christian view of Jesus as a person of final and absolute significance (cf. Cullmann, *Christology*, p. 272). If the centurion in Mk 15 : 39 reflects the hellenistic meaning of the term, it may be significant that Luke (23 : 47 *AV*) changes his confession to read, 'a righteous man'.

2. accuse: cf. 20 : 20.

4. multitudes (*ochloi*)**:** throughout the trial the people are one with their leaders in demanding Jesus' execution (4f., 13ff.). They would support a 'political' prophet or Messiah against the unpopular temple cult. But when Jesus disavows this role, the nation aligns itself with one of two attitudes, the curious indifference of Herod or the outright opposition of the churchmen. The few true friends of Jesus are silenced by fear and disillusionment. See on 4 : 14–30.

8. Herod: see on 9 : 9.

11. soldiers: see on 3 : 14.

13. priests and rulers: see on 14 : 1; 20 : 1; 22 : 54–62.

16. chastise: by warning or light whipping. Cf. Ac. 16 : 22ff.; 22 : 24; Sherwin-White, pp. 27f.

18. Away: see on 5 : 35.

18, 25. Barabbas: in some manuscripts of Mt. 27 : 16f., 'Jesus Barabbas'. Luke may hint at the substitutionary death of Jesus. The one guilty of death is pardoned (*apoluō*; cf. 6 : 37), and the innocent one dies in his stead.

20, 24. Pilate: Luke, perhaps with an eye on Rome, deals lightly with Pilate's guilt. But there is little basis for apologetic arguments that, in turn, minimize the guilt of Judaism and its leaders (cf. Sherwin-White, pp. 35ff., 47n; Stonehouse, *Paul*, pp. 41ff.). Luke allows neither Gentiles nor Jews to evade their role in Messiah's death by pointing a finger. Cf. Ac. 3 : 13.

THE GLORIFICATION OF MESSIAH 23 : 26–24 : 53

Structure. The final section of the Gospel presents in six episodes the death and the resurrection of Jesus. This whole section has sufficient similarities with the Fourth Gospel to suggest the use by both Evangelists of a common source (cf. J. Schniewind, pp. 77–95; Leaney, pp. 28–31). Probably Luke, like John (13 : 31f.), views the death-resurrection-exaltation as one event of redemption. It

is a story of the 'eighth day' of creation, God's new creation of the
messianic age (see on 24 : 13). Thus, on the cross Jesus can say
already. 'Today in Paradise'. And all the resurrection episodes
are placed on the eighth day, i.e. the Sunday of Jesus' resurrection.
See on 9 : 51.

The six episodes are bound together by a series of prophecies or
allusions to prophecies. Only one episode (23 : 50–56) lacks any
explicit prophetic reference. The first prophecy, on 'the way of
the cross' (23 : 26–31), is a judgment upon the old age. The others
concern the 'new age' reality effected by the death and resurrection of Jesus. The central event in Luke's account of 'the crucifixion' (23 : 32–49) is a prophecy of Messiah's exaltation. At the
resurrection 'the message of the angels' (24 : 1–12) recalls a passion prediction of Jesus (9 : 22). The appearances at Emmaus
(24 : 13–32) and in Jerusalem (24 : 33–53) also are dominated
by his interpretation of his death as a fulfilment of prophecy.
The concluding 'great commission' commands nothing more
nor less than to proclaim to all nations what 'is written'
(24 : 46–49).

Teaching. This section, with its thematic emphasis upon prophecy,
is a counterpart to the opening section of Luke's story (1 : 5–2 : 40).
The propheceis in the dawn of the messianic age have found their
fulfilment in the glorification of Jesus. The new age, it is true, still
remains hidden from public view. Corporately Messiah's people
share his victory, but individually they have not yet realized it
(23 : 43). Only 'the pioneer of their salvation' (Heb. 2 : 10) has
been made perfect (24 : 26). Therefore, the glorification of Jesus
is not only a fulfilment but also a beginning (24 : 47). It is a
beginning in which the coming age, now actualized in the resurrection of Jesus, is to effect a total victory over the 'old age' of sin
and death. This road of victory is Luke's *theologia gloriae*. He will
have more to say about it in his second volume, the Acts of the
Apostles.

THE WAY OF THE CROSS **23 : 26–31**

Structure and Background. To the incident involving Simon of
Cyrene (26) Luke appends Jesus' final prophecy against Jerusalem
(27–31). In Judaism the mourning of the dead was an act of

religious merit. Probably the practice of bewailing condemned criminals was related to this. Cf. 7 : 12; 23 : 48; see on 9 : 59f. Although the women lamenting Jesus perhaps included disciples, in the main they were just sincere, religious people earning their salvation. Jesus, however, wants their conversion not their sympathy (Grundmann).

Teaching. It is not without irony that the same religious system that condemned Jesus now laments his death (27). To this religious Judaism the one under judgment gives his judgment. In rejecting and executing Messiah Jerusalem seals its own doom. If its corruption, half-grown, brings forth this act, how great shall be God's judgment when its sin is full (31)?

26f. Luke draws a visible contrast between the women who 'lament' Jesus and Simon who 'follows after'. Probably it is not without a symbolic meaning. To be a disciple demands more than an emotional reaction. It demands 'carrying Jesus' cross' and bearing his abuse. Cf. 9 : 23; 11 : 27f.; 14 : 27.

26. Simon: the father of Rufus (Mk 15 : 21), who perhaps is mentioned in Rom. 16 : 13. He was a Jew from Cyrene, on the north African coast. Perhaps he was 'home' for the feast. But more probably, like Paul's family, he had re-migrated to Palestine. The Cyrenians had a synagogue in Jerusalem, and some became active in the Christian work in Antioch (Ac. 6 : 9; 11 : 20).

cross: probably the cross beam to which Jesus' hands were to be nailed (Manson).

28ff. It is the sixth (or seventh) prophecy against Jerusalem. Two occur only in Luke. See on 11 : 49–51; 13 : 1–9; 13 : 34f.; 19 : 41–44; 21 : 20–24; cf. 20 : 16; Ac. 6 : 14.

30. Cf. Hos. 10 : 8; Rev. 6 : 16.

31. dry: a proverbial saying, not to be pressed to mean 'judgment of fire'.

THE CRUCIFIXION **23 : 32–49**

Structure. The episode consists of the setting (32f.), a contrast of the attitude of the onlookers with that of Jesus (34–43), and the signs and reactions accompanying his death (44–49). Most of the incidents occur in Mark. But Luke, also using another source, rearranges them into a thematic structure.

Teaching. The religious rulers, the soldiers, and the criminal ridicule the idea that this poor creature being executed on a cross could be the glorious Messiah, God's 'Chosen One'. In contrast one criminal takes Jesus' part. More in sympathetic feeling than theological discernment he calls, 'Jesus, remember me' (42). With a sovereign grace reminiscent of earlier days the Saviour bestows the messianic peace.

This incident, found only in Luke, is the core of the episode. In two ways it is especially meaningful for Luke's theme. First, the bandit (Mk 15 : 27 *NEB*) is representative of the type of person Jesus has come to save. Second, Jesus' answer, 'today' (43), shifts the focus of the request from the future kingdom to his present exaltation. At his resurrection Jesus literally was exalted to Paradise. By using this incident, Luke emphasizes that Jesus' 'body'—his people, the messianic Israel—also was exalted there with him (see below).

The prophecy contains a theological interpretation of the Lord's death and resurrection. Appropriately, it introduces the conclusion of the crucifixion scene. The signs accompanying his death announce the effective end of the old age and the accomplishment of his redemptive work (45). The response to Jesus' death by the centurion and the people testifies once again to his innocence (see on 22 : 63–23 : 25).

33. The Skull: i.e. Calvary (*AV*). The name may be derived from a rock formation in the area. It was north of the city just outside the wall (Heb. 13 : 12f.).

34, 43. forgive . . . Paradise: the words of Jesus, which bracket the central segment of the episode, set forth the two main purposes of his mission. The prayer is answered by his death, which brings the forgiveness of sins (Ac. 2 : 38). The promise assures a deliverance from death.

34. they know not: the petition is absent from many manuscripts. The textual evidence argues against the genuineness of the verse. However, other factors shift the weight of probability to its favour. First, Stephen's prayer (Ac. 7 : 60) probably presupposes the present text: Christ's first martyr emulates the attitude of his master. See above, pp. 11f.; cf. Grundmann; Eus. 2, 23, 16. Second, an 'ignorance motif', whose roots are in the Old Testament (Num. 15 : 24ff.), forms a part of Luke's theological emphasis. This verse seems to be presupposed by and to find its

sequel in Ac. 3 : 17 (cf. Ac. 13 : 27; 17 : 23, 30). For Luke, as
well as for other New Testament writers, ignorance does not
mean a deficient mentality or a lack of information but a sinful
moral state. Cf. Rom. 2 : 4; 10 : 3; Eph. 4 : 18; 1 Pet. 1 : 14. It
exists 'in unbelief'. D. Daube (*TU* 79, 1961, 58ff.) has shown that
in Judaism and in the New Testament the sin of ignorance was
approached in two ways. As a prelude to conversion ignorance
is an excuse. But persistent or 'fixed' ignorance is 'a particularly
damnable quality'. See above, pp. 16f.; on 8 : 10; cf. Stonehouse,
Paul, pp. 18–23.

35–39. Chosen, King, Christ: all are messianic titles. See on
3 : 21f.; 19 : 11–27, 28–44. Cf. the 'vinegar' (36) allusion to Ps.
69 : 21 in 1*QH* 4 : 11.

42. 'Remember me' (i.e. at the resurrection) is a prayer
petition on some gravestones from this period. Cf. Kosmala, pp.
418ff.

42f. kingly power (*basileia*): i.e. over Israel. Cf. 23 : 38; Ac.
1 : 6.

when you come . . . today: the shift from a future to a present
manifestation of the kingdom frequently is noticeable in Luke.
See on 11 : 3f., 20; 17 : 20–37; 19 : 5, 9; 22 : 69.

43. Truly: see on 4 : 24.

today, with (*meta*) **me, Paradise:** the meaning of the verse
rests upon these three expressions. A few reasonably early manuscripts place the comma after 'today' and thus continue the
parousia reference of verse 42. But this is against the usage elsewhere: 'today' belongs to the second clause. This does not mean,
however, that Jesus expects an immediate *parousia*. Nor is the
reference to a twenty-four-hour period. 'Today' is sometimes a
technical expression for the time of messianic salvation. Here that
time is Jesus' exaltation at the resurrection. Cf. 2 : 11; 3 : 22
codex D; 4 : 21; 19 : 9; Mt. 6 : 11; 2 C. 6 : 2. See on 22 : 69.

'Paradise', i.e. park or garden, refers in the Old Testament to
the Garden of Eden, which then becomes a type of the future
kingdom of God (cf. Isa. 51 : 3). The image is used similarly in
the New Testament (Rev. 2 : 7; 22 : 2). Some elements of first-
century Judaism use the term to describe the heavenly abode of
the 'soul' between death and resurrection. See on 16 : 23; cf.
SBK IV, 1119. Paul also uses 'Paradise' of a present heavenly
reality to which he was transported physically or in a vision (2 C.

12 : 2). Is the robber, like Paul, to (be resurrected and) accompany Jesus physically to heaven? Most commentators believe that the promise does refer to an individual heavenly journey but that, in common with the Pharisees' view of the intermediate state, Jesus is speaking only of the robber's soul. However, this interpretation apparently is not in accord with Jesus' teachings elsewhere or with the general New Testament view of man and of death. See on 20 : 27–40.

A number of Pauline passages speak of Christians having already been *corporately* crucified, resurrected, and exalted to heaven with (*syn*) Christ (e.g., Gal. 2 : 20; Eph. 2 : 5f.; cf. Ellis, *Interpreters*, pp. 36–40; W. Grundmann, *TDNT* vii, 770–6, 784–9). The same formula, 'raised with Jesus', may be used of the individual's resurrection at the last day (2 C. 4 : 14). But probably the corporate inclusion in Christ's 'body' is what is meant by being 'with Christ' during death (Phil. 1 : 23). If adopted here, this interpretation not only would accord with Jesus' teaching elsewhere but also would explain Luke's omission of Mark's (14 : 58; 15 : 29) temple saying.

The temple saying concerns the Christian's corporate exaltation with Christ. See on 13 : 35. Luke substitutes a saying of similar import that Jesus made to the sympathetic robber. According to a late Jewish writing (*Test. Levi* 18 : 10) Messiah was expected to 'open the gates of Paradise'. Luke declares that in his death and resurrection Jesus opened the gates of Paradise and was exalted there with his 'body'. Cf. E. E. Ellis, *NTS* 12, 1965–6, 35–40. (Although the term 'body of Christ' does not occur in the synoptic Gospels, the concept certainly is present. Cf. D. O. Via, Jr., *SJT* 11, 1958, 271–86). Cf. Ellis, *Eschatology*, pp. 11ff.

44. sixth hour: i.e. noon. It may indicate the hour of Jesus' death. The signs follow immediately upon it. See on 21 : 5–38.

45. the curtain: made from expensive woven materials imported from Babylon (cf. J. Jeremias, *Jerusalem*, p. 38). Of the thirteen curtains used in the temple (*Yoma* 54a), in all likelihood the reference is to the one concealing 'the holy of holies'. Here, the place of God's presence, only the high priest was permitted to go. He entered once a year to make atonement for the sins of the people. The term occurs elsewhere in the New Testament only in Hebrews (6 : 19; 9 : 3; 10 : 20). There it refers to Messiah's atoning death and resurrection.

The cultic usage may have arisen out of the event reported in the Gospels. Of three suggested interpretations of 'the rent veil' each is appropriate to Luke's meaning. It was an omen of the coming destruction of the temple (see on 21 : 5–38; cf. *SBK* I, 1045). It signified that through Christ's death the gates of Paradise, the way to God, were open to all (cf. 23 : 43). It witnessed that the temple rites no longer were necessary for the true worship of God (see the special note at 19 : 45–20 : 18; cf. Jn 4 : 21ff.). Cf. G. Lindeskog, *CN*, pp. 132–7.

46. into thy hands: cf. Ps. 31 : 5.

centurion: perhaps intended to prefigure the conversion of the Gentiles. His reaction is in sharp contrast to that of the people (cf. 23 : 21).

THE BURIAL 23 : 50–56

The Jews were known for the care that they bestowed upon their dead. The acts of Joseph (50–53) and the women (54–56) evidence such a concern. Usually executed persons were buried without honour in a public field (cf. Daube, pp. 310f., 312n). Joseph determined to give Jesus a decent burial, probably at some risk to himself. The initial embalming was his act of love, and the grave was his own new family tomb. Ascertaining that the absolutely necessary acts had been done, the women delayed their ministrations until after the Sabbath.

The funeral rite is elaborated in the Gospels of Luke and John. It emphasizes, perhaps against Jewish calumnies, that Jesus was not buried as a criminal (Daube, p. 310). Also, against docetic tendencies it underlines the reality of Jesus' death. His death was not only an event, it was a state. In its grip decay and dissolution began even though they did not run their course (Ac. 2 : 27). The preserving spices were needed. Here is no platonizing evasion of death's threat. Here is no 'illusion of immortality'. The Jesus who is 'alive for evermore' is the Jesus who 'was dead' (Rev. 1 : 18 *AV*).

51. kingdom of God: cf. 2 : 25, 38; see above, pp. 12ff.

53. wrapped: according to most commentators the earliest (Markan) tradition records no burial anointing. However, it is probable that the wrapping with linen (Mk 15 : 46) involved an initial anointing. The spices were spread on the shroud as it was

wound about the body. John (19 : 40) elaborates the account but
reflects accurately the Jewish burial custom (cf. Bultmann, *John*,
p. 680)

Only in this context would an anointing on 'the third day' be
credible to a reader acquainted with the warm Mediterranean
climate. This would be true especially of a Jewish reader who was
aware that the law did not prohibit the necessary burial anointing
on the Sabbath (cf. *SBK* II, 52f.). The women are performing an
additional act of devotion (23 : 56). Perhaps it is a practice like
that found in the account of Herod's death where spices were
taken to his tomb (Jos. *Ant.* 17, 8, 3; *War* I, 33, 9). Or an analogy
may be found in the modern Samaritan rite in which mourners
visit the tomb for several days after the burial to read and pray
(W. H. Bennett, *ERE* IV, 499; cf. Jn 11 : 31). In this connection
it is of interest that Matthew (28 : 1) mentions no anointing: the
women went to the tomb to 'observe'. In Roman custom the
rich might lie in state for seven days before burial (Toynbee,
p. 45); in Greek custom burial took place on the morning of the
third day (Kurtz, pp. 144f.).

54. Preparation: a technical term for the Friday of passover
week (*SBK* I, 1052; II, 829–32).

THE EMPTY TOMB: THE MESSAGE OF THE ANGELS **24: 1–12**

Structure. The three resurrection episodes are dovetailed into one
another. The first account (24 : 1–12) is virtually repeated in the
Emmaus story (24 : 22–24), and the Emmaus teaching (24 : 25ff.)
is reiterated in the following scene (24 : 44ff.). Each of the episodes
is taken from Luke's Jerusalem traditions, and one may contain a
tradition of the Lord's family (see on 24 : 18).

Chronological sequence and the Galilean appearances are left
aside. Everything occurs in or about Jerusalem on 'the eighth
day' (see on 24 : 13). Yet Luke is aware of a considerable interval
and of other appearances (Ac. 1 : 3). It is likely, therefore, that
he intends to present a theme rather than a chronicle even
though the events could be regarded as a running account. Each
episode sets forth the witness of prophecy as the sufficient and
only persuasive evidence for the resurrection. The prophecies of
Jesus in this regard are equated with those from Scripture. Cf.
24 : 6f., 26f., 44.

The present episode consists of an introduction (1-3), the message of the angels (4-7), the report of the women and the response to it (8-12). Strictly speaking it begins at 23 : 56b. Although there are some partial parallels (4, 9) with Mark, the account is derived from Luke's own sources.

Teaching. The empty grave takes on a redemptive meaning only in the light of the angel's message. In and of itself it could be (and was) explained in many ways (cf. Mt. 28 : 13). Even for the apostles it does not give rise to faith (12). Nevertheless, as Luke will show, the appearances also have no redemptive meaning in themselves (11). The episode of the empty grave is only a prologue, but it is a necessary prologue.

1. spices: see on 23 : 53.

4. two men (= angels, 24 : 23): perhaps a Lukan motif of 'twofold witness' connected (though not identified) with Moses and Elijah. The transfiguration for Luke is a preview of the resurrection. See on 9 : 28-36. Cf. Ac. 1 : 10.

6. Galilee: the women from *Galilee* (23 : 49) are reminded of a prophecy of Jesus of *Nazareth* (24 : 19) given in *Galilee* (24 : 6); cf. Ac. 13 : 31. Luke's selection of episodes arises not from ignorance of or antagonism toward Galilean traditions but rather from his theme. In the Gospel the scene moves from Jerusalem to Galilee to Jerusalem; in Acts, from Jerusalem to *Samaria* to Rome. Cf. Conzelmann, p. 202.

7. sinful men: Gentiles (cf. 18 : 32) or, less probably, Jewish leaders (cf. 24 : 20).

10. women: cf. 23 : 49. Luke alone includes Joanna (cf. 8 : 3), perhaps because he is acquainted with her. According to Mark (16 : 8) the women say nothing. Of course, he presupposes that they did say something (to him, if to no-one else).

apostles: i.e. the eleven and all the rest (24 : 9, 13: *autōn*). See the special note at 9 : 1-9.

11. these words: about the angelic vision. The report of the empty tomb excites a response (12).

12. Because it is absent in a few important manuscripts, most scholars (followed by several modern translations) omit this verse. The vocabulary (e.g., *othonia*) is suspicious, and the verse may be a later insertion from John 20 : 6f. Yet the omission of the 'beloved disciple' mentioned in John is better explained by Luke's repre-

sentative role for Peter than by a later scribe's oversight (cf.
12 : 41). In this section Luke is dependent upon a source also used
by the Fourth Gospel. This fact and the repetition of the incident
in the following Emmaus story also support the genuineness of
this text. Cf. 24 : 24; Schniewind, *op. cit.*, pp. 88–91; Leaney.

A Special Note on the Empty Tomb

Many scholars today believe that the earliest resurrection accounts
concerned 'appearances' and that the 'empty tomb' traditions
formed a later supplement. This judgment is probably correct,
although one should not infer from it that the 'appearances'
traditions, therefore, have a better claim to historical reliability.
The later publication of a tradition (in documents extant to us)
is no evidence that it originated later. The 'empty tomb' tradition,
witnessed to by all four Gospels, derives from pre-Gospel sources
that are not discernably less primitive than the earliest 'appearances' tradition.

In any case the later strata of the canonical tradition placed
more stress on the empty tomb. And one early source (1 C. 15;
c. AD 56) lacks any explicit reference to it. What is the reason for
this shift of emphasis? Usually it is taken to be an apologetic to
Jewish unbelievers. But why should this suddenly become necessary after several decades? It is not an apologetic to unbelievers
at all, for the Gospel accounts admit that an empty grave con-
vinces no one—not even the disciples. But it may be an apologetic
to believers for a particular kind of resurrection, a 'material'
resurrection. Is there any evidence to suggest that the second-
generation Church would have need of this type of apologetic?

It is very unlikely that the earliest Palestinian Christians could
conceive of any distinction between resurrection and physical,
'grave-emptying' resurrection. To them an *anastasis* (resurrection)
without an empty grave would have been about as meaningful
as a square circle. There are several reasons for believing that
this outlook is reflected in 1 C. 15. Paul does not have to say
'empty tomb' because it is implicit in his term resurrection. First,
the *rising* on the *third day* can hardly refer (only) to 'appearances'.
Most probably it presupposes and implies the 'empty tomb'
traditions. Also, the seed analogy presupposes a continuity between the buried and the raised body. 'Spiritual body' refers

to the vitalizing principle and has nothing to do with im-
materiality. Cf. 1 C. 15 : 4, 37, 44; Bultmann, *Theology* 1, pp.
201, 208ff.; Kümmel, *Man*, p. 70; R. H. Fuller, *BR* 4, 1960,
11ff.

Likewise, Paul's opponents, who actually are denying physical
resurrection, are accused of denying simply 'the resurrection'.
That this is their true character is seen in the apostle's assertions.
He writes, 'If the dead are not raised, (they) have perished'; and
'If the dead are not raised, let us eat and drink for tomorrow we
perish'. Cf. 1 C. 15 : 16, 18, 32. This is Paul's alternative. It is
an alternative that would be meaningless to press if his opponents
held this point of view. That the heretical Corinthians believed
in an after-life of some kind is evident from their practice of
'baptism for the dead'. Their objection was to a 'bodily' resurrection (1 C. 15 : 29, 35). The same assumption probably underlies
Paul's assertion that the 'mortal' must put on immortality at the
parousia and that 'then shall come to pass' the victory over death.
That is, these Corinthians believed (wrongly) in an immortality
that one already possessed. Cf. 1 C. 15 : 46–54; Lietzmann-
Kümmel, pp. 79, 192f.; Schmithals, pp. 70–4, 220. It is altogether
probable that, like the later Gnostics or the earlier Platonists,
Paul's opponents in Corinth advocated an after-life apart from
resurrection. At this early stage they did this simply by denying
the resurrection. (The strangeness to the Greeks of the concept
anastasis is shown in Ac. 17 : 18 where some Athenians apparently
thought 'resurrection' was a goddess.)

To such persons, with their depreciation of matter and exaltation of immaterial being, the concept of resurrection was an
offence. Many from this background became Christians. Although
they soon learned to use the Church's terminology, they avoided
its offence by 'spiritualizing' it. Those in 2 Tim. 2 : 18 who said
'The resurrection is past already' witness to this development.
'When the Gnostics speak of the resurrection as having already
occurred (2 Tim. 2 : 18), it is only an attempt to express their
own teaching in traditional Christian terminology' (Schmithals,
p. 71n; cf. Goppelt, p. 172n). Paul's opposition is only the seed of
the later Gnosticism, but Schmithals has identified correctly the
gnosticising character of the Corinthian heresy and its essential
unity with the error in 2 Timothy. In the light of its context this
interpretation of 2 Tim. 2 : 18 seems more likely than its connec-

tion with the error of 2 Th. 2 : 2 (as this writer suggested previously).

In conclusion, the Gospels were written in the 'late apostolic' period when the gnosticizing tendencies of some Christians had become a distinct threat to the Church (see on 1 : 4). One error, crucial for the Church's teaching, was the 'spiritualizing' of Jesus' resurrection. To meet it the Evangelists drew increasingly upon 'empty tomb' traditions. (There is a similar, though less explicit, import to the burial episode. See on 23 : 50–56.) In unmistakable terms these traditions defined for the 'Greeks' the meaning of the resurrection proclamation. Jesus lives because, and only because, he was raised.

Luke's resurrection episodes reflect in considerable measure a consciousness of the above situation. For proof of the resurrection one can neither go to the empty grave nor seek assurance solely from appearances (24 : 12, 24, 37, 41). One's conviction of the resurrection must arise primarily from the conviction that Jesus is Messiah of whose passion and resurrection the Scriptures prophesied and who himself so prophesied (24 : 25ff., 44ff.). That is, for Luke the resurrection is 'confessional history'. This does not mean that it is less historical or a different kind of history in its 'happened-ness'. But it does mean that one's assurance and affirmation of it rest ultimately on the witness of the Word of God and not on a resurrection certificate from the Jerusalem medical society. Thus the resurrection of Jesus can rise above the 'probable' to which all historical verification is subject and become a 'certain' historical event.

The Christian who recognizes this truth is then able to gain from the resurrection stories an insight into the 'manner' of Jesus' victory. The resurrected Jesus is characterized by 'glory' and by 'flesh' (24 : 26, 39; Ac. 2 : 31). He can appear and vanish at will, and he can eat fish (24 : 31, 36, 39, 42f.). He is strangely different and yet he is the same: 'Behold my hands!' He is 'other-worldly' and yet he is very earthy.

Luke's intent is not to 'materialize' an original 'spiritual' experience (Manson) nor to 'historicize' an inner reality (cf. P. Schubert, *NS*, p. 172). These explanations actually read the historical development backwards. The Evangelist relates concrete, 'time and nature' events that reinforce the original meaning of the resurrection proclamation. Gnosticizing Christians had perverted this meaning. With their flesh/spirit dualism they divorced man from the earth, 'resurrection being' from 'material being'. The thrust of Luke's presentation is not unlike 1 C. 15. And it is not impossible that a similar situation is in mind. See on 8 : 31; 24 : 39.

THE EMMAUS APPEARANCE: THE MESSAGE OF JESUS 24 : 13–32

Structure. The opening conversation with 'the stranger' (13–24) is followed by the Lord's exposition of the Scriptures (25–27). The climax occurs at the supper scene (28–32) in which they recognize Jesus and recall how he had 'opened the scriptures' to them.

Teaching. The dialogue is characterized by opposite interpretations of Jesus' death. For the two disciples it is a tragedy, the end of 'a prophet' who they had hoped was Messiah (19–21). From the Scriptures Jesus interprets his death as a necessity, the ordained way in which Messiah was to 'enter into his glory' (25–27). Messiah did 'redeem Israel' and will 'restore the kingdom to Israel' (Ac. 1 : 6). But it is not the 'Israel' of nationalist definition. And his redemption is not the political victory of current messianic expectation.

The two disciples' false interpretation of Jesus' death arose from a false messianic expectation. In turn, this had its roots in a false understanding of the Scripture. To 'know' the events one must 'know' the Scripture. Only after it is 'opened' to them are they prepared to 'see' Jesus in his resurrected glory (31f.). This order is as significant as the occasion of their recognition (30). See on 9 : 9; cf. 16 : 31.

13. That very day: each of the resurrection episodes opens with a time reference to the 'eighth day' (24 : 1, 13, 33). See on 9 : 28; 24 : 1–12; cf. *Barnabas* 15 : 8f.; Justin, *Dail.* 138; Farrer, *Matthew*, p. 87. The symbolism identifies Jesus' resurrection as the beginning of a new creation. Luke takes over from his tradition the time references in the first and last episodes (cf. Jn 20 : 19). In the Emmaus story he may change the setting to fit his theme as he does elsewhere. If one accepts the common tradition of a number of appearances between Passover and Pentecost, Luke's order is not improbable. The Jerusalem appearances would occur at 'feast time', those in Galilee when the disciples were at home.

However, because of the episodic nature of the stories and the Evangelists' lack of interest in the question, no chronological 'ordering' of the resurrection appearances should be pressed.

Emmaus: the site is uncertain, but cf. Jos. *Wars* 7, 6, 6.

16. were kept: blocked or restrained by supernatural power.

18. Cleopas: Jesus' uncle, the brother of Joseph and father of Simeon according to Eusebius (3, 11, 1). Simeon was the leader of the post-70 Jerusalem congregation. If Eusebius is correct, the Emmaus story was originally a tradition of Jesus' family. Cf. Ac. 1 : 14.

19, 21. a prophet . . . to redeem: perhaps the prophet like Moses (Ac. 3 : 22). See on 9 : 35; 19 : 32.

19. deed and word: see on 4 : 32.

21. Israel: in common with Paul, Luke stresses that Jesus brings salvation to 'Israel'. This interpretation is connected to Old Testament prophecies by an altered (i.e. a recovered) definition of Israel. Cf. 2 : 32; 22 : 30; Ac. 1 : 6; 28 : 19f. ('Jews . . . Israel'); Ellis, pp. 136–9.

third day: see on 13 : 32f.

25. the prophets: e.g., 23 : 34ff. (Ps. 22; 69); 20 : 17 (Ps. 118); 22 : 37 (Isa. 53); Ac. 2 : 27 (Ps. 16); cf. Isa. 8 : 14; Hos. 6 : 2; Zech. 12 : 10; 13 : 7; *SBK* II, 273ff. Luke assumes that his readers are aware of these *testimonia*, and he attributes their use originally to the teaching of Jesus.

26. necessary (*dei*): the necessity of the events results from the sovereign purpose of God and the inviolability of his word through the prophets. See on 9 : 22; 20 : 36; the special note at 24 : 1–12.

27. See on 24 : 44.

30. at table: it is the eighth meal episode. See on 14 : 1.

30f. opened: by divine power. See on 24 : 16. Both the broken body (22 : 19) and the fellowship meals and feedings (9 : 16) were a part of Jesus' 'deed and word'; and perhaps both are in their minds. See the special note at 22 : 7–38.

THE APPEARANCES IN JERUSALEM: THE COMMISSION OF JESUS

24 : 33–53

Structure. The introduction (33–35) is followed by a third appearance in which the physical nature of the risen Jesus is made evident (36–43). An appended 'great commission' (44–49) is

climaxed by Jesus' blessing and disappearance (50–53). The commission points to the meaning of the 'death way' of Jesus' pre-
resurrection mission (44–46) and the pattern of his future mission
through the Church (48–49). Beginning from 'Jerusalem' the
disciples, as 'witnesses' endowed with 'power', proclaim 'repentance and forgiveness' to 'all nations'. The book of Acts is an
elaboration of these points and shows the working out of their new
understanding of the Scriptures (cf. P. Schubert, *NS*, pp. 176f.,
185).

Teaching. Like some earlier episodes (see above, pp. 74f., 179, 187)
the thrust of the narrative is in the appended part, the commission
and blessing (44–53). The community of ideas in common with
Matthew and John is noteworthy. In all three Gospels the commission (47), the Holy Spirit (49), and the worship of Jesus
(52, margin) play a part. Jesus' benediction (51) occurs in John.
Cf. Mt. 28 : 16–20; Jn 20 : 21–23, 28. This 'third mission' of the
disciples is not unrelated to the pre-resurrection missions of the
Twelve (9 : 1–9) and the Seventy (10 : 1–20). It is a continuation
of their earlier missions. Also, it is still Jesus' mission, and the
message remains that which was initiated by the Baptist: 'repentance for the forgiveness of sins' (3 : 3; Ac. 2 : 38). But there are
significant differences. This mission includes 'all nations' and is
led by an 'absent' Jesus through the mediation of the Holy Spirit.
See above, pp. 15f.

Luke's story began with a righteous priest giving his blessing
to the congregation of Israel. It closes with Jesus the resurrected
high priest, giving his blessing to the messianic Israel. The priest
Zechariah went into the temple with a petition for the redemption
of Israel. The followers of the resurrected Jesus also go to the
'temple'. But their prayer is one of joy and thanksgiving. The
redemption of Israel has been accomplished, and the messianic
community, the new temple of God, has been established. Cf.
P. A. van Stempvoort, *NTS* 5, 1958–9, 34f.

   33. that same hour: see on 10 : 21; 23 : 43; 24 : 13.
   34. Simon: i.e. Peter. Almost certainly he was not the companion of Cleopas. In a few manuscripts 'who' refers to the
Emmaus disciples, but this is a later alteration. Peter may be
introduced here to answer the question raised by 24 : 12. Cf.
1 C. 15 : 5.

36–43. See the special note at 24 : 1–12. The literary form—Jesus' identity, fear and doubt, doubts answered—is partially parallel to the visions of Lk. 1–2. See on 1 : 5–25. But Luke also is at pains to show that this heavenly being, in contrast to the angelic figures, is not a spirit but is the earthly Jesus.

36c, 40 (margin). Like 24 : 12 these verses are lacking in some manuscripts and have a parallel in John (20 : 19f.). The textual evidence for the omission of 24 : 40 is somewhat stronger than in the case of 24 : 12.

39. my hands: cf. Zech. 12 : 10; Jn 20 : 25.
flesh: Ac. 2 : 31 underscores Luke's affirmation of the resurrection of the flesh of Jesus. Cf. Ellis, *Eschatology*, p. 9n; *Barn.* 6: 9; 2 *Clem.* 9 : 1; Ignatius, *Smyr.* 3 : 1.

41. The sorrow at the death of Jesus gives way to unbelievable joy at his return. Cf. Jn 16 : 19–22.

43. ate: in Jewish tradition eating would not necessarily prove 'materiality'. Cf. Gen. 19 : 1ff.; Tob. 12 : 19. But perhaps it would carry this implication for Luke's Gentile readers. In any case it involves bodily manifestation. Cf. Ac. 10 : 41; Ignatius, *To the Trallians* 9 : 1.

44, 46. Moses, prophets, psalms: the three parts of the Hebrew Old Testament.

47. nations: the mission to the Gentiles is subsequent to Jesus' exaltation and, in part, to the national mission to Israel. Acts details this sequence, which is rooted in the teaching of Jesus. Cf. Jeremias, *Theology*, pp. 245ff. For interesting, though debatable, interpretations of this theme cf. S. G. Wilson (pp. 239–55) and Jervell (pp. 41–69).

49. the promise: cf. Ac. 2 : 16ff.

50. as far as: 'in the neighbourhood of' or 'within sight of'. Cf. Geldenhuys; Funk, p. 125. The geographical reference is not necessarily different from that of the ascension scene in Ac. 1 : 12. But the dissimilar description strengthens the case against interpreting this passage as an ascension scene. See on 19 : 29.
blessed: 'lifted hands' is the posture of a priestly benediction. It may signify the priestly character of Messiah's present exaltation and of his relationship to believers. See on 13 : 32f.; cf. Heb. 8 : 1; Sir. 50 : 20f.; Num. 6 : 23ff.

51. parted from them (*diestē*): probably P. Schubert (*NS*, p. 168n) is correct in paralleling this disappearance with that in

24 : 31. 'Carried up into heaven' (*RSV*, margin) is absent from several important manuscripts and probably is not original. Like Matthew, Luke ended with an interview. The acted parable of the ascension into 'a cloud' (Ac. 1 : 9) is a different event. It does not 'date' Jesus' exaltation but marks the end of the physical appearances. Cf. Ac. 7 : 56; 26 : 15, 19. It also reveals in a graphic picture what occurred at the resurrection and will be revealed publicly at the *parousia* 'with the clouds'. See on 22 : 69.

52*a*. worshipped him (margin): elsewhere in Luke only at 4 : 7f., with reference to a confession of Satan's lordship. The term also may suggest obeisance to a divine or angelic being (cf. Ac. 10 : 25f.). Jesus is the object of worship in Matthew and Mark. The phrase here is omitted by several important manuscripts.

53. temple: see the special note at 19 : 45

INDEX OF AUTHORS

INDEX OF PASSAGES

OLD TESTAMENT

NEW TESTAMENT

APOCRYPHA AND PSEUDEPIGRAPHA

DEAD SEA SCROLLS

ANCIENT CHRISTIAN WRITINGS

(See also Index of Authors)

MISHNAH AND BABYLONIAN TALMUD

OTHER JEWISH WRITINGS